D1740921

THE BEST OF
QUESTIONS
AND ANSWERS

THE BEST OF
QUESTIONS
AND ANSWERS

ANGELUS PRESS
2915 FOREST AVENUE
KANSAS CITY, MISSOURI 64109

Angelus Press has edited some of the answers; they may not appear as they did in their original form in *The Angelus*. All of the entries include the issue in which the questions originally appeared; some answers, although dated, have been preserved for their historical interest and relevance.

Library of Congress Cataloging-in-Publication Data

The best of questions and answers / the Angelus. -- 2nd ed.
    p. cm.
 "Angelus Press has edited some of the answers; they may not appear as they did in
their original form in The Angelus. All of the entries include the issue in which the
questions originally appeared; some answers, although dated, have been preserved
for their historical interest and relevance"--T.p. verso
 ISBN 978-1-892331-68-7
 1. Catholic Church--Doctrines--Miscellanea. I. Angelus Press. II. Angelus.
BX1754.3.B48 2009
 282--dc22

                                                                    2009008066

©2009 by Angelus Press
All rights reserved. No part of this book may be reproduced or transmitted in any form or by any means, electronic or mechanical, including photocopying, recording, or by any information storage and retrieval systems without permission in writing from the publisher, except by a reviewer, who may quote brief passages in a review.

ANGELUS PRESS
2915 FOREST AVENUE
KANSAS CITY, MISSOURI 64109
PHONE (816) 753-3150
FAX (816) 753-3557
ORDER LINE 1-800-966-7337
www.angeluspress.org

ISBN 978-1-892331-68-7
FIRST PRINTING–April 2009

Printed in the United States of America

CONTENTS

FOREWORD XXI

ABOUT GOD THE HOLY TRINITY

We are admonished to forgive our enemies, yet according to His agents (the hierarchy),
God does not forgive His enemies, submitting them to eternal torture in hell. No wrong
can be so bad as to merit unending torture. We are born with no part in the decision.
If we fail to satisfy God, the humane thing for Him to do would be to annihilate that soul.
Does God set a bad example for tyrants to follow against their victims? 1

Supposedly, God knows the future and all things. According to that position,
He already knows if I'll be saved or damned. Who am I even to attempt
to sway the will of God? If I'm due for damnation, any attempt for salvation is futile.
But I don't believe God knows my end yet! Otherwise free will is thwarted. 3

Why does God allow some to suffer mentally and physically more than others? Is this fair? 3

Did the Father and the Holy Ghost suffer like Jesus did on the cross? 4

ABOUT OUR LORD JESUS CHRIST

Is it accurate to say that Our Lord was a Jew? 4

Did Jesus have a brother named James? 5

I understand that Jesus is God and God's Son. Why then would He choose such
a horrible way to redeem mankind when He could have made it so much easier? 6

What do you think of a statement made by an apparition that
"Jesus did not carry the cross, He carried only the cross bar"? 6

What did Christ mean when He said, "Whose sins you shall forgive,
they are forgiven; whose sins you shall retain, they are retained." 7

Why did Our Lord refer to His Mother as "Woman"? 7

Catholics call their priests "father" in spite of the fact that Our Lord says,
"Call no man on earth father" (Mt. 23:9). Isn't this breaking Christ's command? 7

Is altar wine addictive, and if so, how could Christ have used it? 8

When a "born-again" Protestant strikes up a conversation by asking "Who is Jesus?"
and "Do you have a personal relationship with Him?" what is a good way to reply? 9

ABOUT THE BLESSED VIRGIN MARY

If we are to say that Mary is the Mother of God,
must we not also admit that she is Mother of the Divinity? 9

Is the Blessed Virgin Mary "divine"? 10

Is the Church telling the truth when it says of the Blessed Virgin Mary
"thou alone hast destroyed all heresies in the whole world"? 11

Why is it that Catholics adore the wood of the cross, but they do not adore Mary? 13

ABOUT THE ANGELS

What are the cherubim and seraphim? 13

Are angels male or female? What do you say about angels? 14

Why do we call angels "saints"? 14

ABOUT THE SAINTS

Why is St. Stephen considered the first martyr and not St. John the Baptist? 15

ABOUT THE CHURCH

How did the Catholic Church get its name? 15

What is the difference between "dogma" and "doctrine"? 16

Some time ago in the "question and answer" section of one of the foremost "conservative"
   Catholic journals, the answering priest made the categorical statement: "The Church has
   never taught definitively that the soul is infused in the moment of conception." In the dogma
   of the Immaculate Conception, as I understand it, we are taught that the Blessed Mother's
   soul was free from original sin from the very moment of her conception. It would seem,
   therefore, that the Church does, in fact, definitively teach that the soul is infused in the
   moment of conception. I would appreciate your comments on this priest's statement, and
   correct me if I err in my understanding of this dogma. 16

Is it true that the Church frowns on the use of
   the Gothic vestment, preferring the Roman cut? 17

Does the Catholic Church forbid cremation? 18

Is the Catholic Church opposed to war? 20

Has the Church given any conditions for the waging of a just war? 20

Can the Church take donations from companies or individuals
   whose profit is derived from immoral activities? 21

Could you please point to a Church document that requires that financial contributions by the
   faithful be accounted for to them on a weekly or monthly basis, if such a document exists? 22

Protestants say that a tithe of ten per cent of gross income is obligatory
   according to Scripture. Are Catholics bound to keep this rule? 23

Has the Church's position on Freemasonry changed? 25

ABOUT CERTAIN TEACHINGS OF THE CHURCH

The religion writer George W. Cornell writes concerning Charles Curran that
   "Roman Catholicism always has taught the duty of heeding individual conscience,
   when duly informed and seriously considered, even in dissent from official teachings."
   Is that what the Church teaches? 26

T.V., magazines, and newspapers have been plying us with the matters of mercy killing, death
   with dignity, living well, quality of life, *etc.* What is the Catholic teaching on life and death? 26

I was told that at the last judgment everyone will know everyone else's sins.
   How could this be since God forgives sins in confession? I have even heard that
   the devil does not know sins already confessed. 27

ABOUT THE BIBLE AND BIBLICAL MATTERS

If Eve only, and not Adam, had sinned, would we have been born with original sin?.........27

If Adam had not sinned, would we have been born with sanctifying grace?...............28

Why are there different translations of Genesis 3:15, some indicating that the woman's seed
will crush the serpent's head, and others that it is His Mother herself who will do it?......28

Whom did the children of Adam and Eve marry?....................................29

Where did the bodies of Henoch and Elias repose or did they ever die? I have read in
Catholic prophecies that they are able to return to earth to fight the Antichrist..........30

Abimelech was warned by God not to touch Sara, that she was Abraham's wife,
when Abraham was willing to let Abimelech have her. However, He did not warn Abraham
that he had sinned in giving her to Abimelech. It seems incongruous that Abraham should
be revered as our patriarch with such high esteem when he could have done such
a thing, and that God did not punish or admonish him..............................30

Of what evil is God speaking in Is. 45:7 when He says: "I make peace
and create evil: I the Lord that do all these things"? 31

How can it be said that Our Lord came to preach "the acceptable year of the Lord"?.......32

"Blessed are the poor in spirit" (Matt. 5:3): What does it mean?......................33

If the lesson of the Prodigal Son is that God values the repentant sinner
no less than He does one who has tried to live meritoriously,
then why make the effort? It hardly seems fair. 34

What is the proper interpretation of Acts 2:17? "And it shall come to pass in the
last days (saith the Lord), I will pour out my Spirit upon all flesh: and your sons and
your daughters shall prophesy, and your young men shall see visions, and your old men
shall dream dreams." My sister believes we are living in the last days when these
manifestations will take place and quotes this verse often. I would like to respond
to her with the proper interpretation of that Bible passage..........................35

The Gospels speak of St. Thomas as "the Twin." Our pastor spoke of this, saying that
the theory is that we are the twin as no noticeable other twin was mentioned.
He said that we are all doubters. Is this correct? 35

Can the Council of Laodicea be alleged to prove
that the deuterocanonical books are not inspired? 36

The Pentecostal evangelists are preaching an event they claim will happen in the
future called the "Rapture." Literally translating Our Lord's words in Matthew 24:37-44,
"Then two men will be in the field; one will be taken, and one will be left," they state
that after, or right before, the Day of Tribulation (not the Last Judgment), Our Lord will
come and will take all the good and believing people from earth and will bring them forth
to heaven to become immortalized, leaving on earth only those who do not believe.
Is there some truth of this, Father, or is this a deception? 37

ABOUT THE MAGISTERIUM: THE PAPACY, THE POPES, AND PAPAL TEACHINGS

Are Catholics bound in conscience to accept
all papal teachings or just infallible teachings?...................................38

If a pope is neither crowned nor takes the papal oath, is he then the pope
or just an administrator sitting in the Chair of Peter?..............................39

Does the bull *Quo Primum* enjoy infallibility? 40

Are all the texts of an infallible Council infallible? 40

Could the pope institute a new sacrament? 43

When we pray for the Holy Father's intentions when gaining
   a plenary indulgence, for whom do we pray? 44

When was the Council of Trent? What did the Council of Trent do? 44

Are the Church's disciplinary laws infallible? 45

Before Vatican II, popes used to swear fidelity to Tradition under pain of automatic
   excommunication. Does this mean that they would cease to be pope
   if they were to depart from Catholic Tradition? 46

What was the reasoning behind the suppression
   of many vigils and octaves under Pope Pius XII? 47

Where can I find information that the direction given us by the pope is questionable?
   What about our friends who say, "Yes, I see your point (concerning the Mass,
   for example). However, we must stay with Rome." 48

We would like some documented material on Pope John Paul II's "ecumenical" meeting
   in Assisi. What exactly happened there? Was Buddha actually worshipped?
   Did the pope receive on his forehead the sign of some pagan goddess? 48

Do sedevacantists really love the Church? Do they not judge Pope John Paul II
   personally, as they say? 50

In writing an encyclical the pope is not writing as a mere private theologian but as the supreme,
   authoritative teaching authority in the Church. But Pope John Paul II's recent encyclical
   on ecumenism is a practical denial of the Catholic doctrine of the universality of papal
   jurisdiction, of the oneness of the Catholic and Roman Church, outside of which there is
   no salvation. Would it not seem then that he has abandoned his infallibility and that
   consequently it is contrary to our Catholic Faith to maintain that he is still the pope? 50

Is it possible to state that the pope has failed to completely transmit the
   deposit of the faith without being a schismatic? 54

Is it good for laymen, untrained in theology and philosophy, to read papal encyclicals? 55

In what way was Pope John XXII's statement concerning the soul's possession of the
   beatific vision wrong? Surely the souls in purgatory cannot possess the beatific vision. 56

Has the consecration of Russia to the Immaculate Heart
   requested by Our Lady been accomplished? 57

Is a sedevacantist to be considered a non-Catholic? 57

ABOUT THE PRIESTHOOD AND PRIESTS

Must a priest follow certain criteria if he is to refuse Holy Communion to the faithful? 59

What is the status of all those priests who took the Anti-Modernist Oath
   at their ordination and who have now abandoned it and are going along
   with modernism? Are those who took the oath still bound by it
   even though it has since been abolished by the revolutionaries? 61

Can traditional priests absolve from censures in the internal forum? 61

What is the Church's teaching on women in the priesthood? 63

Didn't the early Church have "deaconesses"? 63

Does the non-admission of women to the priesthood
have anything to do with "inferiority" and "superiority"?............................63

About the Mass and the Liturgy

What is the Tridentine Rite?...64

Is it true that only Masses under *Quo Primum* are representative of the Catholic religion? 64

Is the dialogue Mass a "diabolical disorientation,"
and can it be compared to Communion in the hand? 64

What steps are necessary to make a low Mass complete? 66

Is anything more to be gained by hearing two or more Masses
at the same time, rather than just one?...66

What do the three candles on each side of the altar represent?.........................68

Why is it that in the celebration of Mass the psalm *Judica me*
is said before the *Kyrie eleison*? 68

If the Mass is the unbloody renewal of the sacrifice of Calvary,
why does the priest pray the *Orate fratres* at the Offertory of Mass? 69

Does the statement of *Quo Primum* that "none of it be changed
under penalty of our indignation" mean that Masses celebrated
with the name of St. Joseph in the Canon are not Tridentine Masses?..................70

What is the significance of the small piece of host that
the priest drops into the chalice after the *Pater Noster*?............................71

What is a stipend for a Mass? 71

Can the rubrical changes of 1955 and 1962 be compared to the new rite of Mass?..........71

Is it true that a heretic who does not believe in the Real Presence can have
the intention of doing what the Church does and celebrate a valid Mass?...............72

Who has the right to touch the chalice and sacred linens,
namely, the corporal, pall, and purificator?.......................................73

Is it permissible to sing English hymns during Mass, or can this only be done after Mass? 74

Can women be permitted to sing in the choir in church?...............................75

Does this mean that women should not sing in church at all?..........................75

Is it permissible to go to confession during Sunday Mass? 76

Is it permissible to go to the bathroom during Sunday Mass?..........................77

About the Commandments of God and the Precepts of the Church

The opinion has been voiced that a bad deed resulting in good is permissible,
such as the case of the murder of the abortionist doctor in Florida,
comparing it to a just war. In my opinion, this way of thinking is erroneous..............77

Is it permissible to embark on a hunger strike, determined to fast until death,
if one's non-violent political action is not successful?...............................78

Does a Saturday evening "vigil" Mass satisfy the Sunday obligation?.....................79

Is it permissible to publish the sins of deceased persons?............................81

How does one determine what buying and selling is permitted on Sundays? 82

On a holy day of obligation is one required to refrain
    from manual labor the same as on Sundays? 83

Is one allowed to study on Sunday? 84

Is it permissible to attend a concert where music is performed in a Catholic church? 85

How can a person go to hell for lying too long in bed on a Sunday or deliberately
    eating a slice of ham on a day of abstinence? 86

Is a Catholic in mortal sin if he allows more than one year
    to pass since his last confession? 87

Why do Catholics not eat meat on Fridays? 89

Does chewing gum break the ecclesiastical fast? 90

ABOUT THE SACRAMENTS

From an earlier reply in this column it would appear that the "intention of doing what
    the Church does" is implicit in the very act of going through the rites prescribed or
    accepted by the Church, unless a contrary intention is present openly or internally.
    I have read that the "intention of doing what the Church does" need not involve an
    intention "what the Church intends," namely, to produce the effects of the sacrament
    –for example, the forgiveness of sins. Yet the "mere external intention...which is
    directed towards merely performing the external action with earnestness...is
    insufficient" because it is not compatible with the concept of doing "what the
    Church intends." Could you explain this? 92

If intention is necessary for the validity of the sacraments, how can we ever
    be sure that the sacraments we receive are valid? 93

I have a relative in her early thirties who has not been baptized. I was taught
    that anyone can baptize if no priest is available. 94

I know that the Council of Florence taught that three components are necessary for the
    effecting of a sacrament–matter, form, and intention of the minister; and if any one
    of the three is lacking, the sacrament is not valid. I also know, however, that the Church
    teaches that even a pagan can legitimately baptize in an emergency as long as
    he uses water, the correct form, and intends to do what the Church does.
    My question is: How can a minister whose denomination formally rejects
    the very existence of sacraments intend to do what the Church does
    when baptizing a person? In short, should a convert be conditionally baptized?
    Further, if so, should he be conditionally confirmed? The *Novus Ordo* priests that
    I have discussed this with have (predictably) dismissed my entire concern as silly! 95

I do not understand how it can be affirmed that baptism in an heretical church
    gives the character of baptism but does not give sanctifying grace,
    so that person remains with original and actual sins 96

Why is it that the reception of Holy Communion does not break the Friday abstinence? 98

When in confession, should a Catholic mention that he is a member of a third order,
    or that he has made the total consecration to Our Lady? 99

Is it permissible for a private family to have a private chapel
    where the Blessed Sacrament is reserved? 100

How does the Confessor determine the penance
    to give to his penitent in the confessional? 100

Can a person perform the penance received in confession
    after having fallen back into mortal sin?..102
What do you think of the "baptism of the unborn,"
    which is supposedly recommended by some apparition? 103

About Canon Law

What is the authority of Canon Law?...104
Are we to consider all the provisions of
    the 1917 Code of Canon Law to have been abrogated?............................105
I was told that the Church's law permits Catholics to satisfy their Sunday
    obligation at a schismatic Orthodox ceremony, and that this was
    the case both before and after Vatican II. Is this true?............................108
What is the infamous Canon 844 of the 1983 Code of Canon Law? 109
Has this Canon 844 always been the policy of the Catholic Church?.....................110

About Relics

Some scoffers of the religion say that if all the relics of the true cross were
    gathered together from all over the world, there would be sufficient lumber
    to build a three-masted schooner. What is the truth about this? And where
    can one today find the major relics of the sufferings of Christ? 110

About Ecclesiastical Practices and Customs

The month of May is dedicated to our Blessed Lady.
    Do the other months of the liturgical year have a particular significance?..............111
Is it a traditional practice to use the communion rail cloth,
    and if so, should we be using it in our traditional chapel?...........................112
Why light votive candles before the tabernacle or a picture or statue? 113
Which way, and from which side of the church, do the Stations of the Cross start?
    Here they start on the right, and also in Canada. Here on Long Island, some people
    keep moving them to start on the left side. Is there a set rule for them by the Church?...113
What is the history of the nine First Fridays,
    and what are the requirements for making them? 114
What are the history and conditions for doing the five First Saturdays? 114
How can I consecrate myself to the Immaculate Heart of Mary? 114
What benefits can flow from a visit to a Catholic cemetery? 115

About Sacramentals

Does it make a difference whether one makes
    the Sign of the Cross with the right hand or with the left hand? 116
Are there such things as "blessed dresses"?.......................................117

I wear a scapular medal which has the image of the Sacred Heart on one side and that of Our
   Lady of Maryknoll on the other. This medal was blessed by a Maryknoll priest about thirty-five
   years ago. I have asked a Carmelite priest to enroll me, but he tells me that no enrollment is
   necessary. Needless to say, after reading the article concerning the brown scapular in a past
   Angelus I am confused. I would like to do the right thing concerning this most important
   devotion to our Lady. Would you please advise me what to do to ensure this?. 117

What is the prayer that is supposed to be said
   each day by the person wearing the scapular? 118

About the Crisis in the Church Since Vatican II

Is the crisis in the Church primarily a question of the Mass or of doctrine?. 118

How can the seemingly apostate modern Church
   claim to have the four marks of the Catholic Church?. 120

Can we say that the present crisis in the Church has destroyed its indefectibility? 122

Is it true to say that now there is a "conciliar" church? 122

Can Pope Pius XII's clarification of the error of the Council of Florence
   be used as a precedent for refusing the errors of Vatican II?. 124

Here recently I have heard more than once that the Holy Ghost
   was not invoked before or after Vatican II by the Council Fathers.
   Could you inform us of the truth of this remark? 124

What is liberalism?. 125

What is ecumenism?. 126

Just how far will religious liberty go? 128

Ought priests of the conciliar church to be
   conditionally ordained when they come to Tradition? 129

Could you please explain the discrepancies in the ceremonies for Maundy Thursday,
   Good Friday, and Holy Saturday that I see in different traditional chapels? 137

How is it possible to refuse a law coming from the Church, such as the change of
   "for many" into "for all" in the consecration of the Precious Blood at Mass? 138

Christ promised that "the gates of hell shall not prevail against the Church."
   Therefore, should we not just patiently wait? 140

Is it presumptuous to think YOU can save the Church?. 140

Is the *Novus Ordo* Mass invalid or sacrilegious,
   and should I assist at it when I have no alternative?. 140

Please comment on the following situation, which I know exists: people attend the *Novus Ordo*
   liturgy and the traditional Mass on the same day and receive Communion both times. 143

I would like to know if in Aramaic "for all" and "for many" were two separate
   and distinct phrases, and not the same as said by some after Vatican II? 144

Are the brown hosts frequently used in the *Novus Ordo*
   validly consecrated or must the hosts be white?. 144

There is a priest in town who says the *Novus Ordo*. He is unhappy doing so but, for reasons of his own, he continues. At certain times he meets, in secret, with traditional Catholics to say the "true Mass." I have reservations about attending a Mass and receiving sacraments from this priest. What to do?.............145

What is the basis for concelebration of Mass?....................................145

I read an article which stated that the anathemas of the Council of Trent had been abolished by the 1983 Code of Canon Law. Is this true?....................147

Do similar abusive conditions exist in the Byzantine Rite as they do in the *Novus Ordo*? Can a traditional Roman Catholic safely satisfy his Sunday obligation attending the Byzantine Rite even though the Tridentine Mass is available to him? 148

Are the Masses of Thuc-line priests valid, and can we assist at them?...................148

I have been told that I have to accept my daughter's marriage, although she left the Catholic Church in which she was baptized and was married in a Protestant church, since the post-Vatican II Church says it is valid. Can you comment? 150

Can St. Catherine of Siena, St. Teresa of Avila, and St. Thérèse of the Child Jesus be considered Doctors of the Church?..151

A priest told me that cremation is acceptable as long as the body is at the funeral, and that after the Requiem Mass the body can be cremated. Please advise.............154

Nuns nowadays are difficult to recognize. Many of them dress in street clothes. How is that to be explained? 155

Father, can we give any credence to the opinion that Cardinal Siri was the pope? 156

ABOUT ARCHBISHOP LEFEBVRE AND THE SOCIETY OF SAINT PIUS X

How could Archbishop Lefebvre have signed the documents of Vatican II?................157

Some Catholics are disturbed by the election of one of the Society's bishops as superior general. They have read that a superior general has jurisdiction, and they have also read elsewhere that the Society's bishops would be schismatic if they claimed to have jurisdiction. Is it not a schismatic act to elect a bishop as superior general?......158

What is the tenure of the superior general of the Society of St. Pius X? Do the rules allow him to be re-elected? Is a district superior assigned for a specific number of years and, if so, what length of time? 160

If carrying the crosier is a sign of jurisdiction, why do the bishops of the Society of St. Pius X, who claim no jurisdiction, carry it?.....................161

What do the bishops of the Society of St. Plus X do? 162

Does the disobedience of the 1988 episcopal consecrations constitute a schismatic act? 164

Many priests seem to use varying rubrics in offering Mass. Your calendar for the general public promulgates the rubrics of John XXIII. What does the SSPX use? 166

At the beginning of the Canon of the Mass we pray for our pope and our bishop. Which bishop do we pray for? Do we pray for the bishop of our diocese, or a Society bishop, or the repose of the soul of Archbishop Lefebvre? 166

Why do Masses in the churches of the Society of St. Pius X have an additional *Confiteor* before Holy Communion? 167

Why is the second *Confiteor* omitted from the missal published by Angelus Press?.........168

Why does the Society of St. Pius X permit the "pernicious" custom
of displaying the national flag in the sanctuary?................................169

Why does the Society of St. Pius X administer conditionally the sacraments
of baptism and confirmation to those who received them in the *Novus Ordo*?...........169

It seems that it can be argued persuasively that the sacrament of confirmation
ought to be administered before First Holy Communion, somewhere
around the age of seven. What is the Society's position on this matter? 170

When my husband and I were married in 1963, it was imperative that we
have the ceremony held before noon. Why was this? Why is it being allowed
to be held past noon now? What is the practice of the chapels of the SSPX?...........171

Why is it that priests are not assigned to their own countries,
or to their own part of the world even, or to their own language? 172

Does the Society of St. Pius X promote Nocturnal Adoration in the home?.................173

I do not believe that it is right for the Society of St. Pius X to say
"we are not the Church," for the other bishops are all apostates......................173

What kind of men does God call to the Brothers of the Society of St. Pius X?.............174

Some people have stated that Cardinal Ratzinger's decree overturning the
"excommunication" of the "Hawaii Six" is not a precedent and does
not apply equally to other Catholics who attend the Society's Masses. Is this true? 178

How must a Catholic conduct himself at a public forum during the invocation provided by
non-Catholic clergy or even Catholic clergy failing to meet the norm of Catholic prayer?
How do priests of the Society respond when asked to deliver such an invocation? 179

Since the *Novus Ordo* has relinquished its obligation to provide guidance
to parents with regard to movie ratings and since the movie industry
has come out with a new, relaxed rating system, I am wondering if it
isn't time for the Society to come out with a rating system? 180

I think that the Society of Saint Pius X is in heresy. It affirms that the
ordinary magisterium of the Church can err. The proof of this is that it
accepts that the documents of Vatican II are part of the ordinary magisterium,
but it still says that they have errors, does it not? 182

ABOUT PRAYER AND THE SPIRITUAL LIFE

Is it not opposed to free will for our prayers to be answered? 183

Ought we to pray that God lead us not into temptation?..............................184

Why do so many of our most fervent prayers seem to remain unanswered? 184

Are prayers made while in the state of mortal sin useless?...........................185

Are there means of penance other than that which we receive in the confessional?
Often that does not seem adequate, especially for past mortal sins. 187

I quote from the Douay-Rheims version of holy Scripture : "And when you are praying,
speak not much, as the heathens. For they think that in their much speaking they
may be heard" (Matt. 6:7). How is this teaching reconciled with the recommendation
of the Church to pray the rosary daily? Is it not mechanistic and a repetition of words? . . 187

"Novena Never Known to Fail"–a little prayer to the Sacred Heart and to St. Jude.
Then it says "must be said six times each day for nine consecutive days, leaving a copy
in church each day. Prayer will be answered on or before the ninth day. Novena has never
been known to fail to grant favor asked for by ninth day." I found copies of this cluttering
the front pews in church. I wondered what you would say about this sort of thing. 187

When can the Prayer to St. Michael against the devil and the bad angels be recited? 188

May one offer prayers for specific intentions even though
one has made the total consecration to Our Lady according
to the method of St. Louis-Marie Grignion de Montfort? 189

What is holiness? 190

Is holiness possible outside of the cloister? 191

Is there anything wrong with a young person deciding
to stay single for the rest of his or her life? 191

ABOUT RELIGIOUS ORDERS AND THE RELIGIOUS LIFE

What were the Knights Templar, and what was their relation with the Knights of Malta? 193

Can you tell me something about the Legionaries of Christ?
Are they a traditional order? Do they offer the Tridentine Mass
or the *Novus Ordo*? How should one respond to their request for funds? 194

What are the signs of a vocation to the religious life or to the priesthood? 195

Why is it that we have so relatively few vocations amongst traditional Catholics? 195

Would it be morally wrong to dress as a monk even though a layman? Would you consider
someone dressing as a monk a deception? Can a lay person found a monastery?
Even in these times, isn't it imperative that a monastery have ecclesiastical approval?
What suggestions would you give to a young man wishing to join a monastery? 201

Should a traditional religious Sister who is unable to live her religious life
in a post-Vatican II community request to be dispensed from her vows? 202

Can a widow whose children are full grown join a cloister or a convent? 203

ABOUT MARRIAGE, PARENTHOOD, FAMILY LIFE, AND REARING CHILDREN

Is it advisable for a Catholic to marry a non-Catholic? 203

A single woman for grave medical reasons has undergone
a hysterectomy. Can she contract a valid Catholic marriage? 204

A friend of mine was raised a Catholic, fell away from the Church,
and married a non-Catholic person outside the Church.
She has now divorced him. Is she free to remarry? 205

Can it still be affirmed that a wife should be submissive to her husband,
given the changes in modern society? 205

Is it a mortal sin to refuse one's husband or wife the marital debt? 207

Does apostasy of one's spouse from the Catholic Faith give one
the right to refuse the marriage debt and to separate? 208

Is parenthood in itself a great thing? 209

Is a marriage valid if a couple agrees beforehand to limit the number
of children by artificial birth control or Natural Family Planning?.....................210

Is there a Scriptural foundation for the Church's teaching on contraception?..............212

Is it ever permissible to condone artificial contraception
as a means of family planning for a Catholic couple?.............................215

What did Pope Pius XII say on October 20, 1951,
to the midwives of Italy on the subject of temporal abstinence? 215

How do I explain to a total atheist why the Catholic Church
is against both abortion and birth control? 216

Is it permissible for a Catholic wife and mother to take a job outside the home?..........217

How can I get my four-year-old to participate in our daily rosary?.....................218

Is it permissible to send our children to a Protestant grade or high school?..............220

Should the mother or the father be responsible for teaching children their catechism?......222

When a relative is married outside the Church (*i.e.*, invalidly), can we invite him
and his spouse to visit and stay with us or do we have to break off all contact?.........223

Why do marriages fail?...223

Is it wise to give children pocket money? 224

Is one permitted to maintain social contact with apostate family members? 224

Are the television and the movie theater a suitable form of recreation for Catholics? 226

Is it a sin for a traditional Catholic family to have a television in the home?..............227

Should I refuse to speak to my daughter, who is living in sin with her boyfriend? 230

How should Catholics view dancing? 231

About Virtues and Vices

Must we forgive injuries done to God and to others?................................233

Is it not also important to set a good example in the hope of conversions? 234

In order to avoid the error of naturalism, must I despise natural virtues?.................234

Must we always give to those who ask for money, in particular, beggars?.................235

Could you please explain why so many traditional Catholics feel that pants
are improper attire for women and/or girls? Are pants considered immodest?
At what age would a young girl be obligated to wear only dresses?
In what circumstances would pants be allowed for women?.........................236

There is a Catholic standard of modesty in dress for women.
Is there also a standard of dress for men? 236

About Sin and Sins

Why did Our Lord pray from the cross: "Father, forgive them, for they know
not what they do"? My understanding is if we know not what we do,
we are not guilty of sin and therefore no forgiveness is needed. 238

What is slander? Is slandering a priest a grave sin? Is reparation required? 239

Do persons who arrive late for Mass every Sunday commit a sin? 240

Is it true that St. Thomas says that all drunkenness is mortally sinful,
regardless of the extent, for the quantity of wine drunk is but a circumstance?.........240

What is the morality of drug taking? Is the smoking of marijuana a mortal sin?...........241

A priest told me in confession that it is not a mortal sin to use drugs
such as marijuana. What do you think about this? 242

About the Soul and the Body

Is it true to say that the difference between human beings
is in the body and not in the soul?..244

Do you consider sports to be a twentieth-century heresy: the adoration of the body?.......246

About Life after Death: Heaven, Purgatory, Limbo, and Hell

Can the virtue of charity exist alone among the theological virtues
after this life, just as the virtue of faith can exist alone on earth?....................247

Will all men go to heaven? Will everyone be saved? 248

Can the suffering souls in purgatory help people on earth by their prayers? 249

Where will unbaptized children and aborted babies go on the day of the Last Judgment?....250

Does hell exist? What does it seem to mean
for some theologians and teachers in the Church today? 251

Can an apostate from the Catholic Church save his soul
if he dies in the state of unrepented apostasy?..................................252

About Science, Medicine, and Medical Matters

A friend claims that test-tube babies, which are made by men,
have no souls, as God did not create them and breathe life into them.
If this is so, then how can they live if they have no soul?...........................253

Can cloned human babies be used for experiments
and for growing spare parts, to help others?....................................253

What measures must be taken to preserve one's life, in the case of
terminally ill patients or perpetually comatose patients? Who is morally
obliged to have health insurance? Who is morally excused from having it?.............254

Is it not excessive to maintain that the providing of fluids and nourishment
is always obligatory, regardless of the state of a sick person?.......................255

Could you explain the Church's teaching concerning medical treatments
given to those who suffer from fatal illnesses? Whilst I am against euthanasia
and suicide, I am confused as to what treatments I would be obliged to accept..........257

Why is sterilization immoral, and is a reversal procedure ever necessary?................259

Is a vasectomy an immoral operation? When, if ever, is the reversal of this obligatory? 263

As a Catholic nurse, do I have the right to administer
birth control (Depo-Provera) injections?.......................................263

Can the pill be taken for medical reasons? 264

Why also could not a married woman using her marriage rights do likewise?
  Does not the Council of Trent teach that this is permissible, provided that the
  bad effect (*i.e.*, contraception) is not willed and there is no intention to frustrate life? . . . 264

I have a good Catholic doctor, and he did not tell me I had to abstain. 265

I know a Catholic woman who took the pill for years.
  She said that she was advised not to have children during the change of life. 265

Does the Church approve of surgery for an ectopic pregnancy? 266

Is it permissible to induce early delivery in cases of fetal anencephaly? 267

Is there any moral objection for a Catholic mother
  to submit to the practice of amniocentesis? 269

Is it licit to allow one's children to be vaccinated for rubella
  with vaccine manufactured with the help of fetal cells from aborted babies? 269

Is it wrong to be an organ donor? 271

Some physicians use the text of Pope John Paul II's address
  to the International Congress on Transplants, dated August 29, 2000,
  to justify "cadaveric" organ transplantation. Can we accept this? 272

Is hypnosis permissible as a medical therapy? 273

Can a Catholic use acupuncture? 275

Would a person with celiac disease be protected by transubstantiation
  from being harmed by gluten in the host? 275

Is Alcoholics Anonymous penetrated by the principles of naturalism,
  and if so, how can it be justifiable for a traditional Catholic to belong to it? 275

ABOUT THE STATE AND CIVIC DUTIES

Is there such a thing as the Rights of Man? 276

How binding is the "just war" principle on Catholics?
  Can a Catholic, in good faith, be an absolute pacifist? 277

Could a US attack on Iraq be considered a just war? 278

Can the use of nuclear weapons in time of war ever be justified? 280

What is the Church's stand on capital punishment? 281

Is it morally obligatory to vote? 281

Is it a mortal sin to vote for a pro-abortion candidate? 283

Is it permitted for representatives to vote in favor of a law banning partial-birth abortion
  but permitting some exceptions, such as the protection of the life of the mother? 285

Can a US citizen swear an oath of loyalty to a foreign Christian prince? 286

Am I obliged in conscience to pay my taxes? 287

Is slavery evil, and if so, surely the North was right in the American Civil War? 288

ABOUT SOCIAL JUSTICE, BUSINESS, AND WORK

What are the foundations of social justice? 291

What is the Church's understanding of social justice? 292

Is usury a sin? 293

Can a Catholic in conscience declare bankruptcy,
and if so can he consider his debts as forgiven?................................294

Do you accept Belloc's distinction between "productive" and "non-productive" loans?.......296

Is it permissible for a Catholic to speculate on the stock market
or on the international currency exchange market? 296

I have read that the Church has at all times forbidden speculation.
I intended to make a career out of commodities trading and am concerned
this activity is contrary to Church teaching. Can you respond to my doubts?...........298

Can a Catholic invest in a company that makes profit
from immoral products or activities, such as a drug company? 299

Is it permissible for a traditional Catholic to teach in a public school? 299

Could you indicate whether I can perform
classic country acoustic guitar folk music for income?...........................300

What is the purpose of manual labor?...301

Does the Church permit workers to go on strike? 302

Should a Catholic plan his or her retirement? 302

How should a traditional Catholic plan for retirement? 303

Is it permissible for a landlord to rent an apartment
or house to an unmarried couple living in sin? 304

Is it licit to sell on the Internet auction site eBay relics (first, second,
and third class), blessed articles, statues and sacred vessels, and items
of intrinsic value secondarily containing a blessed item or a relic?...................305

Can a Catholic telephone operator give out telephone numbers
to Planned Parenthood and immoral movie theaters?.............................307

About Names and Meanings of Words and Phrases

Is it correct to speak of our "Judeo-Christian" heritage?............................308

What is the origin of the word "Lent"? 310

What is meant by the expression *"sensus fidei"?* 310

Where do we get the word "collation" from?......................................312

Please explain what "slain in the Spirit" is, and how far back
does this date in the history of the Catholic Church? 313

About Other Concerns

What do you think of *The Poem of the Man God* by Maria Valtorta?....................313

FOREWORD

In his Preface to the most famous collection of Questions and Answers on Catholicism, *Radio Replies* by Fathers Rumble and Carty, Bishop Fulton Sheen outlines very clearly the need for such a collection of answers to commonly asked questions:

> If, then, the hatred of the Church is founded on erroneous beliefs, it follows that the basic need of the day is instruction. Love depends on knowledge, for we cannot aspire to nor desire the unknown. Our great country is filled with what might be called marginal Christians, *i.e.*, those who live on the fringe of religion and who are descendants of Christian living parents, but who now are Christians only in name. (1938; I, ix)

Fathers Rumble and Carty were able to do so much good in converting Protestants to the true Faith and to the true Church, for their answers were brief, direct, to the point, practical, and, most importantly, true. It seems to me that the Question and Answer column, present in *The Angelus* magazine from its very inception in 1978 under the title "Ask Me," has fulfilled this function, *mutatis mutandis*, with respect to Tradition. It has given direct answers to simple and commonly asked questions concerning doctrine, morality, the crisis in the Church, and the practice of traditional Catholicism.

The traditional Catholic in the twenty-first century needs knowledge to live his Faith. Unfortunately, there are in our circles not a few good souls who read little and study even less, whose knowledge of the Church, of the crisis, of the principles of theology and morality is quite inferior to their knowledge of secular subjects, who could easily become as marginal with respect to Catholic Tradition as some Catholics in the days of Fulton Sheen were with respect to the Church, who are in danger of becoming nominal traditional Catholics due to lack of nourishment. It is for them that this column has existed in *The Angelus* for now more than thirty years, giving short, precise answers, easy to assimilate and to understand, founded upon the simple principles of the Faith. It is designed to give them in just a few minutes the means to understand, explain and defend many different aspects of traditional teaching, custom and practice. It is in response to the demand to bring these answers into one book, that this collection of questions and answers from *The Angelus* magazine has been assembled.

We owe this book firstly to Father Carl Pulvermacher, O.F.M., Cap., the first editor and printer of *The Angelus* magazine. He started this column and for many years wrote it himself, imparting upon it the gentle, humoristic simplicity that is so typically Franciscan. Now that he has passed to his eternal reward, we can frankly admit how much the Society and the Angelus Press owe to Father Carl, as generations of traditional Catholics affectionately called him. His common sense and down-to-earth faith earned him the right to be not only the friend of everybody, as he certainly was, but also a renowned spiritual director, both inside and outside the magazine.

A succession of priests has tried to walk in Father Carl's footsteps. Father Laisney, as publisher of *The Angelus,* wrote the Q & A column himself briefly (1988-1990). Then Father Doran, as editor of *The Angelus,* wrote it (1990-1992), followed by Father Boyle when stationed in Phoenix (1992-1994). Finally, finding nobody else audacious enough to try to solve all the problems of the world with the stroke of his pen, your servant, then publisher of *The Angelus,* found himself loaded with this task. Indeed, over these past fourteen years I have considered it a great joy and challenge to answer questions, both spontaneous and varied, just as they come to me. These are the questions that concern you, our faithful and our readers. Sometimes they are on the Society and its combat, on our canonical status and the errors of Vatican II and the conciliar church, but just as often they concern Catholic doctrine, or traditional moral principles or Canon Law. Each time has been a good occasion to do a little research and to find the appropriate reference or text, in order to give an answer that is not just a personal opinion, but one which truly reflects the mind of the Church.

It is true that I have not been able to keep up and answer all the questions directed to *The Angelus.* A choice has always to be made, so that an interesting variety of all kinds of questions is put together, with the end result that there is something unpredictable about the column. This collection does not include all the answers given to questions, but is rather a selection chosen amongst those considered most interesting, helpful, informative, topical and presently relevant, divided up and categorized by subject matter, as best can be done. I would like to thank not only the Angelus Press staff themselves, but also Dr. Mary Buckalew, who has not only been a contributor and proofreader for *The Angelus* from its very beginning, but who has also for many years proofread this column, and has spent many long hours proofreading and categorizing the answers published in this book.

Fr. Peter R. Scott

ABOUT GOD THE HOLY TRINITY

 We are admonished to forgive our enemies, yet according to His agents (the hierarchy), God does not forgive His enemies, submitting them to eternal torture in hell. No wrong can be so bad as to merit unending torture. We are born with no part in the decision. If we fail to satisfy God, the humane thing for Him to do would be to annihilate that soul. Does God set a bad example for tyrants to follow against their victims?

There are two questions to be answered in the above query. What is it to forgive our enemies? And secondly, where is God's forgiveness in face of His eternal justice?

Our Lord from the very beginning of His ministry taught the necessity of forgiving our enemies. "Love your enemies: do good to them that hate you: and pray for them that persecute and calumniate you" (Mt. 5:44). The perfection of this doctrine lies in the imitation of the Most High in His equal doing of good to all: "But love ye your enemies: do good, and lend, hoping for nothing thereby: and your reward shall be great, and you shall be the sons of the Highest; for he is kind to the unthankful, and to the evil" (Lk. 6:35). So important is this doctrine that He went so far as to state: "Forgive, and you shall be forgiven; give, and it shall be given to you....For with what measure you measure, it shall be measured to you" (Lk. 6:37-38). Our Lord thus made the measure of our forgiveness the same that Almighty God would mete out to us: "For if you forgive men their offenses, your heavenly Father will also forgive you your offenses. But if you do not forgive men, neither will your Father forgive you your offenses" (Mt. 6:14-15).

"Take heed to yourselves. If thy brother sin against thee, reprove him: and if he do penance, forgive him. And if he sin against thee seven times in a day, and seven times in a day be converted unto thee, saying, I repent; forgive him" (Lk. 17:3-4). When St. Peter asked how many times this was to be done, he thought himself being generous by thinking seven to be more than sufficient (the rabbis of his day believed three times to be a great amount), the Master answered with the key to the question: "I say not to thee, till seven times; but till seventy times seven times" (Mt. 18:22). Therefore the obvious basis of forgiveness is not the one offended but the repentance of the offender. We are commanded by the Savior Himself to forgive as often as there is contrition on the part of the one offending us, without counting the number of times.

This does not counter the necessity of justice, as what is properly due must be kept, at least in public affairs. The criminal may be forgiven but still be required to make restitution for the damage he has committed. In a purely personal matter, though, we are counseled to "turn the other cheek." This disposition of the offender makes clear how God can command forgiveness from His servants and children and Himself mete out justice in hell. God also forgives those who with contrite heart return to Him, and this more than seventy times seven times according to His infinite mercy. Note that the disposition of the offender is here too what disposes the offended to forgive.

It is when the sinner (another name for offender) continues in his original intention that it is impossible to condone his action. He sees no wrong in his works, seeks no forgiveness, and thus receives none. He has sinned against the Holy Ghost; *i.e.*, he has rejected the very source and fountain of forgiveness. "Amen I say to you, that all sins shall be forgiven to the sons of men, but whoever blasphemes against the Holy Spirit never has forgiveness, but will be guilty of an everlasting sin" (Mk. 3:28-29). His blasphemy (insult) is against the Source of all good. His sin remains unpardonable because he seeks no pardon. And this is so not from God's part, but from the part of the sinner. The sinner sets himself on the course to punishment.

Punishment is meted according to the dignity of the person offended. It would be a far greater thing to strike the mayor of a city, or the president, than to do so to an equal. Now, when one commits a mortal sin against God, he offends by breaking His commandments, and gives the honor due to God alone, as last end, to some other of his own choosing. But God's person and majesty are infinite; thus it is just that one suffer forever having sinned mortally.

The man who sins places himself in a state from which only God can rescue him. Therefore, the very fact that he is willing to commit sin signifies that he is willing to remain in that state forever. Thus a man who jumps into a pit from which he would need help to escape could be said to desire to remain there forever, whatever he may have thought himself.

More important is the fact that by mortal sin a man puts his final end in some other than God. Since he directs his life to this end (it is final), it follows that he would remain in this sin forever if he could do so with impunity.

The argument that God should simply annihilate the wicked because existence is the most precious of God's gifts forgets the fact that punishment must also be measured according to the disorder of the fault and not just according to the person offended; otherwise every sin would require a punishment of infinite intensity. Therefore, although a man may deserve to lose his existence for having sinned against the Author of being, from the point of view of the disorder of his act it does not itself demand loss of being. Being is presupposed to merit and demerit. Remember, being is not lost or corrupted by this lack of order in sin, thus the privation of being cannot be the punishment due to any sin.

So much for the attempt of the Seventh Day Adventists and Jehovah's Witnesses to skip the discomforting truth of eternal punishment in hell!

—*Fr. Doran,* July 1992

 **Supposedly, God knows the future and all things. According to that position, He already knows if I'll be saved or damned. Who am I even to attempt to sway the will of God? If I'm due for damnation, any attempt for salvation is futile. But I don't believe God knows my end yet! Otherwise free will is thwarted.**

The divine Intellect contemplates Itself, "He Who Is," in an eternal act of comprehension. This means that the object of God's knowledge is Himself. He sees in one eternal moment—past, present, and future (from our point of view)—all things actual and possible. This means that He sees all things as present to Himself, as present as you are reading these lines.

God thus sees me one hundred years ago, two years ago, ten minutes ago, now, ten minutes from now, two years from now, and in all eternity as all present, and this simultaneously. In fact, all the moments of my existence are present to the view of God in His eternity. To say that God knows the future is to speak in our terms. There is for Him no future. If He sees me in hell, He also sees simultaneously all my free actions which led me there. Free actions, as no one is "due" for damnation.

To deny that God knows my end would be heretical as it would deny that divine attribute of omniscience. It would also be irrational as this is a naturally knowable truth concerning the Supreme Being.

—*Fr. Doran,* April 1992

 **Why does God allow some to suffer mentally and physically more than others? Is this fair?**

God loves some more than others, and He gives His best crosses to those. A cross from God, if accepted willingly, is worth far more than crosses we choose for ourselves. Surely, God is fair. There is no imperfection of any kind in Him. If you think you have more crosses than you deserve, read the Book of Job and be consoled.

—*Fr. Carl,* November 1987

Did the Father and the Holy Ghost suffer like Jesus did on the cross?

It is impossible for God to suffer in His divine nature, for His divinity is immutable and in the all-perfect and all-happy possession of itself. The only way that God could possibly suffer is by taking to Himself a finite, limited, changeable, created nature. God the Son did this in the mystery of the Incarnation, and from that moment on until His death upon the cross He was able to suffer in His human nature. He cannot, however, suffer now in His human nature since it is now glorified in heaven. However, the Father and the Holy Ghost at no time took to themselves a created, human nature. Consequently, they could not suffer and never did suffer. Here lies the mystery of the Redemption. It was in order to be able to pay the debt of our sins with true, human suffering that the Son of God was made man.

When we speak of God suffering on account of the sins of men, we speak of the sufferings of God the Son in His human nature, paying the debt of our sins. If this is said of the Godhead, it is meant improperly to indicate how great is the offense made to the divine Majesty by our sins, but not that God actually suffers from them.

—Fr. Scott, June 2003

About Our Lord Jesus Christ

Is it accurate to say that Our Lord was a Jew?

There are two meanings of the term "Jew." The first meaning indicates that people and nation "chosen by God to maintain acceptable worship of the One True God in preparation for the coming of Him who was to re-establish order in the world by the restoration of supernatural life" (Fr. Denis Fahey, *The Mystical Body of Christ*, p. 150). In this sense "Jesus Christ, Son of David, Son of Abraham" (Mt. 1:1) was most certainly a Jew. Pontius Pilate declares this: "Am I a Jew? Thy own people and the chief priests have delivered thee to me" (Jn. 18:35), as does our divine Savior Himself: "for salvation is from the Jews" (Jn. 4:22). As Fr. Fahey puts it: "Our Lord Jesus Christ, the supernatural Messias, True God and True Man, is at one and the same time the Second Person of the Blessed Trinity and a Jew of the house of David" (*ibid.*). In this sense the Catholic Church succeeded to the synagogue of Israel, applying to all who believe in the Messias the supernatural life of grace, for "there is neither Jew nor Greek … and if you are Christ's, then you are the offspring of Abraham" (Gal. 3:28-29).

However, there is another sense in which we speak of the Jews, both as a religion and as a people. In the same way as the Pharisees of Our Lord's time refused to recognize their Messias and believe in Him as a result of their proud, hypocritical "zeal" for arbitrary interpretations and hairsplitting decisions concerning the law, so also the Jews from their time until now who have refused to convert to the Catholic Church:

> The Jews refused, firstly, to accept that the supernatural life of His Messianic Kingdom was higher than the national life, and, secondly, they utterly rejected the idea of the Gentile nations being admitted to enter into the messianic kingdom on the same level as themselves.... Having put their race and nation in the place of God, having in fact deified them, they rejected the supernatural Messias and elaborated a program of preparation for the natural Messias to come. (Fahey, p. 151)

This is what we call Zionism. In this sense our divine Savior was most certainly not a Jew.

Consequently, it is not at all insulting to call Christ a Jew in the first sense, but rather an aspect of His divine mission. His baptism did nothing to change this origin according to the flesh, but was simply the opportune moment to manifest His divine filiation and nature: "This is my well beloved Son, in whom I am well pleased" (Mt. 3:17). Nevertheless, it would be a complete denial of the mystery of the Redemption to call Christ a Jew in the second sense, or to pretend that we have any faith in common with such modern-day Jews, or that they are in truth sons of Abraham.

—*Fr. Scott,* October 2007

 Did Jesus have a brother named James?

James the Lesser was a cousin of Our Lord, and not at all a son of the Blessed Mother. However, the Greek word for brother, *adelphos*, is also used for close relatives. "Brother" also has a meaning rather like the English word "brethren." The New Testament certainly speaks about Jesus' brethren, but by a false translation Protestants pretend that His brethren were His brothers and make the sacrilegious and blasphemous heretical statement that the Blessed Mother did not always remain a virgin. It is sacrilegious because it speaks of the Blessed Virgin Mary as if she were a regular woman, not one consecrated to be the Mother of God. It is blasphemous, for it treats of the Incarnation of the Son of God as if it were not a divine work, brought about by the overshadowing of the Holy Ghost. It is heretical because it denies the dogma of the perpetual virginity of the Blessed Virgin Mary, first formally defined by the Council of

Constantinople II in 553 (Dz. [Henry Denzinger, *The Sources of Catholic Dogma* (1955)] 214, 218).

—*Fr. Scott,* October 2000

 **I understand that Jesus is God and God's Son. Why then would He choose such a horrible way to redeem mankind when He could have made it so much easier?**

Absolutely speaking, it was not necessary for redemption that God should choose to send His Son to die for the sin of the world. In the eternal and free choice of the Trinity, though, it was decreed that the Word should be incarnate and die in the work of salvation. "No one takes it [my life] from Me [Christ], but I lay it down of myself. I have the power to lay it down, and I have the power to take it up again. Such is the command I have received from my Father" (Jn. 10:18).

Being the Word Incarnate, Jesus Christ is a divine Person. Thus all His actions were of infinite value, done as they were by an infinite Person. His slightest prayer on behalf of mankind could have worked the redemption. His Father commanded, and He chose freely, that He would offer Himself, in the Holy Ghost, as a perfect sacrifice to conquer the devil, sin, and death. This was done to show the horror of sin: it brought about the death of God, who, unable to die in His divine nature, took to Himself a human nature in which suffering was possible. Secondly, this suffering manifested the fullness of the love of God for us. Divine Love appeared in human flesh and poured out its very blood as a sign of its infinite depth. This consummation by His death was the greatest possible giving for the sake of His beloved creatures. The great depth of sin and of God's love are both marvelously seen in the mystery of the Redemption.

—*Fr. Doran,* March 1993

 **What do you think of a statement made by an apparition that "Jesus did not carry the cross, He carried only the cross bar"?**

Leaving aside the question of which apparition, archaeology can answer much of this question.

There were a number of ways in which crucifixion was inflicted. The most probable seems, in the case of our Redeemer, that He was forced to carry the *patibulum*, the cross member. At the site, He would have been nailed to this, which would then have been lifted onto the upright member already fixed in the ground. The feet of the Crucified being nailed to this *stipes*, He was left to die from asphyxiation. The Shroud of Turin would seem to confirm this by the marks seen along Our Lord's back, which would have been caused by the *patibulum* rolling across His back, opening once more His wounds while He fell during the journey to Calvary.

—*Fr. Doran,* September 1992

 **What did Christ mean when He said, "Whose sins you shall forgive, they are forgiven; whose sins you shall retain, they are retained."**

It means only that the confessor is designated as judge in Christ's place, and he judges whether the sinner asking for pardon is truly repentant. If a sinner is penitent the confessor must absolve (forgive). If there is no repentance the confessor must retain, *i.e.*, give no absolution. A sinner who is unwilling to give up an unnecessary occasion of sin is not forgiven, *i.e.*, his sin is retained.

—*Fr .Carl,* November 1987

 **Why did Our Lord refer to His Mother as "Woman"?**

Volumes have been written to explain it. The title "woman," which sounds harsh when used by a son to his mother, is a translation of the Greek word for "lady," a title of respect. Our Lord was not disrespectful to His Mother—formal, but not disrespectful.

—*Fr. Carl,* September 1981

 **Catholics call their priests "father" in spite of the fact that Our Lord says, "Call no man on earth father" (Mt. 23:9). Isn't this breaking Christ's command?**

This is a question that causes some Catholics to stutter and blush. However, there should be no need of this. Our Lord commanded us to honor our father and mother (Mt. 15:3-7). Blessed Mary called St. Joseph "father" to her Son: "Thy father and I have sought thee sorrowing" (Lk. 2:48). The husband of our mothers we normally call "father"—not "pal" or "Joe" or whatever, but "father." St. Paul (Rom. 4:16) calls Abraham the "father" of us all. No man can stand in any way whatsoever as a father unless God holds him up. So Our Lord tells us never to forget that the power of fatherhood is God's above, and no man in any way can add to or detract from that absolute fact. Surely we know as faithful Catholics that an earthly father shares in the wonderful work of the heavenly Father's work of creation in bringing a new life into the world. A priest is surely called "father" because he brings spiritual life to souls—in baptism, confession, and the other sacraments. In some way, God upholds this fatherhood of the priest by the grace of spiritual life which He distributes through the hands of His priests. If the priest does not beget spiritual life, he is not a father, just as an earthly man is no father unless he begets or supports earthly life. Calling anyone a father or master who really does not share the life-giving faculty of God the Father is what Our Lord meant when He forbad the calling of anyone on earth your father. No one reading the Bible carefully should ever wonder about this oft-repeated, stupid question. All fatherhood in earth or in heaven is named after Him, the heavenly Father (Eph. 3:14).

—*Fr. Carl,* April 1984

Is altar wine addictive, and if so, how could Christ have used it?

All alcoholic beverages are addictive in certain persons, namely, in alcoholics, but not in others. Wine is no exception to this. Yet it is certainly true that grape wine is natural and does have some special qualities, recalled even by sacred Scripture. It certainly does rejoice the heart of man, as the psalms say, and it does soothe nerves in those who do not have the predisposition to become alcoholics.

However, with respect to its alcohol content, wine is not any different from other alcoholic beverages, and is easily prone to abuse. Wine-drinking persons can certainly become alcoholics, and frequently do. It is probably true that it is not so frequently abused as whiskey and other spirits and stronger drinks that alcoholics indulge in. Nevertheless, it must be counted with those fermented drinks that can ruin a person.

Our Lord is not responsible for the abuse of this good substance that God in His goodness provided for us, and that our divine Savior elevated to become the species under which He would give us His precious blood. Nevertheless, the wine that was drunk in the time of Our Lord was much weaker than modern-day wine—probably only seven to eight per cent alcohol. Also, the Jews, like all peoples of antiquity, mixed water with their wine in large quantities. Consequently, it was less open to abuse and to cause alcoholism.

Present-day sacramental wine is twelve to eighteen per cent, which higher concentration of alcohol gives the best natural preservation from corruption. The main difference between sacramental wine and table wine is that sacramental wine must be entirely pure from any additives or preservatives, and must not contain any alcohol or other product that is not fermented from or fruit of the vine. This is what the Church has to say:

> In order that wine may be valid and licit matter for consecration, it must be wine which has been pressed from fully ripened grapes, which has fermented, which has been purified of sediment or dregs, which has a vinous alcoholic content of around 12%, which has not been adulterated by the addition of any non-vinous substance, which is neither growing nor

grown bad by acescence or putrefaction. (*Matters Liturgical*, 10th edition [1959], pp. 327-328)

Either red or white wine may be used for altar wine.

—*Fr. Scott*, May 2006

When a "born-again" Protestant strikes up a conversation by asking "Who is Jesus?" and "Do you have a personal relationship with Him?" what is a good way to reply?

I would turn these questions around to the Catholic perspective and rephrase them in terms of the catechism. As they stand, they are in fact Protestant questions, based upon the false assumption that religion is a matter of personal experience. In answer to the question about who Jesus is, I would explain the hypostatic union of the human and divine natures, which makes up the mystery of the Incarnation, upon which our redemption is based. With respect to the question on the personal relationship, I would explain what sanctifying grace is, and how it transforms one's life to be thus filled with the theological virtues of faith, hope, and charity.

—*Fr. Scott*, August 1999

ABOUT THE BLESSED VIRGIN MARY

If we are to say that Mary is the Mother of God, must we not also admit that she is Mother of the Divinity?

It is a Catholic dogma that Mary is the Mother of God, as defined by the Council of Ephesus (431) against the heresy of the Nestorians. The Nestorians refused to acknowledge her title as *Theotokos*, or Mother of God, and only wanted to designate her as Mother of Man or Mother of Christ. For they denied that the divine and human natures were united in the one person of the Son of God, and that consequently Mary is His mother according to His human nature.

This doctrine is well summarized by Dr. Ludwig Ott (*Fundamentals of Catholic Dogma*, pp. 196-197), who points out that the dogma of Mary's motherhood of God contains two truths, namely that Mary truly is a mother, by contributing to the human nature of Christ, and that she truly is the Mother of God, "that is, she conceived and bore the Second Person of the Divinity, not indeed according to the Divine Nature, but according to the assumed human nature." It was precisely the objection of Nestorius that if Mary were the Mother of God, then Christ would have had to have taken not only His human nature but also His divine nature from her, a creature. The answer is that it is not the nature which is conceived and born, but the person.

It is true that there is a contrary heresy to that of the Nestorians, that of the Monophysites, condemned by the Council of Chalcedon twenty years later (451). It maintains that the divine and human natures in Christ are somehow merged together. Since they hold no distinction between the divine and human natures, it follows that Mary is no longer Mother of God simply according to the assumed human nature, as taught by the Councils of Ephesus and Chalcedon. Ott has this to say of this theory, which by mingling the divinity and humanity of Christ ends up by destroying both of them:

> The Fathers also point out the intrinsic impossibility of the monophysite doctrine of unification. It contradicts the absolute immutability and the infinite perfection of God, and by abrogating the true humanity of Christ, leads to the destruction of the work of redemption. (*Ibid.*, p. 147)

It is consequently a doctrine of our Catholic Faith to affirm that Mary is "Mother of God according to human nature" (Dz. 148). If anyone were to say that she were also Mother of the divine nature, he would imply a confusion of the two natures, he would have fallen into the Monophysite heresy, and he would certainly not be a true defender of the honor of the Blessed Mother. This is a good example of the importance of the careful scholastic definitions of such notions as "person" and "nature" to have an accurate understanding of the Catholic Faith.

—*Fr. Scott,* August 1999

Is the Blessed Virgin Mary "divine"?

The word "divine" is an adjective that describes one who has the divine nature, and by consequence the prerogatives, authority, and power of God Himself. Clearly the Blessed Virgin Mary is a creature, finite and limited, whose perfection and fullness of grace and predestination to be the Mother of God are received from Almighty God as gratuitous gifts, not owed to her by nature. Consequently, it would be a blasphemy to call the Blessed Virgin divine, as if to indicate that she had the uncreated and infinite nature of God Himself.

However, the greatness of the Blessed Virgin Mary consists exactly in this, that while retaining her status of a creature, she is by a special grace united to the divinity in such a special way as to be the Mother of the Son and the perfect spouse of the Holy Ghost. It is in this sense that St. Louis de Montfort does not hesitate to call her divine, confounding thereby the small-minded, who, in their effort to reduce the mystery of the Incarnation to a human way of understanding, bring the Blessed Virgin

Mary down to the level of other men. Some have, indeed, questioned St. Louis's audacious use of the title "divine" to describe the prerogatives of the Blessed Virgin Mary. We read, for example, in *True Devotion to the Blessed Virgin Mary*, St. Louis saying in the following prayer directed towards our divine Savior:

> Thou, Lord, art always with Mary, and Mary is always with Thee, and she cannot be without Thee, else she would cease to be what she is. She is so transformed into Thee by grace that she lives no more....She is so intimately united with Thee, that it were easier to separate the light from the sun, the heat from the fire. I say more: it were easier to separate from Thee all the Angels and the Saints than the *divine Mary*, because she loves Thee more ardently, and glorifies Thee more perfectly than all other creatures put together.

St. Louis attributes to Our Lady the title "divine" to indicate that by her inseparable union with her divine Son, a consequence of the hypostatic union and her divine maternity, she truly shares in the prerogatives, the authority, and the power of God Himself. It is for this reason that her prayer is said to be all powerful (*omnipotentia supplex*), although she remains but a creature. St. Louis also explains this in the *True Devotion*:

> Mary, being altogether transformed into God by grace, and by the glory which transforms all the Saints into Him, asks nothing, wishes nothing, does nothing which is contrary to the Eternal and Immutable Will of God. When we read, then, in the writings of Saints Bernard, Bernadine, Bonaventure, and others that in heaven and on earth everything, even to God Himself, is subject to the Blessed Virgin, they mean to say that the authority which God has been well pleased to give her is so great that it seems as if she has the same power as God, and that her prayers and petitions are so powerful with God, that they always pass for commandments with His Majesty, who never resists the prayer of His dear Mother, because she is always humble and conformed to His Will.

Let us, then, not hesitate to attribute to the Blessed Virgin Mary the magnificent title of "divine," which so aptly describes the greatness of this greatest of all creatures, her prerogatives, and her power. And logical with ourselves, let us then not hesitate to consecrate ourselves totally and unreservedly to her.

—*Fr. Scott,* May 2004

 **Is the Church telling the truth when it says of the Blessed Virgin Mary "thou alone hast destroyed all heresies in the whole world"?**

It would be idyllic to imagine a time in which there would be no heresies, no individual persons who place their personal opinions over the Church's authority and magisterium. However, the fact that heresies exist, and that this time has manifestly not come, does not at all mean that this antiphon with which the Church honors the Blessed Virgin Mary is not perfectly and literally true.

For there cannot be a time, this side of the general Judgment, in which heresies will not exist. St. Paul stated this very explicitly in his first letter to the Corinthians: "For there *must* be also heresies: that they also, who are approved, may be made manifest among you" (11:19). The meaning of this antiphon is consequently not that there was or will be a time at which all heresies in the whole world are destroyed, but that at all times the Blessed Virgin Mary destroys all heresies in the whole world in those who are truly and profoundly devoted to her.

The meaning of this expression is very well explained by St. Pius X in his encyclical of 1904 for the fiftieth anniversary of the definition of the Immaculate Conception. He there explains that the dogma of the Immaculate Conception contains in germ all Catholic doctrine and in particular the supernatural order of grace, which man in his proud rebellion refuses to accept. Devotion to the immaculate Mother of God is consequently the only means to preserve the submission to God and to the Church's authority that are the protection against all heresy and every error in the Faith:

> If people believe and profess that in the first moment of her conception the Virgin Mary was free from all stain, they must also admit the existence of original sin, the redemption of mankind by Christ, the Gospel, the Church, and even the law of suffering. These truths will root up and destroy any kind of rationalism and materialism that exists.... This doctrine compels us to recognize that power of the Church which demands intellectual as well as voluntary submission. Because of this intellectual submission the Christian people sing to the Mother of God: 'Thou art all fair, O Mary, and there is no original stain in thee.' For this reason the Church rightly attributes the destruction of all heresies in the whole world to the venerable Virgin alone. (*Ad Diem Illum*, §14)

Archbishop Lefebvre was himself very much aware of the wisdom of this teaching concerning devotion to the Blessed Mother as the great protection for the integrity of our faith, especially for apostles of these last times:

> May devotion to Mary be honored in every house and chapel of the Society, and in all the hearts of all its members! Mary will keep us in the Catholic Faith. She is neither liberal, nor modernist, nor ecumenical. She is impervious to all errors and with even greater reason to heresies and apostasy. (*Spiritual Journey*, p. 57)

—*Fr. Scott,* July 2007

Why is it that Catholics adore the wood of the cross, but they do not adore Mary?

The adoration that is due to God is termed *latria* or divine worship. It is absolutely owed to God Himself, and hence to the Second Person of the Blessed Trinity and to Our Lord Jesus Christ. We adore Christ on the cross as in His glorious Resurrection. Clearly, we do not adore the wood of the cross in the same way, since it is but a creature. However, inasmuch as the wood of the cross is directly and immediately related to our divine Savior, whose precious blood sanctified it and made it the sweet wood that bears the salvation of the world, it must also be honored. Consequently, we owe the wood of the cross a relative adoration. We adore it inasmuch as it is related to the Person of our divine Savior, that is, inasmuch as He died for our sins on this wood. However, the worship of *latria* is not directed to the wood, but to our divine Lord.

The veneration that we owe to the holy Mother of God is called *hyperdulia,* meaning that it is greater than the veneration owed to all the saints put together, on account of her fullness of grace and perfect holiness. She also is holy because of her relation to our divine Savior, and it is her divine Motherhood that is the basis of all her other prerogatives. Nevertheless, the veneration of *hyperdulia* that we owe to her is not a relative one, but an absolute one. We do not adore her as God, but we venerate her for who she is, whereas we adore the cross only because it is our divine Savior's cross, by which He redeemed the world.

Hence it is perfectly true to say that we adore the wood of the cross, but we do not adore Mary, although she is infinitely greater than the wood of the cross considered in itself.

—Fr. Scott, January 2004

ABOUT THE ANGELS

What are the cherubim and seraphim?

Cherubim is the Hebrew plural of the word "cherub." It means roughly "one who blesses, one who prays." They are spirits in the service of the Lord God. They are seen, among other places, after the expulsion of Adam from the garden (Gen. 3:24) and in Ezechiel's vision (Ez. 1-10). They act as guardians in the Old Testament, either in reality (Ez. 28:14) or in representation as in the Holy of Holies over the ark of the covenant. Seraphim is also the plural of "seraph," which means "one who burns." They are seen in the vision of Isaias (Is. 6:1-7) around the throne of God.

They are described as having six wings and prostrate before the divine majesty of the Thrice Holy. These two "ranks" of heavenly beings are considered the two highest "choirs," closest to the throne of God.

—*Fr. Doran,* October 1993

Are angels male or female? What do you say about angels?

Angels are created pure spirits who have a higher intellect and will than man. They have no bodies and therefore cannot be male or female. Each angel is a new species, and there are nine choirs. They do God's will by being messengers and guardians of men, popes, bishops, and towns and countries. I have read where they also perform the work of keeping the universe in clocklike order by guiding the planets and stars in their movements. We know the names of only three: Michael, Gabriel, and Raphael. Since Vatican II, some new theologians have denied the existence of angels because it is an embarrassment to non-Catholics—and this in the face of holy Scripture which speaks of angels on nearly every page!

—*Fr. Carl,* April 1979

Why do we call angels "saints"?

The term "saint" has three meanings. It is used in sacred Scripture for the elect, chosen ones, sanctified here on this earth by sanctifying grace, and "called to be saints" (Rm. 1:7; 8:28), of whom St. Paul considers himself the least (Eph. 3:8). It is used secondly to indicate all the citizens of heaven, all the members of the Church triumphant, who regardless of their previous life are not only now sanctified, but confirmed in sanctity so that they can never lose it. It is used thirdly to indicate those saints whom the Church has canonized, declaring infallibly that they are in heaven on account of their heroic virtue and extraordinary deeds of faith and charity.

All the good angels fall into the second category and are, by their fidelity to the grace they received at the moment of their creation, members of the Church triumphant, offering in heaven the incense of their unceasing praise and adoration. Although no angel has been canonized by decree of the Church, nevertheless the Church has always in her tradition practiced special veneration for those angels who have played a special role in the redemption of mankind, and she consequently calls them saints in the third sense also. St. Michael—prince of the heavenly host, heroic leader of the good angels against Lucifer, with his cry of perfect submission "Who is like God?"—is the greatest of them all, and is consequently honored as the protector of the universal Church. St.

Gabriel is honored next because of his mission to announce the mystery of the Incarnation, the great and holy mystery upon which the redemption of mankind depended. St. Raphael is likewise honored, on account of the role of protection described so well in the Book of Tobias.

—*Fr. Scott,* February 2008

ABOUT THE SAINTS

Why is St. Stephen considered the first martyr and not St. John the Baptist?

St. John the Baptist, having died before Our Lord's redemptive death on the cross, is considered the last of the great prophets and saints of the Old Testament. He is honored as a martyr for having laid down his life in defense of conjugal chastity against the incestuous union of Herod. St. Stephen is thus the first to be killed for his faith in our Lord after His resurrection, and hence Catholicism's proto-martyr.

—*Fr. Doran,* October 1992

ABOUT THE CHURCH

How did the Catholic Church get its name?

The early Christian Fathers recognized the Church founded on St. Peter to be the only Church appointed by Jesus Christ (a) to carry on the work of His Redemption, (b) to carry on His sacred office of preaching and teaching, and (c) to lead the people in the true worship of the Triune God. The combination of the terms "catholic" and "church" is found for the first time in a letter written around the year 110 by St. Ignatius of Antioch and addressed to the people of Smyrna: "Wheresoever the Bishop shall appear, there let the people be, even as where Jesus may be there is the Universal [*Catholic* is the term used in Greek] Church."

There is another interesting reference found in St. Irenaeus, bishop of Lyons in France: "The Catholic Church, having received the apostolic teaching and faith ..." (*Adversus Haereses,* I.x.2).

Furthermore, St. Eusebius of Caesarea in his *Ecclesiastical History,* written in the fourth century, writes: "But the brightness of the Catholic Church proceeded to increase in greatness ..." (bk. 4).

Finally, discussing agreement in the use of the term "Catholic" in *The True Religion,* St. Augustine notes that "whether they wish or not, heretics have to call the Catholic Church Catholic"; and in a more pointed remark the saint remarks that "although all heretics wish to be styled Catholic, yet if any one ask where is the Catholic place of worship none of them would venture to point out his own conventicle." So the term "Catholic" has its origin in the primitive Fathers and refers only to that body we recognize as the Catholic Church.

—*Fr. Boyle,* July 1994

 ### What is the difference between "dogma" and "doctrine"?

Doctrine is "the act of teaching" or "the knowledge imparted by teaching." In this sense it is synonymous with "catechesis" and "catechism," which mean "instruction by word of mouth" or "the act of instructing, the subject matter" respectively. These words are well known and are commonly used by the faithful. The Greek word *didaskalia* is especially used in the pastoral epistles of St. Paul. It is commonly translated as "doctrine."

Dogma, in classical times, referred to philosophical tenets, or doctrines of a particular school of philosophers. It could even be used in the sense of a civil decree or edict (Lk. 2:1), or ordinances (Acts 16:4). The early Fathers of the Church designated "dogma" the doctrines and moral precepts of the Savior or the apostles. The modern use of the term is for a truth appertaining to faith or morals, revealed by God, transmitted from the apostles in the Scriptures or by Tradition, and proposed by the Church for the acceptance of the faithful. It is a revealed truth defined by the Church.

One could say that all dogmas are doctrines, but not all doctrines are dogmas. A dogma is a defined doctrine. Let us finish by saying that St. Paul makes "doctrine" one of the most important duties of the bishop (I Tim. 4:15-16).

—*Fr. Doran,* May 1993

 ### Some time ago in the "question and answer" section of one of the foremost "conservative" Catholic journals, the answering priest made the categorical statement: "The Church has never taught definitively that the soul is infused in the moment of conception." In the dogma of the Immaculate Conception, as I understand it, we are taught that the Blessed Mother's soul was free from original sin from the very moment of her conception. It would seem, therefore, that the Church does, in fact, definitively teach that the soul is infused in the moment

of conception. I would appreciate your comments on this priest's statement, and correct me if I err in my understanding of this dogma.

It is true that the Church has never definitively taught that the human soul is infused at conception. But it is by far the majority of theologians who teach that the body is animated, *i.e.*, the soul is infused, at conception. There are many reasons given for this opinion. It is opposed to the older teaching, held by St. Thomas Aquinas, that the matter was successively animated within the womb. This opinion was based on the scientific data of its age. Our Lady, from conception, was free from any taint of original sin. This is normally taught, that her body was animated at the same time as the conception itself. But the Church's definition is in regards to the freedom from stain (*macula*), not the moment of animation. The exemption from sin, due from our first parent, would still have been even if the soul of the Blessed Virgin had been infused at another moment other than conception.

—*Fr. Doran,* October 1992

 **Is it true that the Church frowns on the use of the Gothic vestment, preferring the Roman cut?**

It is true that when the so-called Gothic vestments appeared early in this century, they were considered to be somewhat of a novelty, capable of causing undue surprise in the minds of the faithful. This was not infrequently because more attention was given to the archaic form than to the sacredness of the vestment. The mind of the Church before Vatican II is clearly expressed in this text of 1957, from the Sacred Congregation of Rites, quoted in *Matters Liturgical*, 10th ed. (1959), p. 207:

> The older or mediaeval style of the Roman chasuble, popularly but erroneously called the Gothic chasuble, may be used with the permission of the local Ordinary. To his prudent judgment the matter is now committed. In making this judgment he is cautioned to consider local and other special circumstances, to have regard to the sanctity and decorum due to divine worship, and not to authorize this change from the present Roman practice except after consultation and mature deliberation. Especially should he be careful to forbid such changes in the form of vestments as are likely to disturb or surprise the faithful.

Over the past forty years the use of the so-called Gothic vestment has become universally accepted. However, there is a grave danger of the sacredness of this vestment being lost, which is what is responsible for the extremely distasteful modernist vestments, which have neither decoration nor symbolism. Consequently, there would no longer be any reason to disapprove of a "Gothic" vestment, so long as it is designed as a sacred vestment, with religious ornamentation, and with a cross on the back, symbolizing the sweet yoke of the cross that the priest must carry if he is to be filled with the all-encompassing charity that the chasuble, a little house that entirely surrounds the body, symbolizes.

Fr. Nicholas Gihr has this to say in *The Holy Sacrifice of the Mass*, first published in 1877:

> Originally the chasuble was an outer garment which fell about the priest and completely enveloped him. The chasuble had an opening in the middle by which it was allowed to come down on the shoulders. As these cloak- and bell-shaped chasubles had much about them which was inconvenient, they began in the eleventh century to shorten or open them at both sides for a freer use of the arms, and this alteration gave the form of the so-called Gothic chasubles, which were still common in the sixteenth century. Although from this period more and more was cut away from the chasuble, it yet remained up to the eighteenth century tolerably long and full of folds, but alas! since that time the vestment has been replaced by a chasuble of still shorter and less graceful pattern.

—Fr. Scott, January 2000

Does the Catholic Church forbid cremation?

At no period in the history of Catholicism was the practice of cremation ever adopted or favored in the Catholic Church. From the very beginning, burial of the dead, *i.e.*, inhumation, was an inviolable practice in the Church, and she struggled constantly against cremation, a pagan custom often accompanied by rites incompatible with the Catholic Faith.

Under Boniface VIII whoever practiced cremation was excommunicated, and the remains even of the corpse were refused Christian burial. With the advent of the French Revolution in 1789 an attempt was made on November 11, 1796, to introduce cremation; it met with no success. It was only as a result of Masonic influence and pressure that in the final quarter of the nineteenth century the idea of cremation became fashionable and certain governments gave it official recognition. The campaign was begun in Italy and the first experiments took place in 1872 by Brunetti in Padua; in April 1873, the Italian Senate gave approval; and, in Milan on January 22, 1876, the first cremations took place. Later in Germany, France, Sweden, Norway, and England the practice was legalized.

The Church reacted strongly. Cremation in itself is not intrinsically evil, nor is it repugnant to any Catholic dogma, not even the resurrection of the body; for even after cremation God's almighty power is in no way impeded. No divine law exists which formally forbids cremation.

The practice is, however, in opposition to the constant, unbroken tradition of the Church since its foundation.

Three decrees emanated from the Holy Office. On May 19, 1886, in answer to two questions posed by the bishops, the Church forbade the joining of cremation societies which were for the most part of Masonic origin and spirit, and it was further condemned to request cremation of one's own body or the body of another. Some seven months later, December 15, 1886, Pope Leo XIII ratified this document. Catholics who destined their bodies for cremation were deprived of a proper Christian burial. On July 27, 1892, the matter was definitively resolved. Priests were requested not to give such Catholics the last rites; no public funeral Mass could be said.

However, in certain strict circumstances the Church tacitly or even expressly authorizes cremation, *e.g.*, in the case of an epidemic where public health safety is in question.

Unfortunately, however, the document of Pope Paul VI, *Piam et Constantem*, of July 5, 1963, introduced a process of reversal of Church practice. Where it is alleged there is no denial of Catholic doctrine, nor contempt for the body, nor hatred of the Faith, cremation is permitted. Hygienic and economic reasons may play a part in this permission.

This paved the way for Canon 1176 of the 1983 Code of Canon Law, §3, in which cremation is permitted though burial is earnestly recommended, but it is only the recommendation of a pious custom. It would seem also that funeral rites are forbidden at a place of cremation. It is also forbidden to scatter the ashes or to have them in one's home; they must be buried or placed in a vault in a cemetery.

What must be our attitude, as faithful Catholics, to this change of legislation? The liberalization of the law forbidding cremation is without a doubt a concession to the ever increasing influence of Freemasons and those who refuse the belief in the resurrection of the body. We have now, more than ever before, the obligation of professing our faith in this important article of the creed.

Consequently, we must adhere to the constant tradition of the Church, which numbers the burial of the dead as one of the corporal works of mercy, so great must be our respect for the body, "the temple of the Holy Ghost" (I Cor. 6:19). We should not either ask for cremation, nor permit it for our relatives, nor attend any religious services associated with it. This is precisely what the traditional (1917) Code of Canon Law prescribed: "If a person has in any way ordered that his body be cremated, it is illicit to obey such instructions; and if such a provision occur in a contract, last testament, or in any document whatsoever, it is to be disregarded" (Can. 1203, §2). It is likewise stated that those who give orders that their body be cremated are amongst those who must be refused "ecclesiastical burial" (Can. 1240, §§1, 5).

—*Fr. Boyle,* December 1994

Is the Catholic Church opposed to war?

In these our times when a false pacifism seems to dominate the thinking of many influential people, it is useful to recall what the Catholic Church's teaching on war truly is. An absolute condemnation of war is something foreign to Catholic tradition. The military vocation is in no way proscribed in the Gospel and has always been practiced by Christians. Were not many holy martyrs and saints men of arms?

The Fathers of the Church considered the military profession and the exercise of it an honorable one. All of Catholic theology from St. Augustine to St. Thomas Aquinas to Pope Pius XII qualifies acts that establish disharmony, disunity, and lack of concord among men as being purely negative and they further determine that it is not always a sin to engage in warfare.

War, however, *is* an evil, though not necessarily the worst of evils, and the Church includes it along with famine and pestilence among the scourges from which men are to be preserved, *e.g.*, the Mass *In Tempore Belli*. For a war to be licit there are certain conditions: that it must be declared by the competent authority, that its true purpose must be to repair the violation of a right, that there is a well-founded hope of success in securing this object, and that the war be conducted with moderation.

The question of total war is more delicate, given the sophistication of modern weaponry and the destruction on a vast scale of which it is capable. A defensive war against an aggressor is always licit, and the morality of war in general is subject to two conditions: that it be just, and that recourse to arms is necessary to repel an aggressor; that it be moderate, for there is no right to wage war outside of the condition of moderation.

—*Fr. Boyle,* July 1995

Has the Church given any conditions for the waging of a just war?

There are invariable Catholic principles for the waging of a just war. The procedure is simple: we simply apply to war the determining factors governing a moral act. In every moral act there are three factors: (a) the object, (b) the intention, (c) the circumstances. All three must be considered morally good; otherwise the act is bad and to be proscribed. In other words, *all* the moral determinants must be good and present.

THE OBJECT

The object must be good; that is, the war must have a just cause. Now, wars are of two kinds, defensive and offensive. A defensive war is just in its cause if waged to defend an essential and fundamental right unjustly denied; an offensive war is just in its action if it is the only means for preserving an essential and fundamental right and justice unjustly denied provided every other peaceful and diplomatic avenue has been exhausted. Furthermore, it is of the utmost seriousness that the importance of the justice to be defended is in proportion to the gravity of the ills which the war will undoubtedly cause. Under no circumstances can a Catholic accept the doctrine "my country right or wrong."

The Intention

The only intention which can justify war is the promotion of the common good and the avoidance of greater evil. In our world the common good will embrace not exclusively the individual nation's good but the common good of the world, for no nation lives in splendid isolation; the order of prosperity of nations is bound up with each other's good.

The Circumstances

War must be good not only in its cause and intention but also in its circumstances or methods. Pope Pius XII declared in March 1937 to the Mexican bishops: "*1)* The methods used for vindicating rights are means to an end, or constitute a relative end, not a final or absolute end. *2)* That as a means to an end, the methods for vindicating rights must be lawful and not intrinsically evil acts." In other words, the end does not justify the means. Robbing the rich to help the poor is not a Catholic moral principle. No advantage, however great, is to be gained at the expense of a violation of the moral law. "*3)* That since the methods for vindicating rights should be means proportionate to the end, they must be used only insofar as they seem to attain that end, in whole or in part and in such a way that they do not bring greater harm to the community than the harm they were intended to remedy."

With this principle in mind, the Vatican rightly condemned the June 10, 1938, bombings of civilian targets in Spain and thus gave greater weight to the world's protests.

It is only when these three questions of morally good end or cause, right intentions, and justifiable methods can be affirmatively answered can war be justified.

—Fr. Boyle, July 1995

Can the Church take donations from companies or individuals whose profit is derived from immoral activities?

This is a question of prudence. Money itself does not have any moral value to it. It is consequently not in itself immoral to receive donations from drug companies or governmental organizations or humanitarian groups who promote immoral products, such as contraceptives, or immoral activities, for example, in AIDS prevention.

However, it is generally extremely imprudent to do so. If such organizations make donations it is not out of charity but out of a determined agenda. It is a pressure tactic and a way to exercise influence. The fact of accepting such a donation is generally interpreted as an approval and a compromise, and would lessen one's ability to defend Catholic moral principles. However, there could be exceptions, for example, when applying for governmental subsidies that are available to everyone and of which the acceptance does not imply a compromise of principle.

—*Fr. Scott,* September 2007

 **Could you please point to a Church document that requires that financial contributions by the faithful be accounted for to them on a weekly or monthly basis, if such a document exists?**

There is no such requirement on the part of the pastor to report the financial status on a weekly basis. Any report given by the one responsible for the church may be freely done, but is not required. It would seem that the only obligation is that those who have donated funds be given records of such for tax purposes when needed.

The offerings given by the faithful at the Offertory of the Mass, or elsewhere, are precisely that—offerings and gifts. These are given to the Church of God. They are not a loan. And one is obliged in justice (with a real obligation of restitution if neglected) to contribute to the upkeep of the Church. Our contribution to the Church is not charity. Charity is over and above the requirements of justice.

Not many of us would go to a relative's house after Christmas and demand to be shown to what use our gifts had been put. We would be considered rude. On the other hand, we would be pleased to see our gift being used. The same is true of the House of God.

The expectation of seeing a weekly report may stem from a lack of trust, or worse yet, a Protestant concept of the Church. The congregational idea of "my" money is not properly Catholic. The Church belongs to God, and not to the congregation. (Thus no need for a monthly report for the shareholders!) The priest is the custodian of the plant and the pastor of the flock. I should not expect to see a weekly report any more than I expect to be shown the use for my gift after Christmas. It goes without saying that I would be pleased to know these things, but to demand such would be excessive.

Any report given by the pastor is gratuitous in justice but, for the sake of prudence, may be recommended.

—*Fr. Doran,* July 1991

 **Protestants say that a tithe of ten per cent of gross income is obligatory according to Scripture. Are Catholics bound to keep this rule?**

The obligation of offering a tenth part of the produce as an offering to God and to His ministers is one of the legal prescriptions of the Mosaic law (Dt. 14:22) that Our Lord did away with when He came to fulfill the law in His own person. It is certainly true that under the new law, as under the old, the faithful owe support to the ministers of the altar. However, since the new law is interior, it is left to the generosity of the faithful in the practice of the virtues of justice and charity to determine the quantity.

In fact, the Church has declared that support is strictly owed in justice to the ministers of the Church, and that it is not pure alms that can be withdrawn at will. The contrary opinion was one of the errors of John Wycliffe condemned at the Council of Constance in 1415 (Dz. 598). This is indeed a part of the natural law that requires that those who minister receive a commensurate remuneration. It is also according to the divine law, as taught by Our Lord, "for the workman is worthy of his meat" (Mt. 10:10), and by St. Paul: "Know you not, that they who work in the holy place, eat the things that are of the holy place; and they that serve the altar, partake with the altar. So also the Lord ordained that they who preach the gospel should live by the gospel" (I Cor. 9:13-14).

Thus it is that the Waldensian heretics had to recant the denial of this when being received back into the Church in 1208 by professing: "We believe that tithes and first fruits and oblations should be paid to the clergy according to the Lord's command" (Dz. 427). Consequently, those who refuse to contribute to the support of the Church and the clergy are guilty of two sins: they are guilty of injustice, by refusing the support that they owe, and they are guilty of a sin against religion by not contributing according to their means to the support of the Church.

In many places during the Middle Ages it became custom and particular law for the ten per cent figure to become obligatory, especially in the East. Bouscaren and Ellis in their *Canon Law: A Text and Commentary* (1946) have this to say: "[This] has long since become obsolete except in a few churches which have kept the ancient custom by reason of local statutes" (p. 747). Consequently, the Church's law gives no precision about the quantity of the donations that are to be given in support of the clergy. The current mind of the Church on the matter is reflected in

Canon 1502 of the 1917 Code of Canon Law: "Local statutes as well as laudable customs regarding tithes and first fruits are to be respected."

When speaking of this issue, St. Thomas Aquinas explains why it is that the Church does not demand the ten percent tithe, and why it would be disedifying and inappropriate to revive this local custom:

> The ministers of the Church ought to be more solicitous for the increase of spiritual goods in the people, than for the amassing of temporal goods: and hence the Apostle was unwilling to make use of the right given him by the Lord of receiving his livelihood from those to whom he preached the Gospel, lest he should occasion a hindrance to the Gospel of Christ.... In like manner the ministers of the Church rightly refrain from demanding the Church's tithes, when they could not demand them without scandal, on account of their having fallen into desuetude, or for some other reason. Nevertheless those who do not give tithes in places where the Church does not demand them are not in a state of damnation, unless they be obstinate, and unwilling to pay even if tithes were demanded of them. (*ST* [*Summa Theologica*], II-II, q. 87, art. 1, ad 5)

This judicious balance of the Angelic Doctor is remarkable. The principle of contributing to the support is maintained, but the Church is not so small-minded as to insist on a certain sum or proportion, although it has the right to do so. It leaves all this in God's hands, knowing that God will provide for all the needs of His true Church, and of the clergy who have consecrated their lives to its service. Protestants who demand a tithe err by acting as if the Mosaic law were still in vigor; by a very materialist conception of the law, centered upon temporal goods; and by failing to give due priority to the Church's true mission—the salvation of souls.

Consequently, no Catholic should feel under any kind of moral obligation to give ten per cent to the support of the Church, and most importantly if it would mean sacrificing the necessities of food, clothing, shelter, and transportation. Yet every Catholic is under the moral obligation to give according to his means, whether his farthing be one per cent, or whether, perhaps, if he is comfortably established in life, it be closer to twenty per cent or even more. It is for each person to decide before God what is a reasonable proportion to contribute to the support of the Church, and the Church's charitable works, concealing his generosity so that, figuratively at least, the right hand does not know what the left hand is doing. Nevertheless, if he is prudent he will also include this proportion, whatever he decides upon, in his budget for the month.

—*Fr. Scott*, September 2003

Has the Church's position on Freemasonry changed?

Despite the fact that in the new (1983) Code of Canon Law no mention is made of the excommunication formerly applied to Catholic members of Masonic groups, the Church still prohibits membership in this secretive and anti-Catholic organization whose principles are totally incompatible with the revealed truths of the Catholic Faith. Eight popes have issued a serious condemnation of its tenets and practices beginning with Clement XII in 1738. His constitution was confirmed and renewed by Benedict XIV.

The same path was closely followed by Pius VII, and Leo XII assumed and ratified all the acts of his predecessors on this matter. It was in the same unambiguous sense that Pius VIII, Gregory XVI, and Pius IX declared their opposition. The most interesting encyclical letter on Freemasonry is *Humanum Genus* by Leo XIII.

In the 1970's a spurious distinction not founded on facts was introduced, a not anti-Catholic Masonic lodge—a contradiction in terms, no doubt, but widely touted among bishops and priests.

In 1980, the Sacred Congregation for the Doctrine of the Faith called this a false perspective and upheld the centuries-old condemnation. The declaration states:

> The Church's negative position on Masonic associations...remains unchanged since their principles have always been regarded as irreconcilable with the Church's doctrine. Hence joining them remains prohibited by the Church. Catholics enrolled in Masonic associations are involved in serious sin [understand mortal sin] and are not to approach Holy Communion.

The declaration further stipulated that no local ecclesiastical authority had the power to diminish in any way the judgment handed down. In this country in 1985, the National Conference of Bishops called Freemasonry "irreconcilable with Catholicism" because the "principles and basic rituals of masonry embody a naturalistic religion active participation in which is incompatible with Christian Faith and practice. Those who knowingly embrace such principles are committing a serious sin."

There is an obligation to make this teaching of the Church known so that there can be no excuse for seeking application to a Masonic lodge to further one's temporal well-being at the expense of one's immortal soul.

—*Fr. Boyle,* October 1994

ABOUT CERTAIN
TEACHINGS OF THE CHURCH

 **The religion writer George W. Cornell writes concerning Charles Curran that "Roman Catholicism always has taught the duty of heeding individual conscience, when duly informed and seriously considered, even in dissent from official teachings." Is that what the Church teaches?**

Conscience is a judgment of the practical reason on the moral goodness or sinfulness of an action. Only if conscience agrees with objective truth is it right. A certain conscience must always be obeyed when it commands or forbids. One may follow opinions of reliable authors (approved by the magisterium), but not of any new theologian who may nowadays dissent from official Catholic teachings. The truth is not something which can be changed by writings of modernist heretics. Truth must be found always side by side with reality. If one is "duly informed" and has "seriously considered," he will not dissent from official teachings of the Church—at least not from dogmatic teachings or from sacred Scripture.

—Fr. Carl, December 1986

 **T.V., magazines, and newspapers have been plying us with the matters of mercy killing, death with dignity, living well, quality of life, *etc.* What is the Catholic teaching on life and death?**

Human life is a creation and gift from God, who maintains His right over it to give or take away. Life comes from the living, and there has never been any proof of spontaneous life from the non-living, no matter how scientifically the evolutionists affirm it. All life therefore belongs to God. It is His creation. The fifth commandment forbids the shortening or taking of any human life. Wanton killing even of plants and animals is forbidden. With our own life and the lives of others in our care, we are obliged to use ordinary means to preserve it. What would be considered extraordinary means need not be used. Therefore all "mercy killing" or "right to suicide" is forbidden by God and so taught by Holy Mother Church. The fifth commandment of God forbids taking innocent life. Human life, from conception to death, is protected by God.

—Fr. Carl, January 1988

I was told that at the last judgment everyone will know everyone else's sins. How could this be since God forgives sins in confession? I have even heard that the devil does not know sins already confessed.

Our blessed Lord said, "For there is nothing hid, that shall not be revealed: nor secret that shall not be known" (Mt. 10:26). This refers to His followers suffering persecutions and their patience being made known. The devil has the powers of an angel and could know sins already confessed. The other part about everyone knowing others' sins is more difficult to answer. Surely God will not make His friends suffer any embarrassment as they stand before His judgment seat, yet all will be revealed to demonstrate God's mercy and to show how devoutly they did penance for their sins. Surely Mary Magdalene would not suffer shame when God reveals the works of reparation she did to atone for her sins. St. Augustine would not stand around and make believe he was always an innocent lamb. His works of sorrow and reparation would not be hidden. Sins that have not been confessed and forgiven will be the true shame of those who have them on their souls at the Last Judgment. All the world will be there to the extreme shame of the non-repentant!

—*Fr. Carl,* July 1985

ABOUT THE BIBLE AND BIBLICAL MATTERS

If Eve only, and not Adam, had sinned, would we have been born with original sin?

St. Thomas Aquinas himself asks this very question (*ST*, I-II, q. 81, art. 5). His answer is clear. Original sin is transferred through Adam and not through Eve, and so, consequently, if Adam had not sinned we would not have inherited original sin, whereas if Adam had sinned, but not Eve, we would still have inherited it.

His answer is based upon sacred Scripture, which states that "by one man," that is, Adam, "sin entered into this world" (Rom. 5:12). Scripture does not say by one woman, nor by two parents, but by one man. Consequently, it is a part of our faith that original sin is contracted only from Adam. St. Thomas explains this by saying that it is through the process of generation that original sin is transferred. However, the mover or the active principle of generation is the father, and not the mother.

Hence it is Adam who transmits original sin to us, although Eve was the first to commit the sin.

—*Fr. Scott,* June 2003

 ### If Adam had not sinned, would we have been born with sanctifying grace?

St. Thomas Aquinas explains that the formal element in original sin is "the privation of original justice, whereby the will was made subject to God" (*ST,* I-II, q. 82, art. 3). This means that what it really and properly consists in is the loss of sanctifying grace, and not the sinful concupiscence and disorders which are the consequence of original sin. Adam sinned as head of the entire human race. Hence if he had likewise preserved original justice as head of the entire human race, then he would not have passed on original sin to his descendants, but instead sanctifying grace. Consequently, if Adam had not sinned, we would have been born with sanctifying grace.

—*Fr. Scott,* June 2003

 ### Why are there different translations of Genesis 3:15, some indicating that the woman's seed will crush the serpent's head, and others that it is His Mother herself who will do it?

After the story of the Fall and of the punishment to be inflicted on sinful mankind, Almighty God curses the serpent and promises the Redeemer, seed of the woman, that is, of the Blessed Virgin Mary, saying that He will place enmities between the serpent and the woman, and between his seed and the woman's seed: "She will crush your head and you will lie in wait for her heel."

Such is the translation of the Vulgate (*ipsa*), namely that she will crush the serpent's head, as confirmed by the translator St. Jerome in his writings. Scripture scholars point out that the Greek text of the Septuagint, and all the original Hebrew manuscripts except two, state that it is he, that is, the seed of the woman, who will crush the serpent's head. How can this be, you might think, since the Council of Trent guaranteed that the translation of the Vulgate is without error? How could St. Jerome have made such an obvious error?

Of course, there is no error at all, and St. Jerome deliberately translated it indicating that the Blessed Mother would crush the serpent's head. Here his translation is guided by the Catholic Faith and makes a little more explicit the role of the Blessed Virgin in destroying the serpent, which role is already manifestly contained in this very text. Clearly, if there is enmity between the serpent and the Blessed Virgin, and not just between the seed of one and the seed of the other, this means that the Blessed Virgin is perfectly united to Our Lord's work of destroying the devil's power. Together with her seed, she crushes the head of the devil. St. Jerome's translation is consequently equally correct, and has the advantage of bringing out a little more clearly the role of Our Lady. It was made in the light of the teaching of the Fathers, without whose interpretation we cannot understand holy Scripture. Pope Pius IX used the patristic application of this text to Our Lady to establish the Immaculate Conception (*Ineffabilis Deus*).

—*Fr. Scott,* November 2002

 ## Whom did the children of Adam and Eve marry?

Adam and Eve handed on to their children the obligations of the natural law. The natural law does indeed forbid the marrying of brothers and sisters as the crime of incest and one repugnant to all peoples.

However, we know it as an article of our Faith that all human beings are descended from our first parents according to the flesh, from whom we inherited original sin. Consequently, the children of Adam and Eve had no choice but to marry close relatives, either brother, sister, nephew, or niece. The theologians explain this by making a distinction between the primary and the secondary precepts of the natural law. The secondary precepts are not so necessary nor so well known as the primary precepts. Consequently, on occasions in the Old Testament God gave dispensations from these secondary precepts for special reasons. Thus it was that He permitted divorce under certain conditions, on account of the Jews' hardness of heart; that he permitted polygamy for the rapid growth of the Israelites; and that for the short period that it was necessary He permitted intermarriage between close relatives. It must be borne in mind, however, that the genetics of the human race were much purer and stronger at that time.

Of course, this temporary permission did not continue, and could never exist under the New Law. The Church recognizes that close consanguinity is an impediment to marriage, and will never dispense in cases of brother or sister or uncle or aunt. With a proportionate reason, she will dispense in the case of first cousins.

—*Fr. Scott,* April 2005

 **Where did the bodies of Henoch and Elias repose or did they ever die? I have read in Catholic prophecies that they are able to return to earth to fight the Antichrist.**

Henoch was the descendant of Adam through Seth. He was the father of Mathusala. It is recorded in Genesis 5:21-24 that Henoch did not die but was taken away by God. It is later stated: "Henoch pleased God, and was translated into paradise, that he may give repentance to the nations" (Ecclus. 44:16). This is the source of the belief that he would later return to combat for the Lord God, along with Elias, as one of the two Witnesses of the Apocalypse. These will fight against the Antichrist. They will be slain but be later resurrected and assumed into heaven. This will be for a judgment on the people as major destruction will accompany their assumption.

Elias's departure was even more spectacular, his having been taken by God in a "chariot of fire," "a whirlwind into heaven," as he walked with Eliseus (IV Kings 2:11).

We do not know the exact location of these two men. Neither died, but the reference to "paradise" in the case of Henoch need not be the Garden of Eden. It could merely refer to a state of peace, or of rest, in which he has been placed.

—Fr. Doran, May 1993

 **Abimelech was warned by God not to touch Sara, that she was Abraham's wife, when Abraham was willing to let Abimelech have her. However, He did not warn Abraham that he had sinned in giving her to Abimelech. It seems incongruous that Abraham should be revered as our patriarch with such high esteem when he could have done such a thing, and that God did not punish or admonish him.**

This episode of Abraham's life is found in the 20th chapter of Genesis. When he settled in the land of Gerara he knew that the beauty of Sara would cause the envy of the men. He also feared that one of them might kill him in order to have Sara as his own wife. For this reason he had Sara say that she was his sister. This in fact was true. She was his half-sister. Both were of the same father.

Abimelech was the king of Gerara. He was taken by Sara's beauty, and upon discovery that she was "the sister" of Abraham he called for her and desired to have her as his wife. It was in a dream that Abimelech learned the truth from God. His sin was real (only material), but he had acted in good faith, *i.e.* "with a sincere heart." The king therefore restored Sara to her husband Abraham and lavished gifts on them for his "fault." He was also instructed by the Lord that he was to ask Abraham to pray for him in order to obtain forgiveness for his transgression and remedy the sterility of his household.

In any judgment of the saints of the Old Testament it must be kept in mind that the fullness of grace and blessings comes only through the death and resurrection of our divine Lord. Pentecost was the outpouring of the Holy Ghost. While all grace, from the foundation of the world, originates in Christ, all periods of time have not benefited equally from it. It is not for us to compare the sanctity of Samson, for example, with that of St. Francis of Assisi.

Any fault on the part of Abraham would be that he did not tell the full truth about the status of Sara. He did not lie. She was his sister. His fear of death at the hands of the pagans in this region caused him to do this (Gen. 20:11). But note Abraham's faith in God. He trusted in the guidance of the Most High. He was in this land following God's directives (Heb. 11:8), thus he believed Him to be in control of events. Here we see that Sara is under divine protection in view of the Promise. It is expressly stated that Abimelech had not "approached her" (Gen. 20:4). This is why Abraham was not only held as innocent in the eyes of God, but that he had to intercede for the pardon of Abimelech, who likely desired Sara from lust.

—Fr. Doran, January 1993

Of what evil is God speaking in Is. 45:7 when He says: "I make peace and create evil: I the Lord that do all these things"?

The difficulty is to understand in what way it can be said that God created evil, and is answered by St. Thomas Aquinas in the *Summa Theologica* (I, q. 49, art. 2). It is interesting to see how he overcomes the ancient dualism of the Persians, the temptation which maintained that there were two principles, one of good and one of evil.

His response presupposes the true explanation of what evil really is, namely, the privation of a good which is due; that is, a defect in that which is done, either in the moral order (=sin, or moral evil) or in the physical order (*e.g.*, sickness, suffering, death). The consequence is that evil is something negative, which cannot exist in itself, but only in something which is good. As Fr. Farrell explains: "The trouble is that evil is not something positive, something one can put a finger on; the very essence of evil demands that it eludes your finger, it is something missing, a defect. To have evil at all, there must be good capable of having holes in it, for evil is precisely a hole in the good" (*A Companion to the Summa,* I, 168).

Clearly, then, God, who is the supreme good, causes the good which evil is in. However, it cannot be by a defect of His action that the defect or hole in the good exists. It is by a defect in the action of the creature which He permits, but does not cause. God permits such defects in the action of creatures in view of "the good of the order of the universe. Now, the good of the order of the universe requires...that there should be some things that can, and sometimes do, fail. And thus God, by causing in things the good of the universe, consequently, and as if it were by accident, causes the corruptions of things..." (*ST*, I, q. 49, art. 2).

This applies also to moral evil or sin. He causes the good which is human life in the sinner, and He even gives the intellect and will power without which the sinner could not sin. However, the sin itself is a defect in the activity of the sinner which comes entirely from the sinner. This gives some little idea of the gravity and perversity of mortal sin.

However, St. Thomas points out that there is another way in which He is the cause of evil, and it is referred to in holy Scripture in passages such as this one from the prophet Isaias. For He is the cause of evils inasmuch as they are a necessary penalty or punishment to maintain the order of justice in the universe: "The order of justice belongs to the order of the universe; and this requires that penalty should be dealt out to sinners. And so, God is the author of the evil which is penalty, but not of the evil which is fault" (*ibid.*).

—Fr. Scott, February 1999

How can it be said that Our Lord came to preach "the acceptable year of the Lord"?

This expression is a part of the prophecy of Isaias (Is. 61:2) that is read by Our Lord on the Sabbath day when He unfolded the scroll of the book of Isaias in the synagogue of Nazareth (Lk. 4:17-19). This is a directly Messianic text, referring to the person of our divine Savior, of which Our Lord Himself stated: "This day is fulfilled this scripture in your ears" (Lk. 4:21).

The complete text from Isaias, as read by Our Lord, is this: "The Spirit of the Lord is upon me. Wherefore He hath anointed me to preach the gospel to the poor, he hath sent me to heal the contrite of heart, to preach deliverance to the captives, and sight to the blind, to set at liberty them that are bruised, to preach the acceptable year of the Lord...."

The meaning of the first part of the text is clear, referring to our deliverance, by our divine Savior, from the blindness and slavery of sin that has bound and bruised our wretched souls. The expression "the acceptable year of the Lord" contained in Isaias 61:2 is in fact a reference to the law of Moses, and in particular to Leviticus 25:10, which orders a Jubilee year to be celebrated every fifty years: "And thou shalt sanctify the fiftieth year, and shalt proclaim remission to all the inhabitants of thy land: for it is the year of Jubilee. Every man shall return to his possession, and every one shall go back to his former family: Because it is the jubilee and the fiftieth year."

This Jubilee year was a time of remission, much more even than the sabbatical year, which came around once every seven years. According to the Mosaic law, at the sound of the trumpet announcing the Jubilee year all debts were abolished and all lands and houses that had been alienated in any way returned to their former owners free of charge, even when the purchaser had promised them to the service of the temple. Likewise, all Israelite slaves recovered their liberty (Lev. 25-27). If it is true that this aspect of the law was most of the time a dead letter, it nevertheless is very clear that it was a part of the Mosaic law, and that it had a profound symbolism, for it indicated to the Israelites that they were not the true owners of the land that God had entrusted to them, that all were effectively slaves of Yahweh, and that no family or corporation could accumulate wealth here on this earth.

However, the real symbolism of this year of grace, the Jubilee, the year of the Lord, is the perfect remission obtained by our divine Savior on the cross when He freed us from the debt of our sins and opened up the gates to the promised homeland, and this not just for the Jubilee year, but for everlasting life.

—*Fr. Scott*, April 2007

"Blessed are the poor in spirit" (Matt. 5:3): What does it mean?

Scripture scholars inform us that the Beatitudes are not merely simple statements of fact: they are, on the contrary, explanations: "O the blessedness of the poor in spirit!" The Beatitudes are not pious hopes of what shall be, they are a confirmation of what already is: it is a happiness which exists here and now, and which cannot be taken from us.

The root meaning of the English "happiness" (chance) is an inadequate translation of the Greek word *makarios*—a joy independent of all the vicissitudes of life. Christian joy is unassailable; it cannot be lost despite sorrow, pain, grief, or even betrayal.

In Greek also there are two words for poor: *penes* and *ptochos*. The former describes one who has nothing superfluous; the latter, the word used in the Beatitudes, refers to absolute abject poverty, the poverty which brings one to one's knees; it embraces those who have nothing at all. So this beatitude is really surprising—it seems to say "O the untouchable joy of the totally poverty-stricken."

It must be remembered also that the Beatitudes were not originally spoken in Greek but rather in Aramaic. The Jewish word *ani* or *ebion* (poor) came to mean "the man who because he has no earthly resources places his entire trust in God."

With this background in mind we can arrive at the meaning of the beatitude. "Blessed is the man who, knowing his own utter helplessness, entrusts himself totally to God." Such at most implies detachment from possessions, for they cannot bring happiness or security, and attachment to God alone, who brings help and hope and strength. The man who is poor in spirit and knows that things mean nothing and that God means everything, the poverty that is blessed therefore is poverty of spirit. To such a poverty belongs the kingdom of heaven; and even more surprisingly, it exists often in the destitute, as many Catholic missionaries realized long before the days of liberation theology so foreign to the true spirit and meaning of the Gospel.

—*Fr. Boyle,* February 1995

 **If the lesson of the Prodigal Son is that God values the repentant sinner no less than He does one who has tried to live meritoriously, then why make the effort? It hardly seems fair.**

Even though there is more joy among the angels over one sinner who repents, this does not take away the great amount of joy we understand there is when the ninety-nine stay on the straight and narrow. The extra joy must come from the unexpected bonus—the saved sinner. Magdalene loved much because much was forgiven her. The father of the prodigal son rejoiced because his "dead" son had come back to life. This means he had been given up for lost. In spite of all these arguments against faithfulness to God, we know in our deepest thought that perpetual fidelity to God is better than a deathbed conversion. You might break a precious vase but it can never be glued back to its former perfection. On the other hand, a just man may advance with a certain slowness while the converted sinner may press on eagerly to his heavenly country. As St. Gregory says: "Whilst such as have been sinners are stung with grief at the remembrance of their former transgressions, and calling to mind how they have forsaken their God, endeavor by present fervor to compensate for their past misconduct. But it must be remembered that there are many just, whose lives cause such joy to the heavenly court, that all the penitential exercises of sinners cannot be preferred before them" (Homily 34).

—*Fr. Carl,* September 1987

 **What is the proper interpretation of Acts 2:17? "And it shall come to pass in the last days (saith the Lord), I will pour out my Spirit upon all flesh: and your sons and your daughters shall prophesy, and your young men shall see visions, and your old men shall dream dreams." My sister believes we are living in the last days when these manifestations will take place and quotes this verse often. I would like to respond to her with the proper interpretation of that Bible passage.**

This quotation is taken from the discourse of St. Peter immediately after the miracle of Pentecost. He addressed himself to the crowds in Jerusalem who had gathered around the house where the apostles were staying because of the sound of the "violent wind blowing." In this sermon the prince of the apostles makes reference to the text of the prophet Joel; this is what you have quoted.

The application by St. Peter is certainly to the events of that morning—the pouring forth of the Holy Ghost. They make no reference to any future events. Though they had been cast in a mode as a prophecy for the end times in the Old Testament, in the apostolic mind the revelation of the Word of God in the Incarnation was the inauguration of "the Day of the Lord." This is why they are applicable to the main events in the work of salvation. This "Day" is the manifestation of God's will from the Incarnation to the *parousia, i.e.,* the return of Our Lord in glory at the of the world. We have been in the "end times" since the revelation of the Son of God, but His physical return will be "as a thief in the night" (I Thess. 5:2). The appearance of "signs" is not the most important element during these events but the events themselves. St. Paul later had to deal with those at Corinth who sought out "signs" and charisms. He reminded them of the relative importance of these spiritual gifts, and that they were to "strive after the greater gifts" (I Cor. 12:31)—charity.

—*Fr. Doran,* November 1992

 **The Gospels speak of St. Thomas as "the Twin." Our pastor spoke of this, saying that the theory is that we are the twin as no noticeable other twin was mentioned. He said that we are all doubters. Is this correct?**

Your parish priest is clearly giving a spiritual interpretation to the name of St. Thomas. This is not the literal meaning of the text. Being called "Twin" does not necessarily manifest any more relation to another than having the name "Victor" need signify the recipient as having been successful in battle.

Whereas it is true that the Faith does always remain somewhat obscure, our eyes being blinded by the brilliance of its light, we must strive to learn ever more profoundly our religion. It is ridiculous to say that we love God but have little desire to know as much about Him, and His revelation, as possible. Ignorance, however, is not equal to doubt. We will always be ignorant of some facet of the knowledge of God. Even in the beatific vision there will remain a divine infinitude for us to discover. Though this is true, we are never allowed to doubt, or to give credence to statements contrary to our religion. Our faith must be firm. This means that, based on God's authority, we hold for true the articles of revelation. Subjective principles are not the foundation. We may be tempted against the Faith, but must never positively foster doubt. This would be to reject the authority of God who has revealed it.

—*Fr. Doran,* August 1993

 **Can the Council of Laodicea be alleged to prove that the deuterocanonical books are not inspired?**

The term "deuterocanonical" was invented as late as 1566 (by Sixtus of Siena) to describe those books of the Bible whose canonical inspiration was denied at one time in the fourth century, but which later became universally accepted as canonically inspired, with the same authority as the protocanonical books. These deuterocanonical books are called "apocrypha" by the Protestants, who do not accept them as divinely inspired. There are seven such books (out of twenty-seven) in the New Testament, and seven (out of forty-six) in the Old Testament, as well as several other shorter fragments.

This hesitation concerning the canonical inspiration of these deuterocanonical books did not exist in the first three centuries of the Church. All books are quoted indiscriminately by the authors of the New Testament, as well as by the Fathers of the Church during the first three centuries, who are unanimous in their acceptation of all these books as divinely inspired. As examples, St. Clement of Rome (96) quotes Judith, Wisdom, and Ecclesiasticus, and the Pastor Hermas (middle of the second century) quotes Ecclesiasticus and the second book of Machabees. Origen, at the end of the second century, defends the canonical inspiration of Tobias and the deuterocanonical parts of Daniel and Esther, and in fact lists as sacred Scripture every single one of the deuterocanonical books of the Old Testament.

It was only from the fourth century on that isolated Fathers of the Church expressed their hesitation about the canonical inspiration of the seven deuterocanonical books of the Old Testament. These Fathers lived principally in the area of Palestine and were greatly influenced by the Jews. After the destruction of Jerusalem in the year 70, the spiritual leadership of Judaism had been taken over by the Pharisees at the Synod of Jamniam (A.D. 90). By applying much more narrow-minded criteria than the Jews of the time of Our Lord, and in fact of the second century before Christ, they eliminated these seven books from their canon, either because they were written in Greek, or because they were relatively late in composition, or because of their prejudice towards a pharisaical, excessively materialistic interpretation of the law. Thus they rejected the version of the Septuagint, which had been the official version of the Old Testament in Greek both in the Diaspora and in Jerusalem, containing as it did all the deuterocanonical books. This is but a consequence of the loss of grace that followed on the rejection of Christ. However, their insistence did cause some isolated Fathers to doubt the canonical inspiration of these deuterocanonical books, in particular that great lover of Hebrew, St. Jerome.

It is alleged that the sixtieth canon of the Council of Laodicea, in the year 360, gives a list of the books of the Old Testament without the deuterocanonical books. This could be explained by the above-mentioned influence. However, most reputable authors dispute with good reason the authenticity of this canon. It consequently cannot be taken into consideration. Furthermore, even if it were authentic, it was only an isolated council, without any authority.

As against this isolated testimony is the constant and universal Tradition throughout Christendom, namely, that the deuterocanonical books were truly inspired by God and a part of sacred Scripture. This was defined by several Councils of Carthage (382, 397, 419), by the Council of Hippo (393), and by Pope Innocent I in 405, and was taught by the quasi-universality of the Fathers thereafter. This tradition of the Church, reflecting its indefectibility in teaching the Faith, was so constant that it was not questioned again for nearly a thousand years, despite the rise of the false apocryphal writings of the fifth century. In 1441 the Council of Florence defined this tradition, namely, that all the books of the Bible were inspired by God and that no distinction could be made between them. This definition was repeated by the Council of Trent.

—*Fr. Scott,* October 2007

 **The Pentecostal evangelists are preaching an event they claim will happen in the future called the "Rapture." Literally translating Our Lord's words in Matthew 24:37-44, "Then two men will be in the field; one will be taken, and one will be left," they state that after, or right**

before, the Day of Tribulation (not the Last Judgment), Our Lord will come and will take all the good and believing people from earth and will bring them forth to heaven to become immortalized, leaving on earth only those who do not believe. Is there some truth of this, Father, or is this a deception?

"And so it was in the days of Noe, so shall also the coming of the Son of Man be." So opens this passage. Our Lord is here emphasizing the suddenness of His return in judgment. This is why the same ends with the verse "Therefore, you also must be ready, because at an hour that you do not expect, the Son of Man will come." His return is synonymous with the Last Judgment and the end of the world. The query of the apostles provokes this explanation of the Master. "Tell us...what will be the sign of thy coming and of the end of the world?" (Mt. 24:3). After the profession of the true Faith by St. Peter in Caesarea Philippi, Our Lord had stated clearly that "the Son of Man is to come with His angels in the glory of His Father, and then He will render to everyone according to his conduct" (Mt. 16:27). This manifests the judgment to take place at the end of the world. No one is left out. Those "left behind" in the verses do not escape judgment; this is merely to point out the immediacy of His return and the necessity of our continual watchfulness, that is, to always live in the presence of God.

—Fr. Doran, April 1993

About the Magisterium: the Papacy, the Popes, and Papal Teachings

 **Are Catholics bound in conscience to accept all papal teachings or just infallible teachings?**

Catholics have a duty to obey all Church teachings. However, there are varying degrees of obligation according to the degree of authority that is attached to the teaching and how it is presented. These distinctions are found in any standard textbook of dogmatic theology. Dogmas defined *ex cathedra* must be accepted under pain of losing the Faith, in such a way that a person who professes the direct contradictory of an act of the extraordinary magisterium defining such a dogma is correctly called a heretic.

Dogmas are frequently taught infallibly by the ordinary magisterium of the Church. We owe them the adhesion of our faith, and a person who would knowingly deny one of these would be a formal heretic. The problem, however, is that of determining what really is a part of the ordinary magisterium (*i.e.,* that which has always and everywhere been taught), and consequently that which really is infallible. This is the work of theology, but since human judgments are involved, errors can enter in. It is consequently often not possible to call a person who denies such a dogma a formal heretic until such time as his error has been condemned by an act of the extraordinary magisterium. This is what was done at the Council of Trent for the Protestant errors, for example, concerning justification and the sacraments.

Other teachings of the Church are neither a part of the extraordinary magisterium nor a part of the ordinary magisterium but are authentically proposed by the Church. These compose the bulk of the teachings in the papal encyclicals. Such teachings of the authentic magisterium are not infallible but cannot be discarded. As Pope Pius XII stated in *Humani Generis*, and as Pope John Paul II has reiterated, such teachings must be accepted with reverential respect:

> Nor must it be thought that what is expounded in Encyclical Letters does not of itself demand consent, since in writing such Letters the Popes do not exercise the supreme power of their Teaching Authority. For … generally what is expounded and inculcated in Encyclical Letters already for other reasons appertains to Catholic doctrine. (*Humani Generis*, §20)

However, since they do not invoke the full authority of the Church and are not infallible, they can be wrong. Needless to say, they can only be rejected or refused if they are in direct contradiction with infallible teachings of the Church's magisterium. This is the case with the teachings of Vatican II, which refused to use its charisma of infallibility. It is an act of the authentic magisterium, which reiterates many dogmas infallibly taught by the extraordinary and ordinary magisterium, but which also includes novelties, such as religious liberty, ecumenism, and collegiality, which must be refused because they are in direct contradiction with the Church's previous teachings (*e.g.,* Pius IX in *Quanta Cura* and Pius XI in *Mortalium Animos*).

—*Fr. Scott,* November 2000

If a pope is neither crowned nor takes the papal oath, is he then the pope or just an administrator sitting in the Chair of Peter?

By the fact of being the bishop of Rome a man is constituted the successor of blessed Peter, the holder of the primacy. After his legitimate election he obtains at once, from the moment he accepts the election, the full power of his supreme jurisdiction, and this by divine right. As a bishop, both of Rome and of the world, he has full power of jurisdiction in matters of faith and morals as well as discipline. He is therefore, by nature, the supreme administrator.

—*Fr. Doran,* July 1993

Does the bull *Quo Primum* enjoy infallibility?

Quo Primum is a liturgical and disciplinary law of the most solemn kind. However, it does not have the infallibility of the extraordinary or solemn magisterium of the Church, for it is not a dogmatic definition.

Nevertheless, it is perfectly true to state that it participates in the infallibility of the ordinary magisterium in an indirect manner. I say in an indirect manner, for underlying the whole decree are the unchanging truths of the Catholic Faith concerning the Mass as a propitiatory sacrifice, renewing in an unbloody manner the sublime act of worship accomplished on Calvary. Inasmuch as the purpose of the bull is to protect these dogmas from the corruptions introduced by the heretics, denying such dogmas as the Real Presence, and inasmuch as these dogmas have always been taught in the Church, it shares in the infallibility of the Church's doctrinal teaching. It is in this sense that universal liturgical and disciplinary laws in the Church are infallible (Vacant, *Le Magistère Ordinaire*, p. 109).

Clearly this does not apply to the "promulgation" of the New Mass, if it ever was promulgated. The reason is that the ideas behind the reform are heterodox novelties and not at all what has always and everywhere been taught in the Church. They are consequently in no way guaranteed by the infallibility of the ordinary magisterium.

—*Fr. Scott,* March 1998

Are all the texts of an infallible Council infallible?

The infallibility of the Church's magisterium is a defined Catholic dogma that is of faith. The general principle is clearly stated by Vatican I's dogmatic constitution concerning the Faith (*Dei Filius*), namely, that "the doctrine of faith...has been entrusted as a divine deposit to the Spouse of Christ, to be faithfully guarded and infallibly interpreted" (Dz. 1800). This infallibility of the Church's magisterium can be exercised either in an extraordinary and solemn manner, such as by an *ex cathedra* definition, or in her ordinary teaching, on a day-to-day basis, without such solemnity, under the proviso that it be truly universal. This is in fact the clear teaching of the same document of Vatican I:

> By divine and Catholic faith, all those things must be believed which are
> contained in the written word of God and in tradition, and those which
> are proposed by the Church, either in a solemn pronouncement or in her
> ordinary and universal teaching power, to be believed as divinely revealed.
> (Dz. 1792)

Note that this can only apply to truths contained in Scripture or Tradition
that she proposes as being divinely revealed.

This infallibility is exercised first and foremost by the pope, in virtue
of his primacy, as is formally defined by the Vatican I document on the
Church (*Pastor Aeternus*) for his extraordinary magisterium:

> The dogma has been divinely revealed that the Roman Pontiff, when he
> speaks *ex cathedra*, that is, when carrying out the duty of the pastor and
> teacher of all Christians in accord with his supreme apostolic authority he
> explains a doctrine of faith or morals to be held by the universal Church…
> operates with that infallibility with which the divine Redeemer wished
> that His Church be instructed in defining doctrine on faith and morals.
> (Dz. 1839)

This definition lists the conditions for the note of infallibility to apply to any teaching: firstly, it must concern a question of faith or morals
that is divinely revealed; secondly, it must be clearly defined, usually by
the anathematization of the contrary condemned proposition; thirdly, it
must be imposed as obligatory for all Catholics, and not just a part of the
Church; fourthly, it must be taught by the pope with his full authority as
teacher and pastor and as successor of the apostles.

The conditions for the infallibility of the pope's ordinary magisterium have not been clearly defined. However, the universality that is inseparable from the ordinary magisterium is interpreted by the theologians
before Vatican II as a universality in time and in place, namely, "that
which was believed everywhere, always, and by all" to use the well-known
fifth-century formula of St. Vincent of Lerins.

The same principles can be applied to the teaching of the bishops
gathered together in an ecumenical Council, to whom, together with
himself, the pope communicates his supreme teaching power for the
duration of the Council. In fact, both the Councils themselves and many
of the popes have frequently defined the supreme authority of such
Councils—as, for example, St. Leo IX did for the first seven ecumenical
Councils, comparing them to the Gospels themselves: "Whatever the
above-mentioned seven holy and universal Councils believe and praise I
also believe and praise, and whomever they declare anathema, I declare
anathema" (Dz. 349).

In fact, the denial of the infallibility of ecumenical Councils is one
of the propositions of liberalism concerning the Church's rights that was

condemned by Blessed Pope Pius IX in his Syllabus of Errors. This is the condemned proposition (Prop. 23): "The Roman Pontiffs *and the Ecumenical Councils* have trespassed the limits of their powers, have usurped the rights of princes, and have even erred in defining matters of faith and morals" (Dz. 1723).

This infallibility of ecumenical Councils is both that of the extraordinary and the ordinary magisterium. It is precisely the principal purpose of an ecumenical Council to define doctrines of faith and morals definitively as being divinely revealed to be believed by all the faithful of the entire Church. In such cases the pope gives the Council the supreme apostolic authority it needs to make infallible *ex cathedra* definitions as acts of the extraordinary magisterium.

However, it is manifestly obvious that not all the texts of the Councils consist in such definitions. There are many other texts that explain the Church's teaching or apply it in the form of disciplinary decisions. Such teachings, however, can also be infallible. If not acts of the extraordinary magisterium, they can nevertheless be acts of the ordinary and universal magisterium. The problem is that it is not so easy to determine what teachings are really a part of the ordinary and universal magisterium, having always been taught everywhere and by all Catholic authorities. It is precisely for this reason that the Church has to resort, from time to time, to solemn definitions. Statements of Councils that reiterate the Catholic Faith as it has always and everywhere been taught are consequently infallible in virtue of the infallibility of the ordinary magisterium, whereas statements that might simply give a theological explanation, or application, while orthodox and having to be respected as a part of the authentic magisterium, still would not have the quality of infallibility.

It is the whole work of Catholic theology to analyze the texts of a Council and thus determine which definitions are infallible in virtue of the extraordinary magisterium, which is easy to determine, and which are infallible in virtue of the ordinary magisterium (propositions that are consequently of faith—*de fide*—but not defined—*de fide definita*). Let us take, for an example, the decree of the Council of Trent on the sacrament of penance. It defines infallibly in virtue of the extraordinary magisterium that penance is truly and properly a sacrament and that it is distinct from the sacrament of baptism. It likewise defines that the words of Our Lord on Easter Sunday "Receive ye the Holy Ghost; whose sins you shall forgive, they are forgiven them; and whose sins you shall retain, they are retained" refer to the sacrament of penance, and then declares that it is especially then that Our Lord instituted the sacrament of penance, as the Catholic Church has always understood from the beginning. However, the object of the definition is not that Christ instituted the sacrament with these words, but that these words refer to penance. Consequently, the teaching of the Council that it was by these words that Christ instituted this sacrament is infallible as a part of the ordinary magisterium inasmuch as it is what the Church has always and everywhere taught, not in virtue of the definition.

Then there are other teachings in the same Session XIV on penance which are theologically certain conclusions, and not properly acts of the ordinary or extraordinary magisterium. An example is the teaching that the three parts of the sacrament of penance are the three acts of the penitent that are the quasi-matter of the sacrament, namely, contrition, confession, and satisfaction. Such teachings cannot be rejected without temerity, but they are not of faith.

The case with Vatican II is particularly confusing. For although it was an ecumenical Council and could have used the charisma of infallibility to make solemn definitions of the extraordinary magisterium, it nevertheless refused to do so, as Pope Paul VI himself clearly declared just after the Council, on January 12, 1966, namely, that the Council "had avoided proclaiming in an extraordinary manner dogmas having the mark of infallibility." This means that only those statements that can clearly be shown to be a repeat of what has always and everywhere been taught by everybody in the Catholic Church can be accepted as infallible in virtue of the ordinary magisterium. Moreover, it is manifestly obvious that philosophical novelties such as the egalitarianism behind religious liberty, and contradictions of Catholic teaching such as ecumenism, are no in way a teaching of the Church, let alone of the ordinary magisterium, and consequently can and must be rejected.

—*Fr. Scott,* June 2008

Could the pope institute a new sacrament?

Admittedly the pope has awesome powers and authority. However, Christ alone instituted the sacraments, and only He can create a sacrament. The pope and the holy Catholic Church can point out what matter and form Our Lord determined were necessary for each of the seven sacraments. The pope could change some of the surrounding ceremonies, but he may never change what Christ has determined. The Eucharist is a sacrament. The pope may never permit a change in the actual words of consecration or the use of non-fermented grape juice in place of grape wine.

—*Fr. Carl,* August 1978

When we pray for the Holy Father's intentions when gaining a plenary indulgence, for whom do we pray?

When we are asked by the Church to offer Mass or to pray for the pope's intentions, we are not being asked to pray for the private or personal intentions of a particular pope. The Church, through the authority given her by Christ and acting in union with the inspiration of the Holy Ghost, determines what the pope's intentions comprise, which are the intentions of Christ Himself: (1) the exaltation of Holy Mother Church; (2) the propagation of the Faith; (3) the uprooting of heresies; (4) the conversion of sinners; (5) peace and concord among Christian nations; and (6) the other needs of Christianity. It is God to whom we are offering the Mass and prayers, and it is God who determines the use to which they will be directed. This must be the case, or how would you gain a plenary indulgence during the time it takes to elect another pope?

—*Fr. Carl,* April 1978

When was the Council of Trent? What did the Council of Trent do?

The Council of Trent, named for the city in northern Italy where it was held, lasted from 1545 until 1563. Called by Pope Paul III to combat the errors of Protestantism, it was especially noted for dogmatically defining original sin and the means of salvation. It declared that the Bible was not the sole rule of faith and that Tradition was the unanimous teaching of the Fathers and Doctors of the Church from the beginning. It commissioned an official catechism called the Roman Catechism to be drawn up, and to this day it is the only official catechism of the Catholic Church. The Council of Trent is rated above Vatican II because it was a dogmatic council and not a pastoral council. Trent set up diocesan seminaries. It ordered bishops to return to and care for their dioceses. It stopped the preaching of indulgences and the collecting of money. It made up the list of forbidden books, called "The Index." The canon of sacred Scripture was dogmatically limited and extended to all those books that are found in true Catholic Bibles today. It corrected with strength and kindness various abuses that had entered into the body of the Church and which had afforded Protestants reason for criticism. Saints were involved with the work of this Trent Council, and they included such greats as St. Pius V and St. Charles Borromeo. A true spiritual renewal was experienced in the Church after this Council. Religious life again flourished and holiness was evidenced in all quarters. In contrast, the Church has suffered nothing but decline since Vatican II. The Bishops' synod of 1985 came out with the insane statement that Vatican II was the greatest grace of this century. Modernist bishops are afraid to mention Trent for fear others will laugh at them! Trent was great. Vatican II was a disaster. They must know it, but they will not admit it.

—*Fr. Carl,* June 1987

Are the Church's disciplinary laws infallible?

This theological question is an important one, and has not yet been adequately treated. Fr. Laisney spoke of it in the March 1997 issue of *The Angelus* (pp. 31-40) regarding the question of the New Mass and the opinion (*a priori*) of those who say that it is infallible since it was "promulgated" by the pope, and that consequently it can contain no error or evil. This is manifestly false, just as it is manifestly false to say that the new Code of Canon Law (1983) and the new Catechism of the Catholic Church are infallible documents and consequently completely exempt from all error.

This is the principle which both sedevacantists and conservatives use against the position of accepting everything Catholic which the pope legislates and refusing that which is not entirely Catholic. This position is but common sense.

It is certainly true that before Vatican II pious theologians proposed that the pope's infallibility should extend to his legislative acts. We know, however, that if such a thesis be accepted it does not and cannot include all his legislative acts, any more than his infallibility can include all his teaching acts.

It is only indirectly that legislative acts teach dogma. It is certainly reasonable that a legislative act of the pope would in this way participate in the infallibility of the ordinary magisterium of the Church. It could not, however, participate in the infallibility of the extraordinary magisterium, for there is not in a legislative act a formal definition of a dogma. It can, therefore, only participate in the infallibility of the ordinary magisterium.

The conditions for the infallibility of the ordinary magisterium are that that which is taught has been taught *ubique, semper, et ab omnibus;* that is, *always, everywhere, and by all.* I refer you to the essays on the infallibility of the ordinary magisterium in *Pope or Church?*, published by Angelus Press.

It could easily be considered that the promulgation of *Quo Primum* does just that, inasmuch as it is a formal codification of a rite of Mass which perfectly expresses the Catholic doctrine taught by the Council of Trent. However, there is no way that new or revolutionary legislation could participate in this infallibility, any more than could the dogmatic decrees of Vatican II participate in this infallibility, for they are not even a part of the ordinary magisterium of the Church when they teach novelties.

Consequently, it comes down to examining the laws (such as the new *Catechism of the Catholic Church*) and seeing what is perfectly in conformity to what has always and everywhere been taught by all Catholics. Such laws express the infallibility of the Church, inasmuch as they express Catholic doctrine even though they do not make a direct definition. Other laws either do not express Catholic doctrine or express something contrary to it (*e.g.*, ecumenism), which means that for serious reasons of faith we may and should question and refuse them.

—*Fr. Scott,* June 1998

 **Before Vatican II, popes used to swear fidelity to Tradition under pain of automatic excommunication. Does this mean that they would cease to be pope if they were to depart from Catholic Tradition?**

When a pope swears his fidelity to Tradition under pain of automatic (that is, *ipso facto*) excommunication, he does not say that he would cease to be pope if he were not faithful.

Excommunication is a canonical punishment, separating a person from the communion of the faithful (1917 Code of Canon Law, Can. 2257), equivalent to the declaration of an anathema, just as Pope Honorius was anathematized by Pope St. Leo II.

However, it does not necessarily make a person incapable of accomplishing acts of jurisdiction or government in the Church. Canon 2264 (1917 Code of Canon Law) explains that acts of jurisdiction done by an excommunicated cleric are illicit but valid, provided that the excommunication was not inflicted by condemnatory or declaratory judgment. It is only if there is such a condemnatory or declaratory judgment that the acts of jurisdiction are invalid. Consequently, a pope who had been condemned or declared by official judgment as excommunicated would be incapable of exercising his jurisdiction. This does not, however, mean that he would not be pope.

But who is going to make a condemnatory or declaratory judgment of the pope? It cannot be done by a Council of the Church. This is the condemned heresy of conciliarism. (*Cf.* Vatican I, *Pastor Aeternus*, Dz. 1830: "Nor is anyone permitted to pass judgment on its judgment. Therefore they stray from the straight path of truth who affirm that it is permitted to appeal from the judgments of the Roman Pontiffs to an ecumenical Council, as to an authority higher than the Roman Pontiff.") Consequently, it cannot be done at all. Hence, even if the pope is a heretic and automatically excommunicated, he retains his jurisdiction, and his acts of jurisdiction are valid, but illicit.

—*Fr. Scott,* April 1999

What was the reasoning behind the suppression of many vigils and octaves under Pope Pius XII?

It is indeed true that Pope Pius XII abolished several of the Church's vigils and octaves that had been observed for many centuries before. The reason given by the Sacred Congregation of Rites in its decree of March 23, 1955, to be effective as of January 1, 1956, was the simplification of the rubrics of the Roman Breviary and Missal.

It is certainly true that the rubrics prior to that time were quite complicated, especially when it became a question of overlapping octaves, and that it was a legitimate aspiration of the liturgical movement to simplify these rubrics in such a way that the ordinary faithful could follow, understand, and participate. Furthermore, periodic elimination of added feasts, octaves, and other liturgical days are not unusual in the history of the Church. Consequently, it is certainly excessive to call this elimination of octaves and vigils a "modernist innovation."

In fact, the three most important octaves are the ones that were retained in 1955, namely, those of Christmas, Easter, and Pentecost. Thus the octaves retain their original meaning as a celebration of the major mysteries of our Faith, the Incarnation (Christmas), the Redemption (Easter), and the Descent of the Holy Ghost (Pentecost). One day alone does not suffice to contemplate these momentous events. The octave corresponds to the observation of octaves in the Old Law by the Jews for the Feast of the Paschal Lamb (Passover) and the Feast of Tabernacles. Thus it is understandable that such octaves as those of the Feasts of St. John the Baptist, Saints Peter and Paul, St. Stephen, and St. John the Evangelist would have been abolished. However, we can personally regret that some of the other octaves were not retained, especially the octaves of the Ascension and Corpus Christi, and perhaps also those of the Epiphany and the Sacred Heart.

The celebration of vigils dates back to the early Church, at which time the early Christians prayed all night, until the celebration of Mass at the dawn of the feast day. The remaining example of this is the Easter Vigil of Holy Week, restored in 1951 to its ancient time and form of celebration. These vigils were very important then and should be important for us now. They were times of watching, as indicated by the Latin word *vigiliae*, and also of praying and fasting, in expectation of the solemnity of the morrow. It is certainly true that the sacrifice of fast and abstinence in the expectation of a great feast, and the preparation involved, greatly helps us to profit from the special graces of the feast.

It is true that some less important vigils were abolished in 1955. Nevertheless, all the important vigils were retained, such as those of Easter and Pentecost, the Ascension, the Assumption, St. John the Baptist, Saints Peter and Paul, and St. Lawrence. However, we can still personally regret also that certain other vigils were not retained, which vigils highlight the special importance of the corresponding feast days, in particular those of the Immaculate Conception, All Saints, and the Epiphany. The Church has compassion on the weakness of this non-penitential age in which we live. This does not prevent us from making the effort to observe the spirit of the Church by preparing the major feast days by recollection, sacrifice, spiritual reading, and fasting.

—*Fr. Scott,* May 2001

 **Where can I find information that the direction given us by the pope is questionable? What about our friends who say, "Yes, I see your point (concerning the Mass, for example). However, we must stay with Rome."**

There are many sources to use in researching this point. For the English-speaking world, books such as *The Rhine Flows into the Tiber* by Rev. Ralph Wiltgen, the Liturgical Revolution trilogy of Michael Davies, and *Peter, Lovest Thou Me?* by Daniel LeRoux (especially concerning the actual Holy Father) are indispensable. Of course, above and beyond all "the facts," an in-depth knowledge of our religion is an absolute necessity in this day and age.

With all of the above "digested" intellectually and spiritually, we must make decisions according to the principles of our Faith. We can in no way condone the general apostasy taking place in our day—no matter its source! We must remain firm on that which is sure.

—*Fr. Doran,* April 1993

 **We would like some documented material on Pope John Paul II's "ecumenical" meeting in Assisi. What exactly happened there? Was Buddha actually worshipped? Did the pope receive on his forehead the sign of some pagan goddess?**

There have been two "Assisi" meetings called by the pope. The first was on October 27, 1986, and the second was on this past 9th and 10th of January [1993]. The initial grouping in 1986 had around 130 religious leaders from all Christian communities and non-Christian religions. "Allow me to begin by thanking you, from the bottom of my heart," the pope stated at his allocution to open the day, "for the open mind and good will with which you have accepted my invitation to pray at Assisi.... The fact of coming together implies no intention to seek for a religious consensus among ourselves....Nor is it to concede to a relativism in matters of religious beliefs, for every human being must follow honestly his right conscience with the intention of seeking the truth and to obey it...."

Here we can ask: if there is to be no religious consensus, then why convene? Though relativism is repudiated, can there be anything more formative of indifferentism than the "parliament of religions" seen at this meeting?

"The fact that we profess different creeds takes away nothing from the signification of this day. On the contrary, the Churches [sic], Ecclesial Communities, and world religions show that they desire profoundly the good of mankind."

How is the "good of mankind" to be accomplished if there is no agreement as to the essence of man's beatitude? At best this "good" is purely natural. A purely natural state man has never been in; as a result, this "good" sought at Assisi must be necessarily disordered since it is not ordered to objective supernatural good.

Following these words each religion separated and held prayer sessions alone. Even the above words do not change the fact that non-Catholic religions used churches dedicated to the true and living God for their false worship, the most disgraceful being the Dalai-Lama's use of an altar in the Church of St. Peter to burn candles and to place on the tabernacle a statue of Buddha. During this time there was no specifically "Catholic" prayer, merely "Christian." John Paul set aside the dignity of the Vicar of Christ and simply prayed, with no distinction, with the Orthodox and Protestants.

In these days of ecumania these events may seem of small occurrence, but we must never forget that as the successor of St. Peter, Pope John Paul II has been commissioned to "feed my [our divine Lord's] lambs." The opening words leave these different religions' adherents with the conclusion that in some way they are justified in a false religion. If the expressions did not do so, the prayer sessions in Catholic churches certainly would.

This is all in keeping with the conciliar document *Unitatis Redintegratio*: "For the Spirit of Christ has not refrained from using them [separated churches and communities] as means of salvation which derive their efficacy from the very fullness of grace and truth entrusted to the Church." And in another place: "it is allowable, indeed desirable, that Catholics should join in prayer with their separated brethren."

On the contrary, the Church had always taught: "It is in no way licit for the faithful in any way to assist actively or to have any part in the worship of non-Catholics" (1917 Code of Canon Law, Can. 1258). A passive presence may be tolerated for certain reasons. And one who formally took part in non-Catholic worship, in an active manner, could become suspect of heresy himself.

The pope did not receive the mark of Shiva, a Hindu goddess, at Assisi but during his voyage to India in 1986. The memorable words of Pope Pius XII set a very different tone: "There has never been, nor is there for the Church any hesitation, or compromise, neither in theory, nor in practice....Her attitude has not changed during the course of history, and she cannot change in differing circumstances which place before her the choice: incense before idols, or blood for Christ."

—*Fr. Doran,* July 1993

Do sedevacantists really love the Church? Do they not judge Pope John Paul II personally, as they say?

It is certainly true that many sedevacantists (*i.e.,* those who believe that the pope has lost the office of the papacy through his heretical actions) think that they love the Church. But they do not love her as she really is, with all the faults and defects to be found in her members. If a man would not love his wife as she really is, but rather a mental picture of how he would like her to be, would he really love her?

Some sedevacantists might state that they do not judge the pope personally. However, to state that his heretical actions remove him from office is to make a public, official judgment. Only a higher authority in the Church can make such a judgment. However, there is no higher authority than the pope, which is why the axiom is to be held *Papa a nemine judicatur*—the pope is judged by no one. By stating that he has lost the papacy, sedevacantists personally judge the pope, as if they had authority over him. This is not Catholic, regardless of the gravity of his materially heretical actions. It is the Protestant principle of personal judgment which is thereby erected into a principle of faith, thus destroying the visibility and hierarchy of the Church.

—*Fr. Scott,* June 1998

In writing an encyclical the pope is not writing as a mere private theologian but as the supreme, authoritative teaching authority in the Church. But Pope John Paul II's recent encyclical on ecumenism is a practical denial of the Catholic doctrine of the universality of papal jurisdiction, of the oneness of the Catholic and Roman Church, outside of which there is no salvation. Would it not seem then that he has

abandoned his infallibility and that consequently it is contrary to our Catholic Faith to maintain that he is still the pope?

The pope's tragic betrayal of the Church in *Ut Unum Sint*, so much more explicit than the documents of Vatican II, has certainly brought to light the whole problem of papal infallibility. It certainly runs against the *sensus fidei*, the Catholic instinct of faith, to maintain that a pope should be so gravely in error. How can this be possible? Would it not, perhaps, be less blasphemous to maintain that he is not the pope at all?

The answer to this dilemma lies in the true understanding of the Church's magisterium, the way it is exercised and the limits of its infallibility.

The magisterium of the Church is its teaching authority, in virtue of the mission given by Our Lord Jesus Christ (Mt. 28:20), to teach divinely revealed truth and thus keep the deposit of the faith (2 Tim. 6:20). This teaching takes places in various ways: in sacred Scripture, interpreted as the Church has always understood it; in the various documents which express Tradition as handed down since the apostles (*e.g.*, the writings of the Fathers); in catechisms and the constant preaching of the Faith; by the common teaching of the theologians; and finally by the teaching and definitions of ecumenical Councils and popes.

What concerns us here is the last expression of the Church's teaching authority—the teaching and definitions contained in encyclicals and other writings of the pope. It is Vatican I which both defines as a dogma of Catholic faith the pope's personal infallibility and also describes its limitations:

> *Porro fide divina et catholica ea omnia credenda sunt, quae in verbo Dei scripto vel tradito continentur et ab Ecclesia sine solemni iudicio sive ordinario et universali magisterio tamquam divinitus revelata credenda proponuntur.* (Dz. 3011)

Further, by divine and Catholic faith, all those things must be believed which are contained in the written word of God and in Tradition, and those which are proposed by the Church, either in a *solemn pronouncement* or in her *ordinary and universal teaching power*, to be believed as divinely revealed.

Infallibility is therefore to be found both in the extraordinary magisterium, that is, in the pope's solemn or *ex cathedra* pronouncements and definitions, and also in the ordinary magisterium, but under different conditions in each case. The four conditions for the infallibility of the extraordinary magisterium are clearly defined by Vatican I: "[T]hat he teaches as pastor of the universal Church in matters of faith or morals by means of a definition which he imposes obligatorily on all Catholics, under pain of mortal sin, that is, by the condemnation of the contrary opinion with an anathema attached to it" (*Pastor Aeternus*, Dz. 3074). It is clear that these four conditions are rarely all fulfilled at the same time. Clear examples include the definitions of the Immaculate Conception (1854) and the Assumption of the Blessed Virgin (1950). It is also very probable that Pope John Paul II invoked the same infallibility in *Ordinatio Sacerdotalis* of May 22, 1994, in which he made a definitive statement excluding once and for all the ordination of women (*The Angelus*, January 1995, pp. 30-32).

Vatican II, however, did not use this charisma of infallibility that it could have had a right to. This was explicitly stated by Pope Paul VI in his discourse to close the Council on December 7, 1965, in which he stated: "Although the magisterium of the Church did not wish to pronounce itself under the form of extraordinary dogmatic pronouncements...." He repeated this again in his Wednesday audience of January 12, 1966, in which he declared that the Council "had avoided proclaiming in an extraordinary manner dogmas having the mark of infallibility." There were many reasons for this; first of all, its many humanistic and liberal principles and ideas which are not at all matters of faith and morals; secondly, its practice of proceeding by manner of confusing ambiguity and refusing to make clear definitions. Thirdly, and most importantly, was its refusal to impose doctrine in the name of the Faith, and to oblige under the pain of sin by the means of contrary anathemas as previous Councils had done. The liberal popes John XXIII and Paul VI, in fact, paralyzed their extraordinary magisterium by voluntarily refusing to condemn error, which refusal is reflected in the lack of any condemnation in the formulae of promulgation of the conciliar documents. Paul VI had, in fact, said in his opening discourse to the fourth session, which promulgated the Decree on Religious Liberty: "The Council, instead of inflicting condemnations against anyone at all, will only have thoughts of goodness and peace."

A simple glance at the encyclicals and other documents of the present pope will clearly show that, with the one exception mentioned above, there is never any formal definition and condemnation of error obliging all Catholics and that consequently they are not documents of the extraordinary magisterium.

But could they be said to be documents of the ordinary magisterium, and as such infallible? The difficulty in answering this question lies in the ambiguity which surrounds the term ordinary magisterium. It is sometimes misunderstood to mean all the teaching that the popes have taught in their official documents. That this is an error (which is at the root of the blindness of those who reject the papacy on account of the liberal ideas contained in these post-conciliar documents) is clear from the definition of Vatican I, which specifically mentions that it is the ordinary and *universal* magisterium which is infallible. These documents only contain infallible teachings of the ordinary magisterium inasmuch as they contain universal teachings on matters of faith or morals. Otherwise, they are given the name of the simply authentic magisterium, which is neither ordinary nor infallible because it is not universal, but which is to be received with respect provided that it is not opposed to the doctrine of faith.

The necessity of universality for any teachings to be truly teachings of the ordinary magisterium and hence infallible has always been believed in the Church. The *Commonitorium* of St. Vincent of Lerins is the most concise and well known statement of this: "In the Catholic Church very special care is to be given that we might hold fast to that which is believed everywhere, to that which has been believed always, to that which has been believed by all" (*Rouet de Journel*, no. 2168). Thus is indicated the universality in the teaching of the same revealed truth throughout the entire Catholic world, the constancy in teaching exactly the same truth through all ages, and the unanimity of Catholics in believing these truths. The indefectibility of the Church requires this infallibility as described by Vatican I.

This very rule needs to be applied to the teachings of the popes. Clearly, to start with, no truth which is not presented as divinely revealed can be part of the magisterium of the Church (*e.g.*, religious liberty). Moreover, truths presented as divinely revealed will only form a part of the infallible ordinary magisterium of the Church if they are universal in all three ways, that is, if they have been taught always in the Church, everywhere, and by all. One example would be the physical resurrection and another the universal mediation of grace of the Blessed Virgin Mary and another the Church's constant condemnation of birth control. However, it could easily be imagined that there can be difficulty in understanding exactly what is guaranteed by the infallibility of the ordinary magisterium. This is precisely why there is the necessity for the solemn pronouncements and the infallibility of the extraordinary magisterium.

It is in the light of the above that we can see how to react to such modernist encyclicals as *Ut Unum Sint*. It is not a solemn pronouncement of the extraordinary magisterium. Moreover, it does not even pretend to present this novelty of ecumenism as obligatory, as it is stated to be, as a revealed truth. Consequently, it is not even an act of the magisterium at all. Even if it did pretend to present ecumenism or religious liberty as a revealed truth, it would be clearly manifest that this would not be guaranteed by the infallibility of the ordinary and universal magisterium of the Church for the very simple and obvious reason that these ideas have not been taught always, everywhere, and by all Catholics in the Church, and that they are a manifest novelty.

In fact, there is no contradiction at all with the Church's and the pope's infallibility for such a document to contain explicit heresy. It is indeed an utter tragedy, destroying within the minds of so many Catholics the very authority on which the Church is built. But it is not a denial of his infallibility. Likewise it is in no way a contradiction to say that the pope has the supreme (but not absolute and arbitrary) authority to teach in matters of faith and morals, and to reject such statements or encyclicals which are manifestly opposed to previous declarations of the Church's infallible ordinary and extraordinary magisterium. Here lies the crux of the mystery of iniquity, of the terrible crisis of faith and conscience which is presently afflicting the Catholic Church. It is a vast and very erroneous simplification of the reality, and denaturation of the Church's magisterial authority, to either maintain that the pope must be obeyed in his modernist errors or that he must be rejected as pope altogether.

—*Fr. Scott,* October 1995

 ### Is it possible to state that the pope has failed to completely transmit the deposit of the faith without being a schismatic?

It is certainly true that the principal duty of the Roman Pontiff is to transmit the deposit of the faith completely, as is taught by Vatican I: "For the Holy Spirit was not promised to the successors of Peter that by His revelation they might disclose new doctrine, but that by His help they might guard sacredly the revelation transmitted through the apostles and the deposit of faith, and might faithfully set it forth" (Dz. 1836). However, if the Holy Ghost is invoked in this manner, and if this divine function of transmitting the deposit of faith can only be done through the help of the Holy Ghost, this leaves it to be understood that there can be many human weaknesses in the exercise of the papacy. This is manifest in the case of popes who have not been as courageous as they should have been in the defense of the true faith, such as Pope Liberius.

However, the holy Council also teaches "that the See of St. Peter always remains unimpaired by any error, according to the divine promise of our Lord the Savior made to the chief of His disciples: 'I have prayed for thee, that thy faith fail not'" (Lk. 22:32; *ibid.*) Note that it is not any one individual that is protected from error or heresy, but the See of Peter. This is why the theologians, such as St. Robert Bellarmine, argue about what would happen if the pope would lose the faith and become a heretic. This would of course be a terrible tragedy, but it is not impossible, since it is the See of Peter and the infallible teachings of its ordinary and extraordinary magisterium which are protected from all error, and not any individual, nor even the pope when he does not use the fullness of his teaching authority, that is, in his authentic magisterium.

Consequently, it is perfectly licit for us to acknowledge the obvious, namely, that through the practice of ecumenism, and through the failure to clearly state such dogmas as the Social Kingship of Christ or that outside the Church there is no salvation, and to condemn the infiltration of modernism in every domain of the Church's life, there have been severe defects in his personal responsibility for the transmission of the faith. This does not, however, mean that the See of Peter has failed, for it cannot. A schismatic would be one who would maintain that the See of Peter has failed, and that it is no longer the center of visible unity in the Church, and not one who acknowledges the reality of the weaknesses and failures of the last four liberal popes.

—Fr. Scott, July 2000

 ## Is it good for laymen, untrained in theology and philosophy, to read papal encyclicals?

It is certainly true that the encyclicals of the popes are addressed to the bishops throughout the world, indicating what they must teach their flocks. The reason for this is that the bishops make up the official teaching Church.

However, this does not mean that they are so complex that they cannot be readily understood by the well-educated Catholic layman. For a Catholic who has studied his catechism in depth has a sufficient summary of theology to be able to understand papal encyclicals. Although they do contain theological concepts that only a theologian can fully understand, their teachings are generally expressed in a way that any educated man can understand. Consequently, they are not exclusively for the bishops, but with the intention that their teachings be passed on, which is most accurately done by the simple publication of the encyclical letter.

In fact, the fundamental reason why the papal encyclicals ought to be studied by all Catholics, in this age when the text is readily available, is that they are the usual expression of the popes' ordinary magisterium or teaching authority. Without being infallible statements (in general), they hand down the deposit of faith contained in Scripture and Tradition, adapting it to the times in which we are living, resolving conflicts and disputes, and condemning modern errors. They must, therefore, be accepted and consented to. This is clearly stated by Pope Pius XII:

Nor must it be thought that what is expounded in Encyclical Letters does not of itself demand consent, since in writing such Letters the Popes do not exercise the supreme power of their teaching Authority. For these matters are taught with the ordinary teaching authority, of which it is true to say: "He who heareth you, heareth Me" (Lk. 10:16). (*Humani Generis*, §20)

If at all times the instructed Catholic could not afford to be ignorant of the content of papal encyclicals, this is more the case since the time of the French Revolution, in which liberal errors infiltrating the Church have been constantly and repeatedly condemned in papal encyclicals. This is the reason Archbishop Lefebvre instituted for his seminarians entering into the first year of their seminary studies, before beginning the study of philosophy and theology, a course called Acts of the Magisterium, a brief study of the most important liberal errors condemned by the popes over the 150 years up until Vatican II. This course of study has been published as the book *Against the Heresies*, in the introduction to which Archbishop Lefebvre has this to say: "Why study the Acts of the Church's Magisterium? Quite simply, in order to grasp the situation of the Church today. One notices, in fact, that for nearly three centuries the popes have always condemned the same errors, those which they themselves called 'the modern errors'" (p. xviii).

A Catholic who wants to save his soul, avoid modern errors, and combat the perversion of liberals, must read the papal encyclicals. Otherwise, he will never understand the errors of Vatican II, the evil of the New Mass, the infiltration of liberalism into the Church, and that modernism is truly "the synthesis of all heresies" (*Pascendi*, §39). It is for this reason that the statutes of the Third Order of the Society of Saint Pius X make it an obligation even for lay people to study the Acts of St. Pius X, which means principally his fourteen encyclicals.

—*Fr. Scott,* May 2007

 ### In what way was Pope John XXII's statement concerning the soul's possession of the beatific vision wrong? Surely the souls in purgatory cannot possess the beatific vision.

The question did not concern the souls who are in purgatory, but the souls separated from the body after the time of their purification in purgatory. From 1331 until 1333 he preached and wrote that these souls could only have a vision of the human nature of Christ, and that they could not see God face to face, *i.e.*, the divine essence. He also taught that the wicked could not go to hell nor the good to heaven before the day of the Last Judgment, on which day the general resurrection of the body will take place. Here precisely lay his error.

On the day before his death, December 3, 1334, he issued a bull (*Ne Super His*) in the presence of the College of Cardinals formally and solemnly revoking this opinion. His successor, Pope Benedict XII, published this document, along with his own constitution *Benedictus Deus* of January 29, 1336, which declared authoritatively and perpetually concerning the matter, namely, that after the purgation (for those who are in need of it) the souls of the blessed "even before the resumption of their bodies and the general judgment...have been, are, and will be in heaven... and have seen and see the divine essence by intuitive vision, and even face to face" (Dz. 1000).

It also defines that the damned will go immediately to hell after their death, where they are tortured by infernal punishments (Dz. 1002).

—*Fr. Scott,* May 1998

Has the consecration of Russia to the Immaculate Heart requested by Our Lady been accomplished?

Our Lady of Fatima asked that the Holy Father consecrate Russia to her Immaculate Heart, together with all the world's bishops (June 13, 1929). Pope Pius XII twice consecrated Russia to her Immaculate Heart himself, in 1942 and again in 1952, but alone. The consecration made by Pope Paul VI in 1964 and those made by Pope John Paul II on May 13, 1982, and March 25, 1984, did not mention Russia specifically. Furthermore, although the world's bishops were invited to join in, many did not participate. This was the point made by Sister Lucy in 1985 when she explained that the consecration requested by Our Lady at Fatima had not been accomplished.

—*Fr. Scott,* October 1998

Is a sedevacantist to be considered a non-Catholic?

It is certainly of faith that Our Lord gave the powers of the keys to the successor of Peter, and that the pope is the Church's visible head. However, it is not of faith that Our Lord would not leave His Church for a time without a visible head. There have been times in past history of up to three years without a pope, and times during which nobody really knew who the true pope was. Consequently, the belief that this particular person is not the pope is not necessarily a denial of the Catholic Faith.

The 1917 Code of Canon Law (Can. 1325, §2) defines a schismatic as one who refuses to submit to the authority of the Sovereign Pontiff. However, given the present confusion of the Church and the fact that we are obliged by our Faith to refuse so many of the liberal, ecumenical statements of Pope John Paul II, it is not necessarily obvious that a sedevacantist actually refuses to submit to the authority of the Sovereign Pontiff, and that he is consequently a schismatic.

Nevertheless, it is preposterous to say, as the sedevacantists do, that there has not been any pope for more than forty years, for this would destroy the visibility of the Church, and the very possibility of a canonical election of a future pope.

Just submission to the pope is a principle of unity in the Church, along with the faith, the sacraments, and the holy sacrifice of the Mass. This is all contained in the definition of the Church contained in the catechism: "The Church is the congregation of all baptized persons united in the same true faith, the same sacrifice, and the same sacraments, under the authority of the Sovereign Pontiff and the bishops in communion with him."

However, he is not the only factor of unity. This is the misconception shared by both modernists and sedevacantists alike. They say that nothing matters but the pope and become modernist like him, or they say that nothing matters but the pope and he is destroying the Church, so therefore there is no pope. The real problem of the present crisis in the Church is that the pope is no longer acting as principle of unity, as he ought, for he is no longer adequately promoting the unity of faith, sacraments, and the Mass that has always characterized the Catholic Church.

It is consequently true that there can be some theological discussion as to whether sedevacantists are formally schismatic or not. The answer to this depends on the degree of sedevacantism. There are radical sedevacantists that call us heretics since we are in communion with a heretic (Wotyla), so they say. These are certainly schismatic, for they clearly reject communion with true Catholics who are in no way modernist. By making their sedevacantism a quasi-article of faith they certainly fall into the second category of persons that Canon 1325, §2 declares to be schismatic: "He is a schismatic who rejects communion with members of the Church subject to him [i.e., the Sovereign Pontiff]." It is consequently by their refusal to be a part of the Church, and effectively making the "church" as they see it consist only in sedevacantists, that they are certainly schismatic.

There are other sedevacantists who do not hold their opinion as a question of faith but just as a private opinion and who do not condemn other traditional Catholics who do not share their opinion. On account of the confusion of the present crisis and the fact that they do not refuse communion with Catholics who have the true faith, it is not unreasonable to hold that such persons are not formally schismatic.

However, the real danger with the sedevacantists, over and above the question of their being formally schismatic, is that they fail to have a

Catholic attitude. Their rash and excessive condemnatory attitude, not only towards the pope and the modernists but also towards Catholics simply trying to live their Catholic life, and other traditional Catholics, leads them to fall into rigorism, formalism, and legalism, and to condemning everybody else. They easily fall into pharisaical pride. They are a real plague to the traditional movement here in the US. Such people have no sense of obedience or submission, and often commit rash judgment. They do not feel at home in the Society's chapels where the Church's faith, sacraments, doctrines, and Mass are preached together with the interior life of charity and self-sacrifice as the means for restoring all things in Christ.

—Fr. Scott, December 2001

ABOUT THE PRIESTHOOD AND PRIESTS

Must a priest follow certain criteria if he is to refuse Holy Communion to the faithful?

A priest does not have the right to refuse Holy Communion arbitrarily. He must follow the requirements of canon law, which prescribes to whom he must refuse Holy Communion, and to whom he must administer it. This law is to be found in Canon 855, §1:

> Catholics who are publicly known to be unworthy (for example, those who have been excommunicated or interdicted or who are manifestly of ill repute) must be refused Holy Communion until their repentance and amendment have been established, and satisfaction has been made for the public scandal which they have given.

The essential part of this law is that a Catholic must be a public sinner, or publicly unworthy, to be refused the sacrament of Holy Communion. This is the case, for example, of a person who has publicly performed abortions, a person who is known to have voted for legislation in favor of abortion, a father who has had his children baptized and raised in an heretical sect, a person who has become a member of the Communist Party, a person who is involved in public concubinage, a person who is divorced and remarried outside the Church, or a person convicted of civil crimes such as pedophilia.

However, the Church is very clear that Holy Communion cannot be refused to a person who is not a *public* sinner, that is, if his sin is not sufficiently well known in the community at the present time. For to refuse

Holy Communion to a person who is not known to many people as one who publicly breaks the commandments of God would be to defame his good name and destroy his reputation, which a person has a right to in justice, even if he is a hidden sinner. It is only by public sin that he loses this right, for he has lost his reputation. However, if such a hidden sinner were to ask the priest in private to receive Holy Communion, or whether or not he can go to Holy Communion, the priest would be obliged to forbid him to go to Holy Communion, and this even though he could not refuse him Holy Communion if he were to request it publicly at the communion rail. This is explained in the second half of Canon 855: "Occult sinners, who secretly ask for Holy Communion, shall be refused by the minister if he knows that they have not amended; if, however, they seek Communion publicly and the priest cannot pass them by without scandal, he shall not refuse them." It is truly sad for a priest to be obliged to administer a sacrilegious Communion, but if he cannot convince them privately to abstain from Holy Communion, then he must do so.

The question can sometimes arise, not of hidden or occult sins, but of public attitudes that persons might take against the Church, but which are not public sins. There are some people who lack respect for their priests, who refuse to follow their advice and counsel, who cause dissension in a parish by gossip and similar means. In general, they are not to be considered as public sinners or publicly unworthy, unless they openly promote teachings that are opposed to Catholic faith and morality or unless they incite other parishioners to direct disobedience and disrespect towards their pastors. On occasion, sedevacantists and Feeneyites have fallen into this category.

Also, when parents obstinately refuse their very grave duty of educating their children in the Catholic Faith, as required by Canon 1113, and instead educate them in a non-Catholic religion, they must be refused Holy Communion. Canon 2319 (1917 Code of Canon Law) states that they are to be treated as excommunicated, and consequently refused the sacraments. This does not apply, though, to those families, as foolish as they often are, who prefer to educate their children at home rather than in a traditional parish school. For as long as they educate their children in the Catholic Faith they are not sinners, let alone public sinners. It is a question of prudence rather than sin, unless they initiate a campaign to attack their Catholic schools or the education received therein, thus undermining the work of the Church and of their pastors.

—*Fr. Scott,* August 2005

What is the status of all those priests who took the Anti-Modernist Oath at their ordination and who have now abandoned it and are going along with modernism? Are those who took the oath still bound by it even though it has since been abolished by the revolutionaries?

To make an oath is to take God as witness of the truth of one's words or of one's promise. Now, the Anti-Modernist Oath ends with these words:

> Therefore I most firmly retain the faith of the Fathers, and will retain it up to the last gasp of my life, regarding the unwavering charisma of the truth, which exists, and has existed, and will always exist in the succession of bishops from the Apostles; not so that what is maintained is what may appear better or more suitably adapted to the culture of each age, but so that the absolute and unchangeable truth preached by the Apostles from the beginning may never be believed or understood otherwise. All these things I pledge myself to keep faithfully, integrally, and sincerely, and to watch over them without fail, never moving away from them whether in teaching or in any way by word or in writing.

All those who made this oath and are unfaithful to it have God as witness of their infidelity. No pope can make that infidelity become fidelity. The priests who have learned the right way and have departed from it (for whatever reason, even the false understanding of "obedience," since there can be no true obedience to change the Faith), not standing up for the truth they knew, have certainly a great responsibility in the disastrous situation of the Church today. Let us pray for them that they return!

—*Fr. Laisney,* January 1991

Can traditional priests absolve from censures in the internal forum?

Censures are canonical punishments that are imposed upon Catholics who have committed grave crimes against God or the Church. There are far fewer censures in the 1983 Code than in the 1917 Code. However, some still remain, such as the automatic excommunication for any Catholic who would perform or in any way cooperate in an abortion (Can. 1398). Normally such a censure, which prevents a Catholic from receiving any of the sacraments, is to be remitted by the ordinary of the diocese. However, both codes foresee the possibility of remission in the confessional, either with delegation from the ordinary, or in the usual situation in which it is spiritually urgent to receive the absolution from the censure so that the sacraments can be received (Can. 2254 of the 1917 Code and Can. 1357 of the 1983 Code).

There are some minor differences between the two codes on secondary questions. One such difference, which concerns the priests of the Society, is the 1983 Code's omission of the possibility of remission of censures by the confessor in the internal forum in the exceptional case of moral impossibility of recourse to the proper superior, as provided for by Canon 2254, §3 of the 1917 Code. Canon 1357 of the 1983 Code is otherwise very similar, permitting priests to absolve from censures in the internal forum, but simply does not speak of the exceptional case of moral impossibility of recourse. Our priests are certainly in this case, given that the bishops and the Sacred Penitentiary regularly refuse to grant the jurisdiction to absolve in such cases. However, it is perfectly understandable that the law could not foresee the case of our priests having to absolve with supplied jurisdiction. Nor need it, for that matter, for nobody can be bound to have recourse when it is impossible, nor does the Church refuse the sacraments in such cases. To the contrary, it always grants the priest the right to absolve from sins, as, for example, in case of danger of death (Can. 882 of the 1917 Code and Can. 976 of the 1983 Code).

The laws concerning correct interpretation are to be followed in such cases, as described in Canons 17 and 19 of the 1983 Code. The interpretation is to be made according to laws in similar circumstances (*i.e.*, the absolution from sins by a priest without jurisdiction in case of danger of death), the general principles of law, and the common practice of the Roman Curia. This interpretation is precisely what is contained explicitly in the 1917 Code. This particular precision is not opposed to the new law but is simply not mentioned in it.

In such cases the 1917 Code helps us to interpret the 1983 Code. The 1983 Code, Canon 6, §2 points out that canons that refer to the old law (this is the case) are to be judged according to canonical tradition, and that customs that are not against the law are to be maintained (Can. 5, §2). Also, Canon 20 of the 1983 Code states that a later law only abrogates an earlier law if it explicitly states so, or if it is directly contrary to it, or if it regulates the whole matter treated by the law. This is not the case with the moral impossibility of recourse, for it is simply not treated. Consequently, this particular detail is not abrogated.

The 1917 Code is more explicit when it states the canonical principle that in case of doubt the prescriptions of the old law are to be retained (Can. 6, §4). Consequently, in such cases there is really no opposition between the codes, but it is simply an application of the more general principles of interpretation and supplied jurisdiction admitted by both codes.

—*Fr. Scott,* December 2006

What is the Church's teaching on women in the priesthood?

The Church's constant teaching can be summarized in three points: *1)* God Himself determines who will exercise the function of the priesthood in the public liturgy. Not even Christ as man takes the honor to Himself, and to the apostles He says, "You have not chosen me, but I have chosen you, and have appointed you" (John 15:16). *2)* God chose men both in the Old and New Testament *exclusively* for the priesthood. *3)* Only men are to exercise the ministerial priesthood, representing all mankind before God in the things pertaining to God.

—*Fr. Scott,* January 1993

Didn't the early Church have "deaconesses"?

Yes, but it is unanimous from early Church documents that the term "deaconess" had nothing to do with the sacrament of holy orders. St. Epiphanius gives unquestionable testimony as to the non-ordination of deaconesses: "They were only women-elders, not priestesses in any sense, and their mission was not to interfere in any way with sacerdotal functions, but simply to perform offices in the care of women" (*Haer.* lxxix, cap. iii).

—*Fr. Scott,* January 1993

Does the non-admission of women to the priesthood have anything to do with "inferiority" and "superiority"?

It has nothing to do with "inferiority" and "superiority" but with the roles which God has ordained for men and women. According to divine plan, God did not call women to the priesthood any more than He called men to motherhood. Our Blessed Mother was the most perfect being ever to walk the earth, outside of the God-Man, Jesus Christ. So much does her excellence surpass all of God's creatures that she is *queen* of angels and saints. Yet Our Lord did not choose her as one of His priests, but twelve unlettered men, one of whom betrayed Him.

—*Fr. Scott,* January 1993

ABOUT THE MASS AND THE LITURGY

What is the Tridentine Rite?

No such rite exists. Quite well did the chancellor of the Memphis diocese answer this: "There is no such thing as the Tridentine Rite." To speak of the "Tridentine Rite" or "Tridentine Mass" is to falsely imply that a new rite has been set up within the Catholic Church. The proper manner to speak of the Mass in question is "The Mass of the Roman Rite according to the Missal of Pope St. Pius V." This Mass existed before Pope St. Pius V or the Council of Trent and only is referred to as "Tridentine"—that is, as codified by Council of Trent. Pope St. Pius V in *Quo Primum* gave in perpetuity this Mass to be said by any priest, without fear of censure.

—*Fr. Carl,* June 1990

Is it true that only Masses under *Quo Primum* are representative of the Catholic religion?

The reason why the New Mass fails to be truly representative of the Roman Catholic religion is not just because it is a break from *Quo Primum*. It is true that *Quo Primum* gives the guarantee that the Tridentine Mass is Catholic and that priests will have the right to celebrate it *"in perpetuity."* But *Quo Primum* does not state that a subsequent pope could not approve a different rite of Mass, and in fact there are many different Eastern and Western rites of Mass which are perfectly Catholic, all traditional, preceding the Council of Trent by 200 years. What makes the New Mass not representative of the Catholic Faith is the fact that it contains modernist ideas and omissions which are in direct contradiction with the Catholic theology of the Mass as defined by the Council of Trent (*cf.* Ottaviani Intervention). This is why it is a grave danger to the Faith, and why priests should not celebrate it, nor should the faithful assist at it, under pain of sin.

—*Fr. Scott,* August 1998

Is the dialogue Mass a "diabolical disorientation," and can it be compared to Communion in the hand?

The custom of the faithful making the responses at low Mass and reciting with the celebrant those parts that they would sing at a high Mass (*e.g.,* Kyrie, Gloria, Sanctus, Agnus Dei) began in 1922 as an outgrowth of the liturgical movement founded by Dom Guéranger and promoted by St. Pius X to bring about an active participation of the faithful in the celebration of the Mass. St. Pius X had requested in 1903, in his *motu proprio* on Gregorian chant, the restoration of the active participation of the faithful in the Mass, outlining this principle, for the glory of God and the sanctification of souls:

> Our keen desire being that the true Christian spirit may once more flourish, cost what it may, and be maintained among all the faithful, We deem it necessary to provide before anything else for the sanctity and dignity of the temple, in which the faithful assemble for no other object than that of acquiring this spirit from its primary and indispensable source, which is the active participation in the most holy mysteries and the public and solemn prayer of the Church.

The so-called dialogue Mass was nothing other than the application of this same principle to the recited Mass, on occasions on which the Mass could not reasonably be sung (*e.g.*, daily Mass for a community of religious). However, modernism did enter into the application of this principle, for the modernists did not see this form of active participation simply as an elaboration of the liturgy but as necessary to it, in virtue of their substitution of the emphasis on the common priesthood of the faithful in place of the ordained, sacramental priesthood. Consequently, they wanted to insist on the people reciting the Mass not simply as an alternative but as an obligation.

As with other excesses of the liturgical movement, the 1947 encyclical of Pope Pius XII, *Mediator Dei*, made the necessary distinctions, condemning the abuses and promoting the correct Catholic understanding of the liturgy. After pointing out the primacy of the interior participation of the faithful uniting themselves with the divine Victim on the altar, it also recommends the outward participation that expresses this union:

> They also are to be commended who strive to make the Liturgy even in an external way a sacred act in which all who are present may share. This can be done in more than one way, when, for instance, the whole congregation in accordance with the rules of the Liturgy, either answer the priest in an orderly and fitting manner, or sing hymns suitable to the different parts of the Mass, or do both, or finally in High Masses when they answer the prayers of the minister of Jesus Christ and also sing the liturgical chant. (§105)

However, the pope at the same time refutes the modernist error of those who make such external participation an end in itself:

> Their [these methods of participation in the Mass] chief aim is to foster and promote the people's piety and intimate union with Christ and His visible minister and to arouse those internal sentiments and dispositions which should make our hearts become like to that of the High Priest of the New Testament. (§106)

He continues, drawing the logical conclusion:

They [these methods of participation] are by no means necessary to constitute it [the Mass] a public act or to give it a social character. And besides, a "dialogue" Mass of this kind cannot replace the High Mass, which … possesses its own special dignity due to the impressive character of its ritual and the magnificence of its ceremonies. (*Ibid.*)

Consequently, one who accepts the teachings of Popes Pius X and Pius XII cannot question the legitimacy of the so-called dialogue Mass, provided that it be done correctly and that it be regarded as just a means to a more perfect interior participation; nor can the dialogue Mass possibly be compared with such sacrilegious and openly modernist practices as Communion in the hand, a practical denial of the Real Presence.

—*Fr. Scott,* April 2006

What steps are necessary to make a low Mass complete?

Your question is a bit vast. The first question is what you may mean by "complete." The very essence of the Mass is the Offertory, the Consecration, and the Communion. Without these it is certain that there would be no Mass.

Every sacrament requires the matter, the form, and the intention of the minister to do what the Church does. For the Eucharist, the matter is bread and wine, the form is the words of consecration, and the intention is to renew the sacrifice offered on Calvary. These parts are the very essence and must be present.

As for "complete," this might encompass any number of things such as a consecrated altar, a chalice and paten in gold, vestments, candles, a missal for the form and ceremonies clothing the essence, *etc.*

—*Fr. Doran,* November 1991

Is anything more to be gained by hearing two or more Masses at the same time, rather than just one?

The multiplication of Masses is of great benefit to the Church and to souls, for each one is a true, propitiatory sacrifice, an unbloody reactualization of the sacrifice of the cross. Consequently, there can be no doubt that a soul has much to gain spiritually by assisting at different Masses successively, even though he can receive Holy Communion at only one of those Masses, since each sacrifice will contribute to the purification of his soul and growth in the love of the cross, by union with the divine Victim.

However, it often happens in large churches or monasteries that several priests will offer the holy sacrifice of the Mass on different altars at the same time. The question of whether or not anything can be gained by assisting at more than one Mass at the same time depends upon whether or not it is really possible to do this. For the assistance at Mass—as, for example, when satisfying one's Sunday obligation—the Church does not just require physical presence. It also requires the intention of worshipping God by assisting at the Mass, and at least some attention to what is going on. This attention is not just external, by the fact of not doing anything else at the same time. There must also be some internal attention, by thinking of the essential elements of the Mass. However, it is in no way necessary to think of everything, which is why involuntary distractions do not destroy one's attention to the Mass.

Now, it is manifestly possible for a person to have the intention of assisting at more than one Mass at the same time. It is also possible to have the necessary attention, for the attention to one Mass does not exclude the attention to what is going on at another altar, at least in the general lines. Consequently, a person who has the intention of assisting at two Masses and who pays attention to two Masses at the same time truly does assist at two Masses, provided that he assists in this manner at all the essential parts of each Mass, or at least the moments of Consecration and Communion. It must be remembered that a person cannot combine different parts of different Masses together to make up the assistance at one Mass, for this is a condemned, laxist proposition (Dz. 1203).

Consequently, a person who had promised to assist at two Masses would truly fulfill his promise by assisting at two Masses being celebrated simultaneously. However, it seems to me that he would not receive as much grace as if he assisted at two Masses successively on account of the weakness and limitations of our human nature, as a result of which we would be better disposed to receiving graces by assisting at two Masses successively, given the additional time for reflection that this would allow.

The other question that could be raised in this regard is whether a person could satisfy the penance of hearing two Masses, received in the confessional, by assisting at two Masses at the same time. Since it is possible to assist at two Masses at the same time, this would seem possible. However, it will depend upon the mind and intention of the confessor who imposed the penance. If the confessor intended to impose two successive Masses, and made this clear, then the penitent would commit a serious sin by omitting this additional circumstance of the succession of the Masses, thus making his penance much lighter. However, if the confessor did not make it clear, then the penance could be interpreted in the same way as other ecclesiastical laws, and in a narrow sense. (Cans. 18 and 19, 1917 Code of Canon Law.) Since all admit that it is perfectly possible to satisfy two obligations at the same time—for example, that of one's penance of assisting at Mass by the same Mass that is the Mass at which one satisfies one's Sunday obligation, or one's family rosary can also be one's sacramental penance—then it follows that a person could satisfy the penance of assisting at two Masses by assisting at both at the same time.

—*Fr. Scott,* September 2004

What do the three candles on each side of the altar represent?

The candles for Mass originated in the catacombs and in the dark cathedrals and were used for needed light in reading the Missal. The bishop, because he might be old and find reading difficult, was customarily given a special candle near the book, called the *bugia*. The candle is also a beautiful symbol of Christ. It sacrifices itself completely to give light as Christ sacrificed Himself to give grace to mankind. It is made of a wick and sweet-smelling beeswax (at least 51%) representing the body and soul of the Redeemer. Normally two are lit for a low Mass and six for a sung or solemn Mass, or according to the solemnity of the occasion or the dignity of the celebrant. At baptism a lighted candle is handed to the candidate or sponsor symbolizing the light of grace. On Easter Vigil the deacon sings the beautiful *Exultet* in praise of the paschal candle which is a figure of our Risen Lord the Light of the World.

—*Fr. Carl,* January 1980

Why is it that in the celebration of Mass the psalm *Judica me* is said before the *Kyrie eleison?*

The ordering of the parts of the Mass is essentially historical in its origin. The Mass did not come into being because somebody sat down and figured out a logical sequence of prayers. Different circumstances were involved in the introduction of the different elements.

Neither the *Kyrie eleison* nor Psalm 42 were a part of the primitive Roman rite. The *Kyrie eleison* was added during the fifth and sixth centuries, coming from Antioch in the East, through Gaul. It was certainly firmly a part of the Roman Mass in the time of St. Gregory the Great at the end of the sixth century. It is the insistent importuning of God's mercy by those who are aware of their unworthiness.

The psalm *Judica me, Deus,* which is Psalm 42, began to be used in the celebration of Mass, together with the other prayers at the foot of the altar, in the eleventh century. However, for several centuries it remained a local custom, becoming more universal as time went on, but not obligatory. It was originally a private preparation of the priest before the celebration of Mass, which is why it was not a part of the Mass prayers properly speaking. Still, in 1550 Pope Paul III simply ordered that this psalm be said aloud or silently in the sacristy before the priest went to the altar. It was St. Pius V with the Tridentine Mass who ordered that it be recited at the foot of the altar.

This psalm is a messianic psalm, referring in its literal sense to David asking God's deliverance and protection from his rebellious son Absalom. It refers, however, in its messianic sense to Christ's offering Himself on the altar of the cross, the accomplishment of His Father's will, the joy of His life. The relevance to the priest in his preparation for Mass is very clear. To mount the altar of God is the joy of his youth, the realization of his every desire, for this altar, on which Christ's sacrifice is reactualized, is the source of all light and truth. With what alacrity does he repeat this psalm that identifies him with Christ Himself, sinner though he is, confident that he will be judged, not on his own merits, but on those of the all-holy Savior in whose person he stands.

Consequently, it might seem a little strange that Psalm 42 precedes the *Kyrie eleison*, and also the *Confiteor*, but when understood as the final preparation for going to the altar, it can be seen how this joyful, confident psalm can precede these professions of sinful unworthiness.

—*Fr. Scott,* December 2004

If the Mass is the unbloody renewal of the sacrifice of Calvary, why does the priest pray the *Orate fratres* at the Offertory of Mass?

The prayer of the *Orate fratres* is offered up that the sacrifice might become pleasing to Almighty God. This does not mean that the sacrifice of the cross was in any way displeasing to God, for it was of infinite value and merit. Nor does it mean that the sacrifice of the Mass is a different sacrifice from that of the cross, for, as the Council of Trent declared, "that same Christ is contained and immolated in an unbloody manner, who on the altar of the Cross once offered Himself.... it is one and the same Victim ... as He who then offered Himself on the Cross" (Session XXII, ch.2; Dz. 940).

The sacrifice is consequently perfectly acceptable in itself, for there is nothing imperfect in the principal Priest, the Victim, or the sacrifice itself. It is our offering of the sacrifice, the manner in which we are associated with the unbloody renewal of the sacrifice, that can mar it and make it unacceptable to the Almighty. This acceptability may seem secondary, and yet it is absolutely essential for it to apply the fruits of the Passion to our souls. It depends upon our disposition of soul, and of how generously we offer ourselves in union with the divine Victim. It is our disposition that limits the varying abundance of the fruits of this sacrifice for our souls, for the value and merits of Christ's sacrifice are unlimited.

This disposition can be defective, both on the part of the human priest's offering of the sacrifice in the person of Christ and also on the part of the laity's participation by offering of themselves from the pew. Hence the prayer: "Brothers, pray that my sacrifice and yours may be acceptable to God the Father Almighty." How we must have an acute awareness of our unworthiness to offer up or participate in this sacrifice, and humbly beg that despite this it may obtain many graces and blessings, and that it might truly be "to the praise and glory of His name, to our own benefit, and to that of all his Holy Church"!

—*Fr. Scott,* February/March 2004

 **Does the statement of *Quo Primum* that "none of it be changed under penalty of our indignation" mean that Masses celebrated with the name of St. Joseph in the Canon are not Tridentine Masses?**

The interdiction of adding or changing refers to the act of any prelate of any rank, by his private preference or authority. It does not forbid a subsequent pope, as supreme legislator, from making changes. In fact, many popes made minor changes, either to the text or to the rubrics, amongst whom Clement VIII and Urban VIII (whose encyclicals explaining their changes are in the front of the Tridentine Missal), Leo XIII, St. Pius X, Pius XII, and John XXIII, whose apostolic letter *Rubricarum Instructum* is also at the front of the *"Missale Romanum ex decreto sacrosancti concilii tridentini restitutum summorum pontificum cura recognitum,"* as it is officially titled; *i.e.,* the Roman Missal restored by decree of the most holy Council of Trent and reviewed by the care of the Sovereign Pontiffs.

The Mass remains the Tridentine Mass for as long as these changes are not substantial, that is, for as long as it remains essentially the Mass restored by decree of the Council of Trent. This was the case until Pope Paul VI's New Mass came out in 1969.

One example of a change which is not substantial and which the pope, and only he, as supreme legislator for the liturgy (as was St. Pius V), could make was the insertion of the name of St. Joseph in the Canon. Already before he was pope, St. Pius X was one of many bishops who petitioned (in 1897) that this take place. It took a long time to come about, and it just happened to be done in 1962, after the promulgation of the 1960 rubrical reform by Pope John XXIII. In fact, it has nothing to do with the new theology, or the new Mass, or Vatican II.

—*Fr. Scott,* August 1998

What is the significance of the small piece of host that the priest drops into the chalice after the *Pater Noster?*

It is called the *fermentum* or *sancta*. It dates back to the days in the early Church when the pope, on Sundays and principal feasts, would send a particle of his host to the local Roman bishops to be dropped into the chalice at their Masses—a sign of unity of their holy sacrifice of Christ with that offered by the pope. Nowadays the practice is for each bishop and priest to break a small particle from his own large host and to drop it into the chalice after the *Pater Noster,* while saying "*Pax Domini sit semper vobiscum.*" I think it is a beautiful reminder of the marvelous antiquity of the Mass of All Time.

—*Fr. Carl,* January 1980

What is a stipend for a Mass?

"A stipend is a contribution toward the support of the priest upon whose acceptance the priest assumes a grave obligation of justice to offer the Holy Sacrifice of the Mass for the intention of the contributor" (Jone/ Adelman, *Moral Theology*). The amount is a matter of agreement, or a rate set by the local ordinary. The idea is not a payment for the Mass or spiritual service but a gift to the priest who agrees to offer it for your intentions. A priest may accept a Mass intention with no stipend. He may also accept a gift of one hundred dollars for one Mass which is still not the payment for the infinite value of one Mass. The Mass is worth as much as Christ is worth, since it is the unbloody renewal of the holy sacrifice of the cross, done through signs and under the appearance of bread and wine.

—*Fr. Carl,* August 1982

Can the rubrical changes of 1955 and 1962 be compared to the new rite of Mass?

It is certainly true that liturgists of modernist tendency, including Fr. Bugnini, had a considerable influence in the Commission for the Reform of the Liturgy from the time of its foundation in 1948. This is what Fr. Bonneterre has to say in *The Liturgical Movement* (Angelus Press, 2002):

> Protected from on high by eminent prelates, the new liturgists took control little by little of the Commission for Reform of the Liturgy founded by Pius XII, and influenced the reforms devised by this Commission at the end of the pontificate of Pius XII and at the beginning of that of John XXIII. (P. 94)

However, until Vatican II these were incidental questions that did not change the liturgy in itself, such as the suppression of certain vigils and octaves, the restoration and change of the times of the Holy Week ceremonies. They did not change the Mass itself in any way, which remained the Mass of St. Pius V, published in virtue of *Quo Primum*, the document with which every Missal of 1962 begins. Some changes were beneficial simplifications, such as the categorization of liturgical days into four classes and the removal of overlapping octaves. Others can be considered regrettable, such as the shortening of the ceremony for the blessing of palms on Palm Sunday. However, Providence and the authority of the Church prevented them from going beyond any such minor rubrical changes, such that Pope John XXIII declared himself dissatisfied with the change of rubrics that he authorized in 1960, wanting a more radical change according to new principles, after the impending Council (*Rubricarum Instructum*). This was to be the New Mass.

Consequently, we are duty-bound to accept these minor rubrical changes, as is done in practically every traditional church and chapel world wide. Whether we personally like them or not, they are not expressions of a new, modernist theology, as is the New Mass, but rather of the same nature as the minor accidental rubrical changes that many popes since 1570 have authorized to the Mass of St. Pius V. The New Mass of Pope Paul VI is evil because it undermines and destroys the Faith, and must be rejected. None of these rubrical changes have any impact on the Mass as a symbol and profession of faith, and consequently there is no objective reason to reject them.

—*Fr. Scott,* April 2006

 **Is it true that a heretic who does not believe in the Real Presence can have the intention of doing what the Church does and celebrate a valid Mass?**

It is certainly true, as St. Thomas Aquinas explains, that faith is not required of necessity in the minister for the sacraments he administers to be valid (*ST*, III, q. 64, art. 9). In the same way that a heretic can validly administer the sacrament of baptism (*e.g.*, a Protestant), and even the fact that he does not believe in original sin does not invalidate this sacrament, so also can a heretic celebrate a valid Mass. He does not have to intend what the Church intends, but only to do what the Church does, which latter is possible even when he has a gross misunderstanding of what the Church really does.

However, this being the case, the existence of heresy can certainly place a shadow of doubt over the intention of the minister giving a sacrament. Before Vatican II it was always the practice to baptize under condition any adult converts from Protestantism. There were several reasons to doubt to some degree Protestant baptisms, one of which is a defective intention of the minister. If the minister had an explicitly contrary intention, namely, if he had explicitly formulated the intention of not doing what the Catholic Church has always done, then the sacrament would be invalid. It is not the fact that he does not believe in original sin that could make the sacrament of baptism invalid, but the fact that his explicit intention is just to give an outward sign, and not to administer a sacrament that removes original sin and infuses sanctifying grace.

The same can be the case with the New Mass, and this even if the priest still believes in the Real Presence. He could have a contrary intention to that of the Church. This would be the case if his intention explicitly refuses offering a true sacrifice, the unbloody renewal of Calvary, and explicitly considers that it is to be only a meal and a commemoration of the Last Supper. Such an intention would be directly contrary to the intention of doing what the Church does. We do not know how often this happens, but it is very reasonable to believe that it is a common occurrence. Consequently, there are probably many celebrations of the New Mass, by priests who are convinced of modernist theories, that are invalid.

This is one reason why we cannot have anything to do with the New Mass. However, the more universal reason is that it is insulting and injurious to Almighty God and to Our Lord Jesus Christ, even if it happens to be valid.

—*Fr. Scott,* September 2002

 ### Who has the right to touch the chalice and sacred linens, namely, the corporal, pall, and purificator?

According to the traditional law of the Church it is normally only clerics who have received the tonsure who can touch the chalice and the sacred linens before they are purified. This is explained in Canon 1306, §1. However, an exception is given. As well as clerics, these items can also be handled by those who are assigned care of them, that is, by the sacristan.

According to the interpretation given in Woywood, *A Practical Commentary on the Code of Canon Law*, 5th ed. (1939), II, 82-83, the authorized sacristan who can touch these objects can be a religious brother or sister or a lay person: "Writing before the promulgation of the [1917] Code, Wernz says that in the course of time the ancient rigor in the matter of touching the sacred vessels was relaxed, so that lay brothers and religious, sisters and laymen acting as sacristans were permitted to touch the sacred vessels."

However, it is not because a person is authorized to touch these items that he should necessarily do so. This is what *Matters Liturgical*, No. 96 (p. 152), has to say: "If the custodian is a lay person [*i.e.*, not a tonsured cleric] it is at least becoming that, when possible and convenient, a veil should be used in handling it [*i.e.*, the chalice and associated linens]." In practice it is much easier to use gloves, and that is what I recommend for my sacristans and altar boys.

Quite different is the practice of the post-conciliar church, which has abandoned all sense of the sacred. Note that in the 1983 Code of Canon Law there are no canons at all which correspond to Canons 1296-1306 in the 1917 Code concerning the sacred objects in the Church. This silent omission of all the Church's provisions concerning the blessing and consecration of sacred objects, and the care to be taken in their use, is one further sign of the desacralization of the post-conciliar church.

—*Fr. Scott,* December 1998

Is it permissible to sing English hymns during Mass, or can this only be done after Mass?

The most complete pre-Vatican II answer to this question is the instruction of September 3, 1958, issued by the Congregation of Rites concerning the practical application to the liturgy of the Church's laws relative to sacred music. It is quoted at length in *Matters Liturgical*. The text concerning vernacular hymns can be found on pp. 47-48 of the 1959 edition. First of all, such popular religious hymns "are greatly to be commended and esteemed, since they constitute a most effective means in directing the minds of the faithful to heavenly things and in imbuing the Christian life with a genuine religious spirit." Strongly to be encouraged for pious exercises, they can only be sung at liturgical functions "when this is expressly permitted."

English hymns are expressly permitted during a low Mass, but in general expressly forbidden during a high Mass: "Hymns in the vernacular are permitted at a Low Mass, on condition that their theme corresponds to the part of the Mass at which they are sung." This means that a theme of sacrifice or offering is retained at the Offertory and of thanksgiving, love of God, or any similar theme at Communion time. However, the singing of vernacular hymns at a sung Mass or *Missa cantata* is manifestly an abuse that can only be tolerated when backed up by a long standing custom that has lasted for over a century: "They [hymns in the vernacular] are permitted at a Mass in chant only in the case of a centenary or immemorial custom which in the judgment of the local Ordinary cannot prudently be suppressed."

Needless to say, this condition is not generally fulfilled in the Society's chapels, which is why only Latin hymns are sung during a sung or high Mass, English hymns being reserved for the processional and recessional. This stands to reason, since Latin is the liturgical language in the Roman Rite, and since these chants are inserted into the liturgy itself, thereby honoring, adoring, and praising God according to their place in the liturgy. The low Mass differs from the high Mass in that the chants are not a part of the liturgical action, there being no ceremony. Such hymns can consequently be permitted as devotional exercises, for the sake of the faithful. Needless to say, it is very commendable to sing Latin hymns during a low Mass, especially when the faithful are familiar with them. Hymns and chants in this sacred language are particularly effective at elevating souls to God.

—*Fr. Scott,* March 2003

Can women be permitted to sing in the choir in church?

The principles are given by Pope St. Pius X in his *motu proprio* on the restoration of sacred music, and in particular of the ancient Gregorian chant. This document of November 22, 1903, is entitled *Tra le solleci-tudine* and is published in its entirety in the March 1995 issue of *The Angelus* (pp. 36-40).

The pope states repeatedly that the sacred chant is an integral part of the liturgy, directed to the glory of God and the sanctification and edification of the faithful (§1). It is consequently not a performance but a part of the act of divine worship. His conclusion follows:

> Except the chant of the celebrant and the sacred ministers at the altar, which must always be sung in plainchant without any accompaniment, the rest of the liturgical singing belongs properly to the choir of clerics....It follows from the same principle that the singers in church have a real liturgical office, and that women therefore, being incapable of such an office, cannot be admitted to the choir. (§§12, 13)

—*Fr. Scott,* April 1999

Does this mean that women should not sing in church at all?

The fact that women cannot perform the liturgical office of singing does not mean that they should not sing in church at all. To the contrary, they should participate in the congregational singing. That such congregational singing is indeed the mind of the Church is indicated by Pope Pius XI in his apostolic constitution of December 20, 1928, "On the Liturgy, Gregorian Chant, and Sacred Music":

In order that the faithful may more actively participate in divine worship, let them be made once more to sing the Gregorian Chant, so far as it belongs to them to take part in it. It is most important that when the faithful assist at the sacred ceremonies...they should not be merely detached and silent spectators, but, filled with a deep sense of the beauty of the liturgy, they should sing alternately with the clergy or the choir, as it is prescribed. (§IX)

There are some exceptions to the rule forbidding women from singing in choirs. One such exception is religious women in their own community. Canon law permits them to sing the chants of Mass, if permitted by their constitutions, but providing that they are in a place where they cannot be seen by the faithful (1917 Code of Canon Law, Can. 1264), since they are not a choir in the liturgical sense.

Another exceptional case (and it is important that it remain exceptional) occurs when there is a dearth of male singers, and when it is necessary for the solemnity of the service that men and women join in the singing (Rev. George Predmore, *Sacred Music and the Catholic Church* [1936], p. 117). However, "we are to make every possible and fair effort to introduce either congregational singing of the liturgy, or to have male choirs. But the service is not to be made unbecoming, distracting, or ridiculous by literal adherence to the law, where the conditions really hinder its decorous observance" (*ibid.*, p. 118).

—*Fr. Scott,* April 1999

Is it permissible to go to confession during Sunday Mass?

It has always been the custom for confessions to be heard during Mass whenever this is possible, preferably during weekday Masses but also during Sunday Masses. This gives some of the faithful the opportunity of going to confession who would not otherwise easily be able to do so. A quick confession during Sunday Mass does not interrupt the assistance at the Mass, for it is a prayer, like the Mass, and does not involve a notable part of the Mass.

However, if a person were to spend a notable part of Sunday Mass in the confessional, for example, receiving spiritual advice and direction from the priest, then he would not have fulfilled his Sunday obligation and would have to stay for the next Mass. A person does not have the right to place himself in this situation, and he ought not to go to confession after the Offertory or before Communion when he anticipates that the confession might take a long time.

Furthermore, there is also the question of respect. In general, the confessor who is hearing confessions during Mass will stop during the sermon so that the penitents also can receive instruction, and he will also stop during the Consecration of the Mass, out of respect for this great miracle. These times should be avoided when going to confession during any Mass.

—Fr. Scott, November 2006

 ### Is it permissible to go to the bathroom during Sunday Mass?

In itself, leaving the church for a couple of minutes for a bathroom stop during Mass does not break the assistance at Mass, for a notable part of the Mass is not missed. However, if a person were to leave for the Canon of the Mass, including the Consecration, he would have missed a notable portion of the Mass.

This being said, it remains very important to maintain the principle of discipline, namely, that one satisfy the needs of nature before and after holy Mass, but not during. Whereas it is understandable that parents with very young children might have to take them out for the bathroom, it is not to be expected that this continue to be the case with children who have the use of reason, and especially not during Sunday Mass during and after the sermon. Parents must teach their children discipline, and adults ought to give a good example in this regard.

—Fr. Scott, September 2006

ABOUT THE COMMANDMENTS OF GOD AND THE PRECEPTS OF THE CHURCH

 ### The opinion has been voiced that a bad deed resulting in good is permissible, such as the case of the murder of the abortionist doctor in Florida, comparing it to a just war. In my opinion, this way of thinking is erroneous.

"Let us not do evil that there may come good" (Rom. 3:8). This is a revealed principle of Christian morality. We also say that "the end does not justify the means." As it is a part of divine revelation, it is often misunderstood, or ignored, by the neo-pagans in the world today. The intrinsic reason for this is that the moral character of an act derives from its object. It is good or evil depending on its accord with right reason and the divine will, or its disaccord with the same. The intrinsic morality of an evil act is not altered by any external motive.

It is not possible to compare this scenario to a just war. A just war requires declaration by legitimate authority. One mob fighting another may be just but does not fit the description of a just war. In shooting the abortionist the man assumed to himself authority proper to legitimate governors. A misuse of power does not forfeit it. It does remain true that the frustration experienced by pro-life people is totally understandable during the present absence of moral integrity of our legislators.

—*Fr. Doran,* June 1993

 ### Is it permissible to embark on a hunger strike, determined to fast until death, if one's non-violent political action is not successful?

The essential question to be resolved here is whether embarking on a hunger strike is to commit suicide or not. Suicide is defined as "the direct killing of oneself on one's own authority" (Fagothey, *Right and Reason*, p. 276).

Suicide is to be distinguished from indirect killing which is only indirectly voluntary, for death is not intended either as an end or as a means to an end, but is only permitted as an unavoidable consequence. Such is the case of deliberate exposure of one's life to serious danger of death. This is certainly permissible but only on condition that the usual rules of the indirect voluntary or double effect apply, namely, that the bad effect of death is quite distinct from the good effect that is desired, that the good effect does not come from the bad effect, and that there is a proportionate reason to justify the bad effect that is permitted as an un-avoidable consequence. Thus it is permitted to place one's life in danger in time of war in order to defend one's country, even knowing that there is a good chance that one may be killed. However, it is never permitted to directly kill oneself, even for one's country, for it is the evil effect of kill-ing oneself which is desired in itself, and the good effect comes from it. This is always wrong, for the ends do not justify the means. Thus suicide bombers certainly commit immoral acts when they kill themselves in order to kill others. They cannot be said to act in virtue of the principle of double effect.

The gravity of the sin of suicide lies in the fact that it is a directly voluntary act in which it is one's own death that is intended either as an end or as a means to an end. Such an act is directly contrary to the natural law, known to all men by their very nature; for by nature we are God's, and He has exclusive dominion over us. It is in the natural law that man, who is subject to God and dependent upon Him for everything, does not have direct or absolute control over himself but only stewardship. For there is no other way for man to attain his end than by belonging to

Almighty God, which a man refuses to do by arrogating to himself God's right over life and death.

A hunger strike is direct suicide. It is death itself that is desired in order to obtain a political change. It is a direct killing of oneself, which is always wrong, regardless of the good that one hopes to attain thereby. It is consequently always a mortal sin regardless of the political gain that could be expected. The only exception to this would be if a person had a revelation from God indicating that it is God's will for him to kill himself, so that it would be an act of obedience and submission to the Author of life rather than an act of rebellion. A person who thought he had such a revelation could possibly be in good faith. However, if he were sane, he would still have to be refused Catholic burial on account of the scandal caused. Furthermore, it is not reasonable to believe that God would ever give such a command so directly opposed to the natural law upon which grace and divine revelation build.

—Fr. Scott, January 2004

Does a Saturday evening "vigil" Mass satisfy the Sunday obligation?

It is of the divine law, prescribed by the third commandment of God, that a day of rest be set aside in honor of God. The theologians teach that the precept that this be observed on the Sunday and no longer on the Saturday is of ecclesiastical law, since at the beginning of the Church the apostles continued to go to the temple on Saturday (Acts 3:1, 5:12). However, the apostles universally introduced the custom of sanctifying Sunday as the Lord's Day, so much so that it had become obligatory by the beginning of the second century (*cf.* Prummer [Dominicus Prummer, *Manuale Theologiae Moralis*], II, 386, §465).

It is certainly true that the liturgical days for Sunday and feast days have always started with First Vespers that are celebrated on the eve of the feast or on Saturday afternoon to prepare for Sunday. But it was never permitted to celebrate a Mass for the feast or for the Sunday on the eve of the day itself, at the time of First Vespers. In fact, the Church's law was explicit on this point, prescribing that Mass could not begin more than one hour before dawn or more than one hour after noon (Can. 821, §1). It was consequently just as inconceivable to celebrate Mass on the eve of a feast to satisfy the obligation of the feast as it was to claim that the law of abstinence from servile work obliged as of the afternoon before the feast. If it is true that in 1953 Pope Pius XII permitted the celebration of afternoon and evening Masses, this was on account of the shortage of priests, to allow for Masses on the afternoon or night of the feast or Sunday itself, rather than for the celebration of a "vigil" Mass to avoid the sanctification of the Sunday or holy day.

The novelty came with the 1983 Code of Canon Law, which permitted the faithful to satisfy their obligation of assisting at Mass on a Sunday or holy day either on the day itself or the afternoon or evening beforehand (Can. 1248, §1). What are we to think of this? It is certainly true that the highest legislative authority in the Church, the pope, technically has the right to modify the first precept of the Church, since it is of ecclesiastical law and not of divine law. It is this ecclesiastical law that obliges under pain of mortal sin, as defined by Pope Innocent XI, and so consequently a person could not be accused of mortal sin for simply availing himself of the privilege of assisting at Mass on the afternoon before a Sunday or feast day.

However, this is not the real issue at stake. The real question is whether this relaxation of the law is in conformity with Tradition, whether it helps protect the Faith, and whether it assures the keeping of the third commandment of God, as it was designed to do. Alas, the response must be negative on each count. Whereas those who were legitimately impeded from assisting at Mass (*e.g.*, by work obligations) were freed from their obligation, there is no tradition in the pre-Vatican II Church of substituting Mass for the offices that are designed to prepare for the feast (with the sole exception being in the 1950's when Pope Pius XII authorized miners who had to work every Sunday to assist at Mass on Saturday evening). It certainly does not protect the Faith or help in the sanctification of Sunday, as experience has shown. What do those Catholics do to sanctify the Sunday, to study and pray their Faith, when they will not even go to Mass on Sunday but prefer Saturday afternoon so that their Sunday can be free for secular activities? Clearly, little or nothing. Gone are the Sunday catechism classes made obligatory by St. Pius X, the study of Scripture, the reading of spiritual books, meditation and prayer, and even the respect for Sunday as a special day, consecrated to the honor of Almighty God. To introduce such a measure into the Church's law is a major step in the secularization of the Church, and in making Catholics' lives entirely indiscernible from those of anybody else in this pagan world.

Consequently, we have a duty to encourage our *Novus Ordo* Catholic friends to stand up against this lukewarm practice, so opposed to the sense of the Church and to the restoration of all things in Christ, and to truly honor the mysteries of the Resurrection and of eternal life that are symbolized by the Sunday rest. Let traditional Catholics not even dream of the hypocrisy of attempting to use this provision of the lax post-conciliar law, unless it be in the case where there is no alternative. For it is a manifest contradiction to pretend to be attached to the traditional

Mass, and to the Church's traditional teachings, and to refuse to even make the effort to attend Mass on Sunday to sanctify the Lord's day.

—*Fr. Scott,* January 2002

 ## Is it permissible to publish the sins of deceased persons?

It is certainly true that a man's reputation is the most precious exterior possession that he can have—as the Book of Proverbs states, "A good name is better than great riches" (Prov. 22:1)—and that he has a strict right to it in justice. It is also true that despite the fact that the modern world considers that a reputation is of little consequence, it is a sign of honor and goodness that a man values the opinion that others have of his excellence. Finally, it is also true that reputation concerns principally a man's practice of virtue and only secondarily his other good qualities, and that this right is not extinguished by death, for a man, having an immortal soul, always has a right to his reputation. Consequently, the deliberate telling or publishing of the sins that a man committed during his life, without proportionate reason, is a mortal sin of detraction both against justice and against charity, even if the facts told are perfectly true.

However, the right to one's reputation is not absolute, and has limitations. Just as we can tell the sins of the living, if it is necessary for their own good (that they might be corrected), or for the good of a third person (to prevent him from being led into error or sin), or for the common good, so also do there exist reasons for relating the sins of deceased persons. In the case of the deceased it is usually the common good that is invoked, and rightly so. In fact, an historian of the Reformation who would not tell the sins of King Henry VIII or Luther could not be considered an historian. He would not tell the truth, and his history would serve no purpose. Likewise an historian of Pope John Paul II who would not tell of his public sin of religious indifferentism at Assisi in 1986 would not tell the truth. History is the master of life, as the saying goes, and to be so it must tell all that pertains to the truth, the evil as well as the good, the faults of Catholics as well as their virtues. Hence the moral theologians are in agreement that for the sake of history itself, there is always a sufficient reason, in virtue of the common good, for relating all certainly true events and backing up with documents (*cf.* Prummer, II, §194).

This applies to all persons who are public, who have a role in history, and notably writers, authors, artists, and men of ideas, and even with respect to acts that were not publicly known while they were alive. It is only by the full picture of their lives that their impact on history can be evaluated. Nevertheless, a disorder can frequently arise in such matters, due to a certain curiosity about evil things that is common to fallen human nature. It is very easy for the mode of telling of sins to be excessive and scandalous, and to become a serious sin against charity.

Such is the case of those who would concentrate on a man's sins before his conversion, or who would describe his sins in a very graphic manner. This is particularly the case with sins against the sixth commandment, in which all detail is an occasion of sin and very dangerous to relate or to read. Some people, however, wrongly take advantage of such sins to promote their own cause. The Internet is easily abused for gossip mongering, and those who went into the details of Gill's moral life on the Internet were sinning against charity by the manner and publicity that they gave to this discussion, and also on account of the scandal that an unnecessary and excessively public discussion of sins against purity does cause.

The key issue is the common good. Persons who have lived a particularly immoral life should only be discussed if the common good requires it, as it does with Luther or Henry VIII. However, the Catholic in charity ought to avoid so doing if it is not really necessary for history. It is for this reason that prudence dictates that it is preferable not to quote from or bring up the subject of such persons, particularly if they are Catholic, on account of the scandal that the telling of historical facts could cause.

—*Fr. Scott*, February 2007

How does one determine what buying and selling is permitted on Sundays?

The traditional Code of Canon Law (1917) is very explicit on this question, stating that "On feast days of obligation [including every Sunday] … one must abstain from public commerce, public gatherings of buyers and sellers [*e.g.*, auctions], and all other public buying and selling, unless legitimate custom or special indults permit them" (Can. 1248). The 1983 Code of Canon Law does not give this precision, but simply states that those things are to be abstained from that impede worship to God, joy proper to Sunday, and due relaxation (Can. 1247). Everything is left to the interpretation of the private individual.

The traditional law is very explicit, and excludes all public buying and selling, such as auctions or major legal contracts. However, it allows for the details to be determined somewhat by local custom. This is not to be understood as what everybody does, but the custom amongst fervent, practicing Catholics. It is certain that private contracts can be entered into, namely, those that do not have any public legal form. It is equally certain that the purchasing and selling of small items is licit, such as milk, fruit, bread, flowers, holy pictures, books, clothing, and other such items that might be available at road-side stalls or at a church bookstall. All agree that those items that are necessary for daily use, such as common food items, can be sold and purchased on Sundays.

The authors also agree that if there is a grave reason to purchase larger items on a Sunday this is permissible, for example, when a person lives a long distance from town and is only able to come in to town on a Sunday. These exceptions, due to necessity, show the Church's attachment to the spirit of the law rather than simply the letter.

There are things that are manifestly forbidden in the traditional law of the Church, such as buying and selling real estate, bidding on important items at auctions (*e.g.*, furniture). Then there are areas that are not so clear cut, such as doing one's grocery shopping on a Sunday. Any one or other of the items could certainly be purchased on a Sunday without any scruple of conscience, and likewise a person who had no other opportunity to do his grocery shopping could do so. However, a person who did a whole week's grocery shopping on a Sunday without necessity would be considered as involved in public purchasing and selling of items of large value, and could not be excused from at least venial sin.

Here, as always, the value of the Church's law lies in the fact that it determines the right means to our end. Our end is to sanctify the holy days and Sundays, for the greater honor and glory of God and the salvation of our souls, which is only possible if we remove the preoccupation with the mundane, temporal things that occupy the rest of our time. We must consequently consider it a grave spiritual obligation to take these means that the Church so wisely imposes upon us. Let us then be determined to abstain from all unnecessary shopping for items of considerable value on Sundays and holy days. In particular, let us protest the opening of grocery outlets on Sundays by refusing to patronize them on Sundays.

—*Fr. Scott,* January 2005

On a holy day of obligation is one required to refrain from manual labor the same as on Sundays?

Yes. Fr. Henry Davis says in *Precepts*: "The Church forbids servile work on all Sundays and holy days of obligation, that we may have time and opportunity for attending Mass, hearing instructions, reading good spiritual books, and incidentally, that we may recuperate body and mind for the better service of God and neighbor." Servile work means manual labor normally, such as plowing, sowing, harvesting, sewing, cobbling, tailoring, printing, building, and all work in mines and factories. Regular shopping, banking, and opening places of business are also forbidden. Permitted are certain arts, crocheting, knitting, *etc.* Also permitted is going walking, riding, driving, rowing, journeying, even though these may be very fatiguing. Sculpting, teaching, and drawing are permitted. About two-and-a-half hours of arduous servile work, moralists say, could constitute grievous matter. Washing clothes in an automatic washer and dryer certainly would not constitute mortal sin. Necessary work, cooking for the family, doing dishes, caring for the children or for the needy or sick—these things are not servile work. In certain cases dispensation can be had from the bishop or the pastor, but only for a time or two.

—*Fr. Carl,* December 1980

Is one allowed to study on Sunday?

The important distinction to be observed in the keeping of the Sunday rest is between servile work, *opera servilia*, and liberal works, *opera liberalia*. Note that the Church's interdiction does not depend on the purpose, or reason, for which the works are done, but on the nature of the work itself. Servile works performed out of charity are forbidden on Sundays, such as mowing a neighbor's lawn or painting his garage, and liberal works are permitted, even if they are done for profit, such as painting pictures to sell.

You might wonder what the difference, then, is between servile work and liberal works, and why it is that servile works should be particularly forbidden. St. Thomas Aquinas explains in the *Summa Theologica* (II-II, q. 122, art. 4, ad 3):

> Servile work is so called from servitude; and servitude is threefold. One whereby man is the servant of sin, according to Jn. 8:34 "Whosoever committeth sin is the servant of sin," and in this case all sinful acts are servile. Another servitude is whereby one man serves another. Now one man serves another not with his mind, but with his body. Wherefore in this respect those works are called servile whereby one man serves another. The third is the servitude of God; and in this way the work of worship, which pertains to the service of God, may be called a servile work.

Clearly Sundays are consecrated to the worship of God, and servile works in this third sense are not only permitted but obligatory. Also, servile works in the first sense of sin are always forbidden, but especially on Sunday, the day that is specially given to the greater glory of God. If servile works in the second sense of physical activities formerly done by servants are expressly forbidden on Sundays, it is because the preoccupation with such matters is a part of the punishment for original sin (Gen. 3:19: "In the sweat of thy face shalt thou eat bread") and hinders the soul from being elevated to the things of God, from contemplating eternity, and from taking care of its eternal salvation and the greater glory of God. Not so the liberal arts, which express the soul's elevation and consideration of beauty, truth, and goodness in varying ways. The Sunday should consequently be used for the soul to express its freedom to know, love, and serve God not only by participating in holy Mass and the Church's offices, but also by its exercise of and/or appreciation for the liberal arts. This is summarized by Jone:

> *Liberal* and *artistic* works (*opera liberalia*) are also lawful: studying, teaching, drawing, architectural designing, playing, music, writing (also typing), painting, delicate sculpturing, embroidering, taking photographs. These works are lawful even if done for remuneration. (*Moral Theology*, §192, p. 130)

However, it may happen on occasion that even the liberal arts hinder the soul's worship of God when they are immoral or an occasion of sin, or if a person is so preoccupied with them that he no longer assists at Mass or attends to his spiritual duties. In such circumstances, study also becomes sinful on Sunday.

—Fr. Scott, February 2001

Is it permissible to attend a concert where music is performed in a Catholic church?

Catholics understand why a church is blessed or consecrated: "By the term church is understood a sacred structure devoted to divine worship for the principal purpose of being used by all the faithful for public divine worship" (1917 Code, Can. 1161). Our Lord declared "My house shall be called the house of prayer" (Mt. 21:13). It is sacred and must be separated from all secular use under pain of becoming "a den of thieves." In consequence: "Business and trafficking, and in general whatever is out of harmony with the holiness of the place, should be excluded" (1917 Code, Can. 1178). Canon 1220, §1 of the 1983 Code says the same.

The question is whether the performance of music in a church which is not for the liturgy takes away from its sacredness. The answer is given by Canon 1264, §1 of the 1917 Code, which simply reproduces a decision of the Council of Trent, but which is, alas, not maintained in the 1983 Code. "Music, whether instrumental, from the organ or other instruments, or vocal, in which there is any tinge of the lascivious or impure, must be entirely excluded from churches."

A clear distinction has to be made between the different kinds of music. Firstly, there is *sacred music*, which is that used in the sacred liturgy, and which is primarily Gregorian chant, but also polyphonic music in the tradition of composers such as Palestrina. Secondly, there is *religious music*, which is not composed or performed for the liturgy but which elevates the soul to the contemplation of divine truths. Thirdly, there is *secular music*, which has no rapport with religion at all. The performance of sacred music is possible within Catholic churches even outside the liturgy under certain conditions:

> Religious music…that seeks to express and stir up pious and religious emotions…is to be greatly esteemed and opportunely promoted, because of its obvious benefits to religion. Religious music cannot be used in liturgical or other sacred functions, since it belongs properly to the music hall or theater, and not to the church dedicated to divine worship. Where no auditorium or hall is available, a concert of religious music may be given in a church, if such a concert can be expected to benefit the faithful spiritually. (Sacred Congregation of Rites, Sept. 3, 1958, *Matters Liturgical*, 10th ed. [1959], p. 49)

Such religious music would include the singing of hymns or the great Masses and oratorios of the Baroque period.

Precautions are taken to avoid disrespect, such as the removal of the Blessed Sacrament and forbidding applause. However, rarely will it be the case that a concert is of purely religious music, with such a spiritual objective in mind, and more rarely yet is it the case that no suitable auditorium is available.

It is not permitted to perform or attend a concert of secular music in a Catholic church, for secular music appeals primarily to the senses. To use a blessed or consecrated church as a concert hall for such music, without regard for its sacredness, would certainly be to steal the honor and glory owed to Almighty God. Catholics must refuse to perform at such concerts or attend them. It is no justification to say that *Novus Ordo* churches are desecrated by secular music in the liturgy itself, as if one person's desecration of a church would justify another to do likewise. These prohibitions do not apply to Protestant churches, which are in no way sacred, provided that in attending one does not partake in any religious ceremony (*cf.* 1917 Code, Can. 1258).

—Fr. Scott, November 2000

How can a person go to hell for lying too long in bed on a Sunday or deliberately eating a slice of ham on a day of abstinence?

The catechism tells us that a mortal sin is a grievous offense against the law of God, and that it is called mortal because it is deadly and deprives the sinner of sanctifying grace. It also tells us that there are three conditions required for the sin to be mortal, namely, that there be grave matter, knowledge of this, and full consent. When all these conditions are fulfilled there is certainly a horrible outrage against the divine order, and against Almighty God Himself. It is a rebellion and, if unrepented before death, will certainly lead the sinner to eternal damnation in hell.

The question is really whether or not the precepts of the Church can constitute such grave matter as to oblige under pain of mortal sin. They most certainly can, since the Church has the authority to bind and loose, which means the authority to govern souls, which means the authority to establish laws which oblige in conscience to such an extent that anybody who knowingly and voluntarily goes against them certainly commits a mortal sin. If the Church did not have the authority to legislate in such a way as to bind the consciences of Catholics, then it would not have any real authority at all.

Some might say that oversleeping or eating meat on a Friday are small matters. The answer is that they are small things in themselves, but when they come under the obligation of a precept of the Church, they become of serious consequence. The Church binds us for our own good, but the Church does really bind us. Consequently, if someone knowingly and deliberately, without any proportionate reason, breaks the Church's precepts, he certainly commits a mortal sin, he scorns the Church's authority, and he rebels against God's order.

There can be no doubt that many souls will go to hell for failing to attend Mass on Sunday and to observe the Friday abstinence. However, it is also true that the Church has the authority to change its laws. It is the present ecclesiastical law which obliges under pain of sin, and not the former law which traditional Catholics respect and observe out of custom, spirit of penance, love of Tradition, and desire to live the spirit of the Church. In most dioceses the obligation of Friday abstinence under pain of mortal sin only exists now on the Fridays in Lent. Likewise, ecclesiastical law now permits the Sunday obligation to be fulfilled on Saturday evening, although we know that the spirit of the Church and the observance of the third commandment of God require that we sanctify the Sunday by assisting at Mass on Sunday.

It is also important to note that the Church has always allowed for the many factors that can excuse a person from the obligation of observing the laws of the Church, such as sickness or distance from the church.

—*Fr. Scott,* April 2000

Is a Catholic in mortal sin if he allows more than one year to pass since his last confession?

It is one of the six precepts of the Church, and explicitly stated in Canon 906 of the 1917 Code of Canon Law: "All Catholics of either sex who have reached the years of discretion, that is, the age of reason, are obliged to confess all their sins accurately at least once a year." Since this is a clear obligation in a serious matter, established by the Church for the salvation of souls, it is clear that it is under pain of mortal sin; and if a person deliberately omits to confess his or her sins, he commits an additional mortal sin.

However, there is a change in the wording of the corresponding canon in the 1983 Code. Instead of all sins, it now says "serious sins" (Can. 989).This leaves some ambiguity, but it must be understood as meaning "mortal sins," to use the precise term employed by the traditional Code of Canon Law. This seems to take away all obligation to confess sins if one thinks that one has no "serious" or mortal sins on one's soul. This is the common practice in the post-conciliar church, in which many practicing Catholics go for many years without seeing the need to go to confession. It is a great tragedy, for their conscience becomes extremely lax. Who are they to judge of themselves that they have not committed any mortal sin? It is hard to understand how one who is familiar with the traditional teachings of the Church could be excused from the sin of presumption.

However, it must be admitted that "strictly speaking, only those are obliged by this precept who have committed a mortal sin" (Jone, *Moral Theology*, §395, p. 279). This is confirmed by Woywood's *A Practical Com-mentary on the Code of Canon Law* (1941), I, 451. It is there pointed out that the obligation of confessing one's mortal sins is of divine law, coming from Our Lord Himself. The time for the confession of sins was specified by Lateran Council IV (1215), but the Council of Trent interpreted this as applying only to those sins that have to be confessed by divine law. The 1917 Code of Canon Law states explicitly (Can. 902) that the confession of venial sins is optional, and one canon cannot contradict another. Hence it was never strictly obligatory under pain of mortal sin for a Catholic who was sure that he had no mortal sin to go to confession every year.

However, putting aside this technical and unreal exception (for who can really pretend to be free of mortal sin when he is so lax as to go to confession only once a year?), it remains that the spirit of the Church is that which is contained in the letter of Canon 906 from the traditional code, and not that contained in the new code, namely, that every Catholic should consider it his duty to go to confession at least once a year.

In fact, it is not just once a year, but frequently that we should confess our venial sins if we hope not only to stay in the state of grace, but also to advance in virtue. This is what Pope Pius XII had to say on this subject in 1943:

> It is true that venial sins may be expiated in many ways which are to be highly commended. But to ensure more rapid progress day by day in the path of virtue, We will that the pious practice of frequent confession,

which was introduced into the Church by the inspiration of the Holy Spirit, should be earnestly advocated. (*Mystici Corporis Christi*, §88)

Condemning the younger priests who "lessen esteem for frequent confession," the pope described some of the many advantages to the soul of the regular confession of our venial sins:

> By it genuine self-knowledge is increased, Christian humility grows, bad habits are corrected, spiritual neglect and tepidity are resisted, the conscience is purified, the will strengthened, a salutary self-control is attained, and grace is increased in virtue of the Sacrament itself. (*Ibid.*)

Is it any wonder that the Church requires that we go to confession eight days before or after gaining a plenary indulgence?

—*Fr. Scott,* April 2001

Why do Catholics not eat meat on Fridays?

The practice of Friday abstinence dates from the very beginning of the Church. The principle of the penitential practice of abstinence, in order to achieve self-mastery, was already outlined by St. Paul himself: "Everyone striving for the mastery must abstain from all things" (I Cor. 9:25) and "Let us exhibit ourselves as the ministers of Christ in labors, watchings, and fastings" (II Cor. 6:5).

Explicit mention is made of the practice of abstaining on Fridays in a document from the end of the first century (*The Didache of the Apostles*) as well as by St. Clement of Alexandria and Tertullian in the third century. It was the universal custom from the very beginning, and Friday was chosen in memory of the Passion of Our Lord as a day on which we should make a special effort to practice penance. It is in recognition of the fact that Christ suffered and died, and gave up His human flesh and life for our sins on a Friday that Catholics do not eat flesh meat on Fridays. Pope Nicholas I made this a law of the Church in the ninth century. In the Latin Church, from the early Middle Ages this one day of abstinence was not considered enough, and Saturday abstinence was added in honor of the burial of Christ and the mourning of the Blessed Mother and the holy women on Holy Saturday. This was made a law of the Church by St. Gregory VII in the eleventh century, but has since fallen out of custom, except by those who desire to profess their devotion to Our Lady in a special way. The Eastern Rite Church also had strict rules for abstinence, given that it was binding for them on Wednesdays and Fridays.

The rules for what can and what cannot be permitted on days of abstinence have also varied with time. St. Thomas Aquinas, for example, indicates that eggs, milk, butter, cheese and lard are forbidden on days of abstinence because they come from animals and have some identity of origin with flesh meat. Present day rules limit the abstinence to flesh meat only.

The abstinence from meat is an ecclesiastical law, but one which has long obliged under pain of mortal sin. Pope Innocent III made this very clear at the beginning of the thirteenth century, and in the seventeenth century Pope Alexander VII anathematized those who would minimize the character of this obligation by declaring that transgressions against it were only venial sins.

It is certainly true that, as an ecclesiastical law, the Friday abstinence can be changed by the Church's sovereign authority. However, the way this important precept has been trivialized by the post-conciliar Church is a great disgrace and shame for Catholics. It is clearly not taught to bind under pain of mortal sin, and the mention of the possibility of substituting any other kind of sacrifice by the 1983 Code of Canon Law has effectively destroyed this very ancient practice. The fundamental reason why the modernists detest the Friday abstinence is that they refuse the need for at least some small works of penance to satisfy for the temporal punishment due to our sins, and they do everything they can to empty out the mystery of the Passion, that is, of the cross, and to replace it by a Risen Christ without suffering and sacrifice. However, it was by suffering, and by offering up His own flesh and blood, that our divine Savior deigned to redeem us, and consequently it is our duty to associate ourselves with Him by the Friday abstinence.

—Fr. Scott, November 2002

 ### Does chewing gum break the ecclesiastical fast?

The ecclesiastical fast is not the same thing as a natural fast, which is the total abstinence from all food and drink. The ecclesiastical fast is the fast that is prescribed by the Church's positive law and is not always as absolute as the natural fast.

There are two kinds of ecclesiastical fast. The first kind is the Eucharistic fast. Until Pope Pius XII's *motu proprio* of 1957, *Sacram Communionem,* the eucharistic fast required by the Church was an absolute fast from the preceding midnight. This excluded the ingestion of any food and drink, even water. It did not allow of even light matter, the ingestion of any food being grave matter and a mortal sin if followed by Holy Communion the same day. Pope Pius XII in the above mentioned decree allowed the three-hour fast, to be counted strictly before the time of Holy Communion. This requires abstaining from all solid food and from alcoholic drinks. The rule was changed to one hour of abstinence from non-alcoholic beverages, and allowed the drinking of water at any time, without breaking the fast. These are the rules that must be kept in Tradition, the one hour fast of Pope Paul VI being truly a farce.

The eucharistic fast does not admit of a venial sin as a result of the small quantity of food ingested, not even a very small quantity being interpreted as nothing. However, it is not broken by particles of food found in teeth and swallowed in saliva, nor by toothpaste. The resolution of the question of chewing gum depends on whether or not it is considered to be a food. If the gum itself is swallowed, it must be said to constitute food. Furthermore, chewing gum has large quantities of sugar, which certainly has food value. Consequently, it must be considered as breaking the eucharistic fast, so that if a person chews gum less than three hours before receiving Holy Communion, then he must abstain from Holy Communion, under pain of sin.

There is no Catholic who believes in the Real Presence who does not see how grave a disrespect it would be to chew gum and then afterwards approach the sacred Banquet. In addition, as Pope Pius XII states, the three-hour fast itself is a special mitigation and concession on the traditional practice (absolute fast from midnight), which is recommended whenever possible, and when we use these mitigations we "are expected to make compensation … by becoming shining examples of the Christian life, and principally by works of penance and charity" (*Matters Liturgical*, 10th ed. [1959], §366).

The question of the ecclesiastical fast prescribed for days of fast is entirely different. Here again, the fast obliges under pain of mortal sin (alas, now only on Ash Wednesday and Good Friday), but allows one main meal and two snacks. Any consumption of solid food outside those times is a breaking of the fast. However, with this fast, there can be light matter when the amount of food ingested is small, so that the sin committed by deliberately doing so is only a venial sin. Moreover, the amount of food ingested can be so little as to be effectively nothing, in which case it could be considered as not breaking the fast at all.

It would seem that the amount of sugar capable of nourishing contained in a stick of chewing gum is not more than that which is allowed in a cup of tea or coffee. Yet we know that this does not break the fast. Consequently, it can be considered safely that the chewing of a single stick of chewing gum on a day of fast would not constitute a sin against this precept of the Church. However, repeated chewing of gum would amount to at least a light matter, and would constitute a venial sin.

Furthermore, any Catholic who understands the most elementary principles of mortification in the spiritual life can see how inappropriate it is to stretch the Church's fasting rules in this way. The chewing of gum, producing oral satisfaction, is a practice that demonstrates little mortification of the sense of taste. It ought, therefore, to be entirely avoided on days of penance, in which we mortify the rebellious senses that lead us into many sins that offend the all pure Sacred Heart of Jesus.

—*Fr. Scott,* January 2008

ABOUT THE SACRAMENTS

 **From an earlier reply in this column it would appear that the "intention of doing what the Church does" is implicit in the very act of going through the rites prescribed or accepted by the Church, unless a contrary intention is present openly or internally. I have read that the "intention of doing what the Church does" need not involve an intention "what the Church intends," namely, to produce the effects of the sacrament—for example, the forgiveness of sins. Yet the "mere external intention...which is directed towards merely performing the external action with earnestness...is insufficient" because it is not compatible with the concept of doing "what the Church intends." Could you explain this?**

Session VII of the Council of Trent taught the necessity for the minister of the sacraments to have the intention of doing at least what the Church does. It laid this down with great emphasis. Contrary to this, the opinion was once defended that the intention to perform deliberately the external rite proper to each sacrament was sufficient. This opinion is no longer held by Catholic theologians. The common doctrine is that a real internal intention is necessary to act as a minister of Christ. It need not be actual (*i.e.*, thought about at the time), but suffices to be virtual (*i.e.*, decided upon previously).

Therefore, when a fully conscious individual (usually an ordained priest, but lay people in the case of matrimony or occasionally in private baptism) goes through the actions required by the Church for a minister of Christ, it implies his intention is to do what the Church does. An individual is judged by his actions, thus one who performs all the ceremonies prescribed is assumed to have acted in accordance with the Church unless proven otherwise by contrary evidence. Only an outward repudiation could prove his internal dissent. Now, what the Church intends is all the effects of the sacraments. These need not be fully willed, nor even known, by the individual, *e.g.*, a pagan baptizing in the case of an emergency. In the case of matrimony, it is the couple themselves who administer this sacrament. Often those marrying may be rather ignorant of all the effects of their vows on the day of their wedding; nevertheless, this does not invalidate the sacrament. A marriage is assumed valid when the prescribed ceremonies are accomplished unless proven to the contrary.

On the other hand, it is not sufficient to merely will the externals, as the Church intends more than this. This does not necessitate the minister to intend all that the Church intends, but that he intend more than mere exterior ceremony. The Church intends more than simple externals and rites. Thus to have a mere external intention, directed towards merely performing the external action with earnestness, would be insufficient. In other words, it is enough to will to function as a minister of Christ, even without actual advertence (*i.e.*, without thinking about what one is doing here and now), but it is not enough to merely to perform the Church's functions.

—Fr. Doran, August 1993

If intention is necessary for the validity of the sacraments, how can we ever be sure that the sacraments we receive are valid?

There can be no doubt as to the necessity of the correct intention for the valid reception of the sacraments. This is explicitly declared by the Catechism of the Council of Trent when it states that the ministers of the sacraments "validly perform and confer the Sacraments, provided they make use of the matter and form always observed in the Catholic Church according to the institution of Christ, and provided they intend to do what the Church does in their administration" (p. 155). The Baltimore Catechism explains what the expression "intending to do what the Church does" really means; namely, "the intention of doing what Christ intended when He instituted the Sacrament and what the Church intends when it administers the Sacrament."

As a consequence, it follows that if a priest has a positive intention against what the Church does, namely, of specifically not intending what Christ intends and what the Church intends, then one of the three elements necessary for the validity of the Mass is absent, and the Mass is invalid. This is effectively stated by Pope Alexander VIII when he condemned the contrary proposition as Jansenist, namely, that baptism is valid when administered by a minister who resolves within his heart not to intend what the Church does (Dz. 1318).

Since none of us can read the innermost intentions of a minister's heart how, then, does any one of us know whether or not the sacraments we have received were valid? In effect, St. Robert Bellarmine points out that we can never have a certitude of faith concerning the reception of a true sacrament, since no one can see the intention of another. However, in truth we can never have such a certitude concerning human events. The greatest certitude that we can have is a moral certitude, which is also the certitude that we can have about any contingent, singular reality.

However, it is perfectly possible to have a moral certitude. In the traditional rites of the sacraments and of Mass the guarantee of this moral certitude is contained in the rites themselves. For the traditional rites for Mass and the sacraments express the intentions of the Church in a very explicit manner, leaving no room for doubt whatsoever. The same is not the case for the new rites, framed explicitly to be ambiguous, and to be just as compatible with a Protestant intention as with a Catholic one. Since they do not express the intention of doing what the Church does, the intention of the priest cannot be explicitly known. Consequently, there is always a doubt as to the intention of the priest in the celebration of the New Mass and sacraments, which does not in any way exist in the traditional rite. The only way to have moral certitude of valid sacraments is to assist at the traditional rite of Mass. Although theoretically it would be possible for a priest to celebrate sacrilegiously in the traditional rite by having a positive counter intention, it is hardly likely, given that the correct intention is repeated several times, which is not the case in the new rite. To the contrary, it is very likely that a *Novus Ordo* priest celebrates invalidly through lack of intention since the full and correct intention is not included in the texts of the New Mass.

Note that the faith is not required for an adequate intention, and that heretics can confer the sacraments validly, provided that they have the intention of doing what the Church does, even though they might not know what that is. This was clear from the third century, when Pope St. Stephen I condemned St. Cyprian's contention that the baptism of the heretical Novatians had to be repeated.

—*Fr. Scott,* October 2003

I have a relative in her early thirties who has not been baptized. I was taught that anyone can baptize if no priest is available.

It is certainly true that a lay person is capable of baptizing validly. However, it is only licit for a lay person to baptize when the unbaptized person is in immediate danger of death and when a priest is not available. Furthermore, a lay person can only give the matter and form necessary for the validity of the sacrament. He cannot administer the other ceremonies, which can only be separated from the sacramental form in the case of danger of death.

In addition, an adult can only be baptized if he believes and embraces all the articles of the Catholic Faith, if he has studied and learned his catechism, if he is sorry for his sins, and if he has requested to be received into the Catholic Church. Only a priest can judge if these conditions are fulfilled. If they are not, the baptism could very well not be fruitful and not give grace.

A case in which a lay person could baptize would be when an unbaptized person is on his death bed and there is no time to call a priest, and he makes acts of faith, hope, charity, and contrition with the dying person, who states that he believes all that the Catholic Church teaches, is sorry for his sins, and wants to become a Catholic. However, every effort must be made to find a good traditional priest to judge the dispositions of the catechumen.

—*Fr. Scott*, August 1999

 **I know that the Council of Florence taught that three components are necessary for the effecting of a sacrament—matter, form, and intention of the minister; and if any one of the three is lacking, the sacrament is not valid. I also know, however, that the Church teaches that even a pagan can legitimately baptize in an emergency as long as he uses water, the correct form, and intends to do what the Church does. My question is: How can a minister whose denomination formally rejects the very existence of sacraments intend to do what the Church does when baptizing a person? In short, should a convert be conditionally baptized? Further, if so, should he be conditionally confirmed? The *Novus Ordo* priests that I have discussed this with have (predictably) dismissed my entire concern as silly!**

When acting on questions dealing with the sacraments, one must be always as certain as possible in clearing a doubt. To leave a doubt when it is possible to resolve it, or to rely on a doubtful solution, is unacceptable, and sinful.

A minister in a denomination which formally rejects the very existence of sacraments could still, with intention, validly baptize as long as the form and matter were correctly applied. As you may well know, a whole new theology and doctrinal expression can be found with each minister you speak to. Because of the vagueness involved, a minister may in fact "intend to do what the Church does." Only a firm contrary opinion and repudiation of the true intention in the will of the minister would invalidate it. Obviously, the pagan has no belief in the effects of supernatural grace, and in all likelihood repudiates the concept of sanctifying grace, but nonetheless can "intend to do what the Church does." Rome forbade the "rebaptism" of Chinese who had received such from the Presbyterians, even when the latter had published their official repudiation of the fact that original sin was cleansed by the sacrament. So there remains, as long as the proper matter and trinitarian form are used, probability of the sacrament's validity.

The Church's general practice in America prior to Vatican II was to conditionally baptize Protestants being received into the Fold. This means that the person was baptized on the condition that the first was invalid. It was conditional, and not absolutely conferred, to avoid the sacrilege of rebaptism. Baptism cannot be conferred twice, and the probability of the validity of the first presents this risk. A second reason for this practice is that it gives tranquility to the conscience of the person who may be tempted to doubt later the fact of having received the grace of Our Lord in baptism.

—Fr. Doran, March 1992

 **I do not understand how it can be affirmed that baptism in an heretical church gives the character of baptism but does not give sanctifying grace, so that person remains with original and actual sins (*Cf.* Fr. Laisney, "Three Errors of the Feeneyites," *The Angelus*, Sept. 1998, pp. 35ff.).**

You are perfectly correct in affirming that the sacrament of baptism is not invalidated by the fact that it is administered by an heretical minister. This is in fact the teaching of the Council of Trent, which anathematized the contrary opinion: "If anyone shall say that the baptism, which is also given by heretics in the name of the Father and of the Son and of the Holy Spirit, with the intention of doing what the Church does, is not true baptism: let him be anathema" (Session VII, Canon 4; Dz. 860). Nevertheless, it does not follow from the fact that baptism by a heretic can be valid that it is always valid. It can be invalid if the minister uses an incorrect matter or form, or if he does not have the intention of doing what the Church does.

However, this is not the essential confusion. A distinction must be made between a valid sacrament and a fruitful sacrament. A valid sacrament of baptism is one which imprints the baptismal character on the soul. However, it does not follow from the fact that it is valid that it is necessarily fruitful, removing sin, infusing sanctifying grace, making a person a child of God, and opening the gates of heaven. There can be an *obex*, or impediment, to the sacrament's infusing grace. In such instances the sacrament will be valid, but fruitless, for as long as the obstacle remains.

St. Thomas Aquinas makes this distinction very clearly in the *Summa Theologica*, III, Q. 68, Art. 8 where he states that "baptism produces a two-fold effect on the soul, *viz.*, the character and grace." He continues to explain that the Catholic faith is not necessary for the validity of the sacrament, that is, for the baptismal character:

> Right faith is not necessary in the one baptized any more than in the one who baptizes; provided that the other conditions are fulfilled which are necessary for the validity of the sacrament. For the sacrament is not perfected by the righteousness of the minister or of the recipient of Baptism, but by the power of God.

However, if the true faith is not necessary for the validity of the sacrament, the absence of the supernatural faith of the Catholic Church will prevent the sacrament from bearing the fruit that it ought: "A thing is necessary for Baptism, as something without which grace, which is the ultimate effect of the sacrament, cannot be had. And thus right Faith is necessary for Baptism...." The knowing and willing refusal to embrace the true faith is, consequently, like the refusal to make an act of at least imperfect contrition, an obstacle to the sacrament's bearing the fruit of sanctifying grace. Hence the valid sacrament does not remit sin.

St. Thomas also considers the case of insincerity, when a person remains attached to a mortal sin, which insincerity is not changed by the sacrament of baptism, which consequently remains valid but fruitless:

> When God changes man's will from evil to good, man does not approach with insincerity. But God does not always do this. Nor is this the purpose of the sacrament, that an insincere man [*i.e.*, attached to mortal sin] be made sincere; but that he who comes in sincerity, be justified. (*ST*, III, q. 69, art. 9, ad 2)

In *Summa Theologica*, III, Q. 68, Art. 9, St. Thomas considers the special case of infants, who are not capable of placing obstacles to prevent the sacrament's bearing fruit, just as they are not capable of having their own intention. It is for this reason that a valid sacrament is always fruitful for them: "Children before the use of reason, being as it were in the womb of their mother the Church, receive salvation not by their own act, but by the act of the Church" (*ibid.*, ad 1). Thus it is that infants when baptized are members of the Catholic Church, even if baptized by heretical ministers in heretical churches, until such time as they embrace the heresy of their Protestant church (which is presumed at the age of fourteen years), and this regardless of "the unbelief of their own parents" (*ibid.*, ad 2), for "the child acquires a good conscience in himself, not indeed as to the act, but as to the habit, by sanctifying grace" (*ibid.*, ad 3). In infants, therefore, the baptismal character is inseparable from the infusion of sanctifying grace and of the supernatural virtue (or *habitus*) of faith, and the remission of original sin, regardless of the church in which a person is validly baptized. (*Cf. ST*, III, q. 69, art. 6, ad 3: "So that children believe, not by their own act, but by the Faith of the Church, which is applied to them:—by the power of which faith, grace and virtues are bestowed on them.")

The final case to be considered is that of an adult who is baptized validly in a Protestant church, but who is not formally attached to the errors of that church, and who does not willingly and knowingly choose to be baptized in an heretical church which refuses the true faith. If he truly believes all that he knows that God has revealed (including at least the Trinity, the Incarnation, the Redemption, and heaven and hell), and on the basis of the supernatural motive of the authority of God who reveals (and not for human, social, or political reasons), and if he would believe everything that the Catholic Church believes and teaches if he knew about its dogmas, and if he would willingly join the Catholic Church if he knew it to be the true Church, then his faith is truly supernatural. It is the right faith (*fides recta*) of which St. Thomas speaks.

This falls into the case of invincible ignorance, which Pope Pius IX describes in the encyclical *Quanto Conficiamur Moerore* of August 10, 1863, which explains the meaning of the dogma *Extra Ecclesiam nulla salus*. As the pope explains, such a person will not be punished for an ignorance for which he is not culpable or responsible, and which he does not have the means to overcome.

If there is no other obstacle (*e.g.*, attachment to mortal sin), then the baptism of an adult with such supernatural faith will also infuse sanctifying grace and remove original and actual sins, even if done in a Protestant church.

—*Fr. Scott,* November 1998

Why is it that the reception of Holy Communion does not break the Friday abstinence?

It is certainly true that the Holy Eucharist contains the Body, Blood, Soul, and Divinity of Our Lord Jesus Christ. However, the catechism reminds us that it is under the appearances of bread and wine. This means that when transubstantiation takes place, the substance of the bread no longer remains, and that instead the substance of Christ is present whole and entire. However, the accidents do not change, and remain the accidents of bread and wine. This means that Christ's body is present whole and entire under each particle of the host, but without all the physical characteristics of the body—namely, the height, weight, color, or even the chemical composition. Every aspect of Christ's body that can be measured is absent, for all that man can measure makes up the accidents or external appearances. His body is present in the manner of a substance, the underlying reality behind the appearances.

With this understanding, we can now determine if the Holy Eucharist truly is Christ's flesh, if to partake of it truly is to eat meat, if it really is cannibalism to consume the Holy Eucharist, as the Jews falsely interpreted His words when they cried out: "How can this man give us his flesh to eat?" (Jn. 6:53).

The Blessed Eucharist is most certainly the flesh of Christ, but present in the manner of a substance, as Christ Himself is present, whole and entire, which is what the Holy Eucharist really is. It is not, however, flesh in the common way of understanding, that is, with the accidents of flesh—namely, its appearance, color, weight, and texture. Consequently, it is not cannibalism to consume the Holy Eucharist, nor is it the eating of flesh meat as indicated by the Church's precept of Friday abstinence. It is to be nourished with the entire substance of Christ, His sacred Humanity as well as His divinity, His human life as one risen from the dead, and His divine life as Son of the Father. It is for this reason that our divine Savior tells us:

> He that eateth my flesh, and drinketh my blood, hath everlasting life: and I will raise him up on the last day. For my flesh is meat indeed [*i.e.*, true, substantial nourishment for the eternal life of the soul, as symbolized by meat]: and my blood is drink indeed. He that eateth my flesh, and drinketh my blood, abideth in me, and I in him. (Jn. 6:55-57)

—*Fr. Scott*, December 2007

When in confession, should a Catholic mention that he is a member of a third order, or that he has made the total consecration to Our Lady?

When we confess our sins we are bound to mention the nature of the sin, nor are we bound to go into any other further details. However, frequently circumstances are involved that increase the gravity of the sin. Such circumstances must be mentioned if they seriously affect the morality of a mortal sin; *e.g.*, stealing from a church, speaking badly against a priest, or sinning against the sixth commandment with a person who is consecrated to God.

Circumstances that modify the morality of a venial sin, or that do not greatly worsen the gravity of the sin, do not have to be mentioned. However, in confessing our venial sins, it is always helpful to confess any additional circumstances that make the sin more culpable. It helps us to humble ourselves and to know the wretchedness of our selfish wills. Consequently, we should mention such circumstances, *e.g.*, that it was a child that I mocked, or that it was my wife that I was verbally abusive towards. In this category also fall extra spiritual obligations that I have taken upon myself and that make more clear to the confessor my refusal to respond to God's graces. In this way, it is desirable to mention that I am a third order member or that I have made the total consecration to Jesus through Mary. This humble avowal will help our confessions to be more profitable for our soul and help us to take seriously the obligations that we have bound ourselves to.

—*Fr. Scott,* October 2002

 **Is it permissible for a private family to have a private chapel where the Blessed Sacrament is reserved?**

This can be done only by way of an Apostolic Indult—that is, permission from the Holy Father. The local ordinary (bishop of the diocese) may give permission for some good reason, but only as long as that reason exists. Whenever the Blessed Sacrament is reserved it must be kept safe with a special person responsible. A priest must be able to say Mass there once a week and the sacred species must be renewed at regular intervals. Of course, there are cases now where, because of the unusual circumstances of the times, something called *epikeia* may be employed. Permission is presumed on the good will of the superior who would give the permission if he fully understood the case. Surely there are *Novus Ordo* clerics who would not agree with me in this, and they would say all our chapels are private and we may never presume to say Mass in them or keep the Blessed Sacrament reserved. The good of souls is ever the highest Church law and takes precedence over all other ecclesiastical laws. Therefore we go ahead on this presumption, knowing full well that the good of many souls depends on this practice. In regard to the mentioned private oratory, it could be that this family has the required papal indult.

—*Fr. Carl,* March 1986

 **How does the Confessor determine the penance to give to his penitent in the confessional?**

The Council of Trent, in its Doctrine on the Sacrament of Penance, gives the principle for the determination of the penance to be given by the confessor: "The priests of the Lord ought, therefore, so far as the spirit and prudence suggest, to enjoin salutary and suitable satisfactions, in keeping with the nature of the crimes and the ability of the penitents" (Session XIV, 8; Dz. 905). This means in practice that the priest is bound to give a heavy penance when the penitent confesses a mortal sin, unless there is a just reason for not doing so, such as the inability of the penitent to do a heavy penance. A heavy penance is a work that would oblige under pain of mortal sin if commanded by the Church, such as five decades of the rosary, assistance at Mass, a one-day fast. A Way of the Cross would also be a heavy penance. However, shorter prayers are light penances, unless they are enjoined to be done several times over.

The precise determination of the penance is not an easy thing to do since prudence demands that it be adapted to the condition of the penitent. In this, two grave dangers are to be avoided. The first is for the confessor to be too lax in giving a very light penance, "lest," as the Council of Trent teaches, "if they should connive at sins and deal too leniently with penitents, by the imposition of certain very light works for grave offenses, they might become participators in the crimes of others" (*ibid.*). Indeed, excessive mitigation of the penance fails to impress on the penitent the need for a true amendment of life, and can lead to routine confessions and repetition of the same sins. The second danger is to be too harsh and demanding on the penitent so as to give excessively burdensome penances that make confession disagreeable, that are not accomplished very willingly, and that can turn penitents away from ready and frequent confession.

In general, the confessor ought to err on the side of giving a lighter penance and of being rather too benign than too harsh, for confession is the sacrament of God's mercy, and he could do much more harm by exceedingly harsh penances than by being too soft. Moreover, it is better that the penitent do a lighter penance more willingly than a heavier penance begrudgingly or with negligence. However, the penitent should want, and can certainly request, a moderately hard penance, providing that he truly is willing to do it and wants to do it out of a sincere desire to make up for his sins.

One of the great challenges for the confessor is to avoid routine in the giving of penances. It is an unfortunate but frequent occurrence that the penitent can almost always predict the penance, and that the penance is the same for nearly any sin. In such cases, the penance does not have the full satisfactory value that it could have had. This danger is overcome by the confessor's effort to apply a remedial penance, namely, one which is at the same time a real atonement for sins and an effective remedy, such as imposing almsgiving on the avaricious or mortification on those who commit sins of sensuality. This is what the Council of Trent has to say: "Let them keep before their eyes that the satisfaction which they impose be not only for the safeguarding of a new life and a remedy against infirmity, but also for the chastisement and atonement of past sins" (*ibid.*).

The confessor who is a little creative in this way will think of different ways in which to impose the three chief kinds of penances, or good works, that satisfy for sins. The first kind are works of religion, such as various prayers; the second are works of charity, such as helping the poor and almsgiving; and the third are works of mortification, such as fasting and abstinence. The penitent should not be surprised to receive as a penance some such work. However, he does have the right to say so if he feels that the penance is too difficult or too demanding for him to accomplish. He can also point out that the priest does not have the right to impose a public penance (which could harm a person's reputation), nor one that is incongruous, inappropriate, or astonishing. Yet all other things being equal, the penitent should thank God for (and even request) a penance which is a remedy for his fault, as also for a penance which is more difficult to accomplish, for it will be more effective in satisfying for his sins.

—*Fr. Scott,* December 2007

Can a person perform the penance received in confession after having fallen back into mortal sin?

The penance received in confession ought to be performed as soon as possible after confession, so that a person who delays for no reason the fulfillment of a heavy penance given for a mortal sin so as to be in danger of forgetting his penance would commit another mortal sin.

It is true that it is not necessary that the penance be performed before going to Holy Communion, and that frequently there is no time to perform the penance and the opportunity of receiving Holy Communion presents itself. There is no reason why such a person ought not to receive the Blessed Sacrament.

However, the penance must be done before going back to confession. If a person were unfortunate enough to lose the state of sanctifying grace before being able to do his penance, or through his own negligence, he would be in a difficult situation. It is probable that the penance performed in mortal sin does not have its full satisfactory value, which depends upon the union of charity between God and the soul, which union has been lost. Yet, the penitent in mortal sin is still bound to do the work of penance before going back to confession. The common opinion of the theologians is that the penance done after falling back into mortal sin satisfies with respect to the work imposed by the confessor, and that it consequently does not have to be reiterated after the person has gone back to confession and recovered the state of grace (Prummer, III, §402). However, a person in such a situation ought to make an act of perfect contrition so as to recover the state of sanctifying grace before doing the penance so that this work can not only fulfill the command of the priest but also have a real satisfactory value to make up for his sins.

—*Fr. Scott,* January 2008

 **What do you think of the "baptism of the unborn," which is supposedly recommended by some apparition?**

It is invalid! The Church always taught that the matter of baptism is water flowing on the body. There can be NO baptism at a distance. To use the very words of the sacraments, which are hereby sacred, in an invalid manner is a serious matter, *i.e.*, matter of a mortal sin.

God is Almighty. As He gave sanctifying grace to St. John the Baptist in the womb of his mother, so He has the power to give sanctifying grace to other children in the same manner. Yet this is not a sacrament, and therefore the words of the sacrament of baptism should not be used for this prayer.

If an "apparition" promotes the use of the sacred words of baptism in an invalid manner, such an apparition should not be followed.

The prayer to ask God to grant sanctifying grace to children who are going to be aborted is not bad, but we must not think that Our Lord Jesus Christ is going to grant it in most cases; if any, it will be in very few cases, and here is the reason: There are some privileges which God granted to chosen souls and does not grant to just anybody. The typical example is that of the Immaculate Conception. It would be a sin for a mother to ask that the children she conceives be "immaculate in their conception." It would be to ask something against the wisdom of God, who bestows grace with order and measure, and who gave to Our Lady as a unique privilege that of the Immaculate Conception, proportionate to her mission of becoming the Mother of God. Since that mission is absolutely unique, so is the privilege of the Immaculate Conception.

The privilege granted to St. John the Baptist has been granted also to the prophet Jeremias, but it was a privilege proportionate to their unique missions of precursor or prophet. It is obviously something extremely rare, and we should not expect it to become the common rule for aborted children. Otherwise, it should rather be given to children naturally aborted by devout mothers without any fault of their own. Yet the Church teaches that for children without the use of reason, the only way to be saved is by the waters of baptism. Adults who are prevented from the reception of the waters of baptism without fault on their part may receive sanctifying grace through a very special grace of the Holy Ghost by an act of living faith in Our Lord Jesus Christ with perfect contrition for their sins. But children cannot do so. Therefore, good mothers pray that the children they conceive be kept safe until their baptism, and they must have their children baptized without delay.

The great principle here is that our prayers must conform to the wisdom of God. For example, we must not ask to go to heaven without having to carry our cross. Such a prayer would displease Our Lord Jesus Christ!

In the same way, what we must ask for the unborn children is not "an easy salvation" but rather that their parents may be converted and that they would lead their children to the waters of baptism: that is the proper prayer. This must also remind us of our duty to work actively against abortion. There is no easy way out.

—*Fr. Laisney,* February 1991

ABOUT CANON LAW

What is the authority of Canon Law?

The Code of Canon Law is the book that contains all the principal laws that apply to the Latin Rite of the Roman Catholic Church. The Eastern Rites have different laws, and for this reason a different Code of Canon Law. The Code of Canon Law reflects the pope's jurisdictional authority to govern the entire Church for those laws that are universal, or the Latin Rite for those laws which are limited to the code of the Latin Rite.

Since the laws contained in the Code belong to the realm of discipline, they are not in themselves doctrinal. They are consequently not *ex cathedra* doctrinal declarations, although they do presuppose the Church's infallible doctrinal teachings as contained in the documents of the extraordinary and ordinary magisterium. Their authority comes from the pope's supreme authority to govern the Church, rather than from his authority to teach.

The consequence of this is that they do not generally meet the four conditions required for an act of the extraordinary magisterium: they are not dogmatic definitions; they often do not directly concern matters of faith and morals; they are often not for the universal Church (but only the Latin Rite); they are not imposed in virtue of the faith. It is consequently not in contradiction with the infallibility of the Church and the magisterium for the Code of Canon Law to contain dangerous and erroneous statements and even laws which jeopardize the salvation of souls. Examples of these abound in the 1983 Code of Canon Law, profoundly penetrated as it is, by the admission of the John Paul II himself, by the ecclesiology of Vatican II—*e.g.*, the reversal of the ends of marriage, the permission of sacramental sharing in both directions between Catholics and non-Catholics, and the new definition of the Church as going beyond the boundaries of the visible Catholic Church.

This means that we have to carefully examine the different laws contained in the 1983 Code to see whether or not these disciplinary determinations are in accord with the infallibly defined Catholic Faith or not, just as we have to do with the pope's particular laws, such as the "promulgation" of the New Mass. If they are a legitimate exercise of the pope's authority, then we must accept them. However, if they are harmful to the Church's teaching (as Communion in the hand destroys faith in the Real Presence), then these laws must be refused. An example of this is the law that permits annulments for psychological reasons, this being a direct attack on the sanctity and unity and indissolubility of marriage. It must always be remembered that if, in promulgating the Code and other laws, the pope exercises his supreme authority to govern (*i.e.*, there is no higher authority on earth), he never has an absolute and arbitrary authority, and that any laws which do not accomplish the end of the law, the salvation of souls, are null and void, and that he received his authority that he "might guard sacredly the revelation transmitted through the apostles and the deposit of faith, and might faithfully set it forth" (Vatican I, *Pastor Aeternus*, Dz. 1836).

—*Fr. Scott,* January 2000

 ## Are we to consider all the provisions of the 1917 Code of Canon Law to have been abrogated?

This question can only be answered with the necessary nuances in two stages. The first and most important response is on the level of the principles of law, without which we cannot determine the value of the letter of the law.

PRINCIPLES

The first principle to be recognized is the universally accepted theological principle that a law is by definition an ordering of reason to the common good. Consequently, a human law (*e.g.*, an ecclesiastical law) that is manifestly unjust because it is opposed either to the common or to the divine law (that is, to the natural law or to divine revelation), is not a law at all, being incapable of attaining the end of the law, "the salvation of souls, which in the Church is always the highest law" (1983 Code, Can. 1752).

The second principle is that the 1983 Code, like all collections of law that preceded it, is a collection of different laws, originating at different times and in different circumstances, although all promulgated at the same time. Consequently, it is perfectly possible to accept one law as just, and reject another as manifestly unjust, and still to respect the legislator who promulgated such a confusing mixture of good and evil.

A third principle is the clear statement made by Pope John Paul II in his apostolic constitution *Sacrae Disciplinae Leges* introducing the 1983 Code, that the "fundamental reason for the novelties" found in this Code is the new ecclesiology of Vatican II. This new ecclesiology, or new understanding of the Church, with its collegiality, religious liberty, ecumenism, and denial of the necessity of belonging to the Catholic Church, outside of which there is no salvation, is manifestly opposed to the divine revelation found in the Gospel and repeatedly taught by the Church's magisterium. We cannot, therefore, accept the new Code as a whole as a law of the Church, on account of the danger to the faith that this would mean, on account of the revolutionary end for which it was instituted, and on account of the liberal spirit that permeates it.

CANONS OPPOSED TO THE FAITH

There are consequently some canons that all traditional Catholics clearly see must be refused, such as Canon 844 that promotes sacramental hospitality with non-Catholics. Such a law destroys the faith in the Catholic Church as the one true Church, and is no law at all, being directly opposed to the common good and the salvation of souls. Another example of a canon that is opposed to the Church's faith is Canon 1055, §1, that redefines the two ends of marriage, in direct contradiction to the constant teaching of the Church, for example in *Casti Connubii* of Pope Pius XI. The consequences are tremendous, particularly in the whole question of declarations of nullity of marriage.

CANONS OPPOSED TO TRADITION

There are other canons that are not directly opposed to a teaching of the Church but are entirely unacceptable because they undermine, destroy, or contradict an age-old tradition of the Church, protecting the sacredness of its sacraments and teaching. The typical example of this is the passage into the Code of Pope Paul VI's 1972 abolition by omission of the tonsure and all the minor orders, and even the subdiaconate (Can. 266), the tonsure having existed for eleven centuries, and the minor orders for at least seventeen centuries. Canon 5 of both the 1983 and 1917 Codes admits the possibility of maintaining centennial and immemorial customs that are not against the law. This is one such case, necessary for the existence of the traditional rite, even in communities that are approved by Rome, but for whose tonsure and minor orders there is no canonical provision.

QUESTIONS OF PURELY POSITIVE LAW

Finally, there are other canons that depend purely and simply upon the will of the sovereign pontiff, the Church's supreme legislator, such as the granting of indulgences, or censures or obligations under pain of mortal sin. In such cases, we are obliged to accept the much reduced protection for the Church, her faith, and her moral life that the 1983 Code provides.

One typical example of this is the law that frees Catholics who have formally apostatized from the Church from the obligation of observing the canonical form of marriage (Can. 1117). This canon is also a tragic betrayal of the Faith. It means that a Catholic can be recognized to have left the Church, that one who is a Catholic is not necessarily always a Catholic; namely, that one has a right to apostatize, which the Church recognizes, permitting a Catholic in such a state to marry validly outside the Church. This causes great confusion, for when such persons return to the Church, usually after the failure of their non-Catholic marriage, they are no longer free to marry in the Church on account of the sins committed in apostasy. However, since the pope does not bind such persons to the canonical form of marriage, neither can we, and consequently we have to accept this canon, as unfortunate as it might be.

The same applies for censures, such as the excommunication against Freemasons contained in the 1917 Code (Can. 2335) but no longer contained, alas, in the 1983 Code (Can. 1374). Those who joined the Freemasonic sect after 1983 cannot, then, be considered as automatically excommunicated.

CONCLUSION

The great difficulty, then, in assessing the 1983 Code will be to consider each canon separately as to its justice and conformity with the teaching and tradition of the Church. Those canons that are not just nor in conformity with the Church's teachings or tradition are not to be observed unless they are questions that depend upon the sole will of the legislator.

Note especially that it is the 1917 Code alone that gives us the mind of the Church and that can be safely followed in questions of morality and the spiritual life. Note, also, the real danger of would-be canon lawyers quoting canons out of context, without understanding the fundamental principles of law and the principles of interpretation. A purely exterior legalism is the consequence, not so different from the attitude of the Pharisees towards Our Lord, refusing to see in Him the Messias because He fulfilled the fundamental reason for the law rather than the external observances that preoccupied them. Such an empty legalism despises the role of theology and tradition in interpreting the law.

—*Fr. Scott,* December 2006

 **I was told that the Church's law permits Catholics to satisfy their Sunday obligation at a schismatic Orthodox ceremony, and that this was the case both before and after Vatican II. Is this true?**

The authority that you quote (Catholic Family Radio) defends the opinion that it was and is permitted to satisfy this obligation of assisting at Mass in a schismatic church before and after Vatican II. It quotes Canon 1258 of the 1917 Code of Canon Law, and the shameful Canon 844 of the 1983 Code of Canon Law on the sharing of sacraments with non-Catholics.

However, I am sorry to inform you neither of these canons is relevant to the question at stake.

To start with the 1917 Code, or pre-Vatican II practice, the canon that you used to justify the possibility of satisfying the Sunday obligation at a schismatic Orthodox church actually means exactly the opposite. Let me quote for you Canon 1258: "It is illicit for Catholics to assist actively in any way, or to take part in, the sacred worship of non-Catholics." Could there be a more explicit prohibition, and could there be any way of interpreting this as meaning that it is permissible to attend an Orthodox, that is non-Catholic, ceremony? Moreover, there is another canon in the 1917 Code of Canon Law that treats of the question more specifically. It is Canon 1249, which states that: "The precept of hearing Mass is fulfilled by being present at Mass celebrated in any Catholic rite...." I cannot possibly see how any Catholic commentary on canon law could interpret "any Catholic rite" as including Orthodox ceremonies since these are manifestly schismatic and not Catholic.

The following is the commentary on this section of the canon, taken from a standard textbook on the 1917 Code of Canon Law (Bouscaren and Ellis, *Canon Law: A Text and Commentary* [1946], p. 635):

> The Mass may be celebrated in *any Catholic rite*; therefore an Oriental may satisfy the precept by hearing Mass according to the Latin rite, and a Latin by hearing it according to any of the Catholic Oriental rites.

The schismatic Orthodox rites are consequently explicitly excluded from the fulfillment of the law, and a Catholic who assists at these ceremonies does not fulfill his Sunday obligation.

Despite all the changes that have taken place in the 1983 Code of Canon Law, this is in fact one thing that has not changed. The appropriate canon to refer to is not Canon 844, but Canon 1248, §1, which states that "the precept of participating in the Mass is satisfied by assistance at a Mass which is celebrated anywhere in a Catholic rite...." Consequently, as before, the presence at a schismatic non-Catholic Orthodox ceremony does not satisfy the Sunday precept. It is true that Canon 844, §2 authorizes Catholics to receive valid sacraments from heretical or schismatic non-Catholic ministers, but this is a betrayal of the unity of the Church. However, it nowhere states that this constitutes a satisfaction of the Church's precept for Sunday and holy days. It is one of the many contradictions that ecumenism has injected into the modernist Code of Canon Law.

—Fr. Scott, April 2000

 ## What is the infamous Canon 844 of the 1983 Code of Canon Law?

This is the canon of the 1983 Code of Canon Law which authorizes sacramental sharing with heretics and schismatics. It is the practical application of the new ecclesiology of Vatican II, particularly the Decree on Ecumenism (*Unitatis Redintegratio*) and of the new definition of the Church as the People of God, that is, without clear boundaries. The pope explains this in the apostolic constitution *Sacrae Disciplinae Leges,* which precedes the 1983 Code of Canon Law. It follows from the fact that the Church does not have clear boundaries, that there are varying degrees of communion with it. Consequently, this canon speaks of giving the sacraments to those who do not have full communion with the Catholic Church, as if it were possible for there to be an intermediary state. This is in direct opposition to the traditional teaching, according to which one is either in communion with the pope and the Catholic Church, or one is not at all in communion.

This canon explains under what circumstances it is to be considered "licit" to receive the sacraments of penance, the Blessed Eucharist, and extreme unction from non-Catholic ministers, and under what circumstances it is to be considered "licit" for Catholic priests to administer these same sacraments "to other Christians who are not in full communion with the Catholic Church." This is, of course, a sacrilegious betrayal of the unity of the one, true Church, outside of which there is no salvation. This is particularly the case for penance, for sacramental absolution cannot traditionally be given to any person who refuses to embrace the Catholic Faith by becoming a member of the Catholic Church, and for the Blessed Eucharist, which symbolizes the very unity of the mystical body of Christ which these heretics and schismatics deny.

Of course, there are no circumstances when this can be done, for the heretic or schismatic must first convert to the Catholic Church before receiving confession and Communion. It is precisely this that the 1983 Code of Canon Law denies, saying that the sacraments can be given in any case "any time that necessity demands it or true spiritual utility suggests it, and provided that the danger of error or indifferentism be avoided."

Of course, we know that necessity or utility can never justify such a betrayal of the unity of the Church, and that in such a case the danger of error or indifferentism could never be avoided.

—*Fr. Scott,* May 1998

 **Has this Canon 844 always been the policy of the Catholic Church?**

This Canon 844 is a total and radical departure from Catholic law, and even from the Catholic faith. According to the Church's traditional law, any of the faithful who receive the sacraments from, and thus participate in the ceremonies of, non-Catholics, would automatically be suspect of heresy. (*Cf.* Canon 2316 of the 1917 Code of Canon Law, which gives the penalty for the *communicatio in sacris* with non-Catholics which is forbidden by Canon 1258 of the same code.) The corresponding canon from the traditional 1917 Code of Canon Law which governs the priests' administration of sacraments to non-Catholics is Canon 731, §2, which states: "It is forbidden to administer the sacraments of the Church to heretics or schismatics, even though they err in good faith and ask for them, unless they have first renounced their errors and been reconciled with the Church." A more direct contradiction with Catholic faith and law could barely be imagined, and yet it is to this extent that ecumenism led Pope John Paul II in 1983, and ever since.

—*Fr. Scott,* May 1998

ABOUT RELICS

 **Some scoffers of the religion say that if all the relics of the true cross were gathered together from all over the world, there would be sufficient lumber to build a three-masted schooner. What is the truth about this? And where can one today find the major relics of the sufferings of Christ?**

Such an assertion is absolutely false. So much of the true cross has been lost that the remains would not make up half the original cross. Enemies of the Church, inspired by Satan, have continually lied about devotions of true Catholics, like they have about the Inquisition. The main pieces of the true cross are found in Rome and the cathedral in Paris. I saw the one in the Church of the Holy Cross of Jerusalem in Rome, and it appeared to be about seven by two by one-half inches. There also was Pilate's inscription tablet. Parts of the crown of thorns are in Notre Dame in Paris, in Rome, and in Toulouse. There were four nails: St. Helena cast one into the Adriatic Sea to calm a storm; one is incorporated into the Iron Crown of the Lombards; one in Notre Dame in Paris; and one in Monza, Italy. The sponge is venerated in St. John Lateran, Rome. Parts of the lance are in Paris and Rome. Veronica's veil is in Rome. The pillar of scourging (the upper part) is in St. Praxedes, Rome. More nails may be seen in replica form because one nail was cut up and pieces were incorporated into twelve certified replicas. The practice was also in vogue of inlaying a sliver of the wood of the true cross into a larger piece of wood—not to fool people but to make it easier to handle and venerate.

—*Fr. Carl,* July 1984

ABOUT ECCLESIASTICAL PRACTICES AND CUSTOMS

 **The month of May is dedicated to our Blessed Lady. Do the other months of the liturgical year have a particular significance?**

Not only the months of the year but also the days of the week: January is devoted to the Holy Name of Jesus, February to the Holy Family, March to St. Joseph, April to the Blessed Sacrament, May to the Blessed Virgin, June to the Sacred Heart, July to the Precious Blood, August to the Immaculate Heart of Mary, September to Our Lady of Sorrows, October to the Holy Rosary, November to the Holy Souls in Purgatory, and December to the Immaculate Conception.

As regards the days of the week, Sunday is consecrated to the Holy and Undivided Trinity, Monday to the Holy Ghost, Tuesday to the Holy Angels, Wednesday to Saint Joseph, Thursday to the Blessed Eucharist, Friday to the Sacred Passion of Our Lord, and Saturday to the Blessed Virgin Mary.

—*Fr. Boyle,* October 1994

 **Is it a traditional practice to use the communion rail cloth, and if so, should we be using it in our traditional chapel?**

I take the answer to this question from the 1959 edition of *Matters Liturgical*, which is the standard source of information on such matters, for it contains all the decrees of the Holy See on liturgical questions. No. 143, on pp. 234-236, cites the texts from the Holy See and from the Missal and Ritual which prescribe the use of the communion rail cloth.

The most important point to note in this matter is that the traditional rules of the Church's liturgy require both the communion plate and the communion rail cloth, not one or the other. I refer to No. 109c in the above-mentioned text, which says: "The communion-plate is not a substitute for, but is required in addition to, the communion-cloth; the latter is prescribed, as noted in n. 143c."

The reason for this is that they have different functions. The communion plate is to catch a host or particle of the host which may fall. The communion rail cloth is not primarily for this purpose, although it does function as an additional backup or safety measure, which is why it is prescribed that it be of linen. The communion rail cloth is really meant to be symbolic of our presence at a divine repast when we receive the Holy Eucharist during the holy sacrifice of the Mass. It signifies the solemnity and dignity of the occasion, the special purity and holiness of the Blessed Eucharist, and our unworthiness to receive it.

The faithful are not to handle the communion rail cloth during the distribution of Holy Communion. They are to hold their hands underneath the cloth and out of the way. This is a practical advantage, for it forces the people, and especially small children, to keep their hands out of the way. Keeping the hands out of the way also increases the sense of respect and dignity which is due to this holy sacrament.

The Church does not determine when the communion rail cloth is to be laid over the communion rail, and this does vary from church to church. It can be laid out before Mass and then removed after Mass. However, this is not the most appropriate way to do it, nor the way it is commonly done. The altar boys will generally have enough time between the *Agnus Dei* and the priest's communion to place the cloth over the communion rail. They will generally have plenty of time after the priest's ablutions, and after having changed the Missal and chalice veil, to fold it back over. If done at these two moments, the movements with the communion rail cloth will not hinder the altar boys from serving the priest at the altar.

—*Fr. Scott,* December 1998

Why light votive candles before the tabernacle or a picture or statue?

This is a practice of devout Catholics. They are like a sign of a prayer one would like to express with love. The little red votive candles speak to God, Our Blessed Lady, or a saint our prayers. They generously consume themselves, sacrifice themselves. They spend hours silently praying our prayer before the ones we love. These little lights represent us before God. They tell Him we want to stay before Him, offering Him the warmth of our love, hour after hour. They tell Him we want to signal all mankind to come and find Him and worship Him. There are many more reasons why people light votive candles, too numerous to mention on this one page, but I hope this gives you some idea why people light votive candles.
—*Fr. Carl,* November 1987

Which way, and from which side of the church, do the Stations of the Cross start? Here they start on the right, and also in Canada. Here on Long Island, some people keep moving them to start on the left side. Is there a set rule for them by the Church?

The indulgences for the Stations of the Cross or Way of the Cross were first given by the pope to the faithful for following the fourteen stations in Jerusalem. It was a devotion born of the early Franciscans who went there following St. Francis's visit to the sultan and the opening of the holy places to the Christian pilgrims of the thirteenth and fourteenth centuries. More recently, a papal indult was granted permitting the stations to be erected in churches around the world, or even outdoors. Faculties for doing so were entrusted to the superiors of the Franciscan order. Still more recently it has been extended to the local ordinaries and bishops of dioceses. To be valid, the fourteen wood crosses must be blessed and erected by one who has this jurisdiction. Normally, a plenary indulgence is granted for one passing from station to station who meditates on the suffering of Christ and another plenary indulgence is given for receiving Holy Communion the same day. If one is in a large group in church, at least one (usually the priest) must proceed from first to fourteenth station while the congregation, in pews, rises and kneels and responds to the prayers. As for beginning in church on left or right—it makes no difference at all. Normally, the pictures or statues are placed so the figure of Our Lord is going forward and not backward. The practice of going from fourteenth to first station is not correct and may be without indulgence. Adding a fifteenth station (the Resurrection) is not correct, but it might not affect the spiritual benefit of the devotion. Shut-ins may

have a wooden cross blessed with the same plenary indulgence as the
Way of the Cross.

—Fr. Carl, March 1985

What is the history of the nine First Fridays, and what are the requirements for making them?

The promise of Our Lord for the nine First Fridays was given to St.
Margaret Mary Alacoque in 1675. Later, Our Lady of the Apparition in
Rome warned Bruno Corrcociolla regarding this practice: "My Son does
not make promises lightly." Now, the promise of the First Friday was
this: "I promise thee in the unfathomable mercy of My Heart that My
omnipotent love will procure the grace of final penitence for all those who
communicate on nine successive First Fridays of the month; they will not
die in My disfavor, or without having received their Sacraments, since My
Divine Heart will be their sure refuge in the last moments of their life."
Eleven other blessings were given at the same time for the reward of nine
faithful First Friday communions. Also, a plenary indulgence under the
usual conditions can be gained on First Fridays for performing a public
exercise in honor of the Sacred Heart. The simple requirement for gaining
this promise is to receive (worthily, of course) Holy Communion on
nine consecutive First Fridays. Our Lord has made no other conditions.

—Fr. Carl, May 1987

What are the history and conditions for doing the five First Saturdays?

In 1917 Our Lady appeared to the three children of Fatima. Among
the many things she revealed was one astonishingly great promise—that
of the five First Saturdays. This was given to Lucy on December 10, 1925.
Lucy, then Sister Marie dos Santos, said that this was said to her by Our
Blessed Lady: "See, my daughter, how my heart is encircled by thorns
with which ungrateful men pierce me at every moment by their blas-
phemies and ingratitude. You, at least, try to console me, and announce
that I promise to assist at the hour of death, with the graces necessary for
salvation, all those who on the first Saturdays of five consecutive months,
confess, receive Holy Communion, recite part of my Rosary, and keep me
company for a quarter of an hour meditating on its mysteries with the
intention of offering me reparation."

—Fr. Carl, May 1987

How can I consecrate myself to the Immaculate Heart of Mary?

At Fatima it was truly one of Our Blessed Lady's requests that we
consecrate ourselves to her Immaculate Heart. According to the message

received by Lucia, we can do this by 1) keeping our souls in the state of grace, 2) doing penance for our sins, 3) saying the rosary, 4) making reparation. Observe these four requirements and you will have fulfilled our Blessed Mother's request for personal consecration to her Immaculate Heart.

—Fr. Carl, January 1982

What benefits can flow from a visit to a Catholic cemetery?

It must first be recalled that a Catholic cemetery is a holy place, being consecrated ground, especially blessed by the Church to receive the bodies, temples of the Holy Ghost, that will rise up to meet Our Lord, the supreme Judge, on the last day. It is for this reason that it was always considered obligatory for the bodies of faithful Catholics to be buried in Catholic cemeteries (Can. 1205, §1 of the 1917 Code).

A visit to a cemetery is consequently an act of religion, as is the special care of the cemetery and of the tombs of those who are buried there. It inspires a Catholic with reverence, awe for God's judgments, respect for the souls of those whose bodies are buried there, with an awareness of the brevity of this earthly life, and of the union of the Church militant with the Church suffering in the mystical body of Christ. Special graces are consequently attached to silent and prayerful visits to cemeteries. It can easily be understood why Church law prescribes that each parish have its own cemetery (Can. 1208) and why it is the traditional custom for it to be physically adjoining the parish.

However, if Catholics love to visit cemeteries, it is especially out of a motive of charity. We long to assist the suffering souls in purgatory by our prayers, sacrifices, and Masses, given that we are united as members of the same mystical body. A physical visit to a cemetery is a great help in inciting us to this duty of charity. It is for this reason that the Church has generously enriched with her indulgences visits to cemeteries. During the eight days from November 1-8, any of the faithful can, simply by visiting a cemetery and praying for the poor souls, obtain a plenary indulgence, applicable to the poor souls in purgatory, under the usual conditions. At other times of the year this is a partial indulgence. The gaining of a plenary indulgence does not mean that one soul is freed from purgatory, but that the power of the Church's suffrages is added to the personal prayers and applied to the poor souls by manner of intercession. How could we refuse to take advantage of the unlocking of the Church's treasury, which simply depends on our visits and prayers?

Let us consequently be generous and regular with our visits to Catholic cemeteries, and let us never pass one by without stopping to recite a short prayer for the poor souls there, or at least reciting such a prayer as we go by.

—*Fr. Scott,* January 2005

ABOUT SACRAMENTALS

 **Does it make a difference whether one makes the Sign of the Cross with the right hand or with the left hand?**

The Roman Missal describes the Sign of the Cross in the following words: "Blessing himself, he turns the palm of his *right* hand towards himself, having all the fingers extended and joined, he makes the Sign of the Cross from the forehead to the breast, and from the left to the right shoulder."

Even left-handed priests make the Sign of the Cross with their right hand. This is the practice of the Roman Catholic Church, which we all should follow. The same is true for genuflection: it should be made with the right knee, down to the ground. It is a real pity to see the negligence, inattention, and carelessness with which these sacred signs are performed by some faithful. Only persons who are physically crippled are excused from this. I remember Archbishop Lefebvre telling us that he had made the prayer to be able to genuflect down to the ground until the end of his life.

Making the Sign of the Cross is a very holy and ancient practice in the Church. The little sign of the cross, with the thumb on the forehead as is done before the Gospel and as the bishop made on us for our confirmation, is from the very beginning of the Church, and refers to the Apocalypse (7:3, 9:4, 14:1). It is a good custom for parents to bless their children in the evening with such a sign on their forehead. The Sign of the Cross is constantly used by the Church in all her blessings.

The Eastern Catholics make it from the right to the left shoulder, and with three fingers joined in honor of the Holy Trinity, the other two folded in honor of the two natures of Christ.

The Sign of the Cross is a sacramental. It gives grace in the measure of the devotion with which we use it. Let us always make it in a worthy manner, respecting the customs of the Church.

—*Fr. Laisney,* February 1991

Are there such things as "blessed dresses"?

The Church, in the Appendix to the Roman Ritual, provides for a whole variety of blessings. Amongst these are found two blessings for dresses, one in honor of the Blessed Virgin Mary and another in honor of Our Lady or of any canonized saint (§§49, 50).

The dress thus blessed can be compared to a scapular, although without the special graces and indulgences attached to the scapular. It becomes a sacramental, provided that it be worn with piety and devotion. The symbolism that must be understood is that a dress is a covering and protection for our fallen human flesh. In the same way as Christ our Lord, for our salvation, took upon Himself the garment of our flesh, so likewise is the wearing of a blessed dress or garment the taking on of the covering of modesty and humility so perfectly demonstrated by our divine Savior when stripped of His garments and nailed to the cross. The Church prays, then, that the person who wears a blessed dress with devotion and holy desire to venerate and honor the Blessed Virgin Mary or another saint may receive the grace of our Lord Jesus Christ to protect her from every evil of mind and body.

The blessing calls the blessed dress a "similar garment of religion," indicating a likeness to the garments of Our Lady or of a religious community. The design of such dresses, although determined by local custom, should observe this likeness. Modesty goes without saying, with full length, long sleeves, and a closed neckline. However, modesty is a part of humility, and a blessed dress ought to reflect that simplicity of soul. It ought not to be extravagant, showy, impressive, nor should the colors be bold, but rather reserved. It would be very appropriate that they be made in the likeness of Our Lady, for example, white with a blue sash such as Our Lady of Lourdes wore, or black such as Our Lady of Sorrows, or brown following Our Lady of Mount Carmel. The color of the religious habit could be used for a dress blessed in honor of a saint of a religious congregation.

Would that our traditional girls and women would make their own dresses truly Mary-like, and ask for them to be blessed by a priest, that, covered by grace, they might serve God alone, far from the vanity and whims of this world!

—*Fr. Scott,* December 2004

I wear a scapular medal which has the image of the Sacred Heart on one side and that of Our Lady of Maryknoll on the other. This medal was blessed by a Maryknoll priest about thirty-five years ago. I have asked a Carmelite priest to enroll me, but he tells me that no enrollment is

necessary. Needless to say, after reading the article concerning the brown scapular in a past *Angelus* I am confused. I would like to do the right thing concerning this most important devotion to our Lady. Would you please advise me what to do to ensure this?

Though since Vatican II the enrollment may no longer be strictly required, it must be remembered that the brown scapular is historically a religious habit. It was meant to be a way for the laity to share in the good works of the religious group for which it was a badge, in this case, the Carmelites. The wearer was invested by a religious authority and was to wear the scapular according to specific prescriptions. Traditionally, a ceremony was celebrated to confer the scapular. In 1910, Pope St. Pius X authorized the use of a blessed medal as a substitute, under certain circumstances, for the cloth scapular. This medal is to have the image of the Sacred Heart on one side and an image of the Blessed Virgin on the other. Investiture cannot be done with the scapular medal. The actual scapular is required. This was very often done in conjunction with First Communion. Any traditional priest will still perform this important rite and would do so if asked.

—*Fr. Doran,* October 1992

 **What is the prayer that is supposed to be said each day by the person wearing the scapular?**

The prayer for gaining the Sabbatine privilege is the daily saying of the Little Office of the Blessed Virgin Mary. Our Blessed Mother has promised that those who are devoted to her and wear her scapular will not leave this life turned away from God. The Sabbatine privilege is extra, and it means to be freed from purgatory on the Saturday following death.

—*Fr. Carl,* October 1989

ABOUT THE CRISIS IN THE CHURCH SINCE VATICAN II

 **Is the crisis in the Church primarily a question of the Mass or of doctrine?**

It is certainly true that the general Catholic in the pews is apt to be shocked much more by the changes of the Mass on a day-to-day and week-to-week basis than by statements of Vatican II or of modernist theologians reinterpreting Catholic teachings in a non-orthodox sense.

However, this does not at all mean that the liturgy comes first, or that the crisis is essentially a crisis of the liturgy of the Mass.

The relationship between the liturgy and Catholic dogma was magnificently explained by Pope Pius XII in his 1947 encyclical *Mediator Dei*, in which he condemned the excesses of the liturgical movement and explained the doctrinal basis for a true Catholic understanding of the liturgy. He there explains that it is not the Mass that comes first and shows us what we must believe, but that it is the profession of faith that comes first and that consequently "the entire Liturgy … has the Catholic Faith for its content, inasmuch as it bears public witness to the faith of the Church" (§47). Hence he condemns "the error and fallacious reasoning of those who have claimed that the sacred liturgy is a kind of proving ground for the truths to be held of faith (§46), and defines (§48):

> The sacred Liturgy, consequently, does not decide or determine independently and of itself what is of Catholic faith.…But if one desires to differentiate and describe the relationship between faith and the sacred Liturgy in absolute and general terms, it is perfectly correct to say: *"Lex credendi legem statuat supplicandi"*—let the rule of belief determine the rule of prayer.

Since faith comes first, and is expressed in the Mass, so likewise does the modernist destruction of the faith come first, and the overturning of the true Mass follow. The historical connection was particularly apparent after Vatican II. The Council promoted the modernist principles of adaptation to the modern world, the evacuation of penance, of the final last ends, of the eternity of the soul, the confusion of the priesthood of the faithful with the ordained priesthood, the undermining of the sacredness of the Mass and the sacraments, and the doctrinal relativism that opened the door to ecumenism and acceptation of Protestantism as a legitimate form of Christianity. The consequence was the New Mass some four years later, which from 1969 started impressing these false principles on the minds of Catholics, destroying their faith.

The crisis in the Church is, consequently, primarily one of faith, and only secondarily one of the Mass. The New Mass is evil because it destroys the Faith, that is, Catholic doctrine. The traditional Mass is Catholic and the banner of our resistance against modernism because it preserves and nourishes the faith.

Some have said that the preoccupation shown by St. Pius X in his condemnation of modernism at the beginning of the twentieth century, and the same preoccupation shown by his disciples in defending Catholic doctrine against modernism, is a distraction from the real issue, that of the Mass, presenting the doctrinal problem of modernism as a "phantom menace." Nothing could be further from the truth. All the novelties and changes contained in the New Mass were deliberately engineered by modernists such as Fr. Bugnini as a means of pushing their modernist agenda.

This point is made particularly well by Fr. Didier Bonneterre in the conclusion to his book *The Liturgical Movement* (Angelus Press, 2002):

> Crushed by St. Pius X, the Modernists understood that they could not penetrate the Church by theology, that is, by a clear exposé of their doctrines. They had recourse to the Marxist notion of praxis, having understood that the Church could become modernist through action, especially through the sacred action of the liturgy. (P. 93)

Consequently the only resistance possible is a doctrinal one, and it is the application of the principles used by St. Pius X in his 1907 condemnation of modernism, *Pascendi Dominici Gregis*. A typical example could be chosen. The turning around of the altar facing the people is not a haphazard invention, but an intentional novelty to express the belief that the Mass is primarily a celebration of the community rather than the action renewed by the ordained priest. This in turn comes from the modernist idea that Christ's presence in religion is immanent and vital, continuously evolving and present subjectively in the community's awareness, and that this experience constitutes religion, not objective doctrine. (*Cf. Pascendi*, §§35-37.) Likewise for the substitution of the vernacular for the sacred language, and for so many other changes. The doctrinal crisis in the Church over the past century is not a phantom, but truly the origin of the destruction of the liturgy.

—*Fr. Scott*, April 2006

 **How can the seemingly apostate modern Church claim to have the four marks of the Catholic Church?**

The term "apostate" has a precise meaning in theology and canon law. It means the total abandonment of all Christian faith in someone who has been baptized (Can. 1325, §2, 1917 Code). Now, it is clear that the modernists who have infiltrated their way into the hierarchy of the Catholic Church have not abandoned all Christian faith. To the contrary, they proclaim themselves to be Catholics and to be faithful to the Church, all the while denying some aspects of the Catholic faith, life, and liturgy by their indifferentism, liberalism, and naturalism. This is the technique of the modernists precisely condemned by St. Pius X in his encyclical *Pascendi*. They are determined to stay inside the Church, so as to change it from within, and not to leave it. Here lies all the confusion of the present crisis in the Church. Many are heretics, but they cannot be considered as formal heretics until they have demonstrated pertinacity, stubbornly denying a doctrine of faith after they have been reproved by authority.

If it is true that the unity of the Church is obscured by the confusion of the present times and the refusal of the modernists to condemn error, it is nevertheless perfectly clear from the constant teaching of the Church in the past. Moreover, as deficient as it may be in performing its duties, the visible hierarchy of the Church remains the proof of the exterior unity of the Church.

If the holiness of the Church is obscured by the naturalism of a teaching of social justice and the rights of man, nevertheless the supernatural teachings of twenty centuries of holy saints and popes concerning the holy sacraments and the holiness of the Mass cannot be denied.

The Catholicity of the Church is likewise obscured by the innumerable variations in modern belief and inculturation. The traditional Latin Mass was a perfect symbol of that universality. However, the deposit of the faith remains the same, despite the betrayals of the modernists, not excepting the pope himself. Catholics still believe what Catholics have always and everywhere believed. Never could the modernists impose their philosophical ravings as points of faith, nor have they. This applies to religious liberty and ecumenism, presented by the modernists as obligatory, but in fact in no way a part of the deposit of the faith, nor consequently of the universality of the Church. Apostolicity is not in question.

Consequently, if the modernist crisis does make it more difficult to identify the Roman Catholic Church as the only holder of the four marks of the Church, and does make it more difficult to convince souls to convert to the one true Church, it is nevertheless not at all impossible. The important question is that of distinguishing what is essential to these four marks from the false human notions of weak, liberal, modernist Catholics, betraying more or less their position in the hierarchy. Christ never promised that every Catholic would be holy, nor that every Catholic would live in perfect union with every other Catholic, nor that there would never be infiltrators attempting to introduce their own notions in the name of the Faith. In fact, the history of the Church is the story of the constant efforts by its enemies, within and without, to undermine its unity, holiness, and catholicity.

The present-day attacks, culmination of over two centuries of revolution, are not the proof that it is has lost its divine constitution, but precisely the proof that it has retained it. For otherwise, it could not possibly have continued to exist, nor would it exist now. The Church is no less divine now in its unity, sanctity, and universality, in the midst of this terrible passion, than Christ was less divine when dying on the cross.

—*Fr. Scott,* October 2004

 **Can we say that the present crisis in the Church has destroyed its indefectibility?**

That the Church will never fail, and that it will always teach the same truths and administer the same sacraments through its visible structure, is a teaching of our Faith explicitly taught by Our Lord: "Simon, Simon, behold Satan hath desired to have you, that he may sift you as wheat. But I have prayed for thee, that thy faith fail not" (Lk. 22:32).

However, Our Lord did not promise that the indefectibility of this visible structure and of the teaching authority might not be obscured through the sins and infidelities of members of the Church's hierarchy. This is precisely what is happening now. The teaching of ecumenism implicitly denies the doctrine that "outside the Church there is no salvation." However, although it has been constantly reiterated, ecumenism has not been taught as a dogma, nor could it be; likewise collegiality and the rethinking of papal primacy, which implicitly mean a denial of the pope's supreme authority of governing and teaching. Yet this has not been taught as a dogma, to deny the official teaching. Likewise, the question of religious liberty as opposed to the rights of the Church and the Social Kingship of Christ. The same can be said of the new concept of justification, to be shared with the Lutherans. Although accepted by a joint statement, this false theory was immediately contradicted by the Congregation of the Doctrine of the Faith.

The end result is complete confusion, obscuring of the visible boundaries of the Church, obscuring of Catholic doctrine, now confused with and overlapped by false, modern, liberal, democratic philosophies. However, this in no way means that the Church has failed, regardless of how many people think that the Church is now different. The reality remains that doctrine has not changed (remember that Vatican II was not doctrinal, nor have the popes since been doctrinal) and that the Church's hierarchy and authority have not changed (although they are not being applied or used). It is simply that few are those now who are able to distinguish true doctrine, authority, and government in the Church from the infiltrated modern errors and liberalism. This is the supernatural miracle of the Church that despite the human weaknesses and betrayals of its members, it does remain indefectible.

—Fr. Scott, 2007

 **Is it true to say that now there is a "conciliar" church?**

The term "conciliar" is an adjective that has long been used to describe those things that relate to Vatican II, such as the documents, commissions, or novel teachings such as religious liberty and ecumenism.

The question raises the objection as to whether this adjective can be used to describe the Catholic Church after Vatican II.

In order to respond to the question, a clear distinction has to be made. If by the term "church" is understood the visible, hierarchical structure founded upon the rock of St. Peter, then clearly there can only be one Church, the Catholic Church. If we were to call the Catholic Church after Vatican II "conciliar" in this sense, then we would claim that it is no longer Catholic at all, but instead a separate visible, hierarchical structure. However, this is manifestly false, both because the adepts of Vatican II have hijacked the visible hierarchical structure of the Catholic Church and because they profess publicly to be Catholics.

However, there is another sense in which the term "conciliar" can rightly be applied to the majority of persons who profess to be Catholic, as well as to their ideas and opinions, profoundly influenced as they are by Vatican II. In this sense "conciliar" refers to the persons who have embraced and who promote the novelties of Vatican II, as well as to the novelties themselves. There are varying degrees of influence of the modern errors, from liberal Catholicism through rash opposition to Tradition to outright apostasy. The term "conciliar" or "post-conciliar" can consequently be applied to the modernist church, not as it is a canonical institution, but inasmuch as, and to the degree that, it promotes the revolutionary errors of Vatican II.

Archbishop Lefebvre understood this reality very clearly and the grave danger brought about by the infiltration of all these modernist principles within the very bosom of the Catholic Church. He had this to say of Rome in 1974, in his famous declaration of November 21:

> We hold fast, with all our heart and with all our soul, to Catholic Rome, Guardian of the Catholic Faith and of the traditions necessary to preserve this Faith, to Eternal Rome, Mistress of wisdom and truth.
>
> We refuse, on the other hand, and have always refused to follow the Rome of neo-Modernist and neo-Protestant tendencies which were clearly evident in the Second Vatican Council and, after the Council, in all the reforms which issued from it.

In his book *Spiritual Journey*, Archbishop Lefebvre explained how the end result of this conciliar church is to separate its members little by little from the true Catholic Church established by Our Lord. By this he means that its revolutionary principles of freedom at all cost separate the clergy and faithful little by little from Tradition and produce indifferentism toward all religions, eventually destroying the Catholic faith in the one true Church, and bringing about a generalized apostasy, even of those persons who outwardly appear to still be members of the Catholic Church:

Certainly, the Church itself guards its sanctity and its sources of sanctification, but the control of its institutions by unfaithful popes and apostate bishops ruins the faith of the faithful and the clergy, sterilizes the instruments of grace, and favors the assault of all the powers of Hell which seem to triumph. This apostasy makes its members adulterers, schismatics opposed to all Tradition, separated from the past of the Church, and thus separated from the Church of today, in the measure that it remains faithful to the Church of Our Lord. (P. 54)

—Fr. Scott, June 2005

Can Pope Pius XII's clarification of the error of the Council of Florence be used as a precedent for refusing the errors of Vatican II?

The question of the error in the Council of Florence's Decree to the Armenians concerning the matter of the sacrament of holy orders is interesting inasmuch as it demonstrates that the infallibility of the Church's magisterium requires as a condition that it be an act of teaching of faith or morals for the universal Church, and not just for one part of the Church. It also demonstrates that not everything taught by an ecumenical Council is infallible, but only those teachings in which the conditions required for the infallibility of the extraordinary or ordinary magisterium are fulfilled. The same applies to the teachings of Vatican II. The novelties, which are not a part of the ordinary magisterium and were never taught by the extraordinary magisterium, can and must be refused if they are in fact contrary to both, which is indeed the case.

—Fr. Scott, August 2000

Here recently I have heard more than once that the Holy Ghost was not invoked before or after Vatican II by the Council Fathers. Could you inform us of the truth of this remark?

The Holy Ghost was certainly invoked before and during the Council, as with any other assembly. It would have had little effect on the Council itself to have invoked the Third Person of the Blessed Trinity after the Council. The confusion seems to be over the issue of infallibility. The Council, precisely because it wished to be "pastoral," avoided defining articles on faith or morals; thus it did not assume infallible teaching authority. The Holy Ghost can be invoked, for example, at the beginning of a class without the teacher's attempting to be infallible in teaching the same class.

—Fr. Doran, November 1993

What is liberalism?

The difficulty in defining liberalism lies in its continual evolving and ever changing ideas, always mutating into new, more or less radical forms. It is often very difficult to seize hold of, penetrating as it does in varying degrees, more or less well camouflaged, into every aspect of human activity and thought.

However, the principles of liberalism are very clear, and once they are understood, the intellectual and moral perversion of this way of thinking and acting can be clearly seen.

Fr. Roussel, in his excellent work *Liberalism & Catholicism*, defines the liberal in this way: "The liberal is a fanatic for independence, and proclaims it in every domain, even unto absurdity" (p. 6). Consequently, it consists not in any particular doctrine, but in a way of thinking. Liberalism is

> a sickness of the mind, an orientation rather than a school, a perversion of sentiment based on pride, or a state of mind rather than a sect. Liberalism appears then as "a disordered affection of man for his independent liberty, which makes him abhor any limit, bond, yoke, or discipline from the law or from authority." (*Ibid.*, p. 8)

The other author whose excellent exposé of liberalism is much recommended is Fr. Sarda y Salvany, in *What Is Liberalism?* He outlines in this way the radical principles which are the basis of its propaganda:

1) The absolute sovereignty of the individual in his entire independence of God and God's authority.
2) The absolute sovereignty of society in its entire independence of everything which does not proceed from itself.
3) Absolute civil sovereignty in the implied right of the people to make their own laws in entire independence and utter disregard of any other criterion than the popular will expressed at the polls and in parliamentary majorities.
4) Absolute freedom of thought in politics, morals, or in religion. The unrestrained liberty of the press. (Pp. 18-19)

It is, consequently, the placing of the individual, society, the people, or freedom as absolutes in themselves, over and above Almighty God. One might wonder how it is that Catholics, who of our nature profess submission to God through our holy religion, could fall into such a trap. The answer is our natural desire of independence, on account of which liberalism is in accord with our fallen depraved human nature, and our natural tendency to follow Lucifer's rebellious refusal to serve. Consequently, we are always inventing ways to compromise the absolutes of our Faith with the spirit of the world, entirely penetrated by liberalism. Hence the development of "Catholic" liberalism throughout the nineteenth and twentieth centuries that Archbishop Lefebvre does not hesitate to stigmatize as "the great betrayal." For an understanding of how these liberal principles became accepted by Vatican II, producing the novelty of religious liberty, the revolutionary idea that all religions should be equally free for as long as they do not impinge on others' freedom, which is nothing short of the denial of the Social Kingship of Christ, I refer you to the magnificent exposé by Archbishop Lefebvre in *They Have Uncrowned Him* (Angelus Press, 1988).

Allow me to sum up by quoting the magnificent 1888 encyclical of Pope Leo XIII, *Libertas Praestantissimum*, in which he describes and condemns the varying kinds and degrees of liberalism, from the radical liberalism of those who refuse the Catholic Faith and the Catholic Church to the moderate liberalism of those who promote separation of Church and State, or maintain that the Church ought to adapt itself to modern systems of government:

> To deny the existence of this authority in God, or to refuse to submit to it, means to act, not as a free man, but as one who treasonably abuses his liberty; and in such a disposition of mind the chief and deadly vice of liberalism essentially consists. The form, however, of the sin is manifold: for in more ways than one can the will depart from the obedience which is due to God or to those who share the divine power. (§36)

—*Fr. Scott,* March 2001

What is ecumenism?

The description of this movement of dialogue and mutual exchange on religious questions with non-Catholics, and this on a basis of equality, is first made in a papal encyclical of Pope Pius XI, *Mortalium Animos* (On Fostering True Religious Unity), published in 1928. This is the pope's description:

> Assured that there exist few men who are entirely devoid of the religious sense, they seem to ground on this belief a hope that all nations, while differing indeed in religious matters, may yet without great difficulty be brought to fraternal agreement on certain points of doctrine which will form a common basis of the spiritual life. With this object, congresses, meetings, and addresses are arranged, attended by a large concourse of hearers, where all without distinction, unbelievers of every kind as well as Christians, even those who unhappily have rejected Christ and denied His divine nature or mission, are invited to join in the discussion. (§2)

Follows immediately afterwards the pope's condemnation of "the pan-Christians," whose "fair and alluring words cloak a most grave error, subversive of the foundations of the Catholic Faith" (§3):

Such efforts can meet with no kind of approval among Catholics. They presuppose the erroneous view that all religions are more or less good and praiseworthy [this is the error of indifferentism], inasmuch as all give expression, under various forms, to that innate sense which leads men to God and to the obedient acknowledgment of His rule. Those who hold such a view are not only in error; they distort the true idea of religion, and thus reject it, falling gradually into naturalism and atheism. To favor this opinion, and to encourage such undertakings is tantamount to abandoning the religion revealed by God. (§2)

In his instruction on ecumenism in 1949, Pope Pius XII ordered that, in opposition to such

dangerous indifferentism...Catholic doctrine must be propounded and explained in its totality and in its integrity. It is not permitted to pass over in silence or to veil in ambiguous terms what is comprised in the Catholic truth on the true nature and stages of justification, on the constitution of the Church, on the primacy of jurisdiction of the Roman Pontiff, on the unique true union by the return of separated Christians to the one true Church of Christ.

And yet, this is precisely what has not been done since Vatican II, in attempting to follow the contrary request not to offend the sensitivities of our "separated brethren" in the Vatican II decree on ecumenism, *Unitatis Redintegratio*. This is how that document defines ecumenism, with none of the precautions laid out by Pope Pius XII against indifferentism:

The term "ecumenical movement" indicates the initiatives and activities encouraged and organized...to promote Christian unity [*i.e.,* the apparent unity, outside the truth, of different denominations or churches getting along]. These are: first, every effort to avoid expressions, judgments, and actions which do not represent the condition of our separated brethren with truth and fairness and so make mutual relations with them more difficult.

The document also lists as other ecumenical activities dialogue, cooperation for the common good of humanity, and common prayer (*U.R.,* §4). These activities are all based upon the belief, already condemned in advance by Pope Pius XI, that all religions are more or less good or praiseworthy, expressed in this way in the Vatican II document on ecumenism: "Separated communities and churches as such...have been by no means deprived of significance and importance in the mystery of salvation. For the spirit of Christ has not refrained from using them as means of salvation" (*U.R.*, §3). Clearly, this leaves no place for the defined dogma "outside the Church, no salvation" (Lateran IV, DS [Denzinger, *Enchiridion Symbolorum* (Schoenmetzer ed.)] 802).

—*Fr. Scott,* October 2000

Just how far will religious liberty go?

Vatican II's decree on religious liberty was the keystone of the liberal transformation. *Dignitatis Humanae* begins with a statement which would resemble a profession of faith if it were not a philosophical postulate quite contrary to the Faith: "The Vatican Council declares that the human person has a right to religious freedom." What interests us here is not the fact that this statement is precisely equivalent to the statement condemned by Pope Pius IX in *Quanta Cura*, namely, that "freedom of conscience and worship is a right which belongs to every man," but what are the consequences of its logical application.

The new universal *Catechism of the Catholic Church* certainly does not overlook this principle of the conciliar church. Having cited this text, it draws the conclusion—namely, that we ought to have a "sincere respect for the different religions which often bring forth a ray of the truth which illuminates all men" (§2104). It does not take a great deal of intelligence to realize that if this were true we could never condemn another religion as being false, nor does it take exceptional brilliance to understand that if there is no such thing as a false religion, then the Catholic religion is no longer the only true religion, outside of which there is no salvation. The logic is implacable.

These principles, alas, were clearly demonstrated during Pope John Paul II's trip to Africa last month. In a public statement in the Sudan he affirmed that "Christians and Muslims alike are called to combat the misuse of religions and to foster reconciliation and dialogue." The misuse of religion is the condemnation of another religion, and Christians and Muslims are presumably alike inasmuch as they have equal rights to freedom. But if it is horrific to think that those who deny the divinity of the Second Person of the Blessed Trinity should have any rights before that same Blessed Trinity, if it is a shameful weakness of faith to even consider any reconciliation with those who deny God Himself, the pope's statements in Benin really demonstrate the iniquity of this religious liberty theory.

Voodooism, the traditional religion of Benin, is one of the most ancient forms of witchcraft and diabolical spirit worship known to man. Speaking to the adherents of this satanic religion, the pope had this to say: "The Second Vatican Council...recognized that in the diverse religious traditions there is something true and good, the seeds of the Word." The pope concluded: "Christians, members of the traditional religion [*i.e.* Voodooism], and Muslims are called to roll up their sleeves and work for the good of the country. This work of solidarity among believers is important for integral development, justice, and human liberation."

One wonders if the Holy Father has ever read the Apostle's words to the Corinthians: "Do not bear the yoke with unbelievers. For what has justice in common with iniquity? Or what fellowship has light with darkness? What harmony is there between Christ and Belial? Or what part has the believer with the unbeliever? And what agreement has the temple of God with idols?" (II Cor. 6:14-16). The pagans are therefore unbelievers with whom we can have neither solidarity, nor fellowship, nor harmony. To pretend anything else is to deny Christ, the object of our faith. How can there be any "integral development" which is not inspired by the grace of the Incarnation? How can there be any justice which is not the fruit of the precious blood of our divine Savior? How can there be any human liberation except that liberation from sin won only on the cross?

Is it any wonder, then, that Catholics have lost the missionary spirit, have lost their sense of identity?

—Fr. Scott, April 1993

Ought priests of the conciliar church to be conditionally ordained when they come to Tradition?

More and more priests ordained in the new rite are turning to the traditional Mass. However, since it is now nearly forty years since the new rite of ordination was introduced, some traditional Catholics question the validity of their ordination and hesitate to receive the sacraments from them. Each case is different in practice, it is true, and is to be decided by the superiors.

However, the following explanation of the principles that form the basis of these decisions can be of help in understanding them.

1) THE THREE SACRAMENTS THAT CONFER A CHARACTER CANNOT BE REPEATED.

This principle was already established with respect to the sacrament of baptism in the letter of Pope St. Stephen I to St. Cyprian condemning the latter's practice of rebaptizing heretics when receiving them into the Church. This was also defined by the Council of Trent, which declared an anathema against those who maintained that the three sacraments that imprint an indelible mark—namely, baptism, confirmation, and holy orders—can be repeated (Session VII, Canon 9, Dz. 852).

2) WHEN IT CONCERNS THE VALIDITY OF THE SACRAMENTS, WE ARE OBLIGED TO FOLLOW A "TUTIORIST" POSITION, OR SAFEST POSSIBLE COURSE OF ACTION.

We cannot choose a less certain option, called by the moral theologians a simply probable manner of acting, that could place in doubt the validity of the sacraments, as we are sometimes obliged to do in other moral questions. If we were able to follow a less certain way of acting, we would run the risk of grave sacrilege and uncertainty concerning the sacraments, which would place the eternal salvation of souls in great jeopardy. Even the lax "probabilist" theologians admitted this principle with respect to baptism and holy orders, since the contrary opinion was condemned by Pope Innocent XI in 1679. Innocent XI condemned the position that it is permissible "in conferring sacraments to follow a probable opinion regarding the value of the sacrament, the safer opinion being abandoned....Therefore, one should not make use of probable opinions only in conferring baptism, sacerdotal, or episcopal orders" (Proposition I condemned and prohibited by Innocent XI, Dz. 1151). Consequently, it is forbidden to accept a likely or probably valid ordination for the subsequent conferring of sacraments. One must have the greatest possible moral certitude, as in other things necessary for eternal salvation.

The faithful themselves understand this principle, and it really is a part of the *sensus Ecclesiae*, the spirit of the Church. They do not want to share modernist, liberal rites and have an aversion to receiving the sacraments from priests ordained in such rites, for they cannot tolerate a doubt in such matters. It is for this reason that they turn to the superiors to guarantee validity.

3) A NEGATIVE DOUBT IS TO BE DESPISED.

This axiom is accepted by all moral theologians. A negative doubt is a doubt that is not based upon any reason. It is the question "what if" that we frequently ask for no reason at all. Such a doubt cannot weaken moral certitude and is not reasonable. (*Cf.* Prummer, I, §328.) Consequently, we cannot question the validity of a sacrament such as holy orders without having a positive reason for doing so; namely, a reason to believe that there might be some defect of one of the three elements necessary for validity: matter, form, and intention.

4) WHEN A DOUBT ARISES IN THE ADMINISTRATION OF A SACRAMENT THAT CANNOT BE REPEATED, IT IS POSSIBLE AND EVEN OBLIGATORY TO REITERATE THE SACRAMENT *SUB CONDITIONE*, THAT IS, UNDER THE CONDITION THAT IT WAS INVALID THE FIRST TIME.

Thus it is that both moral certitude as to the administration of the sacrament is acquired and the sacrilege of simulating a sacrament that has already been administered is avoided. This is frequently spoken of in the rubrics of the Roman Ritual; for example, in the case of adult converts from heresy in whom there is a positive doubt as to the validity of baptism, or even foundlings who "should be baptized conditionally, unless there is a certainty from due investigation that they have already been baptized." The condition is thus expressed: "if you are not baptized ...." In fact, the custom before Vatican II was to baptize all adult converts from Protestantism, its being impossible to guarantee with moral certitude the form, or intention, or simultaneity of matter and form necessary for certain validity. Likewise, it is the custom to administer conditionally the sacrament of confirmation to those confirmed in the new rite, in the frequent case that a valid form and intention cannot be established with certitude.

Under similar circumstances, there is no sacrilege in reiterating conditionally a priestly ordination, as Archbishop Lefebvre himself did many times.

5) THE MATTER AND THE FORM OF THE LATIN RITE OF PRIESTLY ORDINATION INTRODUCED BY POPE PAUL VI IN 1968 ARE NOT SUBJECT TO POSITIVE DOUBT.

They are, in effect, practically identical to those defined by Pope Pius XII in 1947 in *Sacramentum Ordinis*. (In this, priestly ordination differs from the sacrament of confirmation, which in the new rite uses an entirely different and variable form, and one whose validity has been questioned.)

However, this moral certitude may not necessarily exist with vernacular translations of the form, which would have to be reviewed to exclude all positive doubt. One such change was the provisional ICEL translation of the form itself, substituting "Give the dignity of the presbyterate" for the traditional expression "Confer the dignity of the priesthood." Michael Davies comments: "In English-speaking countries the priesthood has never been referred to as the presbyterate" (*The Order of Melchisedech*, 1st ed., p. 88). It is not always easy to determine what English translation was used and whether or not it induces a positive doubt.

Not infrequently, Archbishop Lefebvre is quoted as stating that the New Mass is a bastard Mass and that the same can be said of the new rites for the sacraments, such as holy orders. How could such a Mass and sacraments be valid? In fact, the expression is a poor translation of the French "*messe batarde*," which is correctly translated as "illegitimate Mass," or "illegitimate rites," being the fruit of an adulterous union between the Church and the Revolution, the French expression not having the pejorative force of the English counterpart. Such an expression points out the illicit nature of such a compromise, but does not have a direct bearing on the validity of the rites. He explained this during the sermon he gave in Lille in 1976: "The New Mass is a sort of hybrid Mass, which is no longer hierarchical; it is democratic, where the assembly takes the place of the priest, and so it is no longer a veritable Mass that affirms the royalty of Our Lord" (*A Bishop Speaks* [Angelus Press], p. 271). It is for this reason that he called the traditional Mass the "true" Mass, not meaning thereby to question the validity of Masses celebrated in the new rite.

The new rites of ordination are similarly illegitimate, for they do not adequately express the Catholic faith in the priesthood. By writing very strongly against them, Archbishop Lefebvre did not intend to declare their invalidity. He stated very clearly, in *Open Letter to Confused Catholics*, quoting parts of the ceremony that are certainly not a part of the form of the sacrament and consequently not necessary for validity, that such a ceremony destroys the priesthood:

> Everything is bound up together. By attacking the base of the building it is destroyed entirely. No more Mass, no more priests. The ritual, before it was altered, had the bishop say, "Receive the power to offer to God the Holy Sacrifice and to celebrate Holy Mass both for the living and for the dead, in the name of the Lord." He had previously blessed the hands of the ordinand by pronouncing these words: "So that all that they bless may be blessed and all that they consecrate may be consecrated and sanctified." The power conferred is expressed without ambiguity: "That for the salvation of Thy people and by their holy blessing, they may effect the Transubstantiation of the bread and the wine into the Body and Blood of Thy Divine Son." Nowadays the bishop says: "Receive the offering of the holy people to present it to God." He makes the new priest an intermediary rather than the holder of the ministerial priesthood and the offerer of a sacrifice. The conception is wholly different. (P. 54)

Despite such firm words, the Archbishop has this to say: "The 'matter' of the sacrament has been preserved in the laying on of hands which takes place next, and likewise the 'form,' namely, the words of ordination" (*ibid.*, p. 51). The destruction he is speaking about is of the Mass as it ought to be and of the priesthood as it ought to be. His intention is, consequently, to point out that it is the Catholic notion of the priesthood that is destroyed, not necessarily the validity of the sacrament of holy orders.

6) There can be reasons to doubt the intention of the ordaining bishop in the conciliar church.

The minister of the sacrament does not have to intend what the Church intends, which is why a heretic can administer a valid sacrament. He must, however, intend to do what the Church does. The positive doubt that can exist in this regard is well described by Michael Davies:

> Every prayer in the traditional rite which stated specifically the essential role of a priest as a man ordained to offer propitiatory sacrifice for the living and dead has been removed. In most cases these were the precise prayers removed by the Protestant Reformers [*e.g.*, "Receive the power to offer sacrifice to God and to celebrate Mass, both for the living and the dead, in the name of the Lord"] or if not precisely the same there are clear parallels....Their omission by the Protestant Reformers was taken by Pope Leo XIII as an indication of an intention not to consecrate sacrificing priests. (*Ibid.*, pp. 82, 86)

This is the text of *Apostolicae Curae* (Leo XIII, 1896), §33:

> With this inherent defect of form is joined the defect of intention which is equally essential to the sacrament....If the rite be changed, with the manifest intention of introducing another rite not approved by the Church and of rejecting what the Church does, and what, by the institution of Christ, belongs to the nature of the Sacrament, then it is clear that not only is the necessary intention wanting to the Sacrament, but that the intention is adverse to and destructive of the Sacrament.

If it cannot be said, as with Anglican orders, that the *Novus Ordo* rite was changed with the manifest intention of rejecting a sacrificing priesthood, nevertheless the deliberate exclusion of the notion of propitiation, in order to please Protestants, could easily be considered as casting a doubt on the intention of doing what the Church does, namely, of offering a true and propitiatory sacrifice. Of course, this doubt would not exist if the ordaining bishop had indicated otherwise his truly Catholic intention of doing what the Church does.

However, the difficulty lies in the fact that the accompanying ceremonies in the new rite of ordination do not adequately express either the Catholic conception of the priesthood or the intention, as do the ceremonies in the old rite. The following texts from the Archbishop, taken from spiritual conferences to seminarians, refer to the intention of the priest celebrating Mass. However, the same principles can be applied to the bishop ordaining a priest:

> In the old rite, the intention was clearly determined by all the prayers that were said before and after the consecration. There was a collection of ceremonies all along the sacrifice of the Mass that determined clearly the priest's intention. It is by the Offertory that the priest expresses clearly his intention. However, this does not exist in the new *Ordo*. The new Mass can

be either valid or invalid depending upon the intention of the celebrant, whereas in the traditional Mass, it is impossible for anyone who has the Faith to not have the precise intention of offering a sacrifice and accomplishing it according to the ends foreseen by Holy Church....These young priests will not have the intention of doing that which the Church does, for they will not have been taught that the Mass is a true sacrifice. They will not have the intention of offering a sacrifice. They will have the intention of celebrating a Eucharist, a sharing, a communion, a memorial, all of which has nothing to do with faith in the sacrifice of the Mass. Hence from this moment, inasmuch as these deformed priests no longer have the intention of doing what the Church does, their Masses will obviously be more and more invalid. (*La messe de toujours*, pp. 373-374; in English tr., *The Mass of All Time* [Angelus Press, 2007])

There can be no doubt that Archbishop Lefebvre entertained serious doubts as to the intention of some conciliar bishops when they ordain priests. In *Open Letter to Confused Catholics* (p. 50), he points out that the doubt that overhangs the other sacraments also applies to the ordination of priests and gives examples, asking the question: "Are they true priests at all? Put it another way, are their ordinations valid?" He goes on to explain the reason why he considers that a doubt exists over the ordaining bishop's intention, for it is frequently no longer the intention of ordaining a priest to offer sacrifice:

We are obliged to point out that the intention is far from clear. Has the priest been ordained...to establish justice, fellowship, and peace at a level which appears to be limited to the natural order only?...The definition of the priesthood given by St. Paul and by the Council of Trent has been radically altered. The priest is no longer one who goes up to the altar and offers up to God a sacrifice of praise, for the remission of sins." (*Ibid.*, pp. 51-52)

Hence the Archbishop's affirmation that the whole conception of the priesthood has changed and that the priest is no longer regarded as one having the power to do things that the faithful cannot do (*ibid.*, p. 54), but rather as one who presides over the assembly. This modernist conception certainly casts a grave shadow of doubt over the intention of the ordaining bishop.

7) THE QUESTION OF EPISCOPAL CONSECRATION IN THE 1968 RITE PROMULGATED BY POPE PAUL VI IS EVEN MORE DELICATE.

The difficulty lies in the complete change of the wording of the form of episcopal consecration. The very erudite article of Fr. Pierre-Marie, O.P., published in *The Angelus* (December 2005 & January 2006), establishes that the form is in itself valid. Although radically different from the traditional Latin form, and although only similar, but not identical, to the forms used in the Eastern rites, it is in itself valid, the meaning designating sufficiently clearly the Catholic episcopacy. For the form of holy orders is variable and changeable, this being one of the sacraments established only in general terms. The substance is consequently retained for as long as the words have essentially the same meaning.

However, this does not mean that this new rite of episcopal ordination is valid in every concrete case, for this could depend upon the translation, modifications (now that the principle of change has been accepted), and eventual defect of intention. For the danger of the creeping in of a defective intention, as with the rite of priestly ordination, cannot be excluded. This is what Fr. Nicolas Portail of the Society of St. Pius X wrote in the January 2007 issue of *Le Chardonnet*:

> The authors correctly observe that this rite is the vehicle of a conception of the episcopacy according to Vatican II. It also shows that the functions that are special to the episcopal order (ordaining priests, consecrating churches, administering confirmation...) are not mentioned in the consecratory preface, in opposition to other prefaces in the Eastern rites.

In addition, the specific error of collegiality is explicitly mentioned in the consecrator's allocution. It cannot be denied that this rite is, from a traditional perspective, weak, ambiguous, imperfect, defective, and manifestly illicit.

Yet, even the bishops who ordain priests in the traditional rite were all consecrated bishops according to this new rite. It can easily be imagined how a defect of intention could creep into the episcopal succession, even in the case of "traditional" priests who depend upon conciliar bishops for their ordinations. Fr. Portail quotes a remark by some young priests of the Fraternity of St. Peter who had just been ordained by Archbishop Decourtray to some priests of the Society of St. Pius X: "You are more certain of your ordination than we are of ours" (*ibid.*). It would, indeed, be tragic if all traditional priests did not have moral certitude as to their ordination; and if there existed two different grades of priests, a higher grade ordained in Tradition and a lower grade. It is for this reason that the superiors have the right to insist on conditional ordination for any priest turning towards Tradition, and will only accept ordinations in the conciliar church after having investigated both priestly and episcopal ordinations and established moral certitude.

Archbishop Lefebvre clearly recognized his obligation of providing priests concerning whose ordination there was no doubt. It was one of the reasons for the episcopal consecrations of 1988, as he declared in the sermon for the occasion:

> You well know, my dear brethren, that there can be no priests without bishops. When God calls me—this will certainly not be long—from whom would these seminarians receive the Sacrament of Orders? From

conciliar bishops, who, due to their doubtful intentions, confer doubtful sacraments? This is not possible.

He continued, explaining that he could not leave the faithful orphans, nor abandon the seminarians who entrusted themselves to him, for "they came to our seminaries, despite all the difficulties that they have encountered, in order to receive a true ordination to the Priesthood..." (Fr. François Laisney, *Archbishop Lefebvre and the Vatican* [Angelus Press], p. 120). He considered it his duty to guarantee the certitude of the sacrament of holy orders by the consecration of bishops in the traditional rite, who would then ordain only in the traditional rite.

We must observe the same balance as Archbishop Lefebvre. On the one hand, it is our duty to avoid the excess of sedevacantism, which unreasonably denies the very validity and existence of the post-conciliar church and its priesthood. On the other hand, however, we must likewise reject the laxist and liberal approach that does not take seriously the real doubts that can arise concerning the validity of priestly ordinations in the post-conciliar church, failing to consider the enormous importance and necessity of a certainly valid priesthood for the good of the Church, for the eternal salvation of souls, and for the tranquility of the consciences of the faithful. Given the gravity of these issues, it is not even a slight doubt that is acceptable. Hence the duty of examining in each particular case the vernacular form of priestly ordination, the intention of the ordaining bishop, the rite of consecration of the ordaining bishop, and the intention of the consecrators.

Just as the superiors take seriously their duty of guaranteeing the moral certitude of the holy orders of their priests, whether by means of conditional ordination or careful investigation (when possible), so also must priests who join the Society accept conditional ordination in case of even slight positive doubt, and so also must the faithful recognize that each case is different and accept the decision of those who alone are in a position to perform the necessary investigations. For regardless of the technical question of the validity of a priest's holy orders, we all recognize the Catholic sense that tells us that there can be no mixing of the illegitimate new rites with the traditional Catholic rites, a principle so simply elucidated by Archbishop Lefebvre on June 29, 1976:

> We are not of this religion. We do not accept this new religion. We are of the religion of all time, of the Catholic religion. We are not of that universal religion, as they call it today. It is no longer the Catholic religion. We are not of that liberal, modernist religion that has its worship, its priests, its faith, its catechisms, its Bible....

—*Fr. Scott,* September 2007

Could you please explain the discrepancies in the ceremonies for Maundy Thursday, Good Friday, and Holy Saturday that I see in different traditional chapels?

The key to understanding the minor differences that a traditional Catholic sometimes sees is the restoration of the ceremonies of Holy Week. This was done by Pope Pius XII in two stages, the restoration of the Easter Vigil being decreed in 1951, and of Holy Thursday and Good Friday in November 1955. The changes were not great. The most obvious is the returning of the ceremonies to the original times, times that corresponded with the events that were celebrated. The reason given in the decree of November 30, 1955, *Maxima Redemptionis Nostrae Mysteria*, is to promote the assistance of the faithful, whose customary absence from these ceremonies was a cause of great regret, given not only the extraordinary dignity of these ceremonies but also their special sacramental power and efficacy to nourish the Christian life.

Consequently, it was decided that the Mass of the Lord's Supper (*In Coena Domini*) for Maundy Thursday would be celebrated henceforth in the evening, starting not before 5:00 p.m. nor after 8:00 p.m., this coinciding with the time of the Last Supper. To the Mass was added the optional ceremony of the washing of the feet (previously celebrated separately), symbolizing thereby the charity of Christ towards His disciples that inspired Him to give them His body and blood. The evening procession to the altar of repose is symbolic of the apostles accompanying our divine Lord into the garden of Gethsemane.

The time of the ceremony for Good Friday was also changed to the afternoon, after the time of Our Lord's death on the cross, namely, from 3:00 until 6:00 p.m. The ceremony has barely changed except that the last part is no longer called the "Mass of the Presanctified" but simply a Holy Communion service.

The Holy Saturday Vigil was restored to the original time of a vigil, such that the Mass begins around midnight. The ceremonies were somewhat simplified, notably by reducing the number of lessons from twelve to four, in order to make the ceremony more accessible for the faithful. The above-mentioned decree of the Sacred Congregation of Rites explains the symbolism of this change:

> First of all it is imperative that the faithful should be instructed about the unique liturgical character of Holy Saturday. This is the day of the most intense sorrow, the day on which the Church tarries at the Lord's tomb, meditating about His Passion and death. While the altar remains stripped, the Church abstains from the sacrifice of the Mass until, after the solemn vigil or the nocturnal wait for the Resurrection, there come the Easter joys, the abundance of which carries over to the days that follow.

The intention and purpose of the vigil is to point out and to recall in the liturgical service how our life and grace have flowed from the Lord's death. And so, Our Lord Himself is shown under the sign of the paschal candle as "the light of the world" (Jn. 8:12) who has put the darkness of our sins to flight by the grace of His light.

The experience of the Church has proven the wisdom of this restoration of the primitive custom, of these minor changes, that help us to truly share with Our Lord the sacred moments of Holy Week. These restored Holy Week ceremonies will be seen in all the churches of the Society of St. Pius X. However, there remain some traditional priests who confuse this authentic restoration with the post-conciliar revolution of the New Mass, and who refuse to accept these well balanced and duly authorized rubrical changes. These are in general sedevacantists, who maintain that there has been no pope since Pius XII, and that Pius XII was no longer able to govern during the last years of his papacy. It is true that during the 1950's Fr. Bugnini and the liturgical movement were gathering speed for the liturgical revolution of the New Mass. However, the examination of the text and reasons given for these changes puts the lie to the accusations that they are impregnated with modernism and that Pope Pius XII, who wrote in 1947 a magnificent encyclical, *Mediator Dei*, condemning the abuses of the liturgical movement, had lost control.

—Fr. Scott, April 2002

 **How is it possible to refuse a law coming from the Church, such as the change of "for many" into "for all" in the consecration of the Precious Blood at Mass?**

This particular change in the words of consecration, the most serious in the New Mass, was not a part of the New Mass as "promulgated" (note that properly speaking it was not really promulgated, both from the point of view of the formalities involved and from that of content) by Pope Paul VI on April 3, 1969, in his letter *Missale Romanum*. In the Latin text the words "for many" are retained. This change is consequently one of translation. However, it was manifestly not by accident that in all the modern European languages except Portuguese and Polish this same "error" of translation was committed. It is a manifest effort to undermine the clear teaching found in all three synoptic Gospels that the efficacy of Christ's shedding His blood is limited to many souls and does not include all souls. The reason behind this change is consequently the modernist teaching on universal salvation, according to which Christ saved all human nature by His death on the cross, whether people know it or not.

Since this is a change that manifestly undermines Catholic doctrine, it is equally clear that the traditional Catholic cannot accept it. The objection is then made as to how a Catholic can refuse such a disciplinary law that purports to come from the Church? As Pope Gregory XVI pointed out, since "the Church is the pillar and foundation of truth," how could it "order, yield to, or permit those things which tend toward the destruction of souls and the disgrace and detriment of the sacraments instituted by Christ" (*Quo Graviora*)? It is manifestly impious to think that the Church herself, the immaculate spouse of Christ, can order or command something contrary to the Faith or to the salvation of souls. It is, in effect, a condemned proposition of the heretical Council of Pistoia that the Church "could impose a disciplinary law that would be not only useless and more burdensome for the faithful than Christian liberty allows, but also dangerous and harmful" (Pope Pius VI, *Auctorem Fidei*).

The true Catholic cannot, of course, deny the essential role of the Holy Ghost in governing the Church and its disciplinary laws, that is, its ecclesiastical tradition. However, it is manifestly obvious that this change of "for many" to "for all" is not a disciplinary law of the Church. Although tolerated practically everywhere, it was never "promulgated" by the pope but was simply allowed to happen. Manifestly also, it could not be a law of the Church, for it is opposed to constant doctrinal teaching and liturgical practice, that is, to constant unanimous ecclesiastical and apostolic Tradition. It is consequently not of the Church at all, but of certain churchmen, who have infiltrated it into the vernacular versions of the New Missal. It is an abuse, and it is modernist, and consequently could not possibly be a disciplinary law of the Church.

The same can be said of the other, but less obvious, aspects of the New Mass that express modernism. They cannot be a true law, as St. Thomas Aquinas says (*ST*, I-II, q. 96, art. 4), quoting St. Augustine, because unjust laws are not laws at all. Laws are manifestly unjust that are opposed to the divine Good, that is to the truth, holiness, and sanctity of God, His Church, and the sacraments. Yet this is precisely what the *Novus Ordo* Mass is. It undermines the Catholic teaching on the Mass as a true propitiatory sacrifice, not to mention the sacredness of and devotion to the Blessed Sacrament (Communion in the hand is only one small part of this attack on the Real Presence), and the whole mystery of the Church, the communion of the saints, and reparation for our sins. Consequently, even if it were correctly promulgated by a pope in such a way as to make it appear obligatory (which is not, in fact, the case), it would still be an unjust and invalid law. There is absolutely no contradiction between accepting that the pope truly is pope and rejecting these laws that are manifestly not a work of the Church, nor does it demean the Church's disciplinary and liturgical laws. In fact, it is because of our understanding of these laws, and of the reasons behind them, and of how perfectly they express Catholic doctrine, life, and piety, that we are bound to refuse these pretend laws that are not really Catholic laws at all.

The sedevacantists make much ado about the infallibility of disciplinary laws. It is true that they can participate in the infallibility of the ordinary magisterium inasmuch as they imply a teaching that has always and everywhere been taught by the Church. Such is the case of the bull *Quo Primum*, which most solemnly gives priests the right to celebrate the traditional Mass in perpetuity, precisely because St. Pius V guaranteed the fact that it perfectly expresses the Catholic Faith and spirituality concerning the Mass. However, a defective law, or a law that is unjust and unholy because it does not adequately express the teaching of the Church, manifestly does not participate in the infallibility of the ordinary magisterium, which has to be universal in time and place to be infallible. Consequently, the sedevacantists' affirmation that we cannot accept that the pope is the pope without accepting that all his laws are infallible is manifestly preposterous. To the contrary, it is our duty to pray that the pope use his authority in line with unchanging Tradition, in which case his laws will be infallible. This has happened extremely rarely under John Paul II, but is certainly the case of his refusal to accept the ordination of women to the priesthood.

—*Fr. Scott,* January 2003

Christ promised that "the gates of hell shall not prevail against the Church." Therefore, should we not just patiently wait?

And do nothing? Christ promised that the gates of hell shall not prevail against His Church; He did not promise that the gates of hell shall not prevail against those who do nothing to defend the Church and its Tradition! Remember the useless servant in the Gospel's parable!

—*Fr. Laisney,* February 1990

Is it presumptuous to think YOU can save the Church?

We do not think we can save the Church. We rather want to be saved by the Church and to save many other souls by using the very same means by which the Church has saved so many generations of saints, *viz.,* the traditional Mass and sacraments.

—*Fr. Laisney,* February 1990

Is the *Novus Ordo* Mass invalid or sacrilegious, and should I assist at it when I have no alternative?

The validity of the reformed rite of Mass as issued in Latin by Pope Paul VI in 1969 must be judged according to the same criteria as the validity of the other sacraments—namely, matter, form, and intention. The defective theology and meaning of the rites, eliminating as they do every reference to the principal propitiatory end of sacrifice, do not necessarily invalidate the Mass. The intention of doing what the Church does, even if the priest understands it imperfectly, is sufficient for validity. With respect to the matter, pure wheaten bread and true wine from grapes are what is required for validity. The changes in the words of the form in the Latin original, although certainly illicit and unprecedented in the history of the Church, do not alter the substance of its meaning and, consequently, do not invalidate the Mass.

However, we all know that such a New Mass celebrated in Latin is an oddity, doomed to extinction by the very fact of the reform. The validity of the New Masses that are actually celebrated in today's parishes more than thirty years later is a quite different question. Additives to the host sometimes invalidate the matter. The change in the translation from the words of Our Lord "for many" to the ecumenically acceptable "for all" throws at least some doubt on the validity of the form. Most importantly, however, is the fact that the intention of the Church of offering up a true sacrifice in propitiation for the sins of the living and the dead has been obliterated for thirty years. In fact, most liturgies present the contrary intention of a celebration by the community of the praise of God. In such circumstances it is very easy for a priest to no longer have the intention of doing what the Church does and for the New Mass to become invalid for this reason. The problem is that this is hidden and nobody knows. Whereas the traditional Mass expresses the true intention of the Church in a clear and unambiguous manner so that everyone can be certain of the priest's intention, the New Mass does no such thing. Consequently, the doubt of invalidity for lack of intention, especially in the case of manifestly modernist priests, cannot be easily lifted or removed.

Clearly, an invalid Mass is not a Mass at all and does not satisfy the Sunday obligation. Furthermore, when it comes to the sacraments, Catholics are obliged to follow the *pars tutior*, the safer path. It is not permissible to knowingly receive doubtful sacraments. Consequently, nobody has the obligation to satisfy his Sunday obligation by attending the New Mass, even if there is no other alternative.

However, even if we could be certain of the validity of the *Novus Ordo* Masses celebrated in today's conciliar churches, it does not follow that they are pleasing to God. Much to the contrary, they are objectively sacrilegious, even if those who assist at them are not aware of it. By such a statement, I do not mean that all those who celebrate or assist at the New Mass are necessarily in mortal sin, having done something directly insulting to Almighty God and to our divine Savior.

Sacrilege is a sin against the virtue of religion and is defined as "the unbecoming treatment of a sacred person, place, or thing as far as these are consecrated to God" (Jone, *Moral Theology*, p. 108). The moral theologians explain that sacrilege is in itself and generally a mortal sin (*ex genere suo*), but that it is not always a mortal sin because it can concern a relatively small or unimportant thing. Here we are speaking of a real sacrilege, the dishonoring of the holy sacrifice of the Mass by the elimination of the prayers and ceremonies that protect its holiness; by the absence of respect, piety, and adoration; and by the failure to express the Catholic doctrine of the Mass as a true propitiatory sacrifice for our sins. Here there are varying degrees. Just as it is a grave sacrilege and objective mortal sin for a lay person to touch the sacred host without reason, so it is, for example, a venial sin to do the same thing to the chalice or the blessed linens, such as the purificator or pall.

Likewise with the New Mass. It can be an objectively mortal sin of sacrilege if Holy Communion is distributed in the hand or by lay ministers, if there is no respect, if there is talking or dancing in church, or if it includes some kind of ecumenical celebration, *etc.* It can also be an objectively venial sin of sacrilege if it is celebrated with unusual respect and devotion so that it appears becoming and reverential to Almighty God. This in virtue of the omissions in the rites and ceremonies, which constitute a true disrespect to Our Lord in the Blessed Sacrament and to the Blessed Trinity, and of the failure to express the true nature of what the Mass really is. In each case, the subjective culpability is an altogether other question that God only can judge.

However, regardless of the gravity of the sacrilege, the New Mass still remains a sacrilege, and it is still in itself sinful. Furthermore, it is never permitted to knowingly and willingly participate in an evil or sinful thing, even if it is only venially sinful. For the end does not justify the means. Consequently, although it is a good thing to want to assist at Mass and satisfy one's Sunday obligation, it is never permitted to use a sinful means to do this. To assist at the New Mass, for a person who is aware of the objective sacrilege involved, is consequently at least a venial sin. It is opportunism. Consequently, it is not permissible for a traditional Catholic, who understands that the New Mass is insulting to our divine Savior, to assist at the New Mass, and this even if there is no danger of scandal to others or of the perversion of one's own faith (as in an older person, for example), and even if it is the only Mass available.

—*Fr. Scott,* September 2002

 **Please comment on the following situation, which I know exists: people attend the *Novus Ordo* liturgy and the traditional Mass on the same day and receive Communion both times.**

These are two questions in one. It is good to attend the traditional Mass, but not good to attend the *Novus Ordo*; mixing poison with good food is never the thing to do. It would just lead such people to be more confused. The solution to their dilemma is simple: be attached to the Mass of the saints. One day someone asked a conservative cardinal what was the difference between the Mass of St. Pius V and the Mass of Pope Paul VI. The cardinal answered, "It's very simple: St. Pius V is canonized; Paul VI shall never be canonized. Here you have the difference!"

The second question is that of receiving Communion twice on the same day. Our Lord commanded us to pray thus: "Give us this day our daily bread...." In this petition, we not only ask for the food of our body and other earthly necessities, but above all we ask for the food of our soul, for that "Bread that came down from heaven and gives life to the world." So Holy Communion is our spiritual food for the day: we are thus encouraged by Our Lord to receive Him every day. Yet one Communion is sufficient for the whole day; unless one falls into danger of death and receives the Viaticum, or in the case of a priest offering several Masses on a day of obligation for the necessity of the faithful, to receive Holy Communion more than once a day would be "spiritual gluttony." It is contrary to the practice of the Church.

There is an image of this in the Old Testament. When the Hebrews were fed with manna in the desert, he who gathered more would still have the same measure as he who gathered less, *i.e.*, the measure of a "gomor" which sufficed for one day (Ex. 16:16-18). One should not try to take more than what God wants us to receive.

One should not abuse good things, much less holy things. To receive Communion systematically at every Mass may lead to lack of appreciation of its value. St. Thomas teaches that we should be filled both with fear (reverence and adoration) and with love when approaching Jesus in Holy Communion. Fear would keep us at a distance, and love makes us desire union with Him. Love should always be greater than fear, thus we should not hesitate to receive Holy Communion frequently, even daily if we have the opportunity. But it may be good, from time to time, to abstain just in order to remind us of the infinite majesty of Our Lord hidden in the host.

The modernists have taken away all reverence and adoration. Hence, they have no fear of abusing holy things. Moreover, they consider the Mass just a meal, and it would make no sense to come to a meal and not to eat anything; thus they want to receive Communion at every Mass, even twice a day if one attends Mass twice a day.

The faithful attached to Tradition should follow the age-old practice of frequent Communion, but not more than once a day.

—*Fr. Laisney,* December 1990

I would like to know if in Aramaic "for all" and "for many" were two separate and distinct phrases, and not the same as said by some after Vatican II?

The controversy concerning the translation of the consecration formula in the Mass of the Latin Rite must be centered on the meaning of the Latin. "*Pro multis*" in the official Latin form, even as it remains in the Latin *Novus Ordo*, must be translated "for many" in the consecration of the chalice. The Aramaic equivalents are irrelevant.

—*Fr. Doran,* October 1992

Are the brown hosts frequently used in the *Novus Ordo* validly consecrated or must the hosts be white?

It is Canon 815, §1 (1917 Code) that determines the valid matter that must be used for the consecration of hosts. It is only "*pure wheaten bread*" that is apt for consecration into the Body of Christ at Mass. Canon 924, §2 of the 1983 Code says the same thing. Consequently, bread baked from flour made out of any variety of true wheat is certainly valid matter, whereas flour made out of any non-wheat cereal is certainly invalid matter, such as that made from rye, barley, or millet, as is also bread baked with a notable quantity of non-wheaten flour (*Matters Liturgical*, 10th ed. [1959], p. 320). If anything other than pure water and wheaten flour is included in the mix, then it is of doubtful validity. Likewise if the bread is old and stale and in danger of corruption. Such things are strictly illicit and forbidden.

The usual reason why the hosts used are brown is that they are baked out of whole wheat flour. Such matter is valid and licit, provided that (in the Latin rite) the dough is unleavened. Consequently, it will not in itself be a reason to doubt the validity of the Mass, unless there is a suspicion that other elements (*e.g.*, eggs or butter or sugar) were added. However, it is inappropriate to use brown hosts. The whiteness of the host represents the purity of the immaculate Victim, the perfect Lamb of God, whose perfect offering of Himself is renewed in an unbloody way on the altar. It is most inappropriate for this symbolism to be blemished by the use of whole wheat flour for the baking of altar breads.

—*Fr. Scott,* May 2003

There is a priest in town who says the *Novus Ordo*. He is unhappy doing so but, for reasons of his own, he continues. At certain times he meets, in secret, with traditional Catholics to say the "true Mass." I have reservations about attending a Mass and receiving sacraments from this priest. What to do?

It is not always possible to understand the reasons why priests continue offering a rite of Mass with which they are unhappy. But if the priest has it to heart to offer the "true Mass" for a number of the faithful, his motives would seem to be good.

A Catholic may assist at the Mass of any priest in good standing. Therefore where orthodoxy is genuine there should be no scruple in assisting at Mass or receiving the sacraments in their proper form.

—*Fr. Doran,* September 1991

What is the basis for concelebration of Mass?

The emphasis on the necessity and opportunity of concelebration of Mass by several priests at the same time is a novelty of the modern post-conciliar church, which takes its origin in the conciliar document on the liturgy, *Sacrosanctum Concilium*. It has this to say in the paragraph in which it promotes this practice: "Concelebration whereby the unity of the priesthood is appropriately manifested has remained in use to this day in the Church both in the East and in the West" (§57).

Vatican II consequently makes it sound as if concelebration is a traditional practice. In fact, this is not at all the case. An essential distinction is lacking, and it is between ceremonial concelebration and sacramental concelebration. It is the ceremonial concelebration which has always been traditional. This is the situation that takes place when the bishop is surrounded by his *presbyterium*, that is, his priests, who share in certain ceremonial activities. This happens, for example, during the ceremony of consecration of the holy oils, during which the priests also breathe into the holy oils. It also happens during the ordination ceremony when the priests all impose their hands on the newly ordained priest, together with the bishop. However, the priests present do not consecrate the holy oils, nor do they ordain the ordinand. They are simply present, participating in the ceremonies and showing their unity with their bishop, who alone has the fullness of the priesthood to accomplish these functions.

The same is the traditional practice in the Roman rite. Until the tenth century, priests did not celebrate their own Mass if they were present at the pontifical, or solemn, high Mass. They participated in the ceremonies celebrated by the bishop. It was a ceremonial concelebration. However, only the bishop celebrated the Mass. It was the development of the low

Mass in the ninth century that made it possible for the priests themselves to celebrate every day.

It was during the thirteenth century that the custom of sacramental concelebration developed for two special ceremonies, namely, the ordination of priests and the consecration of bishops. The ordinands to this very day keep this practice by reciting together with the celebrant, not just the words of consecration, but all the words of the Offertory and Canon of the Mass. It is a laborious ceremony, but it demonstrates the union around the altar of the newly ordained priests or bishops with the ordaining bishop.

However, it was never more than a special ceremony for this extraordinary circumstance of ordination. The very same reasons that brought about the introduction of so-called "private" Masses during the ninth and tenth centuries in the Latin Rite, when priests began the custom of celebrating Mass every day, also prevented any consideration of regular concelebration. The development of the understanding of the Mass as an unbloody renewal of the sacrifice of the cross led to a greater understanding of its power to apply to the souls of those present, and to those for whom the Mass is offered, the infinite graces of the Redemption. Since it is the sacrifice itself that is renewed in an unbloody way which applies graces to souls, the more frequently and devoutly the sacrifice is offered the more graces are applied to souls.

This applies to concelebrations, since when several priests concelebrate, there is only one offering of the Body and Blood of Christ, and consequently only one Mass and only one application of the merits of the Redemption. However, if they offer their Masses separately then there are several Masses offered up.

The whole concept of concelebration is an invention of modernists within the liturgical movement, who desire to make the value of the liturgical ceremonies depend upon the social or community aspect of the celebration—namely, the assistance and participation of faithful or of several priests. Consequently, they disdain "private" Masses, as if they were not public acts of worship applying the graces of the cross simply because there is no assistance of the faithful. Likewise they promote concelebration of several priests, thus emphasizing the community aspect of the priesthood. However, in both cases it is the efficacy of the Mass that is despised, as if the unbloody renewal of the sacrifice of Calvary itself, without the assistance of a community, were not all-powerful to atone for the sins of the people and to honor God and to obtain graces for those for whom it is offered, and especially for the entire Catholic Church, for which every traditional Mass is offered.

This is what Pope Pius XII had to say in his 1947 encyclical *Mediator Dei* condemning the errors and excesses of the liturgical movement:

> They assert that the people are possessed of a true priestly power, while the priest only acts in virtue of an office committed to him by the community. Wherefore they look on the Eucharistic Sacrifice as a "concelebration" in the literal meaning of that term, and consider it more fitting that priests should "concelebrate" with the people present than that they should offer the Sacrifice privately when the people are absent. It is superfluous to explain how captious errors of this sort completely contradict the truths which we have just stated above, when treating of the place of the priest in the Mystical Body of Jesus Christ. (§§83-84)

If it is true that the concelebration of priests together is not the same thing as the concelebration of the people with the priest(s), it is also true that the first leads to the second and that the same error about the value of the holy sacrifice of the Mass underlies both practices of concelebration. This is the reason why the 1917 Code of Canon Law (Can. 803) strictly forbade concelebration of several priests, other than in Masses of ordination of priests and consecration of bishops. Not only is concelebration encouraged by the 1983 Code (Can. 902), but it actually forbids the edifying example of different priests celebrating Masses on side altars at the same time as the main celebration. All this is but one more consequence of the failure of the New Mass to express the reality that the Mass is a true propitiatory sacrifice.

—Fr. Scott, December 2004

 **I read an article which stated that the anathemas of the Council of Trent had been abolished by the 1983 Code of Canon Law. Is this true?**

The definitions of Catholic doctrine contained in the Council of Trent (*e.g.,* concerning the Mass, the sacraments, grace, original sin, and justification) are acts of the solemn, extraordinary magisterium of the Church. It is a doctrine of Catholic Faith that such acts are infallible and irreformable, that is, unchangeable (Vatican I, *Pastor Aeternus,* DS 3074). This means that no authority in the Church can change these definitions, not even a pope or an ecumenical Council. Consequently, it is not possible for the 1983 Code of Canon Law to repeal such definitions, nor did it attempt to do so.

It is not possible to say that the definition is infallible and unchangeable but that the anathema is removed. The reason for this is that the anathema (that is, the expression "let him be anathema" for those who hold a doctrine contrary to that which was just defined) is an integral part of the definition. In fact, the obligation of holding the doctrine under pain of separation from the Catholic Church is one of the four conditions necessary for a definition to be an infallible act of the Church's extraordinary magisterium. If it was once an infallible act, it was because it had an anathema attached to it. If the anathema could in some way be removed, it would not be an infallible act, and in fact would never have been.

The anathemas solemnly proclaimed by the Sovereign Pontiffs and the ecumenical Councils of the Church have consequently not been abolished, nor can they be, and they exclude from membership in the Roman Catholic Church any person who falls under their condemnation and who becomes by the very fact a heretic.

—*Fr. Scott,* March 1998

Do similar abusive conditions exist in the Byzantine Rite as they do in the *Novus Ordo*? Can a traditional Roman Catholic safely satisfy his Sunday obligation attending the Byzantine Rite even though the Tridentine Mass is available to him?

In the Eastern countries, the priests have not (yet) been contaminated by the new theology of Vatican II, and thus there are no problems in attending the Eastern rites in such countries. In the Western countries, some of them have been undoubtedly contaminated with these new ideas, though one can still find many good priests in the Eastern Catholic Rites. The Eastern Catholic rites are good and have always been approved by the Church; one does satisfy one's Sunday obligation by going there.

Yet the Church does not favor changing rites, *i.e.*, passing from the Roman Rite to the Eastern Rite on a permanent basis. One born in the Roman Rite should, as far as possible, attend the Roman Rite, *i.e.*, the traditional Roman Catholic Mass.

—*Fr. Laisney,* January 1991

Are the Masses of Thuc-line priests valid, and can we assist at them?

I do not believe that there is a strong reason to doubt the validity of the episcopal consecrations performed by the exiled Vietnamese Archbishop Ngo Dinh Thuc. However, there are several lesser reasons that might be considered sufficient to establish some kind of positive doubt in the matter. These include the absence of correct witnesses during the original ceremony of consecration, which was done in private and in the middle of the night.

Also relevant is Thuc's confused mental state, as evidenced by his public concelebration of the New Mass with the local *Novus Ordo* bishop of the diocese of Toulon just one month before these consecrations in 1981. Also, the lack of conviction can be seen in the fact that twice he consecrated bishops illicitly, and twice he requested absolution from the canonical punishment of excommunication. These frequent changes indicate that he was a man who, to say the least, lacked conviction about what he was doing. This is further confirmed by his failure to join the *Coetus Internationalis Patrum*, the traditional group of bishops at Vatican II, and by a certain liberal tendency that he showed during the Council, speaking out against discrimination directed towards women and in favor of ecumenism. Consequently, although the logical thing would be to presume that he did have the intention of confecting the sacrament of holy orders, the absence of co-consecrators and of a clear purpose does open the door to some astonishment and doubt. Any doubt concerning the first bishops that he consecrated would clearly be passed on to any other bishops and priests ordained as a consequence.

The moral theologians say that we must hold to the *pars tutior*, or safer position, when it concerns the sacraments. Consequently, in case of doubt, it would not be permissible to go to these priests for the sacraments unless there was no other priest available and one was in danger of death.

However, even were there no doubt at all as to validity, it would still not be permissible to assist at the Masses and receive the sacraments from priests of the Thuc line. For they all hold to the radical sedevacantist position that there is no pope, and that if anybody says that there is a pope, or that he is in communion with the Holy Father, then he is in communion with a heretic and a heretic himself. By maintaining such a position, which makes no distinctions and takes no account of the confusion in the Church due to the breakdown of authority, they not only condemn every other Catholic to hell-fire but effectively separate themselves from all other Catholics and make themselves into a church of their own. They are truly schismatic. It is consequently entirely illicit to have any kind of association with them. As a consequence of their loss of the sense of the Church, they abandon all sense of hierarchy and structure in the Church. Any bishop can consecrate any other bishop at any time without any hierarchy of authority amongst them. These bishops constantly ordain to the priesthood men who have no preparation or training, who belong to no religious community, and who are consequently entirely independent of one another and all Church authority. Throwing all canonical norms out the window, they effectively become just as protestant as the modernists they pretend to defend the Church against.

—*Fr. Scott,* September 2000

 **I have been told that I have to accept my daughter's marriage, although she left the Catholic Church in which she was baptized and was married in a Protestant church, since the post-Vatican II Church says it is valid. Can you comment?**

The following principles will allow you to see how to act, despite the confusion of the liberal changes brought about in the Church's law since Vatican II.

PRINCIPLES:

• The revolutionary new canon of the 1983 Code of Canon Law that you refer to is Canon 1117, which states that those baptized Catholics who have abandoned the Catholic Church by a formal act (*i.e.*, formal apostates) are no longer bound to the canonical form of marriage, as they were previously. To the contrary, Canon 1099 of the 1917 Code of Canon Law states that all those who were once Catholics are bound to observe the canonical form of marriage, even if afterwards they abandon the Catholic Church.

• There can be no doubt that this canon is dangerous for the Faith, for it gives people to understand that a person, once a Catholic, can stop being a Catholic in the eyes of the Church. This is manifestly false, for those who are baptized in the Catholic Church are bound by their baptismal vows for the rest of their lives to live as Catholics. However, it is nowhere said, either in the new or in the 1917 Code, that a baptized Catholic can actually cease to be a Catholic before God.

• The 1983 Code does not indicate what a formal act of apostasy really is. Consequently, it must be interpreted in a strict sense. Examples of this would include a written statement saying explicitly that a person abandons all belief in the Catholic Church and its teachings. The difficulty of interpreting a ceremony of initiation in a Protestant church is that these ceremonies (such as altar calls) are very frequent and do not necessarily mean officially belonging to any particular church or denomination or holding to any particular set of beliefs. Consequently, they cannot be necessarily understood as a formal act of apostasy. Likewise, regular attendance at a Protestant church does not necessarily mean formally abandoning the Catholic Church.

APPLICATION:

• We are now in a position to answer your question. Your daughter, who has abandoned the practice of the Catholic religion, must always be considered, before God and the Church, as a Catholic, even though for the time being she is unfaithful to her religion and to her baptismal vows.

• Her marriage outside the Church, without dispensation from canonical form, eighteen months ago, must be considered invalid until proven otherwise, that is, until such time as the fact of a formal act of apostasy from the Catholic religion is established.

• Your daughter is consequently to be regarded as a fallen-away Catholic living in mortal sin. You cannot support or encourage her in this in any way, and in particular you cannot treat her as a married person, but as one living in concubinage.

• If your daughter now commits an act of formal apostasy, her marriage does not for that reason become valid. The validity or not depends upon her state at the time of marriage. The difficulty of determining this illustrates once more the imprudence of this law, in addition to its undermining of the oneness of the Catholic Church.

• Needless to say, it is by your prayers and your charity that you will convince her of the error of her ways and bring her back to our Lord Jesus Christ, His Church, and the Blessed Virgin Mary. Consequently, provided that there is no danger of scandal, and that she and her partner do not spend the night together under your roof, you can maintain contact with her.

—*Fr. Scott,* February 2000

Can St. Catherine of Siena, St. Teresa of Avila, and St. Thérèse of the Child Jesus be considered Doctors of the Church?

The term "Doctor of the Church" is a title of honor that was first attributed to those of the Fathers who were most eminent in the wisdom of their writings and the holiness of their lives. They were consequently extraordinary teachers of the Faith. The original, or great, Doctors were the four Western Doctors—St. Ambrose, St. Augustine, St. Jerome, and St. Gregory the Great; and the four Eastern Doctors—St. Athanasius, St. Basil the Great, St. Gregory of Nazianzen, and St. John Chrysostom.

Additional Doctors have been declared over the centuries, and it was Pope Benedict XIV who laid down the three conditions for such a proclamation: *eminens doctrina, insignis vitae sanctitas, Ecclesiae declaratio*, that is, eminent learning, a high degree of sanctity, and the express declaration of the Church, as Pope Pius XI reiterated at the time of the proclamation of St. John of the Cross as Doctor of the Universal Church in 1926 (*Die Vicesima Septima*). The theologians add that there is a fourth and presumed condition, namely, the orthodoxy of faith (*cf.* Zubizarreta, I, 692).

The Catholic Encyclopedia (1913) has this to say about the conferring of the title Doctor of the Church before Vatican II:

In practice the procedure consists in extending to the Universal Church the use of the Office and Mass of a saint in which the title of Doctor is applied to him. The decree is issued by the Congregation of Sacred Rites and approved by the pope, after a careful examination, if necessary, of the saint's writings. It is not in any way an *ex cathedra* decision, nor does it even amount to a declaration that no error is to be found in the teaching of the Doctor. It is, indeed, well known that the very greatest of them are not wholly immune from error. No martyr has ever been included in the list, since the Office and Mass are for Confessors. (V, 75)

It is not surprising that most of the early Doctors were bishops since the bishops make up the *Ecclesia docens*, the teaching Church, whereas the rest of us make up the *Ecclesia discens*, the Church inasmuch as it is taught or instructed. The reason for this distinction is that the bishops alone have the official function to teach the deposit of the faith, whereas the rest of us have the duty to learn and keep it. It is certainly understandable that the concept of Doctor would be enlarged to also include priests who were saints, for priests participate in the bishops' teaching role. Thus St. Jerome, a Father of the Church, is included, and also other priests such as St. John of the Cross, St. Thomas Aquinas, St. Bernard, and St. Anthony of Padua. It is also reasonable that St. Ephraem, who was a deacon, would also be included. All are Confessors, and the liturgical privileges of Doctors can be applied even to those who are not Pontiffs.

However, the post-Vatican II idea of including these very great women saints in the list of Doctors is a novelty. Liturgically they are not Confessors but Virgins, nor can they be treated as Confessors, for the public teaching of the Faith is not something that can be delegated to women, according to St. Paul: "Let women keep silence in the churches: for it is not permitted them to speak, but to be subject, as also the law saith. But if they would learn anything, let them ask their husbands at home. For it is a shame for a woman to speak in the church" (I Cor 14:34-35).

This being said, it is nevertheless manifestly obvious that the lives of these three great women fulfil all four conditions laid down for the proclamation of a Doctor of the Church, and that they played no less of a leadership rôle for the Universal Church than St. Joan of Arc did for France. No Catholic can doubt their orthodoxy nor their sanctity. Moreover, if they did not have the eminent book learning of sacred theology that is generally associated with a Doctor of the Church, they most assuredly did have infused knowledge from God, allowing their words and writings to make a profound impact on the history and development of the Church.

Furthermore, it must be remembered that there was nothing feminist about these great saints, whose every action defending the Church's magisterial teaching authority, whether it be St. Catherine of Siena encouraging Pope Gregory XI to return to Rome, St. Teresa of Avila laying down the principles of the mystical life and the Carmelite reform for both men and women, or St. Thérèse of the Child Jesus opening up to all souls the little way of childlike abandonment by the incredible story of her soul, thus becoming the patroness of the missions.

We could legitimately ask the question why clergymen would feel the need to expand the notion of a Doctor to include women, and whether there is in this desire a deep-seated influence from the feminist egalitarianism that is one aspect of the post-conciliar revolution in the Church. It certainly seems that this is the real motivation. However, the right of the Church to extend the concept of "Doctor" in an analogical sense to those who share the necessary qualities but who are not actually Confessors, that is, public teachers, but Virgins, cannot be denied. The term "Doctor" still retains a very real meaning, even if the differences, as in every analogy, are greater than the similarity.

This is what is meant by Pope John Paul II in his apostolic letter of October 19, 1997, *Divini Amoris Scientia*, which admits that "in the writings of Thérèse of Lisieux we do not find, perhaps, as in other Doctors, a scholarly presentation of the things of God" (§7) but nevertheless declares that the eminence of her teaching concerning the spiritual life is the basis for this honor: "From careful study of the writings of St. Thérèse of the Child Jesus and from the resonance they have had in the Church, salient aspects can be noted of her 'eminent doctrine,' which is the fundamental element for conferring the title of Doctor of the Church" (*ibid.*). He makes a comparison with the proclamation of St. Catherine of Siena as Doctor of the Church by Pope Paul VI in 1970:

> We can apply to Thérèse of Lisieux what my Predecessor, Paul VI, said of another young Saint and Doctor of the Church, Catherine of Siena: "What strikes us most about the Saint is her infused wisdom, that is to say, her lucid, profound, and inebriating absorption of the divine truths and mysteries of faith...." (*Ibid.*)

We can certainly accept the proclamation of these great saints as Doctors, for as Pope John Paul II says of St. Thérèse, she "appears as an authentic teacher of faith and the Christian life" (*Divini Amoris Scientia*, §8). However, we must be aware that we are not using this term in the same way as it is used to indicate Doctors who are Confessors, whether Pontiffs or not. When applied to a Doctor who is a Virgin, it takes on an analogical and quite different sense to that which it has for a Doctor who is a Confessor. These holy Virgins taught despite themselves, moved by divine inspiration, without having any pretense of having the public function of doing so. Furthermore, these Doctor Virgins can clearly not be assimilated to Doctor Confessors in the texts of the liturgy. However, it is in the liturgical offices that the practical consequences of the title of "Doctor" are most felt, hence the bizarreness of Doctor Virgins, for whom there is no place in the traditional Mass.

—*Fr. Scott,* August 2002

 **A priest told me that cremation is acceptable as long as the body is at the funeral, and that after the Requiem Mass the body can be cremated. Please advise.**

It is false to affirm that cremation is acceptable provided that the body is present at the funeral.

The traditional laws of the Church are very explicit on this point. Those who have ordered their bodies to be cremated are to be refused a Church burial unless they have given some sign of repentance (Can. 1240, §1, 5). This means that they must be refused any kind of Requiem Mass or public ceremony, even an anniversary Mass (Can. 1241). The reason for this strict rule lies in the fact that the Freemasons and enemies of the Church who do not believe in the resurrection of the body have encouraged this practice as a practical denial of respect due to the body as the temple of the Holy Ghost which will rise again on the last day. It is a pagan practice which is abhorrent to the sacredness of the Catholic life.

It is true that this rule was relaxed as early as 1963, during Vatican II. The 1983 Code of Canon Law reflects this change by stating that Catholic burial is only to be refused to those people who have chosen cremation for reasons opposed to the Christian Faith (Can. 1184, §1, 2). This ambiguous expression opened the door to cremation on demand, with the subsequent lack of respect for the body, sealed with the Holy Trinity in baptism.

However, the question is a moot question. For the conciliar church has abandoned Requiem Masses altogether, and not just for those who are to be cremated. Here lies the real tragedy, that the sacrifice of the Mass is no longer being offered for the repose of the poor souls suffering in purgatory.

As far as true Catholics are concerned, cremation is not an acceptable practice, except in extreme cases of danger due to plague or other infectious disease. It must still be regarded as a practical denial of Catholic dogma concerning the body as the temple of the Holy Ghost and the resurrection of the body. Traditional priests must consequently refuse Catholic burial services and the Requiem Mass to all those people who have ordered that their bodies be cremated. Furthermore, traditional Catholics have the duty to explain this to their relatives, so that they may not be in a position of having to implement cremation or to refuse the Requiem Mass.

—*Fr. Scott,* February, 1999

 **Nuns nowadays are difficult to recognize. Many of them dress in street clothes. How is that to be explained?**

The disregard for the religious habit in the present day is a great scandal. The fact that it is the religious themselves who manifest the greatest contempt makes for no little confusion in the Church. Both the Brothers and Sisters, along with the priests, seem only to wear their religious garb when it is to their convenience or profit. They will doubtlessly appear in habit for a public function where they are "expected to look the part." For example, at a recent canonization ceremony in Rome a nun took her place in what was to be the recognition of a *beata* who was supposed to be one of her Sisters. At the end of the events of the day she had only slighting remarks concerning the "heat" and the "discomfort" of wearing the habit. Needless to say, she returned promptly to her street clothes.

A religious habit serves a double function. Firstly, it reminds the wearer of his obligations resulting from his vows of religion—namely, poverty, chastity, and obedience. This, by far, is its most important influence. It reminds the religious—"*noblesse oblige.*"

Recalling the fact that the Church is a visible society, the habit serves a second use. Outward signs and symbols are utilized continually by her. She requires that in the hierarchy of her members all remember their position, and that some are to be paid more respect due to their place in the Mystical Body of Christ. Only an egalitarian spirit would not see the usefulness of this requirement. Because of this obligation certain members are to present themselves as befits their position. Among these are those individuals who have consecrated themselves completely to our divine Lord. The Church has always, and will always, hold in esteem such people. They have chosen the most perfect path in imitation of Our Lord and His Blessed Mother. This being so, they have the reciprocal obligation to manifest this consecration outwardly—hence, in dress. The respect paid to them is primarily to God Almighty, who has given them the grace to walk in such a state of life.

For this reason, those modern day religious who say that they are "no different from anyone else" or that the respect paid to their state is "against humility" have no understanding of the Church's mind. In practice, they choose this position as a means to move about doing whatever they feel like, in many cases causing scandal. They wish to imitate the Incarnate Word of God and live in the world simultaneously. They desire to have the benefits of being a member of the laity and the honor of being a religious. They want to have their cake and eat it too. Our reaction, in turn, should be that any religious who does not want to be recognized as such should be treated like everyone else.

—*Fr. Doran,* November 1992

 ### Father, can we give any credence to the opinion that Cardinal Siri was the pope?

No, not at all. If, *per impossibile,* he had been pope, he was the worst pope in the whole history of the Church! Indeed, if he had been pope, then the last three or four popes were anti-popes and he, the pope, would have submitted to their authority and reforms. Do not forget that Cardinal Siri implemented the reforms of Vatican II, including the reformed liturgy, in his diocese in Genoa; he himself said the New Mass. Had he been the pope, he did nothing to save the Church from the destructive actions of an anti-pope but even co-operated with the latter, saying the Mass according to the rite reformed (and deformed) by an anti-pope! Even the supposition is absolutely incredible.

Archbishop Lefebvre met him several times and never did Cardinal Siri tell him of any claim that he was the pope.

Moreover, he nominated no cardinals, so that it would now be impossible, after his death, for any other pope to be elected. Some are looking for cardinals named *in pectore,* that is, in secret by him. However, their claims would be impossible to verify, and they would thus be incapable of making an election acceptable to the faithful. This would, rather, open doors for opportunists and interminable contentions.

Some poor faithful fall into such errors because they are an apparently easy way to rationalize the crisis in the Church. All the different sedevacantist positions come from this desire to rationalize the present crisis. This desire is sometimes allied with bitter zeal or with some kind of despair. That the successor of St. Peter organized a meeting such as the one held as Assisi is certainly mind-boggling. To judge him immediately as not being the pope is an apparently easy solution but, in fact, it destroys the visibility of the Church.

Our Lord on the cross was disfigured and almost unrecognizable, as is the Church today because of the modernists, but He was still visible!

Some sedevacantists go so far as to prevent the faithful from attending traditional Masses offered by priests who recognize the pope, such as Society of St. Pius X priests. By their fruits you shall know them. To deprive these souls of the traditional Mass is a most grievous (and bitter) fruit.

The Society of St. Pius X rejects sedevacantism.

—*Fr. Laisney,* October 1990

ABOUT ARCHBISHOP LEFEBVRE AND THE SOCIETY OF SAINT PIUS X

How could Archbishop Lefebvre have signed the documents of Vatican II?

The Archbishop himself constantly and repeatedly stated that he signed all but two documents, but did not sign the two worst documents, namely, those on religious liberty (*Dignitatis Humanae*) and the Church in the modern world (*Gaudium et Spes*). When it was pointed out that his signature was on these documents, he responded that it was the list of the bishops present for the vote that he signed, but not the documents themselves.

Bishop Tissier de Mallerais, in his biography of the Archbishop (*Marcel Lefebvre,* pp. 312-313), maintains that he had a memory lapse and that he did in fact sign those documents but afterwards forgot about it. Although this would be comprehensible after a twenty-year interval, it does seem a little surprising to affirm that the Archbishop would have erred on such an important point. Nevertheless, whatever it was that he signed (and it may not have been clear to the bishops at the time), it is certainly true that he continued voting against these two documents every time they were presented until the very day of their promulgation.

Be that as it may, the signing of these documents, if it did actually take place, can easily be understood. For the Archbishop did not state that Vatican II was openly and explicitly heretical, but simply that it contained dangerous errors that favored heresy. It was for this reason that he was willing to accept Vatican II "interpreted in the light of Tradition"—which means excluding those errors that are contrary to the Church's magisterial teaching (such as religious liberty and ecumenism). Consequently, it would not have been in contradiction with his principles to have signed documents that could be "interpreted in the light of Tradition." This is the explanation of his certainly having signed other documents that also contain errors, such as *Dei Verbum,* which contains serious errors on the sources of revelation, and *Lumen*

Gentium, which contains serious errors on the Church. Furthermore, the fact that he constantly and unchangingly stood up against the errors of Vatican II from the very time of the Council indicates that he cannot be incriminated for a moment in adhering to these errors or professing his faith in an ambiguous manner. The question of whether or not he actually signed these documents is, consequently, a rather irrelevant historical detail.

—*Fr. Scott*, September 2006

 **Some Catholics are disturbed by the election of one of the Society's bishops as superior general. They have read that a superior general has jurisdiction, and they have also read elsewhere that the Society's bishops would be schismatic if they claimed to have jurisdiction. Is it not a schismatic act to elect a bishop as superior general?**

In 1994, His Excellency Bishop Bernard Fellay, one of the four bishops consecrated by Archbishop Lefebvre, was elected as superior general of the Society of St. Pius X.

The priests of the Society who elected him were perfectly well aware of the distinction between the power of orders and the power of jurisdiction, and that the power of jurisdiction can only be conferred by the Sovereign Pontiff. They were also perfectly well aware that Archbishop Lefebvre in no way pretended to bestow any jurisdiction on the bishops, and that he consecrated them for the use of the power of orders:

> This is why we have chosen, with the grace of God, priests from our Society who have seemed to us to be the most apt, whilst being in circumstances and in functions which permit them more easily to fulfill their episcopal ministry, to give Confirmation to your children, and to be able to confer ordinations in our various seminaries. (Sermon of June 30, 1988)

It is certainly true that Archbishop Lefebvre thought it best, in 1988, not to consecrate the superior general as one of the bishops. The above statement indicates a practical reason why he thought it less appropriate. He probably also considered it more prudent, in 1988, not to confuse the two responsibilities: that of governing the Society and the sacramental functions of the episcopacy. He might have feared that it could have been falsely construed as the giving of jurisdiction if he were to have consecrated the superior general as a bishop.

However, this was a judgment of prudence. In 1994 circumstances were different. If the priests of the Society chose Bishop Fellay to succeed Fr. Franz Schmidberger as superior general, it was not because he was a bishop. It was because they were convinced of Bishop Fellay's many exceptional qualities, especially his holiness, his quiet prudence, his thorough penetration with the spirit of our founder. They could have chosen any experienced Society priest, and they did. They chose the one the most apt for the position. He just happened to be the priest whose qualities Archbishop Lefebvre had already discerned in choosing him to be one of the bishops. This was not imprudent since it had become perfectly clear over the previous six years that the Society's bishops did not claim any territorial jurisdiction, but in fact shared equally through the entire world the work of confirming the faithful who requested it and ordaining priests to provide them with the sacraments and the holy sacrifice of the Mass.

There is no contradiction in a bishop's fulfilling a post which is normally occupied by a priest. The closest example of that was Archbishop Lefebvre himself. For six years he was superior general of the Holy Ghost Fathers, a position which was normally held by a priest, and which gave him no episcopal, territorial jurisdiction, for he had no diocese.

It is certainly true that the superior general of an approved, exempt religious congregation does have jurisdiction, which he receives from the pope. This is explained in Canon 501, §1 of the 1917 Code of Canon Law and Canon 617 of the 1983 Code. However, it must be understood that this is not a territorial jurisdiction, and is neither exercised over a region nor over the faithful. Moreover, it is not the jurisdiction of a bishop, or local ordinary, over his flock, but one that a simple priest can (and usually does) hold. It is called a domestic jurisdiction, and only refers to those people who are members of the community or live the common life in the houses of the community. It gives him the authority to govern his community, within the limits of his office, and to authorize member confessors to hear confessions of other members. It gives him no authority over the faithful.

The Society claims that its suppression in 1976 was illegitimate and consequently invalid. It also claims to be of Pontifical Right, because it was allowed in the early 1970's to incardinate member priests directly. This means that they did not have to belong to a diocese or religious community, which is tantamount to recognition of Pontifical Right. The consequence would be that the superior general, priest or bishop, has a domestic jurisdiction over the Society's members, and over those only, and not over any of the faithful, except those who might be living in the Society's houses. Modernist canonists, who accept the legitimacy of the Society's suppression, will deny this domestic jurisdiction.

However, this is entirely irrelevant to the question of whether the Society is schismatic. For this jurisdiction has nothing to do with the territorial jurisdiction that schismatics claim to have, maintaining their independence from the Sovereign Pontiff, source of all ordinary jurisdiction.

The dispute as to whether or not, technically, the superior general has domestic jurisdiction over the Society's priests and bishops in no way affects their apostolate, which is based upon supplied jurisdiction. For the Society's apostolic work with the faithful is entirely founded upon the need which the faithful have for the traditional Mass and sacraments, and the complete and entire handing down of Catholic Tradition and doctrine. Neither priests nor bishops nor the superior general claim to have the authority to govern, in the name of the Church, any area of the world or any group of faithful.

Consequently, the fact that the priest elected as superior general in 1994 also happened to be a bishop is entirely accidental to the Society's status within the Church. This is notwithstanding occasional articles previous to this election, which used the fact that the previous superior general was not consecrated a bishop as proof that the Society's bishops were not claiming jurisdiction. The above explanation shows that this is not a relevant argument, except inasmuch as the Society's superior general, whether bishop or simple priest, has never pretended to have ordinary jurisdiction over the faithful who attend the Masses celebrated by the Society's priests.

There is consequently no break at all with the position of Archbishop Lefebvre, who had this to say to the bishops he was to consecrate:

> Hence we declare our attachment and our submission to the Holy See and to the Pope. In accomplishing this act of consecration we are aware of continuing our service to the Church and to the papacy exactly as we have striven to do ever since the first day of our priesthood. The day when the Vatican will be delivered from this occupation by Modernists and will come back to the path followed by the Church down to Vatican II, our new bishops will put themselves entirely in the hands of our Sovereign Pontiff, to the point of desisting if he so wishes from the exercise of their episcopal functions. (Oct. 19, 1983; *The Angelus*, July 1988, p. 37)

—*Fr. Scott*, May 1999

 **What is the tenure of the superior general of the Society of St. Pius X? Do the rules allow him to be re-elected? Is a district superior assigned for a specific number of years and, if so, what length of time?**

The superior general, along with his two assistants, are elected by the general chapter for twelve years. These may be re-elected. A district superior is named by the superior general, after consultation with his assistants in council, for six years.

—*Fr. Doran*, January 1993

 **If carrying the crosier is a sign of jurisdiction, why do the bishops of the Society of St. Pius X, who claim no jurisdiction, carry it?**

In heraldry the crosier is an external ornament to the shield and not to be confused with the processional cross of an archbishop. The crosier is, as it has always been, the pastoral staff, a sign of episcopal dignity and traceable to the fourth century and used by abbots in the fifth.

The crosier is thus an ecclesiastical ornament conferred on bishops at their consecration, or on mitred abbots at the investiture, and used in the performing of certain solemn and sacred functions.

It is also a symbol of authority and jurisdiction.

The notion is unambiguously expressed in the rite of episcopal consecration in the Roman Pontifical, 77: "Receive the staff of your pastoral office, *etc.*" It is then, as Durandus comments, "borne by prelates to signify their authority to correct vices, stimulate piety, administer punishment, and thus rule and govern with a gentleness that is tempered with severity" (*The Catholic Encyclopedia* (1913), IV, 515).

Cardinal Bona in his *Rerum Liturgiarum*, XXIV, says that the crosier is to bishops what the scepter is to kings. In regard to this symbolism, bishops always carry the crosier with the crook turned outwards while lower prelates hold it towards themselves.

The crosier has many functions: a sign of the bishop's pastoral solicitude over his flock, an ecclesiastical ornament in important sacred liturgical functions, a sign of authority and jurisdiction.

The bishops of the Society of St. Pius X have no *ordinary* jurisdiction, *i.e.*, no jurisdiction attached to their office and as of right, flowing from that office. They have never claimed, in fact deny, such an authority to govern by virtue of their office; they have no diocese to govern and do not establish parallel structures of jurisdiction, recognizing thereby the legitimate authority of the local ordinary appointed by the Holy See. They are bishops in a time of unprecedented crisis and confusion both doctrinal and moral.

They possess, however, an undoubted moral authority over those who seek their guidance and pastoral care and furthermore enjoy supplied jurisdiction in the light of the evident collapse of faith and virtual apostasy in the Catholic world at large. The legislator of the Code of Canon Law has not foreseen the circumstances of the present emergency. Since there is no express law concerning the grave situation, the rule must be taken from laws promulgated for similar circumstances, the general principles of canon law itself, and recourse to the mind of the legislator, who never wants his legislation to be too burdensome.

Should the present difficulties in the Church be ignored, minimized, or even trivialized, then a refusal to apply the mercy and goodness of the Church will follow. The Church supplies jurisdiction for the spiritual good of the faithful. This jurisdiction is possessed by our bishops and priests.

There is, therefore, no conflict between the carrying of the crosier and supplied, extraordinary jurisdiction which comes not from the hierarchy, normally its legitimate channels, but from the Church herself. What matters is the good of the faithful, the salvation of souls being the supreme law. This topic is well discussed in an *Angelus* supplement on supplied jurisdiction, "Supplied Jurisdiction and Traditional Priests," written by His Excellency Bishop Tissier de Mallerais.

—*Fr. Boyle,* May 1995

What do the bishops of the Society of St. Pius X do?

In his sermon for the consecration of the four bishops, on June 30, 1988, Archbishop Lefebvre explained very clearly the state of necessity in which Tradition existed then—and still exists now. It was as a consequence of the state of necessity that he stated:

> I think it is my duty to provide the means of doing that which I shall call "Operation Survival"....If I had made this deal with Rome, by continuing with the agreements we had signed, and by putting them into practice, I would have performed "Operation Suicide." There was no choice, we must live!

Unable to confer upon them the power of jurisdiction, Archbishop Lefebvre was nevertheless able to confer the fullness of the power of holy orders so that they could fulfill an episcopal ministry, "to give Confirmation to your children, and to be able to confer ordinations in our various seminaries." These are the two sacraments that the four bishops have constantly administered ever since, thus guaranteeing the continuing of the work of Tradition, of the Society of St. Pius X, and insuring that it would never be watered down, absorbed by, or taken over by the modernist infiltration in the Church. As the Archbishop himself stated on June 30, 1988:

> When God calls me—this will certainly not be long—from whom would these seminarians receive the Sacrament of Orders? From conciliar bishops who, due to their doubtful intentions, confer doubtful sacraments? This is not possible.

However, the function of the bishops of the Society of St. Pius X is not limited to the simple administration of the two sacraments of confirmation and holy orders. There are many pontifical blessings and consecrations in the Church's liturgy that are reserved to bishops, and these they regularly perform, such as the consecration of the holy oils used for the sacraments of baptism, confirmation, holy orders, and extreme unction; the consecration of chalices, altar stones, and churches; and the consecration of holy virgins.

Moreover, through reception of the fullness of the power of holy orders they receive a radical power to teach and to govern the flock of Christ, even before a special portion is entrusted to them by ordinary jurisdiction, which can only be done by the Sovereign Pontiff. However, although the Society's bishops have not received this jurisdiction, they still retain their responsibility for the Catholic Church of which they are bishops. As Pope Pius XII stated in the encyclical *Fidei Donum* of 1957, a Catholic bishop is "as successor of the Apostles, jointly responsible for the common good of the Church." This is what Archbishop Lefebvre explained on June 30, 1988: "I am simply a bishop of the Catholic Church, who is continuing to transmit Catholic doctrine." It is precisely because of his teaching and Catholic principles, reiterating what the Church has always done, that traditional Catholics listened to him and followed his leadership and direction. In so doing, he exercised a supplied jurisdiction to teach and to govern, the jurisdiction being supplied to him by the need of the faithful.

Bishop de Castro Mayer explained likewise, at the episcopal consecrations of 1988, that his presence was the exercise of his power to teach, an obligation for him as a Catholic bishop:

> My presence here at this ceremony is caused by a duty of conscience: that of making a profession of Catholic Faith in front of the whole Church... because the conservation of the priesthood and the Holy Mass is at stake, and in spite of the requests and pressures of many, I am here in order to accomplish my duty: to make a public profession of Faith.

The four bishops they consecrated have exactly the same power and functions as bishops of the Catholic Church. Thus it is that the Regulations of the Society of St. Pius X state that the bishops of the Society, devoid of all territorial jurisdiction, have, nevertheless, the necessary supplied jurisdiction to exercise the powers that are attached to the episcopal office and certain acts belonging to the ordinary episcopal jurisdiction.

Two such episcopal functions were created already in 1991 and have functioned ever since, to the great benefit of the traditional movement, namely, the Canonical Commission, headed by His Excellency Bishop Tissier de Mallerais, and the bishop responsible for religious, who is presently His Excellency Bishop de Galarreta. It was Archbishop Lefebvre himself who requested these, in a letter dated January 15, 1991:

> As long as the present Roman authorities are steeped in Ecumenism and Modernism and seeing that all their decisions and the 1983 Code

of Canon Law are influenced by these false principles, it will be necessary to form authorities of supplied jurisdiction that will faithfully preserve
the Catholic principles of Catholic Tradition and Catholic Canon Law.
It is the only way of remaining faithful to Our Lord Jesus Christ, to the
Apostles, to the deposit of Faith that was handed down to their legitimate
successors who remained faithful until Vatican II.

The bishops of the Society of St. Pius X are consequently bishops in
every sense of the word, although they lack ordinary jurisdiction. They
fulfill the function of sanctifying through the sacraments of confirmation
and holy orders, the function of teaching wherever they preach the entire
Catholic faith as bishops of the Catholic Church, and the function of
governing inasmuch as they are called on by necessity to resolve difficult
questions.

—*Fr. Scott,* July 2008

 ### Does the disobedience of the 1988 episcopal consecrations constitute a schismatic act?

The consecration of the bishops was not an act of disobedience at
all, but, to the contrary, an act of the most painful and exact obedience,
which virtue sometimes requires obedience "to God rather than men"
(Acts 5:29) who contradict Him, as the apostles answered the high priest,
and which virtue sometimes requires that one resist the highest abuse of
authority, as St. Paul did to St. Peter, the first pope: "But when Cephas
was come to Antioch, I withstood him to the face, because he was to be
blamed" (Gal. 2:13).

The apostolic mandate, read as a part of the ceremony of the consecration of bishops, confirms that it was not at all an act of disobedience,
but, to the contrary, an act of obedience to the Church:

> We have this mandate from the Roman Church, always faithful to the
> Holy Tradition which She has received from the Holy Apostles. This Holy
> Tradition is the deposit of Faith which the Church orders us to faithful-
> ly transmit to all men for the salvation of their souls. Since the Second
> Vatican Council until this day, the authorities of the Roman Church are
> animated by the spirit of modernism. They have acted contrary to Holy
> Tradition....

However, even if the consecration of bishops were an act of disobedience, it would not follow that it is schismatic. The question of whether or
not it was a schismatic act is an entirely different one. Schism is defined in
the Code of Canon Law as the refusal to submit to the Sovereign Pontiff
or the refusal of communion with the members of the Church who are
subject to him (Can. 1325, §2 of the 1917 Code and Can. 751 of the
1983 Code). Disobedience, real or apparent, is consequently not the same

thing as schism. In the same way as a child who refuses to obey his father when he orders him to steal candy from the store practices a true virtue of obedience (to God rather than men), nor does he in any way deny that his father is truly his father, so likewise do the episcopal consecrations not at all imply the rejection of the authority of the Holy Father, nor a refusal to submit to it. There is one clear proof of schism, and it exists when a bishop claims for himself jurisdiction over a portion of the Church. It is because all authority in the Church flows from the pope that this is a direct refusal of the pope's universal authority to govern the Church. This the bishops of the Society have never done, never claiming anything but a supplied jurisdiction, coming from the need of the faithful.

Consequently, Pope John Paul II was quite simply in error when he claimed, on July 2, 1988, that the episcopal consecrations were an act of disobedience such as to imply in practice the rejection of the Roman primacy and to constitute a schismatic act. Much to the contrary, it was because of Archbishop Lefebvre's unshakable belief in Roman primacy that he held to the constant, repeated, infallible teachings of the popes who condemned for two centuries the errors later adopted by Vatican II. This is true obedience and true communion with the Church.

However, there is a reason for every assertion, and there was a clear reason why it was that Pope John Paul II accused this act of being schismatic. It was because he had an entirely different notion of tradition. For the Catholic, Apostolic Tradition is one of the two sources of divine revelation. It has as its objective content the deposit of the faith, unchanged since the death of the last of the apostles, that it transmits down to us.

Not so for modernists, for whom "tradition" is a subjective, evolving, changing experience of how the Faith is lived in every moment of the Church's history. This is what St. Pius X had to say in 1907 in the encyclical *Pascendi*: "Tradition, as understood by the Modernists, is a communication with others of an original experience...stimulating the religious sense...renewing the experience once acquired" (§15). It cannot, therefore, be the simple passing down of a fixed truth, but rather the living of a communicated personal experience, as a consequence of which St. Pius X says: "Thus we are once more led to infer that all existing religions are equally true, for otherwise they would not survive" (*ibid.*).

Ecumenism is the immediate consequence of this new notion of tradition that approves every religious experience. Thus it is that Pope John Paul II in *Ecclesia Dei Adflicta* states that "the root of this schismatic act can be discerned in an incomplete and contradictory notion of Tradition." He considers that Archbishop Lefebvre's notion of Tradition is incomplete because it is not "living," meaning that it is not an experience, allowing for the possibility of evolution, change, and adaptation to the times. It is simply a transmission. He considers that it is "contradictory" because it goes against collegiality that is the present teaching of Rome and the bishops, which is an essential part of the modern-day experience that they call tradition. It was, consequently, precisely because he adhered to what the Church has always taught that Archbishop Lefebvre was condemned as being schismatic.

Can one be schismatic for refusing the modernist notion of tradition condemned by St. Pius X? Clearly not. Can one be schismatic for believing in the unchanging, objective nature of the Catholic Faith, as always taught? Clearly not. Can one be schismatic for refusing to obey the destruction of the Faith and the Church? Clearly not. Can one be schismatic for standing up to a pope who has become the instrument of the liberalism and modernism so often condemned by more than two centuries of popes? Clearly not.

—*Fr. Scott,* July 2008

 **Many priests seem to use varying rubrics in offering Mass. Your calendar for the general public promulgates the rubrics of John XXIII. What does the SSPX use?**

The International Society of St. Pius X uses officially the rubrics and liturgical books of 1962, therefore promulgated by Pope John XXIII.

—*Fr. Doran,* September 1992

 **At the beginning of the Canon of the Mass we pray for our pope and our bishop. Which bishop do we pray for? Do we pray for the bishop of our diocese, or a Society bishop, or the repose of the soul of Archbishop Lefebvre?**

All must pray for the local ordinary, that is, the diocesan bishop. This regulation is even for exempt religious, who are not immediately connected to the bishop. The ordinary is the head of the local church and as such the direct link with the Church Universal. Prayer for these individuals manifests the hierarchical nature of the Church. It is not a statement of worthiness of the man.

The Society bishops do not have, nor claim to have, any ordinary jurisdiction. They head no local churches. Their consecrations were to ensure the continuance of the traditional sacraments. We should pray for them (the tasks they have undertaken for our spiritual welfare are difficult) but not as the local ordinary. We should pray for both the repose of the Archbishop's soul and for a speedy recognition of his glory!

—*Fr. Doran,* May 1993

Why do Masses in the churches of the Society of St. Pius X have an additional *Confiteor* before Holy Communion?

St. Pius X in his bull *Quo Primum* in 1570, codifying the Tridentine Mass, included an additional *Confiteor* before Holy Communion in those Masses in which Holy Communion was to be administered to the faithful. In so doing, he accepted a custom that was already immemorial. However, it is certainly true that in the ancient Roman rite there was no additional *Confiteor* before Communion, but simply the two confessions at the beginning of Mass, one for the priest and the other for the ministers and faithful. The incorporation of an additional *Confiteor* derived from the ceremony of Holy Communion outside Mass, where such a confession is prescribed. Custom then introduced this ceremony into Masses in which Holy Communion was administered.

We can certainly understand how providential is the prayer of the *Confiteor* before Communion, and why the faithful have always appreciated it. It expresses the duty of examining one's conscience before approaching to receive Holy Communion and is a reminder that those who are unworthy because of mortal sin must not receive Holy Communion. It is also a very salutary reminder for all Catholics that we ought to have a profound sorrow for our venial sins, deliberate or not, and that it is only through this contrition that Holy Communion can become, as defined by the Council of Trent, "an antidote, whereby we may be freed from daily faults and be preserved from mortal sins" (Session XIII, 2; Dz. 875).

One of the changes introduced by Pope John XXIII in 1960 was the omission of this additional *Confiteor*. The Society priests are consequently accused of mixing rites and showing an arbitrariness in picking and choosing what pleases them, given that they use the rubrics of 1960 but maintain also the *Confiteor* before Holy Communion.

In fact, there is no arbitrariness at all, nor the presumption of picking and choosing amongst the rubrics. Far from it. It is a question of custom, which has force of law if it is reasonable and it has been constantly observed for the required period of time (forty years in the 1917 Code and thirty years in the 1983 Code). In fact, this practice is a custom which is centennial and immemorial, having been constantly practiced for at least five centuries.

If custom is a source of law in every area of Church discipline, it is particularly the case with the liturgy, the prescriptions of which are not contained in the Church's canon law. Provided that such customs have not been explicitly reproved, it is up to the local ordinary to judge whether they are to be retained or not (Can. 5 of the 1917 & 1983 Codes). Moreover, general laws (*e.g.*, omission of the additional *Confiteor*) do not abolish particular customs, nor do they abolish centennial or im-memorial customs, unless they make explicit mention of it (Can. 30 of the 1917 Code and Can. 28 of the 1983 Code). Such is the case of the particular custom in the churches of the Society of St. Pius X of retaining the additional *Confiteor*.

It must be remembered that this custom did not come into existence by anybody's arbitrary decision but by the general observance of the great majority of traditional Catholics. Just as the 1960 rubrical changes were generally accepted by traditional Catholics the world over, not bringing about any substantial change in the Tridentine Mass, so likewise was the abolition of the final *Confiteor* not generally accepted. This became a question of a particular custom, to maintain the centennial practice approved and accepted by St. Pius V.

All that the Society did was to acknowledge this general custom and thus explain that it had become a particular law in its churches. This was done by Archbishop Lefebvre in Ecône, Switzerland, on September 21, 1979, meeting with his council, stating that since this practice already existed in many priories in different countries, all ought henceforth to conform to this custom in all the Society's houses and chapels. As superior general, he had the ordinary authority over the priest-members of the Society to permit that such a custom be recognized as law.

—*Fr. Scott,* November 2006

 ### Why is the second *Confiteor* omitted from the missal published by Angelus Press?

The 1962 *Roman Catholic Daily Missal* published by Angelus Press in January 2005 is essentially a re-typeset version of the *Ideal Missal* of 1962 with the addition of certain commentaries and prayers. The publisher did not make any modification to the rubrics of the Mass, as published on July 25, 1960.

In these rubrics of 1960 the second *Confiteor*, the one immediately preceding the Holy Communion of the faithful, was abolished. The reason for this abolition was that it was a late introduction into the Mass (sixteenth century) from the ceremony of administration of Holy Communion outside of the Mass. It is certainly true that the second *Confiteor* is not necessary to the integrity of the Mass, being simply a repetition of what the altar boy recited at the beginning of the Mass.

In the first years of the Society of St. Pius X, the second *Confiteor* was not recited, in accordance with the rubrics. However, the universal custom beforehand was to recite the second *Confiteor*. This universal custom was maintained even after the introduction of the rubrical changes of 1960. The reason for this can easily be understood. It is a perfect preparation for Holy Communion, and it helps the faithful to examine their conscience to determine if their soul is in the state of grace, in order to receive worthily the Most Blessed Sacrament and, if it is, to renew their sorrow for the deliberate venial sins that could be an obstacle to the reception of grace from Holy Communion.

In the Church, custom has force of law unless it is expressly reproved (*cf.* Cans. 5, 28, and 30 of the 1917 Code). Archbishop Lefebvre, then superior general of the Society of St. Pius X, acknowledged the universality of this custom of reciting the second *Confiteor* before Holy Communion and in 1978 determined that the priests of the Society of St. Pius X would follow this universal custom amongst traditional Catholics.

However, this being said, the Society of St. Pius X has no authority to modify the Church's liturgical books, nor does it pretend to do so. This is why Angelus Press did not modify this rubric in the publication of its 1962 *Roman Catholic Daily Missal.*

—Fr. Scott, March 2005

Why does the Society of St. Pius X permit the "pernicious" custom of displaying the national flag in the sanctuary?

The national flag is a symbol of one's country and is honored and revered everywhere by men of true patriotic spirit. Patriotism is a Catholic virtue, and Church law permits the display of the national flag in the church. Banners of societies neither condemned nor against the Faith may also be allowed in church and, if requested, out of regard for the church, may even be blessed. The Congregation for Sacred Rites pronounced on this matter, reference number 4390, as well as the Holy Office on March 31, 1911. The custom is to place the American flag on the gospel side of the sanctuary, the Vatican flag on the epistle side.

—Fr. Boyle, May 1995

Why does the Society of St. Pius X administer conditionally the sacraments of baptism and confirmation to those who received them in the *Novus Ordo*?

It is forbidden for a priest to administer a sacrament conditionally unless there is some doubt about the validity of the sacrament already received. A mere suspicion does not suffice, but any real doubt does (*i.e.,* when there is a positive reason to think that the sacrament might have been invalidly administered) since the sacraments are so necessary for the salvation and sanctification of our souls.

In general, there is no doubt as to the validity of the sacrament of baptism administered in the post-conciliar church since the matter and the form are very simple and have been retained, despite the whole new theology replacing the washing of original sin (and actual sin in adults) from the soul with the nebulous social concept of belonging to a community. In general, there is no reason to doubt that the priest has the intention of doing what the Church does, even though he may have a false notion of what this is. However, it will happen from time to time that the sacrament is administered in such a sacrilegious way as to place in doubt even the matter or form or even the intention of doing what the Church does. In such rare cases, in which even the rules of the *Novus Ordo* are not followed, it may be necessary to administer the sacrament of baptism conditionally in order to guarantee validity.

The bishops of the Society administer the sacrament of confirmation conditionally when the faithful request it, that is, when they have a reasonable doubt as to the validity of the sacrament that they received and this doubt cannot be resolved, as is usually the case. This is the case if oil other than the sacred chrism is used, or an oil other than olive oil (highly doubtful, since at variance with the divine institution of using olive oil) as is now permitted in the new rites, or if the signing with the sacred chrism and the imposition of the hand were not done at the same time, or if there is a doubt about the words used. Since there is a great variety in the words used, and since the traditional words "I sign thee with the sign of the cross and I confirm thee with the chrism of salvation, in the name of the Father and of the Son and of the Holy Ghost" are never used, there is very frequently a doubt about the validity of the administration of this sacrament. This is the reason why the Society's bishops do not hesitate to administer it conditionally when asked to do so.

—*Fr. Scott,* October 2002

 **It seems that it can be argued persuasively that the sacrament of confirmation ought to be administered before First Holy Communion, somewhere around the age of seven. What is the Society's position on this matter?**

The three sacraments of baptism, confirmation, and the Holy Eucharist are known as the sacraments of "initiation." This term is somewhat abused these days but is appropriate as it describes the means by which an individual is brought into the Mystical Body of Christ, the Church. The ancient custom is that they be conferred in the above order. Even to the present day there are some regions and rites in the Church where all three are administered even to an infant. The lower age of First Holy Communion brought about by St. Pius X introduced a change in this order. Confirmation began to be conferred after First Holy Communion. This, however, was not to be normative.

The 1917 Code of Canon law stipulated that confirmation be postponed until about the age of seven, but it did permit earlier conferral in danger of death, or if the minister of the sacrament himself judged to do so for grave reasons. Canon 788 did not, however, contemplate the sacrament to be postponed beyond the age of seven. The later age of reception, usually twelve or fourteen, was in many cases tolerated by the bishop as a centennial or immemorial custom in accord with Canon 5. This is similarly allowed even by the new Code of Canon Law. This lack of proper order, however, in the reception of the sacraments, *i.e.* Holy Communion, then confirmation, was recognized by Rome: one who had already received First Holy Communion without being confirmed was not to be impeded from the Eucharist, but it was stated, in 1952, that an episcopal law delaying confirmation until the age of ten could not be sustained. The mind of the Church is therefore clear that Catholics are to receive the sacraments in proper order and that confirmation should be received around the age of discretion.

The Society has no other position than that prescribed by the tradition and law of the Church. It accepts the common custom of delaying confirmation till the age of eleven years. But would it not be highly desirable and would it not be opportune these days, when children are so often forced into adult roles, for children to be well enough instructed to make possible a return to the ancient tradition, enshrined in canon law, of being confirmed as soon as possible after the age of seven years?

—*Fr. Doran,* October 1993

 **When my husband and I were married in 1963, it was imperative that we have the ceremony held before noon. Why was this? Why is it being allowed to be held past noon now? What is the practice of the chapels of the SSPX?**

Evening and afternoon Masses are of recent occurrence, permission being first granted in 1953. This is why weddings, followed by Mass, were held in the morning and were followed by a customary breakfast given by the parents for the bridal party. Your pastor was simply keeping this prescription. Permission was first given for evening Masses to allow the assistance of those normally impeded as a result of employment, as a result of great distance, or because of the large number of the faithful. It was not allowed for the benefit of mere private individuals or simply to enhance the external solemnity of the feast. This privilege was originally for the common good of the faithful. To the best of my knowledge, following a later, less stringent interpretation of this permission by Rome, most chapels served by the Society have afternoon nuptial Masses, especially those which are still of mission status where it is difficult for the priest to be present on a Saturday morning.

—*Fr. Doran,* April 1993

 **Why is it that priests are not assigned to their own countries, or to their own part of the world even, or to their own language?**

Although there is a multitude of different factors that superiors have to take into account in assigning priests, and although these include the natural capacities of the priest and his understanding of the culture, language, and historical background of the people to be administered to, there is another much more profound reason according to which priestly assignments must be seen as the work of divine Providence.

This reason is precisely the maintaining of the profoundly supernatural quality of our work to restore all things in Christ. This is why it is that the assignment of priests is not uniquely, or even primarily, on account of language or natural gifts and talents. There can be no place for personal empires and endeavors in a Society such as ours. Each of us must, like St. John the Baptist, "decrease" that Christ might "increase" (Jn. 3:30). The priest's willingness to accept this is the sure sign that his work is Christ's work, the work of grace.

Likewise the willingness of the faithful to accept the transfer of priests is essential to the success of our work. Frequently, there will be no apparent reason. In fact, often times, it will simply not make sense at all according to any human calculations, on account of the difficulties of dealing with priests who may not be familiar with the language, culture, history, or customs of the souls entrusted to them, or on account of the great sacrifices of self-denial required by both priests and faithful.

However, the great treasure is that it is precisely through such reassignments that the work remains profoundly and fundamentally the same, and that the supernatural unity of our Society, living its motto *Cor unum et anima una,* having "but one heart and one soul" (Acts 4:32), is maintained. Indeed, for the soul who understands the Faith and spiritual things, there is one common language that transcends all else, and it is that of the Faith. It is a great consolation to know that regardless of what part of the world we come from; which language we speak; what be our social, educational, economic, or cultural background, we share, promote, preach, teach, live the same supernatural inheritance. It is this religious spirit that is essential to the supernatural work of our Society.

—*Fr. Scott,* September 2004

Does the Society of St. Pius X promote Nocturnal Adoration in the home?

The Society of St. Pius X does indeed promote Nocturnal Adoration in the home. This apostolate is a part of the Enthronement of the Sacred Heart in the Home, as promoted by Father Mateo Boevey-Crawley and by all of our priests. However, it is not obligatory but is an additional practice that very generous families will choose to offer to Our Lord. It consists of taking a nocturnal hour once a month, sometime between 9:00 p.m. and 6:00 a.m., in order to make reparation to the Sacred Heart. Many mothers are involved in this apostolate of prayer and sacrifice, and that is why the Nocturnal Adoration is organized by the Catholic Mothers Exchange. However, not only mothers, but any Catholic can watch for an hour with Our Lord once a month. Contact information can be obtained from the district office.

—*Fr. Scott,* October 2000

I do not believe that it is right for the Society of St. Pius X to say "we are not the Church," for the other bishops are all apostates.

The statement that "we are not the Church" is made in answer to the accusation that we in the Society of St. Pius X believe that outside the Society there is no salvation. Now, this is a manifestly preposterous statement. Society priests do not have a monopoly of the Catholic Faith. There are many other Catholics, in all the Rites, who accept all that the Church teaches.

The problem with many of the modern-day Catholics and bishops who have effectively apostatized, since they deny one or more doctrines of faith (a recent study showed that only 17% of Catholics between twenty and thirty-nine years of age agree with the pope that only men can be priests), is that they are still members of the visible Church. They perform functions in the Church and they hold authority in the Church (which they abuse by spreading their modernist errors), although they are dead and corrupt members (separated from the principle of union, Christ, by their lack of faith and supernatural charity). However, since they have not been publicly condemned as having separated themselves from the Church, they remain within the visible structure of the Church.

Furthermore, there are many faithful and priests in the post-conciliar church who do not understand the gravity of the modern errors but who are yet in good faith and have supernatural faith and charity. As a result of ignorance, they fail to understand the contradiction of the new humanistic ideas with the Catholic Faith. The motive of their faith is still intact, that is, the authority of God who reveals. They are not only visible members, but also living members, of the mystical body, and some of them have a sanctity which puts to shame some traditional Catholics who have regular access to the traditional sacraments and the true Mass.

—*Fr. Scott,* August 1998

 ## What kind of men does God call to the Brothers of the Society of St. Pius X?

One of the reasons why a strong, virile, thoughtful young man might shy away from a religious vocation is the feeling that the Brother's life is horribly constraining, that it is made up of unbearable restrictions, that it stands in the way of being able to do as one wants, that it prevents one from developing one's personality, that it stifles all natural feelings, that it makes one into little better than a slave, that it takes all the fun out of life and gives very little in return.

Nothing, indeed, could be further from the truth. Far from hampering personal freedom, far from holding a man back in a state of puerile dependence, the religious state has the exact opposite objective, and truly accomplishes it. It is a state of perfection, in which a man commits himself to take the means necessary to strive for perfection every day. This is in fact what makes the religious free, free to make a total and perfect gift of himself, free from the obstacles of his own disordered attachments, free to love God, free to place the divine honor, glory, and holy will over and above every created thing, free to make of himself "a sacrifice of perpetual praise to the divine majesty" (Brothers' Profession).

THE RELIGIOUS IS SUPREMELY FREE

Indeed, the religious who is not a priest has the ultimate freedom, for without the direct responsibility for others' souls, he gives himself entirely to the striving for personal perfection through the living of the vows of poverty, chastity, and obedience. If the Church presumes the priest to be free through his detachment and through his consecration to God, the religious actually takes the means to become so. This is why the religious vocation is radically different from the priestly vocation, and why the religious is not at all to be considered as a man who does not have the aptitude for seminary studies and who cannot become a priest. His is quite simply a different vocation. The priest is consecrated to the service of the Church, so that no man has a right to priestly ordination. This is why it is the first duty of the seminary rector to exclude from ordination any seminarian who does not have the requisite learning, piety, and uprightness of life. However, every Catholic man has a right to the religious life, provided that he seeks it for the right reasons, uses it to strive for perfection, and has no impediments. Furthermore, if it is true that no religious can be lazy, some are more educated and others less so. There is absolutely nothing to stop a more educated Catholic who is not called to the priesthood from applying to enter the religious life. Indeed, it would be a great blessing for the Brothers of the Society to receive as vocations men with academic degrees, for it would enable the Brothers to play an even more active role in the education of boys.

THOUGHTFULNESS AND MERIT IN THE RELIGIOUS

By practicing obedience to the rule as to the will of God and to his superiors as to God's representatives, the religious in no way loses his own will, nor do his acts become any less voluntary and meritworthy. Much to the contrary. For it is by his own generous sacrifice that he embraces the rule as the will of God, that he joyfully and generously sees in the commands of his superiors the manifestation of God's plan of divine providence for his life and activities. Indeed, just as the vow of poverty makes voluntary and meritworthy the religious's state of possessing nothing of his own, so likewise does the vow of obedience make more willing and meritworthy everything that he does. The rule of life, including the Divine Office, prayers, meditation, and common meals is embraced as the signified will of God and the decisions of superiors as God's will of good pleasure. However, in both cases the religious knows with absolute certainty the will of the Almighty, and this gives to his acts and duties a willingness impossible for those who are wandering uncertain, and often aimless, amongst the vagaries of the world.

Nor is there anything childish about the Brother's dependence. It is a whole and complete abandonment to the will of Almighty God. This is accomplished through the living of the vow of poverty, which is nothing less than the generous response to the invitation of our divine Savior mentioned in the brothers' profession ceremony: "If thou wilt be perfect, go sell what thou hast, and give to the poor, and thou shalt have treasure in heaven: and come follow me" (Mt. 19:21).

Truly, the religious life makes a man free.

Nor is it to be thought that the religious life somehow discourages a man from thinking for himself or making his own decisions. Again, the truth is entirely the opposite. Obedience is not at all a blind virtue, and the religious learns to always consider the ultimate reasons for decisions and duties as they fall into God's plan. The religious is thus trained in the virtue of prudence, namely, how to govern himself for heaven and how to govern those for whom he is responsible. This requires the humble seeking of counsel both from his own spiritual director and from his superiors; it requires the ability to make the right judgments as to how to overcome his faults, bad habits, and disordered attachments as well as to fulfill his duties; it requires, finally, follow-through, or the ability to execute both with respect to his own spiritual duties and with respect to his responsibilities for the apostolate and for the community. These are the three acts of prudence that the Brother must be trained in, as a thinking man, without which he cannot be faithful to his vocation.

THE JOY OF THE RELIGIOUS

The practice of poverty and detachment, of willing and obedient submission, necessarily presupposes a community in which the religious lives, along with superiors and fellow religious. A community is both a mortification, as is any family life, but also and especially a great treasure, for it is a supernatural family that shares its life together. The community is indeed an incomparable consolation for the religious who has vanquished his self-centeredness.

Archbishop Lefebvre had this to say about the Brothers' living of community life when he wrote their rule:

> Let the Brothers make efforts to manifest in the community their profoundly religious spirit, one of silence, of union with God, of fraternal charity, of zeal to give service to others, but without neglecting the service of God. May all those whom they approach, and all those in the midst of whom they live, be edified by their behavior, and never disedified. Let them be like the guardian angels of our communities. (§20)

There is certainly nothing inhibiting in such an ideal, nor could there be anything sad, depressing, or lonely about a community of men who share together the same magnanimity, who live side by side the absoluteness of self-sacrifice. Indeed, if natural family life is enjoyable and consoling, how much more is the supernatural family life that is open to the man who has willingly offered up the passing natural joys of this earth for the unchanging ones that will never perish. This is powerfully impressed upon the soul by the following counsel, also contained in the Brothers' Rule, namely, that the Brothers

> strive to understand the profoundly supernatural nature of this life....May they find in this conviction and in this reality, more heavenly than earthly, their unchangeable joy, their unceasing consolation, their steadfast serenity. (§§ 4-5)

MANLINESS IN THE RELIGIOUS

The modern world holds the mistaken idea that the man who is willing to make the vow of perpetual chastity is somehow lacking in virility, that he is less of a man, that he hates women, or is someone who finds it difficult to love, or who refuses to take the responsibility of supporting a family. Again, nothing could be further from the truth. Such a person, not a real man, could never be a candidate for the religious life. Furthermore, manliness is not just a prerequisite of the religious life, but the religious formation positively strives to develop and perfect it. Grace does not suppress nature, nor does the religious life suppress the manly desire to support, help, and cherish the weak, especially the sick and the elderly, women and children. But it does purify it from all disordered or self-centered attachments, and it does encourage the elevation of the sensitivity by the appreciation of art, music, and beauty, starting with the liturgy and Gregorian chant, in which all the Brothers are trained.

Modern psychology uses the term *sublimation* for what it describes as a psychological process, without understanding any of the reality, considering it to be but the substitution of one emotion or interest in order to make up for the lack of another. However, in the etymological sense of tending towards the sublime, it is eminently true of the religious life. Far from suppressing natural feelings, life in community and the vow of chastity indeed elevate them to a much higher plane. They are not substituted for, but purified from, the selfishness so easily inherent in purely human relationships. The religious is indeed indifferent with respect to himself, but he cannot afford to be with respect to others. He must have a true concern, affection, and care for the members of his community, as for all souls with whom he enters into contact.

Thus a Brother is in no way unmoved by suffering and hardship. To the contrary, he is very familiar with it, thanks to his constant meditation on the Passion of our divine Savior. Without in any way denying the reality of human pain, he will constantly strive by his words and example to encourage others to sanctify it by offering it up in reparation for their sins and in union with our divine Savior on the cross. His human feelings find their perfection in their union with those of Our Lord. In this he learns to scrupulously avoid all particular friendship, destroying as it does any true community and undermining his ability to imitate Our Lord, who loves all without exception, "who will have all men to be saved, and to come to the knowledge of the truth" (I Tim 2:4). Sublimation it is, if by this is meant the lifting of the natural affections to the sublime affections of God truly made man, the bearing in one's heart of His own love of truth and beauty, and of His hatred for the ugliness of sin.

However, it is especially in the formation of a sense of responsibility that this manliness consists: responsibility for one's own soul, for one's spiritual family, for edifying one's neighbor, and in the seminary for the edification of the priests and major and minor seminarians. This sense of responsibility is characterized in particular by the manly moral virtue of fortitude, manifest in the strength of character of the mortified religious.

The Brother constantly emulates the martyrs, who lived this virtue to perfection, for the religious life, a constant dying to oneself according to the words of St. Paul "I die daily" (I Cor. 15:31), is an ongoing martyrdom, as said St. Anthony of Egypt, disappointed when he could not endure the martyrdom of blood. This manly fortitude is manifest in his striving for perfection in the ordinary duties of state of every day.

WHO IS CALLED?

I think, then, that it is clear what kind of men God calls to the religious life. It is not the weak, inconstant, effeminate who cannot make a go of it in the world, who do not have the desire to marry and to raise a family. No, God calls to the religious life strong, virile, responsible men; men whose feelings, convictions, and passions are firm and unshakable, yet under control; men who would like to raise a family if it were the will of God, but men who would like much more to consecrate themselves to His service, to His honor and glory, if this is the will of God; men who would much prefer to joyfully and willingly "humbly ask for the favor of consecrating myself totally to God the Holy Trinity, to Our Lord Jesus Christ, and to the Holy Church by the three vows of religion" (Brothers' Profession). God is seeking those truly prudent men who are willing to devote all the energy of their manhood to striving for perfection, to the practice of the holy virtue of religion.

—Fr. Scott, January 2007

 **Some people have stated that Cardinal Ratzinger's decree overturning the "excommunication" of the "Hawaii Six" is not a precedent and does not apply equally to other Catholics who attend the Society's Masses. Is this true?**

It is true that when Our Lady of Fatima Chapel in Honolulu was founded in 1987 it was not a part of the Society of St. Pius X and that it did invite in some traditional priests who were not members of the Society. However, as of 1990 it has been regularly and entirely serviced by the priests of the Society. Consequently, the faithful whom Bishop Ferrario attempted to declare "excommunicated" on January 18, 1991, were so treated directly on account of their attachment to the Society of St. Pius X.

This is in fact confirmed by the formal Canonical Warning itself. Of the three grounds listed in it by Bishop Ferrario, two directly concern the Society. The first does not, being the incorporation of a traditional chapel. The second concerns the radio program "aligning yourselves with the Pius X schismatic movement." The third directly concerns the visit of His Excellency Bishop Williamson, one of the Society bishops invited to Hawaii to administer the sacrament of confirmation. This visit was supposed to have communicated, as if it were an infectious disease, the censure of excommunication:

> Whereas on May 1987 (actually 1989) you performed a schismatic act not only by procuring the services of an excommunicated Lefebvre bishop, Richard Williamson, who performed *contra iure* illicit confirmation in your chapel, but also by the very association with the aforementioned bishop incurred ipso facto the grave censure of excommunication.

When Cardinal Ratzinger as Prefect of the Congregation for the Doctrine of the Faith overturned this "excommunication" by a decree dated June 4, 1993, he indicated that he understood that the essential reason was the charge of schism, which was entirely related to procuring the services of and association with Bishop Williamson, for this was the only part of the accusation that involved the charge of schism. These were his words: "on the grounds that she had committed the crime of schism and thus had incurred the *latae sententiae* penalty." The cardinal went on to say that the charge was false, and since Mrs. Morley did not commit this crime of schism the so-called excommunication was null and void.

It is entirely ingenuous to pretend that because she was not a "member" of the Society of St. Pius X this decree does not apply to the Society's faithful. It is only the priests who are members of the Society. The faithful parishioners are all in the exact situation now as Mrs. Morley was then. They are not members, and they do not belong to the Society any more than she did then. They simply assist at the Masses of priests whose doctrine, integrity, Catholicity, and Masses they can trust and depend upon. Cardinal Ratzinger's decision that Mrs. Morley did not commit a crime of schism by inviting Bishop Williamson for confirmations and by associating with him consequently applies just as much to them now as it did to her then.

—*Fr. Scott,* June 2001

 **How must a Catholic conduct himself at a public forum during the invocation provided by non-Catholic clergy or even Catholic clergy failing to meet the norm of Catholic prayer? How do priests of the Society respond when asked to deliver such an invocation?**

Your question is probably a concern with what is known as *communicatio in sacris*. This matter was dealt with in the 1917 Code of Canon Law (Can. 1258). The "*communicatio*" signifies a common action with another in prayers and functions of worship. "Active" communion is to take a real part in a non-Catholic rite. Active participation in non-

Catholic services is always intrinsically unlawful because it is at least an external denial of the true religion. It brings with it the danger of perversion for the Catholic, scandalizes fellow Catholics, and confirms in error the non-Catholic. For a sufficiently grave reason, *e.g.*, the funeral of a non-Catholic of close acquaintance, passive assistance is allowed, as long as the danger of perversion and scandal are removed. This participation is a merely physical presence at the service with no involvement whatever.

Whenever a canon involving restrictions is interpreted, it is to be read in the strict sense of the words. Now, these public invocations, while being religious, would hardly seem to be classified as true worship in the sense of a ritual cult rendered to the Divinity. It is more or less a civil form of introduction—these days little more than a watered down "acknowledgement" of the Great Architect of Freemasonry. The canon would thus not be strictly applicable. Its spirit is, however, to be kept. Therefore, a Catholic would not be guilty of *communicatio in sacris* during these invocations if "bowing the head," but all the same the spirit of the Church is rather to spurn these weak, and often false, expressions. Thus, while it is not necessary to make a mountain out of a molehill, silence would be a better answer than "bowing the head" to these invocations.

When invited to give one of these invocations the clergyman is reminded that his audience is a mixed one. It follows that he is not to "offend" anyone present. The result is obvious. No priest of the Society has, to my knowledge, ever given one of these invocations. In fact, what could be his possible response when he is faced with only the chance of rendering a prayer to the Most Holy Trinity which must consist of only monosyllabic words empty of all meaning?

—*Fr. Doran,* August 1991

 **Since the *Novus Ordo* has relinquished its obligation to provide guidance to parents with regard to movie ratings and since the movie industry has come out with a new, relaxed rating system, I am wondering if it isn't time for the Society to come out with a rating system?**

The only films I would recommend for viewing would be the videos distributed by Keep the Faith: lives of the saints, conferences of Bishop Fulton Sheen, *etc.* However, while a video is allowed, Archbishop Lefebvre does not allow television for the members of the Society of Saint Pius X—not only priests, Brothers, and Sisters, but also for members of the Third Order. As for all the faithful, the Society strongly advises the faithful not to have a television.

Our Lord Jesus Christ has spoken about television! Yes, indeed! He said: "If thy eye scandalize thee, pluck it out. It is better for thee with one eye to enter into the Kingdom of God, than having two eyes to be cast into the hell of fire: where their worm dieth not, and the fire is not extinguished" (Mk. 9:46-47). Now, I ask every one of the readers to be honest with himself: if television is an occasion of sin for you, these words of Our Lord apply to you. What is easier for you?—to pluck out your eye or to throw away your television? Do not say that you may use your television for good purposes; you can use even more your eye for good purposes; yet, if it becomes an occasion of sin for you, do not spare it, pluck it out! So, if your television becomes an occasion of sin for you, do not throw it away without self-pity, *true* self-pity, pity for your soul!

If television is an occasion of sin for your children, have pity on their souls, too, and throw your television away.

Remember that there is not just one commandment, but there are ten of them—and all of them are violated repeatedly on television. Do not think just of the impurities on television, but also of all the violence, of all the disrespect for parents and legitimate authorities, of all the misuse of the holy name of God—so common, so common! Think of all the bad, vulgar, and dirty language. Think of the worldly spirit of pursuit of earthly goods with no regard for eternal salvation (and you certainly have this in sports, too: the most ardent pursuit of money and earthly glory!). One could go on and on.

Now, if you rate all the films which offend against one or another of the Ten Commandments, then I really doubt whether there will be one out of a thousand that will be acceptable. The Society cannot preview all of these evil films to find the improbable one which will be acceptable.

Television very often harms and can even destroy family life. Without television you will find time to help your spouse, to be with your children, to help them with their lessons, and even to play with them. Your children will not develop a passive attitude in front of the television, but they will rather develop an active attitude, helping their mother or reading good, wholesome literature. You will learn to listen to each other instead of listening to the television. We must return to the fervor of the early Christians. The television of their time was the games of the circus. The Fathers of the Church were very strongly opposed to these games. The Society of St. Pius X continues their tradition.

—*Fr. Laisney,* February 1991

 **I think that the Society of Saint Pius X is in heresy. It affirms that the ordinary magisterium of the Church can err. The proof of this is that it accepts that the documents of Vatican II are part of the ordinary magisterium, but it still says that they have errors, does it not?**

It is certainly true that on page one of Michael Davies's booklet *Archbishop Lefebvre and Religious Liberty*, published by Angelus Press in 1980, it is stated: "The documents of Vatican II come within the category of the Church's Ordinary Magisterium which can contain error in the case of a novelty which conflicts with previous teaching." There follows a reference to Dom Paul Nau's study on the ordinary magisterium, published in 1998 by Angelus Press under the title *Pope or Church?*

This statement by Michael Davies is erroneous. This expression is a common misunderstanding of the ordinary magisterium and just the opposite of Dom Nau's true teaching concerning the ordinary magisterium. Dom Nau's whole point is that the definition of the infallibility of the solemn magisterium by Vatican I has overshadowed the just as real (but perhaps less clear) infallibility of the ordinary magisterium, of which Vatican I also spoke: "It is a duty to believe with divine and Catholic Faith all that is contained in the word of God, whether written or transmitted by Tradition, that the Church puts forward to be believed as revealed truth, either in a solemn judgment or by her ordinary and universal Magisterium" (*Dei Filius*).

The term ordinary magisterium is commonly used for any teaching that is not solemnly defined. This is where Michael Davies's error lies. The Society certainly does not follow him in this. The ordinary magisterium is of its nature both universal and infallible. If it is not universal, it is not ordinary magisterium and it is not infallible. The term we give for teaching which does not have continuity with the past is the authentic magisterium. This kind of teaching is not at all infallible, and it is to this that the novelties of Vatican II belong, not to the ordinary magisterium.

Listen to what Dom Nau says of the ordinary magisterium:

> The infallibility of the Ordinary Magisterium, whether of the Universal Church or of the See of Rome, is not that of a judgment, nor that of an act to be considered in isolation, as if it could itself provide all the light necessary for it to be clearly seen. It is that of the guarantee bestowed on a doctrine by the simultaneous or continuous convergence of a plurality of affirmations or explanations; none of which could bring positive certitude if it were taken by itself alone. (*Pope or Church*, p. 18)

Consequently, there are some statements in the documents of Vatican II that belong to the ordinary magisterium, and that are infallibly true. These are the doctrinal statements that simply repeat what the Church has everywhere and always taught. However, there are many other statements that do not do this, and that do not belong to the ordinary magisterium, but rather to the authentic magisterium, which simply means that they authentically come from the Council or the pope who has authority in the Church. Under normal circumstances they would be accepted with reverence, but never as infallible. At the present time, it is clear that many of these are radical modernist novelties, such as religious liberty, ecumenism, collegiality, and the adaptation of the Church to the modern world. Since they are clearly in direct contradiction to infallible statements of the solemn and ordinary magisterium, these novelties can and must be refused.

The consequences of this confusion concerning the question of the ordinary magisterium are very far reaching. On the one hand, those who follow Michael Davies draw the conclusion that these documents are all a part of the ordinary magisterium, although they still have a few errors. They end up by accepting their contents (even if rather reluctantly), just as they have ended up by accepting the legitimacy of the New Mass, alas.

On the other hand, the sedevacantists say that all that Vatican II and the post-conciliar popes say is the ordinary magisterium. However, these documents contain errors that are incompatible with the infallibility of the ordinary magisterium. The conclusion is that Vatican II was not a Church Council and that the subsequent popes were not popes. A small error of principle leads them to entirely distort the reality, and refuse its real complexity for their *a priori* mindset that all teaching is infallible. The correct understanding of the ordinary magisterium is consequently of the utmost importance in the present crisis. I strongly recommend the reading of the book *Pope or Church?*

—*Fr. Scott,* November 1999

ABOUT PRAYER
AND THE SPIRITUAL LIFE

Is it not opposed to free will for our prayers to be answered?

When we pray for others we do not require of God to take away their free will or to compel them in some way against their will. We pray, to the contrary, that God's grace might move, inspire, and actualize their free will, so that no longer being slaves to their passions, they might act out of free will. We pray as God's instruments, exerting the influence of our prayers to bring about the will of God. We pray out of docility to grace that others might be docile also. Far from taking away free will, our prayers, which are directed to God, from whose majesty all graces come, play the role in divine Providence of obtaining for souls all the graces they need in order to be free.

—*Fr. Scott,* October 2003

Ought we to pray that God lead us not into temptation?

The correct understanding of the sixth demand taught by our divine Savior in the Our Father, when He taught us to pray, is this: "Allow us not to fall into temptation."

If we translate it as "lead us not into temptation," it is because this is a direct translation from the Vulgate Latin text: "*Et ne nos inducas in tentationem.*" The verb *inducas,* or "lead us," is a translation of the Greek *eisphero,* which means literally "to bring into." However, it has a second-ary or causative meaning, namely, "to make or command one to enter into," and from that also is derived a permissive meaning, namely, "to allow one to enter into"; for by allowing one to enter in (*e.g.,* a building), one becomes a cause of his entering into it. This is the meaning here: namely, "do not allow us to enter into" or "allow us not to succumb to" (*cf.* Zorell, *Lexicon Graecum,* p. 384).

This interpretation is confirmed by multiple texts in sacred Scripture that indicate that God, who is all good, cannot tempt man in the sense of inducing him to fall into evil. St. James states this explicitly: "Let no man, when he is tempted, say that he is tempted by God. For God is not a tempter of evils, and he tempteth no man" (Jas. 1:13). This is likewise confirmed by St. Paul: "Let no temptation take hold on you, but such as is human. And God is faithful, who will not suffer you to be tempted above that which you are able: but will make also with temptation issue, that you may be able to bear it" (I Cor. 10:13).

The three sources of temptation are the world, the flesh, and the devil, but not God. Hence, when we pray "lead us not into temptation," we should understand thereby, "allow us not to succumb to temptation."

—*Fr. Scott,* August 2006

Why do so many of our most fervent prayers seem to remain unanswered?

Prayer, our catechism taught us, is a raising up of the mind and heart to God; and we know that God never turns a deaf ear to a genuine prayer. All prayer, especially the prayer of petition, is answered not on our terms, in accordance with our desires, but in the light of the designs of God's eternal providence upon each and every individual soul. A true and proper understanding of God's will is the key to a Catholic comprehension of prayer. It is not only the raising of one's mind to God but the raising of one's mind to embrace and accept the will of God. We must beware of trying to impose upon God our human understanding of things. God is not like us. He is unchanging and eternal. His will is unchanging and His love also. In God His will and His love are one reality. God wills our eternal happiness and everything that leads to it. There is no opposition or contradiction between His will and His love. A mother may well love her son injudiciously by giving in to his pleadings. Her will is opposed. She knows it to be wrong. She gives in, using love as an excuse. She wills the lesser good. Not so with God. No such conflict can exist in Him. Our prayer cannot force the hand of God; it cannot make Him give what from all eternity He has not willed to give. Our necessary prayer, however, can bring God's will into play and very often to our surprise our prayers are granted. Even if He has apparently refused, God has said "no" for the greater welfare of our soul. We always receive in prayer; above all, we receive the grace, through faith and perseverance, to accept in all things the divine will rather than a positive response to a particular petition. This is the essence of all prayer, as Christ taught us: "Thy will be done on earth as it is in heaven."

—*Fr. Boyle,* July 1994

Are prayers made while in the state of mortal sin useless?

It would seem that prayers offered while in mortal sin, that is, in rebellion against God and His law, would be ineffective and useless, for the sinner is not a friend of God, and has nothing supernatural in common with Him.

This is, however, by the grace of the good Lord, entirely false. As St. Thomas Aquinas explains with precision (*ST*, II-II, q. 83, art. 15), there is a twofold efficacy of our prayers, namely, that of meriting and that of impetrating. Prayers offered to God in the state of grace are certainly vastly more powerful because they are meritorious, meriting an effectiveness that is infallible, provided that we are asking for graces necessary for our own salvation, and with piety and perseverance. This is the meaning of the wonderfully consoling words of our divine Savior: "If you abide in me, and my words abide in you, you shall ask whatever you will, and it shall be done unto you" (Jn. 15:7), and of St. John: "Dearly beloved, if our hearts do not reprehend us, we have confidence towards God: And whatsoever we shall ask, we shall receive of Him: because we keep His commandments and do those things which are pleasing in His sight" (I Jn. 3:21-22).

Yet even when a man is not in the state of sanctifying grace the second effect of his prayers still remains, the effect that our prayers have as a petition begging God's help and grace. This can only be attributed to the divine mercy, but is the whole reason for our justification; for if God did not listen to our prayers when we were dead in our sins, how would we receive the actual graces to accomplish His holy will? This is how St. Thomas puts it:

> As to its efficacy in impetrating, prayer derives this from the grace of God, to Whom we pray, and Who instigates us to pray. Wherefore Augustine says: "He would not urge us to ask, unless He were willing to give"; and Chrysostom says: "He never refuses to grant our prayers, since in His loving-kindness He urged us not to faint in praying." (*ST*, II-II, q. 83, art. 15)

St. Thomas further points out that in the soul that is not in the state of grace, this efficacy of petition or begging derives chiefly from faith, "because it is through faith that man comes to know of God's omnipotence and mercy, which are the source whence prayer impetrates what it asks for" (*ibid.*, ad 3). This is most evident in the prayers of sinners that sacred Scripture tells us were heard, by which prayers the sinners attained justification. This is the case of the publican who went home justified after having prayed "O God, be merciful to me a sinner" (Lk. 18:13). It is also the case of the thief whom we call "good" because he converted and was justified on the cross, after having prayed: "Lord, remember me when thou shalt come into Thy kingdom" (Lk. 23:42).

We must not, therefore, minimize the extraordinary and divine power of prayer, even that made when in the state of mortal sin. For this is a power that derives entirely from God's mercy, and it has no limit. Such prayers will be heard on account of the faith and the importunity of the soul begging God's help, grace, mercy, and forgiveness, as our divine Lord Himself promised when He said, "Ask, and it shall be given to you: seek and you shall find: knock, and it shall be opened to you. For every one that asketh, receiveth; and he that seeketh, findeth; and to him that knocketh, it shall be opened" (Lk. 11:9-10). No greater service can we render to our neighbors and friends than inspiring and encouraging them to pray to Jesus and through Mary, whatever the state of their soul.

—*Fr. Scott,* December 2007

 **Are there means of penance other than that which we receive in the confessional? Often that does not seem adequate, especially for past mortal sins.**

How true! The small penances given by a confessor are more like a token. For mortal sin, the death sentence would be too little. However, if a fit penance were always given, few sinners would avail themselves of the sacrament of God's mercy. Just because Father is "easy" in the box, we must not be led to believe that works of penance are no longer important. For every sin committed there is a temporal punishment due, and the sacrament does not completely remove this. A genuine follower of Christ truly needs both interior and exterior penances. And the gift of tears is a real grace.

—Fr. Carl, September 1980

 **I quote from the Douay-Rheims version of holy Scripture : "And when you are praying, speak not much, as the heathens. For they think that in their much speaking they may be heard" (Matt. 6:7). How is this teaching reconciled with the recommendation of the Church to pray the rosary daily? Is it not mechanistic and a repetition of words?**

A mother kisses her baby very repetitiously. One kiss could never be considered enough for her! Devotedly prayed, a rosary is much like a good child kissing a good and wonderful mother. Should a child be satisfied to give only one kiss? The danger of mechanistic rote is ever present, but that is not the ideal way to pray the beautiful prayer of the rosary.

—Fr. Carl, May 1983

 **"Novena Never Known to Fail"—a little prayer to the Sacred Heart and to St. Jude. Then it says "must be said six times each day for nine consecutive days, leaving a copy in church each day. Prayer will be answered on or before the ninth day. Novena has never been known to fail to grant favor asked for by ninth day." I found copies of this cluttering the front pews in church. I wondered what you would say about this sort of thing.**

It is superstition masquerading as true Catholic devotion. Like a chain letter, it is a sin against the first commandment, against the virtue of religion. Devout Catholics sometime become entangled in schemes like these. Our religion is not magic. God always hears our prayers and grants them if we ask for what is good with humility, perseverance, and confidence. My advice is not to become involved with superstition but to practice your faith as the saints did, with childlike simplicity and devotion.

—*Fr. Carl*, May 1985

When can the Prayer to St. Michael against the devil and the bad angels be recited?

This powerful prayer, written by Pope Leo XIII in 1888, was incorporated into the Roman Ritual in 1925 (tit. XI, cap. 3) with the rubric that it can be recited by bishops or by priests who have received the authority to do so from their ordinaries. However, this rubric concerns the public prayers of the Church that are contained in the Roman Ritual. The same restriction does not apply to the private recitation of this prayer by any individual priest, or any of the faithful, for that matter, as many bishops permitted and encouraged before Vatican II.

The Church's traditional teaching concerning the recitation of private exorcism prayers is contained in the moral theology manual of Dominicus Prümmer (II, 463):

> It is not only clerics who can pronounce an exorcism in a private and secret manner, enjoying a special power over the devils in virtue of the order of the exorcistate, but also the laity themselves. It is in no way forbidden to the laity nor does any inconvenience arise from it. Thus we read in history how several lay persons, such as St. Catherine of Siena and St. Anthony of the Desert, cast out devils.

Consequently, it is in no way inappropriate for the laity to recite the exorcism prayer of Pope Leo XIII, provided that they do so privately. It will certainly be very powerful in overcoming the temptations and evil snares of the devil.

One wonders why it is that post-Vatican II authors have scruples concerning the recitation of this magnificent prayer, stating that since the 1983 Code of Canon Law it is no longer permitted. In fact, the same rule of the necessity of permission for public exorcisms is retained (Can. 1172). There is, however, no determination concerning the private recitation of an exorcism prayer, which is consequently perfectly permissible. Of course, we all know why it is that the modern church has changed the rites of exorcism, done away with the traditional powerful prayers, and discouraged all such commands in the name of Christ against the power of evil: it is that the devil is henceforth treated more as a mythical figure than as a reality that we must deal with every day, as St. Peter teaches: "Be sober and watch: because your adversary the devil, as a roaring lion, goeth about seeking whom he may devour" (I Pet. 5:8).

The gravity of sin, the danger of eternal damnation, and the personal power of evil that the devil is able to exercise in this corrupt world, the corruption of the Church, and its infiltration by its enemies, even to the papacy, are so many realities pushed aside by the modernists, but of which we are reminded in this prayer:

On men depraved in mind and corrupt in heart the wicked dragon pours out like a most foul river the poison of his villainy, a spirit of lying, impiety, and blasphemy; and the deadly breath of lust and of all iniquities and vices. Her most crafty enemies have engulfed the Church, the Spouse of the Immaculate Lamb, with sorrows, they have drenched her with wormwood; on all Her desirable things they have laid their wicked hands. Where the See of Blessed Peter and the Chair of Truth have been set up for the light of the Gentiles, there they have placed the throne of the abomination of their wickedness, so that, the Pastor having been struck, they may also be able to scatter the flock. Therefore, O thou unconquerable Leader, be present with the people of God against the spiritual wickednesses which are bursting in upon them: and bring them the victory.

Is it any wonder that the modernists consider this prayer "dangerous" for the soul? In fact, to the contrary, it is the refusal to pray in this way that is dangerous for the soul.

—*Fr. Scott,* July 2005

 **May one offer prayers for specific intentions even though one has made the total consecration to Our Lady according to the method of St. Louis-Marie Grignion de Montfort?**

The total consecration to Jesus through Mary is just what it says: a total offering of all that we are and have, both interior and exterior, including merits and prayers: "I deliver and consecrate to thee (*i.e.*, Mary), as thy slave, my body and soul, my goods, both interior and exterior, and even the value of all my good actions, past, present and future; leaving to you the entire and full right of disposing of me…" (Formula of Consecration). Consequently, the consecrated soul has nothing of its own. Here lies the totality of the consecration:

[Y]ou abandon your own intentions and operations, although good and known, to lose yourself, so to speak, in the intentions of the Blessed Virgin, although they are unknown. Thus you enter by participation into the sublimity of her intentions, which are so pure. (*True Devotion to Mary* [London: Burns & Oats, 1904], p. 162)

The totality of the consecration consequently means that we cannot have any specific intentions of our own. Living by Mary, our intentions are entirely lost in hers:

In order that the soul may let itself be led by Mary's spirit, it must first of all renounce its own spirit and its own proper lights and wills, before it does anything. For example, it should do so before its prayer…because the darkness of our own spirit and the malice of our own will and operation, if we follow them, however good they may appear to us, will put an obstacle to the spirit of Mary. (*Ibid.*, pp. 184-185)

A distinction must, therefore, be made in what is meant by "specific" intentions. If by this I mean something that is specific to me, as distinct from Mary, then it is precluded and forbidden by the total consecration. If it means that I am asking for a special grace that it is Mary's will to obtain for me because it is God's will to bestow it, then it is perfectly permissible.

Consequently, souls that are consecrated to Mary can certainly pray for their own friends and relatives, for the state of their own soul, for their priests and those who are in need of prayers, for the Church and for vocations, but all of these "specific" intentions must be understood as an extension of Mary's intentions.

Inasmuch as we do not know Our Lady's intentions, then the condition under which any such prayer must be uttered by the one who is totally consecrated is "in so far as it is Our Lady's desire and will." In this way, the practice of the true devotion obtains for us the grace of perfect detachment from our own will, manifest even in our prayers, the gaining of merits, and intentions behind our good works. This is the condition for union with Our Lady. Frank Duff, founder of the Legion of Mary, put it this way:

> That union is a life, and just like the common life of the body, it demands the regular beating of the heart, the steady movement of the lungs, the stimulus of periodic nourishment. These are the impulses of prayer, ejaculation, act, practice, thought, and other reminders, which warm and renew the soul and preserve in it the spirit of consecration. (*The De Montfort Way* [Bay Shore, NY: Montfort Publications, 1947], p. 24)

The totally consecrated soul is consequently not at all indifferent to the specific needs of his soul and others, but to the contrary filled with a burning desire to pray for them, to the extent that this is the will, intention, and desire of the Blessed Virgin Mary.

—*Fr. Scott,* March 2005

What is holiness?

Holiness is at the same time a *state*, the state of sanctifying grace which renders us agreeable to God, and a *virtue*, charity which makes us perform acts of love of God and our neighbor.

Holiness does not consist in extraordinary things which theologians call *gratis datae*—for example, performing miracles, predicting the future, having apparitions, *etc.* It consists in this gift of God, which theologians call *gratum faciens,* that renders him who possesses it agreeable to God and permits him to perform supernatural and meritorious acts for heaven.

When the Church canonizes saints, she does not do it because they had apparitions of the Blessed Virgin or of the Sacred Heart, or because they performed miracles. She canonizes them because they practiced all of the virtues in a heroic degree.

Therefore, holiness is Christian perfection, that is to say, the perfection of the theological virtues—faith, hope, and charity—and of the cardinal virtues that accompany them. As the resumé of Christianity is the love of God and of our neighbor for love of God, we can say that holiness is nothing other than the perfect practice of charity.

But in order to avoid any sentimental error, let us quickly add that in the present life, love of God and of our neighbor cannot be practiced without renouncing an inordinate love of self. Therefore, in order to arrive at holiness, we must necessarily fight against our triple concupiscence.

"If anyone love Me, he will keep My commandments."

"If any man will come after Me, let him deny himself, take up his cross, and follow Me."

—Unknown, February 1993

Is holiness possible outside of the cloister?

Yes, holiness is possible outside of the cloister. It is possible in all social conditions and every state of life. Age, health, and sickness do not oppose it; and even the greatest sinners can aspire to it, providing that they convert.

Our Lord calls all Christians to holiness: Be perfect as your heavenly Father is perfect!

And, whatever our past might have been, St. Paul assures us that where sin abounded grace did more abound.

—Unknown, February 1993

Is there anything wrong with a young person deciding to stay single for the rest of his or her life?

The decision as to one's state in life is a very personal one. However, there is a much more fundamental question that must be answered before this question is answered, and upon which the answer depends. This question is whether or not I want to strive for perfection, as our divine Savior encourages all of us to do: "Be you therefore perfect, as also your heavenly Father is perfect" (Mt. 5:48). This is not a counsel of optional extra. It is a necessary and immediate consequence of our Catholic life. If a person cannot answer this question affirmatively, he (or, of course, she) needs a conversion; he needs to follow an Ignatian retreat. If he does not do so, then there is no way that he will be able to discover the will of God for his state in life.

The next question that a Catholic must ask himself (or herself) is whether or not a religious vocation is the means for him to strive for perfection. The religious state is a state of tending towards perfection, which every Catholic should desire, if it is possible for him. The reason for this is that the religious life is a state in life which most disposes the Catholic soul to the perfection that grace inspires in the soul, defined as it is by canon law: "a permanent manner of living in community wherein the faithful, in addition to those things that are of precept, engage themselves by vow to observe the evangelical counsels of obedience, chastity, and poverty" (Can. 487). However, it very often happens that a generous soul, willing to follow God's will, discovers that the religious life is not for him (or for her). This can be for any of a number of reasons, whether in the natural or supernatural order, whether they be impediments or simply prior background, whether they be character quirks or special gifts, whether they be eccentricities or simply being too set in one's ways to adapt to community life. None of these things is an impediment to such a person's striving for perfection, nor is a person to consider himself in some way inferior or a failure because he cannot join a religious community. Far from it, it remains the will of God for him to sanctify himself in his state in life, which may not be a state of perfection, it is true, but which nevertheless provides him with all the means necessary to sanctify his soul.

After this has been resolved, the next question that a young Catholic should ask himself (or herself) is that given that he does not have a religious vocation, should he enter into the married state or not. There is in the mind of some people the idea that this is in some way an inevitable consequence. Far from it. The essential question is: What is the best means for me to strive for perfection in the world? For most people, it is the married state, because matrimony is a sacrament that sanctifies, gives grace, and conforms to Christ in His Passion; and because the duties of the married state, both towards a spouse and towards children, are the best guarantee against the egocentric self-centeredness that a single person can otherwise be prone to.

However, the married state is not necessarily the best means for his (or her) perfection. We need to be wary of a romantic glorification of marriage that almost prescribes it. There have always been some souls who are called to strive for perfection in the world in the single life. It gives them the freedom to devote themselves to a cause; in particular, a spiritual work of mercy, such as education, nursing, taking care of elderly parents, and the like. It also prevents them from becoming so overwhelmed by the burdens of daily life as to be prevented from devoting the time and attention to the things of God, as they so long to do. This is the "tribulation of the flesh" from which St. Paul so wants to spare us (I Cor. 7:28).

Such generous souls have always been of great assistance to the Church and have on many occasions achieved high levels of sanctity, striving for perfection by all the ordinary means at their disposal, especially their daily Mass, meditation and spiritual duties, and frequent reception of the sacraments. They have only one goal, the greater glory of God, through the sanctification of their own soul, through the edification of their neighbor by works of charity, and seeking not the passing joys of this earth, but considering that "that which is at present momentary and light of our tribulation, worketh for us above measure exceedingly an eternal weight of glory" (II Cor. 4:17). They should by no means feel that their life is a missed opportunity or in some way unfulfilled. Such is a purely naturalistic conception. Once such persons are firm in their resolution for their state in life, they can increase the merit of their service of God by a private vow of chastity, although it is by no means necessary.

—*Fr. Scott,* November 2003

ABOUT RELIGIOUS ORDERS
AND THE RELIGIOUS LIFE

What were the Knights Templar, and what was their relation with the Knights of Malta?

The Templars, or the Knights Templar, were a military order, namely, a religious order that added to the usual three vows of religious the vow of taking the cross as Crusaders. They followed the rule of St. Benedict and wore the white Cistercian habit. They were founded in 1118 to defend the recently established Catholic kingdom of Jerusalem. After the fall of that kingdom, the order became popular, and also quite powerful and wealthy. It was considered to be a threat by King Philip IV of France, who ruthlessly attacked its members, even as he had ruthlessly attacked the recently deceased Pope Boniface VIII. Although history has argued about the truthfulness of the gross, incongruous, and contradictory accusations made against the Templars, and although many Templars confessed under torture, they mostly repudiated their confessions in the presence of the representatives of the Pope Clement V. Eventually, in 1312 the pope bowed to the political pressure from the king of France and suppressed the whole order, without accepting the truth of the accusations or condemning the members.

The members of the order who were not so accused were allowed to enter the Order of the Knights of St. John of Jerusalem, or Knights Hospitallers, and it is in this way that the two orders became one. The Knights of St. John were founded for nursing and hospital work but were also crusading knights in the Holy Land, Cyprus, Rhodes, and Malta. They still exist to this day, but the so-called "O.S.J." is not a part of the Knights of St. John, being a schismatic, counterfeit break-off from the Knights of Malta under Czar Paul I of Russia in 1798.

—*Fr. Scott,* October 2004

Can you tell me something about the Legionaries of Christ? Are they a traditional order? Do they offer the Tridentine Mass or the *Novus Ordo*? How should one respond to their request for funds?

The Legionaries of Christ were founded in 1941 in Mexico City by Fr. Marcial Maciel, who is presently stationed in Rome. The main objective of this congregation was to establish Christ's kingdom in society. They work in many diverse fields: counseling, the media, summer camps, and schools.

The Legionaries stand out to many as a traditional order because of their appearance and reverence still preserved among their members. They do, in fact, offer the *Novus Ordo* and accept at face value all the documents of Vatican II, including *Dignitatis Humanae.* They are conservative rather than traditional. They strive to reconcile the shift since the Council with the Tradition of the Catholic Church. Thus they have no profound understanding of the crisis of faith with which the Church is presently afflicted. They hold an absolute, blind, one could say unthinking, obedience to the Holy Father. This in normal circumstances would be laudable, but when, for example, the pope himself calls false religions to worship in the house of the living God (as he has recently done for the second time in Assisi), we cannot see the inspiration of the Holy Ghost behind this. They would accept this on faith as being an action in accord with the position of the Vicar of Christ. To a hypothetical papal mandate (one would hope hypothetical!) to say a "clown Mass," one priest of the Legion has answered that he would "spend all night practicing in order to do it perfectly in the morning!"

This conservatism serves to cover the more reprehensible elements of modern, post-conciliar Catholicism, with the result that many are deceived by these novelties.

—*Fr. Doran,* June 1993

What are the signs of a vocation to the religious life or to the priesthood?

Four gifts God gives to those He calls to serve Him in the religious life or the priesthood. The first is the attraction to this state of life. Secondly, a physical soundness or integrity. Thirdly, mental balance, or a wit and talent equal to the demands of the calling. And fourthly, spiritual health. For the priesthood there is also the calling of the Church. Religious orders or the Church are neither obliged to accept someone with a vocation, nor is any person obliged to answer this call. A vocation remains a calling, therefore, and not a command.

—Fr. Carl, October 1980

Why is it that we have so relatively few vocations amongst traditional Catholics?

Inspired by a May 24 letter on the subject of vocations written by Fr. Troadec, Rector of the Society's seminary in France (Flavigny), I would like to investigate the six requirements for successful ecclesiastical vocations, so rarely present simultaneously in our young men. It is this that explains why we do not have the same number of vocations as existed in the Church before Vatican II and what our families can do to encourage vocations.

1) Understanding Why God Made Us

The first reason why few seek after a vocation is a false notion of what a vocation is.

> Many of the faithful think that a vocation consists in a very strong call felt in the depth of the soul that would persuade the young man that he is called by God. Archbishop Lefebvre stood up against this opinion, affirming that "a vocation is not the fact of a miraculous or extraordinary call, but the development of a Catholic soul, attaching itself to its Creator and Savior, Our Lord Jesus Christ, by an exclusive love, and sharing His thirst for the salvation of souls." Two elements must coexist to awaken vocations: the love of Our Lord and the love of souls. (Fr. Troadec)

Vocations, consequently, lie principally not in a personal experience or subjective call, but in the intelligence, in a more profound understanding of the reason why God made us—to know, love, and serve Him—and in the will, in the determination to put this into practice regardless of the cost. Here lies the love of God and the love of souls that inspires in a young man the ideal of imitating the Sacred Heart, and serving the Church and souls through the priesthood. It is, consequently, a possibility upon which every fervent young Catholic man should reflect, nor should he exclude it because he does not "feel" any particular call.

Here is how Fr. Troadec puts it:

> God has given us an intelligence and a will, but He has also given us a heart. This heart is made, above all else, to love Him, and this with a preferential love. Thus, young men who enter the Seminary perceive everything that God has done for them more deeply than others. Meditating on the life of Our Lord and His Passion, considering His death on the Cross, they repeat with St. Paul that Christ "loved me and delivered himself for me" (Gal. 2:20). Seeing how Our Lord's love was not an empty word pronounced in the air, but that it was concrete, bringing about heroic acts and unspeakable sufferings, young men say to themselves: No, I do not want to live as if God had not come on this earth; I do not want to live as if Our Lord had not died for me. In response to that love, I am not satisfied with living a simply honest life in the world. I want to respond to His love by a love that is exclusive, total, and perpetual, and which embraces all my strength, all my energy, my entire life.

2) DIVINE FRIENDSHIP

There is a second reason why our young men are afraid to try a vocation. They have a narrow notion of friendship, one which is limited to this world. The idea of giving up legitimate earthly friendships seems too much, too difficult, too overwhelming, nor do they consider sufficiently the incredible grace of the divine friendship, of the intimacy with our divine Savior, to which the priest is called, becoming the instrument for applying the graces of the Passion to souls, offering the holy Sacrifice, standing in His place, in His very person. This is a friendship that surpasses every other friendship as much as heaven surpasses the earth. They tend to ask themselves whether or not they can do without the friendship of a woman, rather than the much more fundamental question as to which friendship is going to change them, as to which friendship they are going to give priority, which friendship it is that "may give you power to attend upon the Lord without impediment" (I Cor. 7:35).

There can be no doubt that the young families in our traditional circles are very edifying by the sacrifices that they make to have many children and to give them a Catholic education. However, there can sometimes be found a certain romanticism of the married state, as if it were a guarantee of the elusive earthly happiness that man in his old age realizes can never be obtained on this earth. Indeed, if there could be any true lasting happiness attainable on this earth, St. Paul would not have written: "The time is short; it remaineth, that they also who have wives be as if they had none; and they that weep, as though they wept not; and they that rejoice, as if they rejoiced not; and they that buy, as though they possessed not; and they that use this world, as if they used it not..." (I Cor. 7:29-31).

If there were any doubt as to the penetration into our families of the world's glorification of sentimental attachments, it would immediately be dissipated by listening to the shamefully superficial gossip concerning adult, or even teenage, boyfriends and girlfriends that can be heard around any of our groups of young traditional Catholics, not to mention the vain and trivial pastimes to which they devote themselves, not counting the occasions of sin. Such peer-group pressure is an obstacle to any young man seriously contemplating a vocation, closing his mind to the possibility of an intimate divine friendship. The modern substitution of sweet sentimentality in family life for virtue, discipline, obedience, and submission cannot but play a major role in the unmanly closing of the mind to the greatness of true friendship.

This is how Fr. Troadec explains the friendship that is offered to the generous young men who consent to follow a divine call:

> Once they pronounce their generous, magnanimous, complete, and final yes, these young men are abundantly recompensed. In effect, God does not wait for heaven to reward them, for He gives Himself right away, especially to those who consecrate themselves to Him. From that very moment He binds Himself to an exchange of friendship with those who accept to live intimately with Him. For God is not an abstract being, but a concrete one, the most concrete of all beings. We have sometimes the tendency to believe that He is far removed from us, lost in the clouds, whereas in fact He is very close to us. He is in fact in us when we are in the state of grace, and He is in us above everything else as a faithful friend, and not as an implacable judge.
>
> Every person in the state of grace is a friend of God. St. Ambrose said it; St. Thomas Aquinas confirmed it. But there are degrees in friendship. Thus it is that God loves all souls in the state of grace, but He loves more those who attach themselves to Him by an exclusive, perpetual love. He promised, even in this early life, a hundredfold to those who abandon all to follow Him. What is this hundredfold if not the life of friendship in which the soul enjoys already the first fruits of the happiness of heaven? Without a doubt, some very beautiful souls live in the world, but oftentimes they are rather overwhelmed by their preoccupation with material things, and by family and professional worries, so that it is very difficult for them to enjoy the recollection and the intimacy tasted by souls who live withdrawn from the world.

3) The Idealism of Love

There can be no getting around it. The consecration of one's life to God, and the vows of poverty, chastity, and obedience are sacrifices to which no-one feels a natural attraction. There is only one possible explanation for why a young man would be willing to do this. It is, as St. Paul says, that *"caritas Christi urget nos,"*—"for the charity of Christ presseth us" (II Cor. 5:14), impels, drives, forces, inspires even our rebellious wills. It is the infused virtue of charity, directed primarily towards God, and secondarily towards souls, the two being united together in the redeeming Passion of our divine Savior, which calls us to become "fishers of men." Crucial importance is here played by the mystery of the mystical body of Christ, the Catholic Church, in which the mystery of the Incarnation is continued, and for the sanctification of whose members the priest gives himself whole and entire. He loves the Church as he loves Christ, and will do no less for the Church than he does for Christ. Likewise essential to this consecration to the Church is the young man's love of the Blessed Virgin Mary, from whom he will learn the nature of true self-giving, compassion for souls, adoration of the divinity of Christ, and devotion to His sacred humanity in His Passion.

If a young man really knew how to love, how to yield his heart to the manly urge to offer himself for what is truly good and beautiful, how could he hold himself back from serving the Church? However, here also we see a frequent defect in our youth. Enamored with the love of sport and practical skills so helpful for a boy's growing up, they nevertheless rarely develop the love and appreciation of the most sublime realities—being, truth, goodness, and beauty—that is so necessary for a man. How rarely do we find in our boys the aspiration for excellence in those activities that most develop this appreciation—academic studies, languages, history, music, art, and literature!

Would that our young men loved knowledge for knowledge's sake, that they appreciated philosophical and theological truth for its very transcendence over day-to-day life, that they admired the beauty of true music, art, and literature, that they had the psychological intuition of the heroism of a life of virtue, prudence, fortitude, and self-control, and in particular of the sublime virtue of purity! How often indifference, or a know-it-all cynicism, to these highest of values paralyzes the idealism—ultimately the idealism of love—upon which every vocation is built! How often innocence is lost, impediments to a vocation are formed, and this by a failure of parents to train their children in the appreciation of true beauty!

4) SPIRIT OF FAITH

Clearly we cannot love what we do not know. There can be no response to a call to a life entirely penetrated by the supernatural without the spirit of faith. Much more is required for this than simply having the faith, or even saying our morning and night prayers together. We only have the spirit of faith when the principles of faith penetrate all our daily thoughts, activities, and recreations, when our family life is penetrated by the desire to promote the Social Kingship of Our Lord Jesus Christ, when we live in total dependence on divine Providence and the Blessed Virgin Mary. A much greater effort is to be made in our families. They all teach the Faith, the truths of the catechism, but few are able to impart to their children the spirit of faith.

Allow me to quote once more from Fr. Troadec's letter:

> To encourage the growth of the spirit of Faith amongst our youth, it is important that children feel, from a very early age, that God occupies the first place in their family. They must be aware that their parents' important decisions are made in the presence of God, that all trials are borne with a profoundly supernatural attitude, that the critical spirit is banished from their home, especially with respect to religious Brothers and Sisters, and priests. Breathing a supernatural perfume from their earliest childhood, children acquire the supernatural spirit that enables them to respond generously to God's call.... And so, parents cannot nourish the spirit of Faith in our youth if they are not themselves penetrated by it.... In effect, whatever be our vocation, we are all made for God, and if God does not occupy in our life all the place that is due to Him, it will be the devil that will take over, for it is natural for a void to be filled in.

5) Spirit of Sacrifice

We are painfully aware of how self-centered our young people have become, of how much their youthful energy and desires are directed towards "fun," "pleasure," "having a good time," "experiencing life." While many folks laugh about such attitudes, attitudes that they consider normal in youth, it seems to me that we ought to be saddened at such superficiality, so far removed from the ideals that youth ought to hold on to. When egocentrism has become a way of life, it is practically impossible to break, such a young man wanting the spiritual indeed, but counting the cost as carefully as if it were a dangerous pill, holding back from giving up all his time, energy, health, abilities, life, and his whole self. These are the souls that give up on a vocation when the going gets tough. Such a frame of mind does not happen by chance. It happens due to overindulgence, self-will, lack of discipline, absence of mortification, not being trained to go without, and loss of the spirit of poverty, none of which were possible in large families a century ago, and all of which are characteristic of our large and small families these days. Is it any wonder that our boys are deaf to the invitation: "If any man will come after me, let him deny himself, and take up his cross, and follow me. For he that will save his life, shall lose it; and he that shall lose his life for my sake, shall find it" (Mt. 16:24, 25)?

Fr. Troadec has this to say:

The spirit of sacrifice must be joined to the spirit of Faith. Paul Claudel wrote: "Youth is not made for pleasure, it is made for heroism." Youth is not made for pleasure, for pleasure is not an end in itself. Pleasure ought not necessarily be rejected. However, it must not be sought after for itself. If we seek it for itself, we desire to satisfy our ego, and we fall little by little into narcissism. But we are not made for ourselves. We are made for God. Youth is consequently not made for pleasure, but to strive after a high ideal. Instead of feeding himself with earthly pleasures, man ought to give himself to imitate the example of the Good Shepherd, who gave His life for His sheep. This is why priests and seminarians who have been faithful to their vocation are so complete in their personality.

But in order to have the strength to leave all to follow Our Lord, we must be detached. It is here that the spirit of sacrifice enters in…. Young men must have as early as possible the spirit of sacrifice, in order to develop their generosity and to help them in responding one day to God's call, if they receive this grace. This spirit of sacrifice must be present in families, and can also be nourished by meditation and by recourse to a spiritual director.

6) EQUILIBRIUM

Balance is a rare jewel at any time, but in particular in the instability of the modern, rapidly changing world. However, a priest-to-be must have the supernatural balance established among the virtues, especially those of humility, docility, obedience, and fortitude, by infused prudence, completing in its turn a naturally balanced character. Here lies the integrity that a priest must have, for he is necessarily a leader, not by his own efforts, nor by his own knowledge, nor by his own judgments, nor by his own temperament. He is a leader because he represents Christ, stands in the place of God, in his teaching, governing, and sanctifying of souls.

This precious equilibrium is, more than anything else, the product of a balanced family environment. More often than not it is undermined or destroyed, and this not only by mixed and broken marriages, but also by families in which the father refuses to take responsibility, the mother refuses docile submission, and both refuse to discipline themselves and their children. When ongoing conflicts, surging emotions, dysfunction, disorder, instability, unpredictability, and sentimentality are the order of the day, it is very difficult for a young man to have the integrated personality and spiritual life so necessary for the priestly life. Families that neglect to consider that grace builds on nature, that omit to cultivate natural virtue and emotional stability, who think that piety is a remedy for everything (and God knows how numerous such families are in our chapels) do not produce vocations.

Fr. Troadec remarks:

To enter the Seminary, one ought not to wait for a revelation from St. Michael the Archangel or the Blessed Mother. It suffices that one has the desire and the disposition to cooperate in the great work of the Redemption. A minimum of physical health, a good psychological equilibrium, intellectual and spiritual aptitude, and common sense must be joined to the desire of giving oneself to God. Finally, one must have a character that is neither too soft nor too violent. These are the dispositions that must be acquired in order to be capable not only of following the Seminary formation, but especially of becoming the holy priest that the world needs so badly.

These, then, are the six aspects of a priestly vocation that are all absolutely necessary, and that are little known and appreciated among our faithful. The absence of any one of them will make it impossible for a young man to persevere. May our families live their Catholic lives in such a way as to promote all these qualities of true vocations.

—*Fr. Scott,* August 2003

 **Would it be morally wrong to dress as a monk even though a layman? Would you consider someone dressing as a monk a deception? Can a lay person found a monastery? Even in these times, isn't it imperative that a monastery have ecclesiastical approval? What suggestions would you give to a young man wishing to join a monastery?**

A religious life is one of consecration to our divine Lord and as such requires the guidance of Our Lord's authority here on earth, which is the Church. Hence, all endeavors of a consecrated life by the evangelical counsels is strictly subject to the direction of the ecclesiastical power.

There is a certain false and romantic idea of the religious life among some. They seem to forget that the evangelical vows are to conform us more closely to Jesus Christ who was crucified. The religious life is to be a sublime gift of self-donation to God. Anyone considering the religious life must faithfully follow the direction of a spiritual guide, usually his confessor. And such a grave decision could never be made without serious thought and prayer. This would especially require a retreat.

Though it would certainly be deceptive to don a religious habit without ecclesiastical approval, it may not be gravely sinful except insofar as the individual is attempting to deceive and say, for example, was soliciting funds for "his monastery." Most whom I have encountered of this ilk, unfortunately too many times, are a little off the wall, to say the least. They too often consider themselves more versed in Church matters than the priest and are stubborn. They also give a very bad idea of religious life and scorn for the Church when they meet others, especially those outside the Fold. God will judge them according to their knowledge and mental capacity, but in the meantime they are to be forbidden such eccentricities as they damage the true religious life.

Yes, it is imperative that a monastery receive some type of ecclesiastical approval—even in these times.

—*Fr. Doran,* November 1991

Should a traditional religious Sister who is unable to live her religious life in a post-Vatican II community request to be dispensed from her vows?

No. If a religious sees the crisis in the Church, she will only ask to be dispensed from her vows if she is paralyzed by legalism and by the false notion of obedience that this legalism engenders.

The real solution of a traditional Sister in a modernist congregation is not to request a dispensation from her vows. It is precisely the contrary that a traditional Sister is obliged before God to do—to live faithful for life the vows that she made before God. It is precisely to keep her vows that she must leave the modernist community. It is precisely because she is determined to keep to her religious vows that she is obliged to adhere to Tradition. Consequently, it makes no sense at all for her to abandon those vows or ask to be released from them. These vows are not an impediment to her sanctification, but the means for it.

It is certainly true that in normal times one does not have the right to leave one's religious community to join another without dispensation or permission from both superiors. However, the proof that we are not living in normal times is the fact that the rule has changed radically and in its entirety since the religious made profession. Her profession is of a rule that the modernist community no longer keeps. Consequently, she is obliged in virtue of her profession, and the virtue of religion, to leave her modernist community and to establish herself in a traditional community in which the spiritual life is compatible with her vowed constitutions. By not keeping the rule, and not watching that others keep it also, the modernist superiors lose their authority to govern. The religious is no longer bound to them in obedience and can transfer her obedience to another authority.

A Sister who has left a modernist community to join a traditional community is consequently not disobedient at all. She has the true virtue of obedience, which is a part of justice, and directly related to the virtue of religion, by which we submit ourselves to God. She is obedient to her rule and to the superior that God gives her to live that rule. She is obedient. The decision as to just how bad it must be before a religious is forced to leave her community is not in itself an easy one. A simple moral disorder or laxity is not enough. It must be the despising or abandoning of the traditional rule that the religious professed and of the religious life altogether. This is an easy decision to make in the vast majority of communities at this time in history.

—*Fr. Scott,* October 1999

Can a widow whose children are full grown join a cloister or a convent?

Anyone desiring to enter religious life must first of all be Catholic and have the right intention. This intention cannot be interpreted without reference to a divine vocation. All religious institutes must therefore in some manner discern this vocation.

The general law of the Church is that the individual be seventeen (previously fifteen), in sufficient physical and mental health to accomplish the work of the institute, and be unmarried. Separation or civil divorce from a spouse is not sufficient. Consequently, a divorced or separated person cannot enter the religious life, whereas a widow or widower can. There is no general age limit set for entrance into religion. It is important to remember that these are only the most general norms for entry; each religious institute is free to set its own requirements and regulations, within the laws of the Church.

—*Fr. Doran,* October 1993

ABOUT MARRIAGE, PARENTHOOD, FAMILY LIFE, AND REARING CHILDREN

Is it advisable for a Catholic to marry a non-Catholic?

Marriage, surely one of the most difficult and trying of vocations and at the same time most rewarding and fulfilling, is rendered even more difficult when serious unresolved differences exist even before the solemn exchange of vows.

In the *Forum* of June 1929, a non-Catholic woman wrote an article entitled, "What It Means to Marry a Catholic." "The wisest ruling the Roman Catholic Church ever made," she said, "was that of forbidding the marriage of a Catholic with a non-Catholic. If it could enforce this decree, many tragedies would be averted."

Why a tragedy?—because two persons holding with equal sincerity and conviction opposing religious views, especially in relation to the concept, nature, and intimacies of married life, are destined to be in perpetual conflict and continuing opposition. Disagreement over fundamental issues is a very unsure foundation for marital union and happiness. The problems in many cases increase as the marriage progresses, and divisions abound with no real meeting ground possible for solution or compromise because basic principles are not held in common.

There is no situation that calls for more clear thinking than the situation of mixed marriages. The dispensation to marry a non-Catholic is only a toleration of, not a solution to, such a marriage, which will inevitably bring in terms of tension and uneasiness over questions of the Faith, Catholic upbringing and education of children, birth control, divorce, *etc.*

Even in an "ideal" mixed marriage, there is an element of secret sorrow on the part of the Catholic because his or her marriage partner is excluded from the essential, true, and fruitful participation in the one thing that alone matters and unites, the holy Catholic Faith given us by Christ Himself.

—*Fr. Boyle,* December 1993

A single woman for grave medical reasons has undergone a hysterectomy. Can she contract a valid Catholic marriage?

Catholic marriage is defined as the lawful contract between a man and a woman by which contract the exclusive and perpetual right is given and accepted to those mutual bodily functions which of themselves are suitable for the generation of children. What concerns us here in this definition is the right to the marital act, *i.e.,* can the marriage act be accomplished fully as to its proper function and end.

For a man, impotency is an invalidating impediment to marriage. In the case of hysterectomy, the absence of the uterus does not constitute impotency but sterility. Canon 1068, 1917 Code of Canon Law, §3, clearly states that sterility neither invalidates marriage nor renders it illicit. This is really the issue raised in the question. Thus it is clear that such a person can validly marry, but with respect to Canon 1098 of the new Code of Canon Law she must inform her future spouse of her condition; this is also restated in the new code, Canon 1084, §2.

—*Fr. Boyle,* January 1994

 **A friend of mine was raised a Catholic, fell away from the Church, and married a non-Catholic person outside the Church. She has now divorced him. Is she free to remarry?**

You are perfectly correct in stating that a Catholic is obliged to the canonical form of marriage, and that this is, according to ecclesiastical law, under pain of invalidity of the marriage. Before Vatican II the marriage of a Catholic by a justice of the peace or by a Protestant minister was always invalid. The couple was not married in the eyes of God until such time as the marriage was regularized before a Catholic priest.

There are, however, two shamefully liberal exceptions which are permitted by the 1983 Code of Canon Law, and in which cases the marriage would presumably be valid. One case is where the Catholic party formally apostatizes. In the new code, he is no longer obliged to the canonical form to enter into a valid marriage, as if once a Catholic he is not always obliged to be a Catholic. The other shameful exception is the dispensation from canonical form, which the parish priest can now give, that a person might be married in the church of the non-Catholic party. Such a marriage is valid, but it is founded on indifferentism, and the children suffer, for they have no chance of being raised Catholic in such a case.

Presuming that the marriage was never regularized, and that neither of these two cases applies, your friend's marriage was invalid.

However, these are quite a few presumptions to make. Consequently, a person is not allowed to judge in his own case, and he must seek a decision from an ecclesiastical tribunal, which will consider all the circumstances, and if it truly is the case that the marriage is invalid, will grant an annulment for lack of canonical form.

—Fr. Scott, September 1999

 **Can it still be affirmed that a wife should be submissive to her husband, given the changes in modern society?**

The due submission of a wife to her husband can be considered on two different planes: firstly, that of the natural law, man and woman having each a profoundly different function in the building block of society which is the family; and secondly, on the supernatural plane.

This second perspective is by far the most important and illuminates all of married life. For if the submission of a wife to her husband is totally clear in the natural law to any woman who has not been tainted by the rebellious principles of liberalism, it was explicitly confirmed in the New Testament. St. Paul, in the fifth chapter of his epistle to the Ephesians, lays down the principles. A husband has, in virtue of the sacrament of matrimony, always to imitate Christ in His love for the Church, and a wife has always, in virtue of the same sacrament, to imitate the Church in her love for Christ. Thus a man is really the head of his wife, and has the duty to take leadership, whereas the wife must strive to be the heart responding to and dependent upon the head.

Pope Leo XIII treats of this question explicitly in his encyclical *Arcanum Divinae Sapientiae* of February 10, 1880:

> The husband is the chief of the family, and the head of the wife. The woman, because she is flesh of his flesh and bone of his bone, must be subject to her husband and obey him: not, indeed as a servant, but as a companion, so that her obedience shall be wanting in neither honor nor dignity. Since the husband represents Christ, and since the wife represents the Church, let there always be, both in him who commands and in her who obeys, a heaven-born love guiding both in their respective duties. For "the husband is the head of the wife, as Christ is the head of the Church.... Therefore as the Church is subject to Christ, so also let the wives be to their husbands in all things" (Eph. 5:23-24). (*Papal Teachings: Matrimony*, selected by the monks of Solesmes, p. 141)

Since man's nature cannot change, neither can the natural law; and since divine revelation was completed with the death of the last of the apostles, neither can this supernatural plan change either. In order to resist the corruption of nature and God's supernatural gifts, husbands and wives need to remember that they do not belong to this world, otherwise modern-day liberalism will succeed in destroying the family. Husbands will consequently take responsibility and leadership, even when they feel inadequate, and wives will take delight in denying their own will and obeying their husbands.

These questions have been treated often in *The Angelus*, and I would like to take the opportunity of recommending the following articles, which treat explicitly of this subject: "When Mothers Need Mothering" and "Flesh of My Flesh," in *The Angelus,* June 1997; and "The Leadership of Fathers" and "What Is a Mother?" in *The Angelus,* October 1995.

It is this authority of a man over his wife (not of men over women) which the liberals detest, and which, alas, Pope John Paul II has fought against on the basis of the false rights of man. In his analysis of this change of teaching, author Luigi Accattoli does not hesitate to affirm (approvingly) that the pope "corrects the teaching of St. Paul" (*When a Pope Asks Forgiveness* [Alba House, 1998], pp. 105-108).

In regard to the radically feminist nature of the assertion of the equality in marriage of husband and wife, it suffices to quote some passages from the above author, based as they are on the pope's September 1988 encyclical *Mulieris Dignitatem*:

> The boldest stroke is also found in *Mulieris Dignitatem*, which contains a summation of the biblical references to individual women and even cor-

rects two thousand years of interpretation of the passages in St. Paul which describe man as the "head" of the woman. He even corrects St. Paul—or what is based on antiquity in his writings—when he states: "All the reasons in favor of the subjection of woman to man in marriage must be understood in the sense of a mutual subjection of both out of reverence for Christ." (Accattoli, citing *Mulieris Dignitatem*, §§9, 24)

Accattoli is certainly accurate in pointing out that this is a radical transformation in the Church's teaching. Nobody could possibly doubt that the letter and sense of St. Paul is of a one-sided submission, and that the pope, by reinterpreting it as a "mutual subjection," is both emptying the text of all sense and going directly against divine revelation for the sake of his humanistic and false principles on the equality and dignity of man.

Truly feminine wives will consequently abhor this feminist perversion of Catholic truth, and practice the submission and obedience which both nature and grace incline them to.

—*Fr. Scott,* October 1998

Is it a mortal sin to refuse one's husband or wife the marital debt?

Conjugal relations are rightly called the "marriage debt," which each spouse owes the other in justice the relations that are apt to engender children. It is this very particular right over one's body that is given up to one's spouse by marriage vows. St. Paul is very explicit about this:

> Let the husband render the debt to his wife, and the wife also in like manner to the husband. The wife hath not power of her own body, but the husband. And in like manner the husband also hath not power of his own body, but the wife. (I Cor. 7:3, 4)

A debt in justice obliges under pain of mortal sin when a serious matter or quantity is owed. However, marriage relationships are a serious matter and of great importance. Furthermore, the refusal of the marriage debt may cause a danger of incontinence. Consequently, it is a mortal sin to deprive one's spouse of these relationships whether it be the husband or the wife who refuses the debt. The typical example of this is when a wife feels that she is justified in withholding the marriage debt because her feelings are hurt or she is not appreciated enough. Nevertheless, there is no excuse for the husband to withhold the affection and care for his wife's feelings, for he is responsible for them as head of the family.

However, it is possible for the couple to agree, by mutual consent, to abstain for a short period of time, for example, for penance during Lent. However, it must be by mutual consent, and on the understanding that either spouse can withdraw this consent at any time. St. Paul speaks of this also: "Defraud not one another, except, perhaps, by consent, for a time, that you may give yourselves to prayer" (I Cor. 7:5).

There can, however, be good reasons that excuse a husband or wife from rendering this marriage debt, such as adultery of the other spouse, or unreasonable demands (*e.g.*, frequency, intoxication, recent birth of a child), or grave danger to health or life (*e.g.*, by the possible communication of infectious diseases), or in the case where the husband refuses to perform his duty of supporting his family (Jone, *Moral Theology*, pp. 557-558). There can also be special circumstances that reduce the culpability of refusing the marriage debt, so that it is only a venial sin, for example, "if the petitioner will readily renounce his right, or if rendering it is only briefly postponed, or when the use of the marriage right is frequent and its refusal is only rare" (*ibid.*).

—*Fr. Scott,* June 2001

Does apostasy of one's spouse from the Catholic Faith give one the right to refuse the marriage debt and to separate?

It is truly a very sorrowful time when a husband or wife either abandons all Christian faith (=apostasy) or abandons the Catholic Church and joins a heretical sect (=heresy). This poses immense problems for the Catholic spouse, for when a person abandons the faith that he has once held, he generally becomes very bitter and antagonistic towards it. Perseverance in cohabitation with such a spouse can be a great danger to the faith of the Catholic spouse, constantly exposed to opposition and perversion. It can also be a grave danger to the faith of the children, whom the apostate will frequently turn away from the Catholic Church.

It is for these reasons that the Church has considered, since the time of Pope Urban III in the twelfth century, that spiritual adultery can constitute a sufficient reason for separation. It is by analogy with physical adultery, that Our Lord Himself considered sufficient reason for separation (Mt. 19:9). Adultery is called "spiritual" when a person abandons the one true spouse of Our Lord Jesus Christ, the Roman Catholic Church, and adheres to a false religion, sect, or atheistic belief. It is called "adultery" because it is a betrayal of the whole mystical symbolism of marriage: the union between Christ and the Catholic Church consummated on the cross. However, marriage vows are not thereby dissolved, and if the apostate later returns to the practice of the Catholic Faith, then the Catholic party is obliged to resume the common life with him (or her) and render the marriage debt.

This is summarized in Canon 1131 of the 1917 Code of Canon Law. In fact, it is the first of several reasons given that could justify a Catholic for separating from his spouse, the others being the insistence on giving a non-Catholic education to the children, or living a criminal and shameful life, or threat of grave danger to body or soul, or abuse that makes the common life unbearable. The canon, however, reminds Catholics that such a separation can only be undertaken with the authorization of the ordinary of the place, and not on one's own authority, unless perhaps the facts are certain and there is a danger in delay. It is interesting to note that eight centuries of ecclesiastical tradition and common sense have been done away with in the 1983 Code (Can. 1153), which carefully excludes abandonment of the Faith or adhesion to a sect from the reasons that justify separation. It is difficult not to see here a clear sign of the indifferentism to the true Faith that characterizes the modern church.

This being said, it does not follow from the above that in the case of one's spouse abandoning the Faith one must separate. Far from it. In general, this will neither be necessary nor prudent. Frequently, the rebellion against the Faith and the Church will be a temporary temptation or spiritual difficulty, and patience on the part of the Catholic party is the best way to handle the passing problem. Not infrequently, the rejection of God and faith will also be a personal thing and will not affect directly the religious life of the Catholic party or the children. In such cases, it is imperative that separation not take place, on account of the grievous psychological harm that such a separation is wont to engender in the children, and the bitterness in the spouses. In short, every effort must be made to keep the cohabitation for as long as there is no danger of perversion of the faith or moral life of either the Catholic spouse or the children. Likewise, no effort must be spared to obtain the counseling necessary to bring about an understanding, even on a purely natural level, so as to keep the married life together. By courageously bearing these crosses the Catholic spouse will most effectively sanctify the person whom on earth he is most bound to love, as St. Paul teaches:

> And if any woman hath a husband that believeth not, and he consent to dwell with her, let her not put away her husband. For the unbelieving husband is sanctified by the believing wife; and the unbelieving wife is sanctified by the believing husband. (I Cor. 7:13-14)

—*Fr. Scott,* February 2008

 ## Is parenthood in itself a great thing?

Parenthood is so noble that to understand its greatness we must rise above all creatures, including the angels, and go up to God Himself in His own life.

God the Father begets a Son to whom He gives all that He has: His own substance and all of His attributes, so that the Son is, in truth, the image of God, the brightness of His glory, and the figure of His substance. He is that so perfectly that the Father was well-pleased in His Son because He finds Himself in Him. Henceforth, to see the Son is to also see the Father.

So, in becoming a father, man receives from God a participation in His paternity. "And," said Msgr. Bougaud, "this is possibly one of the meanings of this word of God. 'Let us make man in Our image and likeness.' May he be a father in time as I am in eternity."

To become a father is to beget a son. But man, not possessing "paternity" in himself, needs an assistant similar to him in order to become a father.

By paternity man participates so much in the very power of the Creator that in the natural order he is the father, the direct representative of God with his children, the pontiff ("*pontem fecit*"—he who makes the bridge) who reconnects them to God. Also, in the Ten Commandments, directly after the first three precepts concerning God Himself, we find before all of our other duties, that of honoring our father and our mother.

In the plan of God, in becoming a father, man is crowned with a halo of divine glory, of this same glory from which all paternity proceeds.

Without difficulty we understand that such a great thing demands holiness: "Be ye holy for I the Lord your God am holy." "Look for holiness without which no man shall see God."

—Unknown, February 1993

 ### Is a marriage valid if a couple agrees beforehand to limit the number of children by artificial birth control or Natural Family Planning?

The Church's teaching is summarized in Canon 1013 of the 1917 Code of Canon Law, which states that "the primary end of marriage is the procreation and education of children." The intention of having children, provided that this is possible, is consequently essential to the very substance of the matrimonial contract, which is for "acts which are in themselves capable of engendering children" (Can. 1081, 1917 Code of Canon Law).

The importance of children as the primary end of marriage was again stressed by the Holy Office under Pope Pius XII:

> To the question: "Whether the views of certain recent writers can be admitted, who either deny that the primary end of marriage is the procreation and education of children, or teach that the secondary ends are not necessarily subordinate to the primary end, but are equally principal and

independent," the reply was: In the negative. (Bouscaren and Ellis, *Canon Law: A Text and Commentary* [1946], p. 400)

Yet the 1983 Code of Canon Law embraces the personalist conception condemned less than forty years earlier by not only placing the two ends of marriage on an equal and independent level, but even listing first the secondary end (*i.e.*, mutual support, or the personal good of the spouses): "The matrimonial covenant, by which a man and a woman establish between themselves a partnership of the whole of life, is by its nature ordered towards the good of the spouses and the procreation and education of offspring" (Can. 1055, §1).

It is ultimately this new concept of marriage, as being for the couple themselves, and not so much for children, which has resulted in the refusal of Catholics since Vatican II to have large families. Artificial birth control, which is the destruction of Catholic families, is no longer condemned as a mortal sin, for marriage is now considered in a selfish way, as being for the couple themselves, rather than an outpouring of love desiring to participate in God's work of creation and sanctification of His children. The so-called practice of Natural Family Planning (NFP), propagated in the post-conciliar church as a "Catholic" method of contraception, derives also from the same contraceptive mentality. Since marriage is considered primarily for the couple itself, they consider themselves free to determine the number of children and their spacing. This can be a mortal sin if NFP is employed without sufficient reason, as approved by the Church (*e.g.*, serious eugenic, social, or medical reasons, such as danger to the life of the mother through additional children). Whether it be through artificial or natural means that the first purpose of marriage is frustrated, such couples who are not willing to accept all the children God sends them do indeed fail to live up to their marriage vows.

However, this does not mean the marriage vows with the condition of limiting children by artificial contraception or NFP are necessarily invalid. The exclusion of children is certainly a grounds for a declaration of nullity, but only when there is an explicit, provable, and positive act of the will to avoid children, that is, only when the obligation of having children, as being the fulfillment of the first purpose of marriage, is explicitly excluded. For this is an intention contrary to the substance of marriage itself. The difficulty in such cases is to determine whether it is the obligation of having children which is refused, or whether it is simply the fulfillment of this obligation (*cf.* Bouscaren, *Canon Law Digest*, I, 532-533).

Those couples who accept the obligation of having children are certainly validly married, even if they do not always fulfill this obligation, *e.g.*, by limiting the number of their children. This is the case of those selfish couples, without faith in divine Providence, who are determined to limit the size of their family for reasons of convenience or simply because they prefer it that way. They commit a grave sin, even if it is by NFP that they presume to do this. They are truly married, but they will never be able to communicate to their children generosity, the spirit of sacrifice, the love of the cross, of souls, and the Church.

Moreover, even if a couple deliberately excludes all children, the Church always presumes, until proven otherwise, that it is the fulfillment of the duty that is excluded, and not the obligation of having children itself, and that consequently the marriage is valid.

—Fr. Scott, May 2002

Is there a Scriptural foundation for the Church's teaching on contraception?

The importance of this question lies in convincing Protestants of Catholic truth on this question. For, if they sometimes see the evil of abortion, in general they approve of contraception.

It is true that in the Bible there is only one explicit reference to the sin of contraception, from which it receives its technical name of Onanism. The text that describes the sin of Onan, the second son of Juda, is found in Genesis 38:8-10:

> Juda therefore said to Onan his son: Go in to thy brother's wife and marry her, that thou mayst raise seed to thy brother. He knowing that the children should not be his, when he went in to his brother's wife, spilled his seed upon the ground, lest children should be born in his brother's name. And therefore the Lord slew him, because he did a detestable thing.

Protestant apologists, however, maintain that the sin for which the Lord God slew Onan was not specifically that of spilling his seed, but spilling his seed so that he would not raise up children to his brother. However, this latter was a grave obligation promulgated in the Mosaic law. It was called the law of the levirate, according to which a man had the obligation of raising up children for a deceased brother by taking his brother's widow for his own wife and engendering and raising children in his brother's name, who would legally be his brother's (Deut. 25:5-10).

The first problem with this explanation is that Onan lived in the time of the patriarchs, before the departure into Egypt, and four hundred years before Moses and the promulgation of the Mosaic law that is described in the book of Deuteronomy. If it is true that the Mosaic law legally acknowledged and approved a much more ancient custom, it cannot be said that Onan's refusal to observe this custom was a crime punishable by death by law.

A further objection is that even the Mosaic law did not consider the refusal to take one's deceased brother's wife as punishable by death. The punishment prescribed in Deuteronomy 25:9-10 is nothing more than a public humiliation:

> The woman shall come to him before the ancients, and shall take off his shoe from his foot, and spit in his face, and say: So shall it be done to the man that will not build up his brother's house. And his name shall be called in Israel, the house of the unshod.

Canon Clamer has this comment to make on this obligation:

> The obligation that arose from the law of the levirate was not so rigorous that one could not escape from it. If for one reason or another a brother-in-law did not agree to take his sister-in-law, the law, without obliging him, allowed the abandoned and outraged widow to inflict upon him a humiliation which became the sanction of law. (Pirot-Clamer, *La Sainte Bible*, II, 670)

Catholic exegetes dispute as to what degree Onan was punished for breaking the law of the levirate and to what degree it was for his use of contraception. Nevertheless, it must be a combination of the two, for it can hardly be considered just for Almighty God to have punished Onan by death for a crime condemned by custom only and not under pain of death. Furthermore, Onan did not refuse to take Thamar, his brother's wife, but did actually go into her (Gen. 38:10). Consequently, the evil crime that he committed consisted not in his refusal to marry her, but in his refusal to engender children, namely, his frustration of the procreative act. This selfishness, inspiring as it did a sin against the very nature itself of the marriage relationship, is manifestly the reason why God struck him dead. Consequently, this text can certainly be used, as it always has been, to establish the biblical foundation of Catholic teaching on contraception.

It ought not to astonish us that other texts on this subject are not found in sacred Scripture. The reason for this is that it is such an evident and obvious conclusion of the natural law, that it is presupposed for the supernatural revelation condemning sexual immorality. The Church has always taught that contraception is wrong because it is against nature, that is, against the natural law. A few texts will establish this. In 1679 Innocent XI *condemned* the proposition: "Self-abuse is not prohibited by the natural law. Hence, if God had not forbidden, it could have been often good and even sometimes obligatory under pain of mortal sin" (Prop. 49, DS 2149). Self-abuse is effectively the same thing as contraception, since it produces a spilling of the seed.

Furthermore, in 1851 the Holy Office condemned the proposition that contraception could sometimes be justified for good reasons as "scandalous, erroneous, and contrary to the natural law of marriage" (DS 2791). Of the proposition that contraception is not prohibited by the natural law, it stated: "Scandalous, and elsewhere implicitly condemned by Innocent XI's proposition 49" (DS 2792). In 1853, the Holy Office repeated its condemnation of contraception, giving as its reason that it is "intrinsically evil" (DS 2795). If something is intrinsically evil, it is perverse, against the natural order. There consequently can be no doubt that the Church's firm condemnation of contraception is for this reason.

Pope Paul VI repeats this teaching in his 1968 Encyclical *Humanae Vitae*, pointing out the intrinsic evil that makes it against the natural law even if done for a "good" intention:

> Excluded is every action which, either in anticipation of the conjugal act, or in its accomplishment, or in the development of its natural consequences, proposes, whether as an end or as a means, to render procreation impossible.... It is an error to think that a conjugal act which is deliberately made infecund and so is intrinsically dishonest could be made honest and right by the ensemble of a fecund conjugal life. (§14)

When entering into discussion with Protestants, it is imperative to understand the reason why the Catholic Church condemns contraception. For Protestantism is based upon the philosophy of nominalism, which denies the common sense and obvious fact that we can know the real natures of things. If there are no natures of things, then the distinction between nature and grace does not make sense; nor the mystery of the Trinity, three Persons with one divine nature; nor the Incarnation, one Person having two natures; nor the Real Presence or the whole concept of Transubstantiation, a change of substance. Equally difficult for them to comprehend is the natural law, established by the Creator, a moral ordering that is inscribed in man's nature itself and from which he cannot escape. For them, morality is purely positive; it is simply being told what to do and what not to do, and then having to abide by it, without anything being intrinsically good or evil in itself.

The Protestant will consequently not be convinced of the objective truthfulness of the Church's teaching on contraception until he has come to understand that there is an objective order of things that we call the natural law. Just as this manifestly exists in the ordering of creation in nature, and can be clearly established, so also does it exist in the moral realm, and it regulates man's actions and his relationships with others. Once he has understood this, he will see that there is such a thing as an intrinsically perverse act, and that contraception is such an act, taking away from the nature and final purpose of the marriage act, inscribed in nature, which is to procreate children. He will then understand why Almighty God did not repeat in sacred Scripture this self-evident truth.

—Fr. Scott, June 2007

Is it ever permissible to condone artificial contraception as a means of family planning for a Catholic couple?

The simple, direct answer to this question is No. It is never permissible to break God's laws nor advise an act which in itself is intrinsically evil, *i.e.*, which is always evil by its very nature, and nothing nor anyone can ever excuse it. The marriage act, willed by God, must respect the divinely established order: Catholic parents are co-creators with God and must never, by any practice whatsoever, prevent God's will which is that every marital act must be open to the transmission of life. Procreation is the primary end of marriage and is always to be respected. The secondary end of marriage—for in marriage there is a hierarchy of ends—is the mutual love and companionship of husband and wife. These ends are not opposed to each other nor can they be inverted, as has been done in the new conception of marriage, without grave damage to the divine concept of the sacrament itself. Such a practice prompts the question asked and the response duly given. Birth control is a misnomer as Chesterton rightly observed. There is nothing to control—except our wayward passion—but there is a possible birth to prevent. Artificial contraception is birth prevention, which is clearly opposed to God's laws. Therefore it can never be approved nor advised. It is contrary to the Church's traditional teaching from the beginning as Pope Pius XI reminds us in his encyclical *Casti Connubii*, January 9, 1931: "Those who in exercising the conjugal act deliberately frustrate its natural power and purpose sin against nature and commit a deed which is sinful and intrinsically vicious."

—Fr. Boyle, January 1994

The question of Natural Family Planning again. What did Pope Pius XII say on October 20, 1951, to the midwives of Italy on the subject of temporal abstinence?

The teaching of the Church which Pope Pius XII clearly expressed on this matter of temporal abstinence is the following: Temporal abstinence is only allowed if there are grave motives, independent of the good will of the couple. Then, only for serious reasons the married couple may avoid conception with timed continence. As the pope says, these serious reasons can be of medical, economic, or social order, through the circumstances of life (*i.e.*, the mother is ill, the family is poor, there is a war). God shows each family how many children He wants them to have. This family planning doesn't come from men but from God. If there is no serious reason, it would be surely against justice or charity for a couple to avoid having children even with this method of timed continence.

—*Fr. Carl,* May 1984

How do I explain to a total atheist why the Catholic Church is against both abortion and birth control?

Speaking to an atheist you must first prove the existence of God before discussing God's Institution, the Church. You will be wasting your time speaking of Church doctrine to one who does not believe in the Church. Fortunately, abortion and birth control are both natural subjects, that is, they form part of the natural law. The Church speaks on these matters because she expounds and defends both the supernatural order and that of the natural order which affects the religion and morality of men. The natural law is the participation of rational beings in the eternal law of God. This is thus part of morality. As humanity moves farther and farther from God, their minds become more and more dimmed by sin. This crass ignorance gives the result that the Church of God alone defends many truths which are, in fact, knowable by natural reason. Therefore, the so-called "Catholic doctrines" against abortion and birth control are in reality the natural law. Men can know the truth concerning them by the use of natural reason; divine revelation is not needed. Abortion is intrinsically evil because it is the termination of an innocent human life. The child in the womb, regardless of defects or helplessness, is human life. It is an individual created in the likeness of God. Though still in development it remains a human person in its fundamental reality. Even genetically the individual is complete only days after conception. It remains only to grow, and this we all do during our lives. Need for growth does not remove this child's right to life. Destruction of this child is to obliterate the created image of God and is therefore a mortal sin against the Creator. It is also a grave injustice against the child and his parents. Finally, it is a serious offence against society. Any community which kills the most helpless of its members will die.

Artificial birth control is a thwarting of the primary end of the union of a husband and wife. Man and woman are married primarily for the education of children, the continuation of the human race. It is not necessary to be married to have a baby. Nor is it necessary to be married to express affection. One can love a parent or a friend without marrying him. But to educate correctly a child requires the stability of a family. Therefore, marriage is primarily instituted for this end. (We do not even speak of any sexual union outside of marriage, which is always illicit.

Human beings are to be governed by intelligence, their highest faculty. They are not barn animals.) The artificial obstruction of the generation of children is therefore always gravely wrong as it violates the primary reason for the union itself. It is a sin against nature. To remove the ultimate reason for the union of man and woman artificially is to reduce that union to a mere source of pleasure, and all too often reduces it to a selfish misuse of one another.

Note well that both of these questions can be dealt with without reference to the positive law of God. All men, keeping all things in proportion, should see their truthfulness.

—*Fr. Doran,* March 1993

Is it permissible for a Catholic wife and mother to take a job outside the home?

It cannot be accepted as something normal and approved by the Church for a wife and mother to be free to take employment outside the home for as long as her children are still dependent upon her care.

The working of mothers outside the home for a salary is called by Pope Pius XI "economic emancipation" in his 1930 encyclical on Christian marriage, *Casti Connubii:*

> This, however, is not the true emancipation of women, nor that rational and exalted liberty which belongs to the noble office of a Christian woman and wife; it is rather the debasing of the womanly character and the dignity of motherhood, and indeed of the whole family, as a result of which the husband suffers the loss of his wife, the children of their mother, and the home and the whole family of an ever-watchful guardian. More than this, this false liberty and unnatural equality with the husband is to the detriment of the woman herself, for if the woman descends from her truly regal throne to which she has been raised within the walls of the home by means of the Gospel, she will soon be reduced to the old state of slavery (if not in appearance, certainly in reality) and become as amongst the pagans the mere instrument of man. (§75)

Towards the end of the same encyclical the pope is even more explicit. He talks about the evils and the injustices that discourage married couples, and compares the evil of mothers having to work with that of not being able to find a suitable home:

> If families, particularly those in which there are many children, have not suitable dwellings, if the husband cannot find employment and means of livelihood; if the necessities of life cannot be purchased except at exorbitant prices; if even the mother of the family, to the great harm of the home, is compelled to go forth and seek a living by her own labor...it is patent to all to what an extent married people may lose heart. (§120)

Clearly, we cannot judge the particular situation of mothers who experience the need to work outside the home. There can be many reasons that could make this a necessary evil, such as sickness and unemployment of the husband, or a husband not receiving a just salary, sufficient to support the family. There can also be psychological and professional reasons why a wife and mother might be obliged to stay in the workforce outside the home. However, the Church clearly teaches that this is an evil. We cannot pretend that it is a good thing, or that it is indifferent, or that it is not going to do any harm to her children and family. Moreover, no woman can be liberated from the home in this manner without changing her very awareness of what it is to be a Catholic wife and mother.

Consequently, it can only be tolerated as an unavoidable and necessary evil, and provided that it be only considered a temporary, short-term arrangement, and that the utmost effort is made by the working mother and her husband to minimize the negative effects. However, it would be very wrong to claim that this is a good thing, or approved and allowed by the Church. It is at best an unavoidable and necessary evil that one ought to be apologetic for and never brag about.

—*Fr. Scott,* April 2007

How can I get my four-year-old to participate in our daily rosary?

The prayer of little children is a very delicate thing. Not unlike the disciples, who rebuked those who brought little children to be blessed by Our Lord, we find it difficult to understand that children can do what we find so difficult ourselves, namely, prayer. Yet Our Lord was clear: "Suffer the little children, and forbid them not to come to me: for the kingdom of heaven is for such" (Mt. 19:14).

Children can indeed pray, but only within the limits of their capacities—namely, their understanding, concentration, and attention span. Moreover, their prayer must retain childlike simplicity to be genuine, that is, spontaneity in asking for what they need, in praying for Mommy and Daddy, in telling Jesus they are sorry for their faults, *etc.* Mary Reed Newland's article "Teaching Children to Pray" in *Raising Your Children* (Angelus Press, 1995) has some practical suggestions:

> Children have such simple faith in the efficacy of prayer that it is easy for them to form the habit of praying on all sorts of occasions ... occasions of minor crises during the day .... They will voice their prayer aloud, matter of factly, and with the simplicity of the faith that is as a grain of mustard, they wait for the mountain to be moved.... It is very easy to plant the habit, and their world is so much more secure, because of this faith that God is ready and willing to help them on every hand, that calling on Him is second nature to them. (Pp. 137-138)

If the family rosary is not to become an interminable chore for little children, these principles must be applied. It must first be recognized that every family and every child is different. There are some families and some children, used to a more strict discipline, who will kneel or sit quietly during the recitation of the rosary. There are others who find it impossible to stay still. The discipline required for the rosary must be in proportion to the discipline required for the rest of their lives. If family life as a whole is disciplined, little Johnny will know how to sit still and be quiet during the sacred time of prayer. However, flexibility needs to be shown on the exterior details, depending upon the individual circumstances for each child (*e.g.*, age, temperament, and maturity) and each family.

Furthermore, unless they be malicious disruptions, distractions and lack of concentration should not be punished lest prayer become onerous and painful. The emphasis should rather be given to positive rewards for good efforts, such as a fun activity or a treat after the recitation of the rosary. The active involvement of the children, according to their age level, is crucial. This does not just mean saying the Our Father's and Hail Mary's when they are able to do so. Each decade could be preceded by a very brief discussion of the mystery, and the children could be asked their intentions for each particular decade. A special virtue can be asked for, as well as sorrow for a fault. In this way the spontaneity can be renewed at the beginning of every decade.

Another key help to profiting from the daily rosary is to take advantage of children's ease in praying always, as Our Lord suggested. Their trust in Providence can be so profound, their sense of right and wrong so acute, that it can bring on a spontaneous prayer for God's help or forgiveness. Very short but fervent prayers can punctuate the day. A parent can do well to take advantage of this and spread out the mysteries of the rosary during the day.

However, above all else in importance is the example of the parents themselves. If the parents are bored and distracted during the recitation of the rosary, irritable and picky towards their children, and if they recite the rosary in a mechanical and routine manner, without unction or fervor, then the same will be found in their children. However, if they are recollected and fervent, able to verbalize the object of their meditation and the graces to be obtained, and if the parents find this an enjoyable time in God's presence, rising above the million and one interruptions of fidgety children, then their children will strive to follow their example.

—*Fr. Scott,* July 2002

Is it permissible to send our children to a Protestant grade or high school?

Pope Pius XI, in his encyclical *Divini Illius Magistri* on Christian education (December 31, 1929), explains why Catholics cannot attend "neutral" schools, from which religion is excluded, or "mixed" schools, in which children of different religions are educated side by side:

> From this it follows that the so-called "neutral" or "lay" school, from which religion is excluded, is contrary to the fundamental principles of education. Such a school moreover cannot exist in practice; it is bound to become irreligious....We renew and confirm their declarations [Pius IX's and Leo XIII's]...in which the frequenting of non-Catholic schools, whether neutral or mixed, those namely which are open to Catholics and non-Catholics alike, is forbidden for Catholic children, and can be at most tolerated, on the approval of the Ordinary alone, under determined circumstances of place and time, and with special precautions. Neither can Catholics admit that other type of mixed school...in which the students are provided with separate religious instruction, but receive other lessons in common with non-Catholic pupils from non-Catholic teachers. (St. Paul Editions, pp. 42-43)

The pope goes on to explain why it is that the fact of receiving some religious instruction does not make a Catholic education or a fit place for Catholic students. He goes on to explain: "To be this it is necessary that all the teaching and the whole organization of the school, and its teachers, syllabus, and textbooks in every branch, be regulated by the Christian spirit..."(*ibid.*). The simple answer is, consequently, that it is not permissible to send one's children either to public or to Protestant schools.

This is solidly backed up by the 1917 Code of Canon Law, which explains that it is not sufficient that nothing be contrary to the Catholic religion and morality, but that the principle function of education is the religious and moral instruction that only the Catholic Church can give (Can. 1372). However, it is clearly apparent that Protestant schools, no less than secular public schools, teach a great deal which is contrary to the Catholic religion and morality. In fact, it is even more perverse inasmuch as it is done in the name of God and of a false religion. That is why Canon 1374 strictly forbids Catholic children from attending all non-Catholic schools, except with the permission of the ordinary. Needless to say, there is no such forbidding in the equivalent canon of the 1983 Code of Canon Law (Can. 798).

An instruction of the Holy Office of November 24, 1875, explains the kind of conditions under which the ordinary of a diocese might have granted permission to attend a non-Catholic school:

It will usually be a sufficient reason if there is either no Catholic school at all available, or only one which is inadequate for the suitable education of the children according to their condition. In that case, in order that the public school may be attended with a safe conscience, the danger of perversion which is already more or less connected with its very nature must, by appropriate remedies and safeguards, be rendered remote (Bouscaren and Ellis, *Canon Law: A Text and Commentary* [1946], pp. 705-706).

Exceptions to this general rule can consequently only be granted if there is such strong faith in the home, such regular religious practice, such fidelity to the reception of the sacraments, such a religious spirit in the family, that there is no proximate danger for the faith. Clearly, in this present day and age, the modernist ordinary of the diocese cannot be contacted or trusted. Consequently, parents must consult their traditional priest or pastor to give an objective assessment as to whether the danger of perversion is truly only remote or whether it is proximate. Clearly, also, there must be strong reasons to justify even the remote danger, such as no other possibility of education because of the absence of a true Catholic school and the impossibility of home schooling in a particular family. Parents who are able to do so but deliberately refuse to make use of either of these two means of giving a Catholic education to their children cannot be excused from mortal sin and must be refused absolution, as is stated in the above-mentioned decree of the Holy Office:

> Parents...who, although there is a suitable Catholic school properly equipped and ready in the locality, or, although they have means of sending their children elsewhere to receive a Catholic education, nevertheless without sufficient reason and without the necessary safeguards to make the proximate danger remote send them to the public schools—such parents, if they are contumacious, obviously according to Catholic moral doctrine cannot be absolved in the Sacrament of Penance. (*Ibid.*, p. 706)

Those who might claim that these strict rules no longer apply are sadly misled. The present grave moral and religious crisis in the world and in the Church makes youth more than ever susceptible to the perversion of their minds by error and vice. Parents and all those who have responsibility for children are obliged to protect them, and this can only be done by Catholic schools and home schooling. Unfortunately, the denial of the dogmas of our Faith has become so widespread in the modernist Catholic school system that these schools must be considered equivalent to Protestant schools. The Faith is in grave danger of perversion, and all the more as the errors are being spread by those who are looked up to as having authority—namely, priests and religious.

There is consequently no sacrifice too great for the Catholic education of your children, preferably in a traditional Catholic school, but

if not, at least by an effective, organized, disciplined home school program.

—*Fr. Scott,* July 1999

 **Should the mother or the father be responsible for teaching children their catechism?**

The very formulation of the question presupposes a false dichotomy, since both are responsible. Yet both are not responsible equally and in the same way.

Since the father is the head of the family, he has the responsibility for planning, and foresight is his prerogative and duty. His is the responsibility to look to the future and to plan out the religious formation of his children, just as it is his duty to lead the family in prayer and other religious activities. He has no right to opt out of all involvement on the grounds that he is not home long enough, but must act towards his family as Christ, who is the invisible head of the mystical body, the Catholic Church. His paternal prudence requires that he determine how and when his children's religious education is to take place, even if he is not able to do it himself.

Ed Willock had this to say a half century ago:

> Few fathers realize their own dignity as fathers, and few see the unique role that the Church insists that they play in this work of revolutionary change (*i.e.*, the formation of character in children). He should recognize that the American tradition of the last quarter century, which assigns to him the role of eternal adolescence, is a belittlement of his vocation. He is the bridge between Church and State. He is the bridge between State and family. He is the bridge between family and Church. (*Fatherhood and Family* [Angelus Press, 1999], p. 81)

However, the mother is the one who is responsible for the daily imple-
mentation of her husband's foresight. She is the one who will teach them the holy names of Jesus and Mary at her knees, and who will repeatedly go over their catechism questions with them by heart.

Nevertheless, as the children grow older the father's role in the actual teaching of the Faith ought to increase, inasmuch as it is possible. It is he who ought to lead family discussions defending the great teachings on the Faith, and who must instruct his children on how to defend their faith out in the world, and how also to defend the Church. By so doing, his authority and leadership will make the learning and expression of the Faith a profound reality in the lives of his children instead of a superficial veneer.

—*Fr. Scott,* December 2000

When a relative is married outside the Church (*i.e.*, invalidly), can we invite him and his spouse to visit and stay with us or do we have to break off all contact?

When a relative is living in an objectively sinful state, one may not condone it. If there is a direct responsibility, one must try to bring the culprit to his senses. On the other hand, it is not obligatory, nor even prudent, to constantly remind a relative of his sinful life. One would be condoning the situation by allowing them to remain at the house as spouses, and thus this would be forbidden, as it would be to visit them if this would give the impression of accepting the union as legitimate. There is no obligation to break off all contact; in fact, charity and good example would be the best course of action.

—*Fr. Doran,* November 1993

Why do marriages fail?

It is often said, with justice, that to know someone you have to live with him or her. Many a wonderful fellow at the office or recreation center is a perfect boor or bear at home. Many a delightful, charming woman in company is a spitfire and sarcastic cat once she begins to carry out her role of wife and mother. How revealing and shocking are the disclosures of the divorce courts!

Failure to appreciate candidly the nature and responsibilities to be assumed in marriage, the necessity of having to make concessions to each other in many areas of conjugal life, is a distant reason for the tragic failure of so many marriages. Such unions are built on a too romantic or idealistic notion of what is involved. This is due to lack of maturity—sometimes of both partners—and the failure to follow an adequately proper course of marriage instruction. These factors are not readily evident prior to the commitment given but become apparent later.

There are two broad areas of marital breakdown within marriage: a lack of communication between the spouses and an inability or unwillingness to talk, to discuss matters of mutual concern; and difficulties and disagreements over finances.

Since every effect must have a cause, the causes of marital failure can be attributed to the following, as many outstanding court judges and psychologists point out causes well known to every priest for generations: (1) meddling and obnoxious relatives; (2) deliberate and selfish birth prevention; (3) boredom, frustration, disappointment; (4) rash marriages; (5) differences of religious beliefs and neglect of the spiritual and prayerful dimension of marriage; (6) jealousy; (7) emotional, intellectual, and physical immaturity; (8) nagging; (9) the "love" triangle, *i.e.*, infidelity;

(10) sex ignorance and increasing signs of disinterest and lack of affection; (11) drink, gambling, and drugs. It is largely within these areas that marriages fail.

—*Fr. Boyle,* December 1993

Is it wise to give children pocket money?

A judgment of prudence consists in taking the right means to attain one's goal. Pocket money must be given for a reason, and that reason is certainly not to placate children, or so that they can be like their friends, or so that they can have everything that they want. The reason why children would be given pocket money would be to teach them a sense of responsibility in the use of the means placed at their disposal in the best way possible. It is important for a parent to realize that it is not because he has given his child pocket money that he is free from all responsibility as to how it is spent. The parent should not only know, but also supervise, the spending of this money, and make it quite clear that he has the authority to forbid unnecessary, wasteful, or worldly use of pocket money.

It is also important for children to learn from an early age that privileges such as pocket money need to be earned, and that this particular privilege will be suppressed for behavior problems. It is also a necessary education to give it as a payment for on-time, joyful, and good performance of chores, so that pocket money is not something to be taken for granted.

The age at which pocket money is given and the sums given are highly variable, depending upon culture, the family's economic status and lifestyle, and the parents' methods of education. It is doubtless preferable to err on the side of austerity and poverty, as is usually the case with large families.

—*Fr. Scott,* January 2001

Is one permitted to maintain social contact with apostate family members?

The question here concerns what is called by the theologians communication with heretics. Here it concerns profane or civil communication, namely, that concerning commerce, business, and friendly conversation, as distinct from communication in sacred things pertaining to the worship of God, and prayer. Active participation of this latter kind is forbidden by the traditional law and practice of the Church (Can. 1258, §1 of the 1917 Code), but encouraged by the post-conciliar Church in the name of ecumenism (Can. 844 of the 1983 Code).

There was a time in the history of the Church when the Church's law forbade communication in civil or friendly matters with those who were or who had become notorious heretics, and who apostatized. However, the sad conditions of modern society, in which we must constantly live alongside heretics and apostates, forced the Church to mitigate this law. Consequently, the injunction to avoid civil communication with heretics and apostates only applied to the special class of excommunicated persons classified as having to be avoided in the 1917 Code. Furthermore, even then such civil communication was permissible for any reasonable cause, such as necessary commerce (Can. 2267). In addition, the same canon explains that the forbidding of civil communication does not apply to a person's spouse, parents, children, servants, or subjects, since manifestly such communication cannot be avoided.

Nevertheless, although the Church's law does not bind us to avoid all personal and friendly contact with apostates, and especially not with relatives, such contact is frequently highly dangerous to the faith of Catholics, bringing with it the possibility of indifferentism. For, in practice, such contact presumes that the Faith is not discussed, and the beliefs or not of the apostate person are accepted as such. For this acceptation is the basis of ordinary friendly, social contact. In such instances, contact even with relatives would be opposed to the natural law, and even to the divine law. St. Paul is, indeed, very explicit: "A man that is a heretic, after the first and second admonition, avoid" (Tit. 3:10). Likewise St. John, the apostle of charity: "If any man come to you, and bring not this doctrine, receive him not into the house nor say to him, God speed you. For he that saith unto him, God speed you, communicateth with his wicked works" (II Jn. 10-11).

However, this being said, it cannot be denied that there is no true Catholic who is not zealous for the conversion of heretical or apostate relatives to the true Faith, and that if there were no friendly contact or conversation there would be no human possibility of initiating that conversion. It will consequently depend upon the virtue of prudence to balance the possible advantage of maintaining some contact with the grave danger of indifferentism of keeping up that contact, either affecting one's own soul, or giving one's relatives the impression that religion does not matter, or, finally, inducing other persons or relatives into indifferentism by the example of such contact.

The prudent man will generally resolve this question by using the opportunity of a social contact to speak openly and frankly about the true religion and faith in an attempt to encourage the apostate or heretical relative to show interest in it. In so doing, he will faithfully fulfill Our Lord's command: "Everyone therefore that shall confess me before men,

I will also confess him before my Father who is in heaven" (Mt. 10:32). If this effort brings a positive response, then he will maintain the contact, speaking regularly about the Faith. If it does not, but rather seems futile, then he will avoid all friendship but simply limit his contact to social necessities, thus fulfilling the recommendation of St. Paul: "Bear not the yoke with unbelievers. For what participation hath justice with injustice? Or what fellowship hath light with darkness? And what concord hath Christ with Belial? Or what part hath the faithful with the unbeliever?... Wherefore, go out from among them, and be ye separate, saith the Lord" (II Cor. 6:14-17). Indeed, for what do we have in common with those who refuse to believe in supernatural realities, in God, His grace, the teachings of the Church, and the cross, our only hope.

This being said, the prudent man will always be ready to practice charity towards his relatives, even apostate, and in case of need he will always be available to provide physical help or emotional support, even when the spiritual is rejected, as St. Paul teaches: "Be not overcome by evil, but overcome evil by good" (Rom. 12:21).

—*Fr. Scott,* January 2005

Q Are the television and the movie theater a suitable form of recreation for Catholics?

This is for many people a controversial issue, a serious bone of contention in numerous homes. There is one dangerous pitfall to be avoided from the outset. It serves no useful purpose to attribute to an instrument, which television is, emotions, feelings and powers which belong to humans. Television is merely an instrument like so many others which can be used for good purposes or immoral ones.

This is a distinction made by Pope Pius XI in his encyclical *Divini Illius Magistri,* in which he deplored "the potent instrumentalities of publicity [such as the cinema] which *might* be of great advantage to learning and to education were they properly directed by healthy principles [and which] often unfortunately serve as an incentive to evil passions and are subordinated to sordid gain."

This is a truly prophetic judgment on the part of the pope. Despite reasonable arguments in favor of televised sports, documentaries, and other laudable programs, the indisputable fact remains that television and the cinema ignore Christian morality and even human morality based upon the natural law. The fundamental purpose of art is to help perfect the moral personality of man, and for this reason it must itself be moral. Television is not an influence for good morals; on the contrary, it is for the most part a purveyor of Hollywood filth, responsible for the degradation, destruction, and ruin of souls. Television is for many an occasion of sin; it presents a false view of life; it obscures ideals; it perverts true love and undermines respect and fidelity in marriage; and it educates in a subtle fashion the viewers into a toleration and passive acceptance of every vice contrary to the law of God and nature.

Where the television remains in a Christian home there is the most serious of obligations incumbent upon parents before God to re-evaluate their position and prevent the corruption of their children, rather than be responsible for it through a lack of vigilance and parental neglect. Television is a profoundly anti-Christian medium and has to be recognized and rejected as such.

—Fr. Boyle, August 1994

 ## Is it a sin for a traditional Catholic family to have a television in the home?

I do not believe that the question is asked in the correct way, which would be: Is it the will of God for a traditional Catholic family to have a television in the home? I think that simply by rephrasing the question the answer becomes much more obvious. Nevertheless, let us answer the question as posed.

It is manifestly obvious that in itself the television is but an electronic gadget, and the fact of owning such a gadget is neither morally good nor morally evil. It is indifferent. The morality comes from the end for which the television exists in the home and from the associated circumstances that inseparably accompany the existence of such a gadget in the home.

It is equally obvious, and every traditional Catholic will admit it, that the regular watching of television for children is an occasion of sin, and this not just because of the obvious sins of impurity but especially of materialism, concupiscence of the eyes, the loss of the Faith, and the perversion of the mind by the parading of the false ideals of subjectivism and liberalism continually before the eyes of the young. He who exposes himself deliberately to a proximate occasion of sin commits a sin, and it will be a mortal sin if the proximate occasion to which he exposes himself is of a mortal sin. How much more serious is the culpability of those parents who expose their defenseless children to the perversions presented as ideals by the world of television!

However, there are many traditional Catholics who admit the above principles, but who still feel that they can keep a television in their home. After all, they are intelligent people, and they are perfectly capable of controlling the use of television to only good, approved shows, and it enables them to watch videos which are entirely within their control. Why would this not be licit, they maintain.

Such an abstract consideration of the use of television fails to consider an essential circumstance that substantially modifies the morality of the use of television. It is profoundly addictive, for it panders to our desire for visual self-satisfaction and to our inborn laziness. Any person who claims that he can control its inroads into his own life, let alone his family's life, is sadly deceiving himself. He denies the ugly reality of the wounds of original sin, which we all have to live with. Furthermore, television, in the practical use to which man puts it, necessarily provokes the capital vice of sloth. For it preoccupies man with transitory, visual, material things; paralyzes his ability to think and to elevate his soul to spiritual things; and prevents him from rejoicing in the things of God, in divine truth, and in heavenly aspirations. This is precisely how St. Thomas Aquinas defines the capital sin of sloth. By promoting sloth, television destroys recollection, the interior life of prayer, and union with God. How rare indeed is that situation in which, in practice, it is not at least an imperfection or venial sin for a traditional Catholic man to allow a television to remain in his home!

Some folks object to this radical conclusion by stating that they only use their television for watching videos, and especially religious videos, and that there is no sin at all in watching such videos. This is all perfectly true, and there may indeed be some families in which there is such strict discipline that there is no temptation to use this means other than for such edifying videos, and in which such audiovisual means are kept so carefully under control that there is no danger of provoking sloth. In such circumstances there is manifestly no sin at all, but we all know how infrequent and fragile such a situation is.

Furthermore, a family that is truly God-centered, a family that strives to maintain an interior life, a family that desires to distance itself from the world, is going to have a horror for this terribly effective instrument for the perversion of modern society. It will realize that the television is a destroyer of all family life, of shared activities of all kinds, as well as of the supernatural life. It will see that the little benefit to be gained by an occasional video is far outweighed by the grave danger of placing such an occasion of worldliness in their midst, and will reject it outright.

It is precisely for this reason that the television is forbidden in religious communities, which furthermore have the discipline that could potentially prevent its abuse. Archbishop Lefebvre was a great example in this regard. After he fought against the introduction of the television into the Holy Ghost Fathers during the 1960's, he had the wisdom to include this very categorical prescription in the Statutes of the Society of St. Pius X:

> They shall take care to break with the habits of the world, which has become a slave to radio, television, vacations, and costly leisure. Hence, there shall be no television set in our communities....Our true television is the Tabernacle, where dwells He Who puts us in communication with all spiritual and temporal realities. (VI, 7)

Note that the Archbishop does not just forbid television in our houses, but also gives the reason why. If such a rule is good enough for the spiritual family of the Society, why would it not be good enough for traditional Catholic families, in which there is much greater danger of abuse?

Our holy founder had likewise the same wisdom when it came to writing the rule of the Third Order of the Society of St. Pius X. Not only did he list "to abstain from television" amongst the personal obligations of third order members, he also listed it again under the obligations of the married when he described how their home should be and when he listed television as one of two examples of things that can harm the souls of children. Here is the full obligation:

> To make of the family home a sanctuary consecrated to the Hearts of Jesus and Mary where evening prayers are recited in the family and, if possible, the Rosary. Liturgical life should be paramount on Sundays and feast days. Avoid everything that could harm the souls of children: television, unclean magazines.

Surely this means that televisions should not even be present in the home, in the same way that a Catholic man would detest the thought of having unclean magazines somewhere hidden in his home.

It is this aspect of the rule of the Society's third order that has most discouraged the faithful from joining. They consider that it is too difficult, radical, too different from the ways of the world. They consider that it would be much easier to join one of the other older third orders, which do not have this in their rule, such as the Carmelite, Franciscan, or Dominican. They seriously deceive themselves, for if the exclusion of television is not a part of these third order rules, it is not that it is any less important for these third orders than it is for the Third Order of the Society of St. Pius X, but simply that the television did not exist when the rules were written. Any person who is serious about his own and his family's spiritual life, and who desires to join a third order, will have a great desire to rid himself of the television and will consider that the little gain of being able to watch videos is nothing compared to the grave danger of having such an instrument of perversion in the midst of his family.

This elimination of the television from the homes of third order members is in fact an illustration of the great value of the Society's third order. Not only is it adapted to the real times in which we are presently living, but in addition it unites the laity to the priests in their daily Masses, spiritual life, and sacrifices, so that they can share in the special grace of the Society to fight for the Social Kingship of Our Lord Jesus Christ, and contribute their own merits to this combat. May there be many generous families willing to rid their homes of the television, grave impediment to their spiritual life as it is, in order to live the supernatural life of grace more profoundly.

—*Fr. Scott,* July 2003

Should I refuse to speak to my daughter, who is living in sin with her boyfriend?

Certainly it is your duty to avoid anything that would give the impression of supporting or helping her to commit this sin, whether you do it materially or emotionally, directly or indirectly. Any such encouragement is certainly matter for confession. It is furthermore your grave duty to inform her that she knows that you abhor such behavior, so offensive to God and scandalous to other souls, including siblings. You cannot allow the two of them to come to family gatherings as if they were married. This would be to approve the scandalous situation. Alas, this is frequently not enough to force them to separate.

However, I am concerned that the approach of cutting off all conversation and contact until she ceases living in sin is not psychologically sound and will not be the right approach to touch her soul. The best that could come from it would be that it would force her to get married. The worst is that it could turn her away from our holy religion. However, neither of these is what you desire. I have seen many situations like this. The young people involved are always blinded by passion and shortsighted. They ought not to be forced or coerced into marriage. It does not work to approach the matter head-on and in a frontal manner. Such an approach is often counter-productive. It makes the sinner feel personally attacked and threatened.

My approach to this situation would be quite different. Firstly, I believe that it is very important that you maintain contact, and that you speak frequently to your daughter, and express your concern and affection for her. Secondly, there is no point belaboring the point of her sin and pushing her further into her obstinacy or into getting married without due preparation. Thirdly, you must take a positive tack. Speak about your own spiritual life, the graces that you receive, and how God has taught you to carry your cross.

Speak about love, and how the roses and thorns are inseparable in your own marriage. Encourage her positively in the practice of virtue. Remember that all virtues are connected together, and by encouraging her to practice charity, meekness, humility, thoughtfulness, *etc.*, you are effectively encouraging her to practice chastity without saying so. Encourage her especially in her daily prayers. Talk about spiritual reading, and give her the very correct impression that she also can pray, even though she is not in the state of grace. Encourage her to recite her rosary every day, or the Litany of the Blessed Virgin Mary, to know the will of God (but be very careful not to tell her what the will of God is; she has to figure this out for herself). Speak to her about Mass and the spiritual high points in the year, and you can expect that when she starts reciting her rosary every day, she will go to Mass.

All of these things will have a much more profound effect upon her soul than any reproach or harsh words. If you can get her to pray, you will not have to say anything about the horror and scandal of living in sin. She will see it for herself. This must be your goal. I have often given instructions to a couple living in sin (*e.g.*, one would like to convert). I do not wait until they separate to start the classes. I simply teach them the catechism. If they follow through with their prayers, it does not take more than three months for them to ask what they need to do about their living situation.

—*Fr. Scott,* September 2002

How should Catholics view dancing?

The morality of recreational or social dancing is not a new subject, but one which saints and moral theologians have treated at length. The difficulty lies in the fact that the style, fashion, and manner of dancing are in a continual flux, and that this affects its morality.

All agree that dancing, in itself, is morally indifferent, and consequently that it is not in itself sinful, and that dancing of the right kind, under the right auspices can *in itself* be an innocent and even beneficial diversion. However, it is equally clear that it is very commonly a proximate occasion of sin in virtue of the circumstances that accompany the dancing, such as place, time, immodesty, company, let alone the sensual nature of many dances and the intimate physical contact which is an immediate peril for the virtue of purity and entirely opposed to the respect which is owed to the body, temple of the Holy Ghost.

The *Catholic Encyclopedia* of 1913 summarizes in this way the Church's teaching:

Undoubtedly old national dances in which the performers stand apart, hardly, if at all, holding the partner's hand, fall under ethical censure scarcely more than any other kind of social intercourse. But aside from the concomitants—place, late hours, décolleté, escorting, *etc.*—common to all such entertainments, round dances, although they may possibly be carried on with decorum and modesty, are regarded by moralists as fraught, by their very nature, with the greatest danger to morals. To them perhaps, but unquestionably still more to masked balls, should be applied the warning of the Second Council of Baltimore against "those fashionable dances which, as at present carried on, are revolting to every feeling of delicacy and propriety." (IV, 619)

Such is the Church's teaching concerning ballroom dancing, despite the fact that it can be a form of art. It must, at least in general and for most young people, be considered a proximate occasion of mortal sin and consequently forbidden. However, square dances and folk dances, in which there is not the same intimate physical contact and pairing off, nor the same danger of bad company, are not a proximate occasion of sin and are consequently permissible. Ballet, as an art form and expression of beauty, can be licit and permissible. However, it must be remembered that it is a sensual art form, and one in which the displaying of the body can be an occasion of sin both for performers and for the audience, and one in which vanity plays a large part, *e.g.*, the ultra-slim figure required. It is consequently not an art form to be encouraged or patronized.

It goes without saying that modern dancing as commonly done these days, being animalistic and extremely sensual by its exclusive emphasis on rhythm at the expense of any ordered, harmonious, bodily movement, is always to be excluded as a proximate occasion of serious sin, in virtue of the music and dance itself, as well as the company and other circumstances. This includes dancing to rock music and dancing to jazz accompaniment (*i.e.*, swing dancing).

If any young people are so taken with the craze of dancing as to hesitate to accept the Church's wisdom on the question, I suggest they read the following passage from the saint who liked to meekly catch flies with honey, and not vinegar, and whose understanding of the situation of people in the world is so clearly manifest in his spiritual direction. St. Francis de Sales had this to say:

In themselves, dances and balls are indifferent things. However, in actual practice they tend strongly toward the side of evil, and therefore are dangerous.

People dance at night, and in darkened rooms. This favors certain familiarities. People stay up late and this results in their rising late the next day, causing the morning to be wasted. Consequently, they miss opportunities of serving God. Is it not foolish to turn night into day and day into night and to replace useful work with frivolous pleasure? Finally, at balls everyone tries to outdo everybody else in vanity, and vanity is favorable to the evil affections and dangerous loves which dancing so easily spawns.

Philothea, what physicians say about mushrooms or pumpkins I say about dances: The best of them are not worth much! However, if you must eat pumpkins, be careful how they are prepared, eat only a little of them, and that rarely. In the same way, if you cannot give up going to balls, be careful how you dance, doing so with modesty, dignity, and the right intention. Attend balls rarely, because no matter how carefully you conduct yourself at them, there is danger of excess in them, by becoming too attached to them.

Because they are spongy, mushrooms are said to attract the surrounding rot. The same is true of balls and other such night-oriented gatherings. They usually attract sin: quarrels, jealousies, mockery, sensual loves. These activities open the pores of the heart to be poisoned by some loose word or some folly or some wanton glance of love. Yes, Philothea, such amusements are usually dangerous. They scatter one's spirit of devotion, weaken one's strength, and chill one's charity. They awaken countless evil affections in the soul. Because of all this, use them with great caution.

After eating mushrooms, one is advised above all to drink some good wine. I personally advise you to think some holy and good thoughts after a ball. These will counterbalance the bad impressions you may have received there.

What are some such holy and good thoughts? While I was dancing, some people were burning in Hell for sins committed at dances or occasioned by their dancing. While I was dancing, monks, nuns, and other fervent Christians were chanting God's praise and contemplating His beauty, thus using their time far more profitably than I was. While I was dancing, many souls departed from this world in great anguish; thousands were suffering dreadful pains in hospitals.... While I was dancing, the time of my earthly life was hurrying by and death was approaching nearer. See how he mocks and invites me to his dance! In that dance I shall take but one step from this life to the next.

—*Fr. Scott*, March 2000

ABOUT VIRTUES AND VICES

 **Must we forgive injuries done to God and to others?**

The obligation of forgiveness, even of our enemies, is fundamental to the new law of charity instituted by our divine Savior. We all have heard many times of Our Lord's response to St. Peter's question: "Lord, how often shall my brother offend against me, and I forgive him? Till seven times? Jesus saith to him: I say not to thee, till seven times; but till seventy times seven times" (Mt. 18:21-22). We constantly pray in the Our Father that God might forgive us, as we forgive those who trespass against us (Mt. 6:12). We know that regardless of the insults directed against us, we must pray for our persecutors, as Our Lord Himself did on the cross: "Love your enemies: do good to them that hate you: and pray for them that persecute and calumniate you" (Mt. 5:44).

However, it is not for us to forgive injuries done against Almighty God or against others. We are not those who have been offended, insulted, attacked, calumniated, and it is not our honor that is in question. It is consequently not for us to forgive, but for God Himself, or for the persons concerned. In such instances, of course, we have the duty to pray for the enemies of God, that they might convert and ask for pardon, that they might understand the gravity of the insults directed against God and His friends, or against the Blessed Virgin or the Church. However, it is not in our power to forgive an injury that is not directed against us. How frequent this situation is with respect to God, and how great a desire of making reparation it enkindles in our hearts! Yet only God, who is offended, can forgive, and then only when pardon is requested of Him.

—*Fr. Scott,* June 2005

 **Catholics must always strive to set a good example. Of course this is key for obvious reasons, but is it not also important to set a good example in the hope of conversions?**

"If you love Me, keep my commandments"—so Our Lord spoke to His apostles. It is supernatural charity which must give vitality to all our actions. Good example necessarily follows. Charity is the source of the "good fruit" of the "good tree." When the tree is good its fruit must be good. Obviously then, bad example and lack of virtue immediately manifest the "bad tree."

The supernatural desire to love God above all things, and thus to serve Him in all things, is not incompatible with the additional motive of conversions. On the contrary, this desire is to draw more individuals to the Highest Good for His honor and their salvation. Good example therefore lays the foundation to practice the spiritual works of mercy.

—*Fr. Doran,* September 1993

 **In order to avoid the error of naturalism, must I despise natural virtues?**

The Church has defined, against Jansenism, that there is such a thing as natural virtue, that it is good, and that it is consequently not to be despised. However, it cannot possibly be of itself any help towards attaining a supernatural goal, the supernatural domain being infinitely above the natural.

This being said, the naturally acquired cardinal virtues of prudence, justice, fortitude, and temperance, learned by repeated efforts, and the natural virtues associated with them, are a marvelous preparation for the infused, supernatural virtues. When the supernatural virtues are received, they immediately take advantage of all the acquired good habits, which give the facility in the exercise of supernatural virtue. A person who practices natural temperance, for example, will become very generous in practicing the supernatural virtue when in the state of grace, and he will have an especial ease and joy in so doing, that a person who has never practiced natural temperance would not have.

This applies to the public, social order of the State also. When a State promotes natural virtues, such as temperance, fortitude, and justice, then the citizens will have a certain preparation and facility in the supernatural order if they should receive the Faith and the state of sanctifying grace. Consequently, Catholic men should do all in their power to bring about a social order that is based upon the practice of natural virtue, *i.e.*, that is based upon the natural order. It is a great help to the Church for the salvation of souls. Strange though it may seem, it is precisely the error of naturalism that prevents this because it denies the natural order and the importance of natural virtue. Denying the reality of human nature and the natural law as well as original sin, its wounds and its consequences, naturalism arrives at the strange paradox of denying the very existence of natural virtue. This perversion of nature makes it very difficult to accept the Church and supernatural revelation, given that grace builds on nature.

—*Fr. Scott,* March 2007

 **Must we always give to those who ask for money, in particular, beggars?**

We are obliged in charity to give of our surplus to the genuinely needy, and in some cases to deprive ourselves provided our primary obligations have been met and we don't renege on our particular duties of state, especially those that apply to family and our local church. Prudence dictates that we don't give money to drunks or drug addicts, *etc.* One must also beware of the con artist and the sob story which is patently untrue. This knowledge comes with experience. Not everyone who asks deserves to receive. There must be a practical, down-to-earth approach and even limitation to giving. Almsgiving is a particularly Christian practice, but remember, all charity begins at home.

Only charitable institutions which respect the law of God and do nothing contrary to it should be supported, in particular religious works of truly traditional Catholic nature.

—*Fr. Boyle,* February 1995

 Could you please explain why so many traditional Catholics feel that pants are improper attire for women and/or girls? Are pants considered immodest? At what age would a young girl be obligated to wear only dresses? In what circumstances would pants be allowed for women?

"A woman shall not be clothed with man's apparel, neither shall man use woman's apparel: for he that doeth these things is abominable before God" (Deut. 22:5). This quotation is very often the basis of the thought of many Catholics that pants are never permissible for women.

The crux of the matter is whether or not pants are uniquely masculine. Fashions, it must be remembered, are relative to the age. But modesty is never out of fashion. From just this column it is impossible to pass judgment on every set of trousers that exist whether they are, or are not, immodest.

The age at which a young girl should wear pants is dependent on the circumstances of the family and its lifestyle. A pink frilly dress would seem hardly appropriate in the sandbox. If work or play do not dictate modesty, not always possible in a skirt, the little girl should be trained as a young lady as early as possible. In any case, it should be kept in mind that culottes are the normal replacement for sports.

—*Fr. Doran,* September 1991

 There is a Catholic standard of modesty in dress for women. Is there also a standard of dress for men?

Absolutely there is, for exactly the same principles apply for men as for women.

Modesty is a moral virtue, and a part of the virtue of temperance, by which a person brings moderation to his outward and inward actions (inasmuch as they can be reflected by certain exterior signs) in order to keep them under the control of right reason (*ST*, II-II, q. 160, art. 2). St. Thomas Aquinas lists four kinds of modesty, in ordinary matters, that are obligatory for everybody:

One is the movement of the mind towards some excellence, and this is moderated by humility.

The second is the desire of things pertaining to knowledge, and this is moderated by studiousness which is opposed to curiosity.

The third regards bodily movements and actions (including words), which require to be done becomingly and honestly, whether we act seriously or in play.

The fourth regards outward show, for instance in dress and the like. (*Ibid.*)

If all four aspects of modesty are equally important, there remains no doubt that the last two, which have no special name, are most commonly understood by the term "modesty." Moreover, it is most especially the last that is referred to by "modesty" on account of the disorder of fallen human nature, which is most easily overcome by a disordered attraction to the last kind of immodesty.

Clearly, men have an equal duty as women to avoid provocative words or actions and to avoid any kind of dress that might show off their person or their body, leading to vanity. Like women, they are hence forbidden to display their bodies in public in an unseemly manner, or in a way that might produce a disordered attraction in the opposite sex. Men should always wear a shirt for gymnastics, and shorts should not be worn in public, but only be used for athletics, and should not be too brief or too tight. Likewise, men should dress modestly for Sunday Mass, with shirt, tie, jacket, trousers—all of which symbolize a man's sense of responsibility, leading his family by the orderly self-discipline of modest dress, and doing his duty in the true worship of God.

However, there are two important differences in the application of these principles to men, as compared to women, and which are the reason why the Church's documents on the subject refer to modesty in women. The first is that the nature of a woman makes her much more prone to the temptation of vanity, to show off her body, and the nature of a man makes him much more tempted by seeing this. Consequently, the gravest and most dangerous offenses against modesty, understood in its fourth and most restricted meaning, namely, as against purity, are by women.

It is for this reason that the Church has been so much more adamant about women's dress, as in the following quote from a decree of the Sacred Congregation of the Council of January 18, 1930:

> His Holiness, Pius XI, has never ceased to inculcate in word and writing that precept of St. Paul (I Tim 2:5, 10)—"Women also in decent apparel; adorning themselves with modesty and sobriety … as it becometh women professing godliness with good works."
>
> And on many occasions the same Supreme Pontiff has reproved and sharply condemned the immodesty in dress which today is everywhere in vogue; even among women and girls who are Catholics; a practice which does grave injury to the crowning virtue and glory of women, and moreover unfortunately leads not merely to their temporal disadvantage, but, what is worse, to their eternal ruin and that of other souls.
>
> It is no wonder, then, that Bishops and other Ordinaries of places, as becomes ministers of Christ, have in their respective dioceses unanimously resisted in every way this licentious and shameless fashion and in doing so have cheerfully and courageously borne the derision and ridicule sometimes directed at them by the ill-disposed....

There is a second reason why modesty of dress is especially applicable to women over men. It is that there is a special form of immodesty that is characteristic of our modern times, and it is the immodesty of women wearing men's clothes, most notably pants and shorts. This undermines a woman's psychological perception of herself and of her difference from a man, which in turn de-feminizes her, erodes natural respect between men and women, removes the defense to over-familiarity, and eventually degrades the relationships between men and women to the level of sensuality. It is this form of immodesty which is ultimately by far the most destructive of human relationships and of the virtue of purity.

If, therefore, there is certainly a standard of modesty for men, it must always be remembered that the battle for women's modesty is both much more crucial and much more difficult to win.

Real men will, however, teach and lead by their example. If they have a difficult time insisting on the modesty of their wives or daughters, they will remember to practice very precisely all the four kinds of modesty mentioned above and their admonitions will bear fruit.

—*Fr. Scott,* December 1999

ABOUT SIN AND SINS

 **Why did Our Lord pray from the cross: "Father, forgive them, for they know not what they do"? My understanding is if we know not what we do, we are not guilty of sin and therefore no forgiveness is needed.**

If one would see God face to face, as the angels and saints do in heaven, he could not sin because he could not have any motive to turn away from God, whose infinite goodness he would behold. Any sin, therefore, includes a certain ignorance (see I Cor. 2:8, I Tim. 1:13, *etc.*).

Yet not all ignorance is invincible. First, ignorance can be the punishment of other sins (II Cor. 4:3-4; see Is. 6:10). Thus, ignorance of Christ in New Caledonia for eighteen centuries was certainly the punishment of their sin of cannibalism: they who refused to see "thou shalt not eat thy neighbor" deserved to remain in darkness concerning the Savior, though God in His mercy did not leave them in darkness forever.

Secondly, not all ignorance is total. Some see some truths which they reject, and thus remain blind on other truths. Though the Pharisees, who knew the prophecies, could easily recognize Our Lord as the Messias, their pride blinded them. Our Lord said: "For judgment I am come into this world; that they who see not, may see; and they who see, may become blind. And some of the Pharisees, who were with Him, heard, and they said unto Him: Are we also blind? Jesus said to them: If you were blind, you should not have sin: but now you say: We see. Your sin remaineth."

Thirdly, some ignorance is sometimes directly willed; thus, many people may come close to the Church, attracted by the grace of God, then they learn that the Church forbids contraception and they go away. Their ignorance of many truths of religion is far from excusing them.

Every sin contains a choice to disregard the truth (the true good according to the law of God) in order to turn towards apparent goods according to one's will. Yet the more one knows, the more one is guilty!

—*Fr. Laisney,* January 1991

What is slander? Is slandering a priest a grave sin? Is reparation required?

Everyone has the right to his good name. Any good esteem is the opinion which men express in words regarding the excellence of another. This esteem is violated by defamation, which is to blacken another's good name secretly. (Contumely, insult, is the sin committed in the person's presence.) If it is a true but hidden fault, the sin is called detraction. If it is a lie about someone's reputation, the sin is called calumny. Slander is the sin of calumny.

Now, a man's reputation is his greatest possession. All the wealth in the world will not amount to much if no one has a good opinion of him. Therefore, unjust defamation is a grave sin contrary to justice and charity (which admits, however, of slight matter).

Each has the right to his good name. Even when his good reputation is false, I still do not have the right to blacken it. It is the same as when one may possess something through theft. Even though he retains the object unjustly, I do not have the right, for that reason, to steal it from him. Defamation also threatens the welfare of society because it gives rise to quarrels, disputes, and other things against charity.

The dignity of the person slandered can, and does, aggravate the gravity of the sin. Thus, the slandering of a priest is more grave because he is more likely to suffer grave injury to his name.

A person who defames another is obliged to make reparation. He must repair 1) the loss of good esteem; and 2) all the material losses foreseen, at least vaguely, from the defamation. One who calumniates must also make a public declaration that he has lied. The detractor must use all the lawful means at his disposal to excuse the faults which he has unjustly revealed.

—*Fr. Doran,* July 1991

Do persons who arrive late for Mass every Sunday commit a sin?

Many lukewarm Catholics ignore the two aspects of their Sunday obligation. The first is to be present physically from the beginning until the end of Mass. The second is to assist at Mass with attention, that is, in a prayerful manner. Persons who deliberately and through their own fault fail in either of these duties do not fully satisfy their Sunday obligation.

The theologians agree that a person who misses a substantial part of the Mass through his own fault commits a mortal sin, and a person who misses a lesser part of the Mass commits a venial sin; but it is still sinful if it is culpable, through negligence or deliberation. It is considered a substantial part of the Mass if a person arrives after the Offertory, whereas it is considered a lesser part if he arrives at any time up until the Offertory. In such a case, the person ought to wait for the next Mass, if there is one, and assist at the part of the second Mass that he missed at the first Mass. Clearly, anybody can arrive late once in a while simply because he is not well organized. However, a person who regularly arrives late every Sunday cannot be excused of culpability; and, furthermore, he gives grave scandal to his fellow parishioners. How, indeed, can somebody rush into church off the street, enter Mass when it is well advanced, and then truly be recollected to pray and offer it as he ought? Such a practice rapidly engenders indifference to sacred and holy things.

—*Fr. Scott,* September 2006

Is it true that St. Thomas says that all drunkenness is mortally sinful, regardless of the extent, for the quantity of wine drunk is but a circumstance?

I think that the misunderstanding concerning the comparative gravity of imperfect and perfect drunkenness lies in the use of the term "objection." St. Thomas does not at all agree with the objection that the quantity of wine drunk is but a circumstance. He simply presents this objection, as always, in order to adequately answer it. His answer is that what makes drunkenness a mortal sin is that it removes the use of reason. This means that only perfect drunkenness is a mortal sin. Consumption of alcohol to a lesser extent, or imperfect drunkenness, is consequently only a venial sin. It is therefore false to say that the quantity of alcohol consumed is but a circumstance.

Hence, the moderate consumption of alcohol, without any excess or drunkenness, is not a sin at all. The consumption of alcohol to excess, such that one becomes tipsy and loses some physical self-control, but not the use of reason, is but a venial sin. The knowing and willing consumption of alcohol to such an extent as to remove the use of reason is a mortal sin.

St. Thomas consequently keeps the balance between the imbibers and the teetotallers, as does St. Paul when speaking to St. Timothy. A little alcohol, without excess, is not at all offensive to God and may be good for mind and body. A small excess of alcohol is certainly offensive to God, but only a venial sin, and a voluntary large excess removes sanctifying grace from the soul.

—*Fr. Scott*, March 1999

What is the morality of drug taking? Is the smoking of marijuana a mortal sin?

"Neither the effeminate, nor sodomites, nor thieves, nor the covetous, nor drunkards...will possess the kingdom of God" (I Cor. 6:10). Drunkenness is a deliberate excess in the use of intoxicating drink or drugs to the point of forcibly depriving oneself of the use of reason for the sake of gratifying an inordinate desire for such drink and not for the sake of promoting health. This is contrary to the virtue of temperance, and specifically sobriety. Sobriety regulates man's desire and use of intoxicants, and is vitally necessary for an upright moral life. The evil of intoxication lies in the violence committed against one's nature by depriving it of the use of reason. He deprives himself of that which makes him specifically human—his ability to think. The drunk, or in this case the drug user, desires this loss of reason because of the feeling of liberation which accompanies it precisely from this lack of control of the will over the reason. It is unnatural, contrary to sleep, which also deprives one of the use of reason but in a natural manner.

Drug use gives an illicit means of escape. Besides being a sin, it also manifests an immaturity on the part of the user. Through an act of violence against himself, he escapes from the responsibility of decision making and control in his life. When this deprivation is complete, *e.g.*, actions totally contrary to normal behavior, incapability of distinguishing between good and evil, *etc.*, it is a grave sin. "*In vino veritas*," said the Romans, not without reason. Any state short of complete drunkenness, without sufficient reason, is of itself venially sinful, but even in this case it may be a mortal sin if it causes scandal, injury to health, harm to one's family, *etc.* It is important also to note that a man is responsible for all the sinful actions committed while intoxicated which he had, or ought to have, foreseen.

According to Jone/Adelman in *Moral Theology*, the use of drugs in small quantities and only occasionally is a venial sin if done without sufficient reason. This could be the case, for example, with sleeping pills. Obviously, deprivation of the use of reason through narcotics is to be judged as alcohol. The use of most drugs is complicated by the fact that they are illegal. This also signifies the will of the user to break the law, an offense against social justice. This compounds the sin. The speed with which a drug alters one's consciousness also aggravates its use. This rapidity risks a greater potential to deprive oneself of the use of reason and thus to pass on to stronger intoxicants for increased effect. Therefore, adding to the violation of the virtue of justice, the grave scandal caused, the grave danger of addiction, and the stronger consciousness-altering ability of marijuana, it is difficult to excuse one of mortal sin. Moreover, experience tells us that its use is frequently an occasion of mortal sin, especially sins of the flesh and the use of narcotic drugs. But to willingly and knowingly place oneself in an unnecessary proximate occasion of mortal sin is to commit a mortal sin.

—*Fr. Doran,* September 1993

 **A priest told me in confession that it is not a mortal sin to use drugs such as marijuana. What do you think about this?**

The old text books do not speak of this new problem of the modern world. However, the immorality of drug abuse can be clearly deduced from the principles which allow an evaluation of the malice of alcohol abuse. The distinction is made between imperfect drunkenness, the fact of making oneself tipsy deliberately, which can only be a venial sin, and perfect drunkenness, which is drinking until one is drunk. This is a mortal sin because a drunken person loses the use of reason. This is St. Thomas Aquinas's response to the objection that the quantity of wine drunk is but a circumstance, which cannot make a venial sin into a mortal sin:

> With regard to drunkenness we reply that it is a mortal sin by reason of its genus: for that a man, without necessity, and through the mere lust of wine, makes himself unable to use his reason, whereby he is directed to God and avoids committing many sins, is expressly contrary to virtue. That it be a venial sin is due to some sort of ignorance or weakness, as when a man is ignorant of the strength of the wine, or of his own unfitness, so that he has no thought of getting drunk, for in that case the drunkenness is not imputed to him as a sin, but only the excessive drink…. (*ST,* I-II, q. 88, art. 5, ad1)

The consumption of illegal drugs, even those called soft drugs, is comparable not to becoming tipsy on a little wine but to perfect drunkenness. For these drugs have their effect by causing a "high," that is, an emotional experience when a person escapes from the demands of reality. For a brief period he lives in an unreal, euphoric world. All the other effects, such as relaxation, come as a consequence of this "high," or unreal euphoria. If this state does not always prohibit all use of reason, it most certainly does always impede the most important use of reason, which St. Thomas just explained to us "whereby he is directed to God and avoids committing many sins." All drugs deaden the conscience, and obscure the practical judgment as to right and wrong and what we must do. With respect to morality, their effect is consequently equivalent to the removal of the use of reason, and is a practical refusal to direct all of man's acts to God through reason.

Drug abuse is consequently much worse than the pure seeking of pleasure or relaxation that some claim it to be. It is a denial of the natural and supernatural order, according to which God has created us in His image and likeness that our acts might be ordered to His honor and glory. Moreover, it goes without saying that the abuse of drugs is directly opposed to the Catholic spirit, which spirit of sacrifice, the practical application of the spirit of the cross, is essential to the living of our faith.

As previously mentioned, the principal evil of drug abuse is the destruction of moral conscience. It follows that the atrocious consequences of drug abuse are inseparable from it, and are willed together with the drugs themselves. This includes the breaking of the law in the consumption of drugs; and in the means of obtaining them, such as theft; and in the effort to sell them in turn to others, often minors or children. Other consequences include the incredible self-indulgence which accompanies the almost insatiable desire for always more titillating experiences, sins of blasphemy, the often satanic rock music, and the sins against purity and chastity, which are the consequence of the loss of shame and conscience. Sins against charity and justice abound, such as disobedience to parents and refusal to do one's duty at school or work, not to mention the bad company-keeping which is the breeding ground of all vices. Long term results are also willed in their cause, and they include such things as emotional and physical addiction, the passage from soft to hard drugs, the damage done to the body and to general health by prolonged drug use, culminating in the "fried" brains of the person who cannot even reason clearly, let alone make a moral judgment. It is a mortal sin to place one's physical and spiritual health in such proximate danger, even if a person is to pretend that he is immune from this danger and that "it could not happen to me."

Even the often liberal and ambiguous *Catechism of the Catholic Church*, published in 1994 in application of the principles of Vatican II, acknowledges this:

> The use of drugs inflicts very grave damage on human health and life. Their use, except on strictly therapeutic grounds, is a grave offense.

Clandestine production of and trafficking in drugs are scandalous practices. They constitute direct co-operation in evil, since they encourage people
to practices gravely contrary to the moral law. (§2291)

This does not, however, exclude the use of narcotic drugs for therapeutic
reasons. Their use, under medical supervision, is justified by a sufficiently
grave and proportionate reason, even if they do deprive a person temporarily of the use of reason. (*Cf.* Merkelbach, *Summa Theologiae Moralis*, II,
925). For it is not the loss of reason which is willed. It is only an indirect
consequence, so that there is not necessarily a disorder with respect to the
final end of man. The typical example is pain control.

In conclusion, therefore, the use of marijuana, like any hard or soft
drug, must be considered a mortal sin. If on occasion some people might
be in ignorance as to the gravity of this sin, it is clearly evident that the
matter is objectively serious. Consequently, it must be confessed as a mortal sin, and a person is obliged to confess drug abuse under pain of a bad
or sacrilegious confession. If he forgot to confess the sin, he must then
confess it at the first possible opportunity that he has. The priest who
claimed that this was not a mortal sin has fallen into the trap of laxity.

—*Fr. Scott,* January 1999

ABOUT THE SOUL AND THE BODY

**Is it true to say that the difference between human beings is in the
body and not in the soul?**

St. Thomas Aquinas, following Aristotle, explains that man is a
composite of body and soul. Both together make up the substance of his
being, the soul giving the form or determination of human nature, the
body being the material element, but both inseparably making up human
nature. In this man differs from the angels, who are pure spirits, and not
at all a composite of matter and form, of body and soul. It is because
they are pure spirits that each angel has a different nature from all the
other angels. Since they are all pure spirits, they share no common nature
(except the fact of being pure spirits), as men do. This is in turn why there
is a natural hierarchy amongst the angels, in which they are of greater or
lesser natural perfection as pure spirits.

It follows from this that what makes one man different from another
is not the soul, but the body. If we all share the same human nature, and
if the mystery of the Incarnation is precisely this, that our divine Savior
took upon himself our human nature, it follows that the natural difference between one man and another is not in the soul but in the material

element in which the soul exists, namely, in the body and everything that relates to the physical aspect of our existence. Taken separately, our souls are all identical in nature. Of course, there is also the supernatural difference of grace that is infused into the soul, and in the case of Our Lord this is the grace of the hypostatic union. Nevertheless, what makes a man an individual separate from every other man is not that he has a different soul but that his soul, of a common nature, is united to a particular body.

The consequence is that it is not only a man's sensitive faculties that depend upon his health and bodily well-being, but also the spiritual faculties of his soul, namely, his intelligence and his will. These spiritual faculties can only be educated and formed in a well-balanced physical life and emotional life, for the emotions, coming from the body, are part of the physical make-up of a person. This is a fundamental principle for all education. The conclusion is drawn by Fr. C. Spicq, O.P.:

> Parents engender a human body that will be the instrument of a soul and that will determine the initial practical value of that soul. God will intervene afterwards, and He does so, but a man's ancestors determine the initial energy, the fundamental orientation of a human life … even spiritual! (*Ce que Jésus doit à sa mère*, p. 30)

This philosophical principle has some fundamental consequences in the mystery of the Incarnation and in the role of the Blessed Virgin Mary as unique source of the body of our divine Savior. Explaining St. Thomas Aquinas, Fr. Spicq has this to say: "Since all souls are equal and the quality of their bodies makes the difference between souls, we can understand how extremely important it was that the body of Our Lord was perfect, as an organized body, as a body destined to be united to a soul" (*ibid.*, p. 31). He could not have been our Redeemer without being a perfect man, and He was a perfect man because He received His physical human nature from a woman who had been miraculously preserved from the stain of original sin. He had the integrity lost by Adam and hence perfect health of body, perfect and delicate sensitivity, perfect balance of emotions, perfect control of passions. It could not have been otherwise, and we see here the appropriateness of the Immaculate Conception of the Blessed Virgin Mary:

> If a special Providence of God had not watched over the bodily formation of the Mother herself, on the day of the Incarnation of the Son the Holy Ghost would have had to multiply miracles to preserve the Child Jesus' organism from the hereditary stains that his Mother would have—involuntarily but necessarily—transmitted to Him. But since the body of Mary was perfect, that of Christ was also. (*Ibid.*, pp. 31-32)

We do not often think of it, but when we honor the Blessed Virgin Mary as the Mother of God, and we acknowledge that Christ had no human father, and that consequently He received his genetic and physical makeup entirely from His mother, we at the same time admit that everything that makes Him different from the rest of us in the natural order He received from His mother. He could not help resembling her in all things, not just in physical beauty but also in the natural harmony and perfection that made Him so lovable. It was from Our Lady's extraordinary power of compassion that He received His own delicate and very human mercy and compassion for sinners, encountered on every page of the Gospel (*e.g.*, to the adulteress: "Go and now sin no more" [Jn. 8:11]).

The same can be said of the brightness of His human intelligence and the firmness of His human will, spiritual faculties that were molded by his inheritance from His Blessed Mother:

> If Jesus was the greatest genius of the human race, He owes it to His Mother; for let us repeat it again and again: his human soul was worth exactly as much as our own. It is only because it was united to a perfect body that it had a value that ours does not have....Jesus understood in the blinking of an eye all the truth that is hidden under appearances. His acquired knowledge was developed with unheard of facility and rapidity. (*Ibid.*, pp. 51-52)

St. Louis de Montfort had a real intuition of these simple truths when he related the captivating beauty and the ineffable gentleness of Incarnate Wisdom to His Holy Mother:

> He was born of the sweetest, the most tender, and the most beautiful of all mothers, the Immaculate Mary. If you would appreciate the gentleness of Jesus then consider first the gentleness of Mary, His Mother, whom He resembles by His pleasing character. Jesus is Mary's Child; in Him there is no haughtiness, no harshness, no unpleasantness; and still less, infinitely less, in Him than in His Mother because He is Eternal Wisdom; He is gentleness and beauty itself. (*Love of Eternal Wisdom*, §118)

—*Fr. Scott,* April 2008

Do you consider sports to be a twentieth-century heresy: the adoration of the body?

There can be little doubt that sports play an overwhelming and even exaggerated role in contemporary society. This is true particularly of professional sports, which can no longer be considered a legitimate form of entertainment and relaxation. It is a multi-billion dollar business linked to advertising which promotes values at variance with Christian ethics; win at all costs, for it is winning that counts no matter how. The sports stars, frequently anti-heroes bathing in public adulation and promoted to the status of supermen earning excessive wages far beyond their limited intellectual abilities, are in the forefront of liberal causes undermining even basic natural morality. These champions of physical exercise, whose exploits singularly fail to reflect the attitude of Juvenal, "*orandum est ut sit mens sana in corpore sano*—we should pray for a healthy mind in a healthy body," are the new gods: the new inadequate role models that replace the saints. The Church has always approved, supported, and encouraged sensible physical recreation. The body needs to be exercised, strengthened, recreated and this has a beneficial effect on the whole person; amateur sport has been an important factor in fostering good community spirit on a local level in an atmosphere of friendly rivalry and enjoyment. In Ireland, for example, the Church is directly responsible for the preservation of native games and amateur sportsmanship.

Physical education in the schools can serve to promote sound character, team spirit, a spirit of healthy competition and co-operation, values that have their counterpart in other aspects of social life. Sport itself is not a promoter of such values. Sport is an aspect of bodily health and enjoyment; it is not the perfection of the human person. This false view so prevalent in our time was refuted by Pope Pius XII on November 8, 1952, while addressing the National Scientific Congress of Sport. Sport as an end is subordinated to the perfection of the human person in God. Today we can see that it is in direct conflict with the teaching of the Church and it has become an end, a supreme end in itself—a twentieth-century heresy.

—*Fr. Boyle,* August 1994

ABOUT LIFE AFTER DEATH: HEAVEN, PURGATORY, LIMBO, AND HELL

Can the virtue of charity exist alone among the theological virtues after this life, just as the virtue of faith can exist alone on earth?

It is certainly true that the virtue of faith can exist alone on this earth, namely, without hope and charity. However, this is a very abnormal situation, given that generally in justification, as in baptism, the three theological virtues are infused at the same time. Furthermore, such faith without hope and charity is very imperfect and very unstable, liable to be lost all together, because it is dead, without the life of sanctifying grace. It is for this reason that the Council of Trent teaches:

> Faith, unless hope and charity be added to it, neither unites one perfectly with Christ, nor makes him a living member of his body. For this reason it

is most truly said that "faith without works is dead" and is of no profit....
(Dz. 800)

However, the fact that the theological virtue of charity exists alone in heaven is neither abnormal nor imperfect. It is, to the contrary, a sign of the perfection of the state of the blessed. There is no possibility of the theological virtue of faith, for faith is the assent to that which we cannot see, on the authority of God who reveals. But in heaven the blessed see everything in God, including all the truths and dogmas of the Faith. They are self-evident, in virtue of the beatific vision, and there is no longer any possibility of faith. Likewise for hope, which is the assurance of obtaining a future difficult good, based upon the divine Omnipotence. The blessed in heaven possess God Himself, and consequently are filled with every good. There is no further good to long for, no good to hope for. It is not possible for them to have hope.

However, the poor souls in purgatory have all the three theological virtues and necessarily so. If they did not have the theological virtue of charity, they would have been condemned to hell. Yet despite their certitude of one day doing so, they do not at the present time see or possess God. They consequently have the infused supernatural virtues of faith and hope, by which they believe what they will one day see, and hope for what they will one day possess.

—*Fr. Scott,* June 2004

Will all men go to heaven? Will everyone be saved?

Though the sacrifice of Jesus Christ offered once for all on Calvary and made present at each and every valid Mass is more than sufficient to save all men without exception, it does not follow that all men will consequently be saved. It is a fundamental doctrine of St. Paul that salvation can be acquired only by the grace merited by Christ, and St. Peter himself testified before the High Council that "neither is there salvation in any other" (Acts 4:12).

Furthermore, this is the significance of the dictum "outside the Church there is no salvation." Outside of Christ there is nothing, for "the gods of the Gentiles are devils" (Ps. 95:5).

Ignorance, even if invincible, is not in itself an infallible means of salvation. There is the most serious of obligations to seek the truth, incumbent upon all who are not of the household of the Catholic Faith.

The grace of Christ is always given and must not be refused, and Christ established only one Church in which God is worshipped in spirit and in truth.

It is the deliberate and studied ambiguity of recent texts which causes confusion and leads into the path of error; all religions are not equal, all religions are not good. There is no regard for truth, the truth of Christ, in much recent ecclesiastical teaching.

In a recent review of *Crossing the Threshold of Hope*, an English journalist writes that reports of the pope's infallibility are somewhat exaggerated. Everything the Holy Father says is not infallibly true, especially in his remarks on other religions. I will quote Noel Malcolm at length:

> He talks [the pope] in relation to other religions—as if spirituality were just an aspect of human experience as such, something which can be found among Hindus, Confucians, and ancestor-worshipping aborigines. He even suggests that having the rudiments of spiritual experience connects such people with Christianity and makes them eligible for salvation— a claim which I believe teeters on the edge of heresy. (London *Sunday Telegraph*, November 6, 1994)

If such a person, who is not Catholic, can understand, why cannot our pope and bishops see the truth that they all professed at one time for most of their lives, but now seek to reinterpret in true revisionist fashion, reminiscent of a supposedly fallen regime?

—*Fr. Boyle,* January 1995

 ## Can the suffering souls in purgatory help people on earth by their prayers?

There are two opinions on this question. The first is founded on St. Thomas Aquinas, who explains why it is that we do not generally pray to the souls in purgatory as we do to the saints in heaven.

> Those who are in purgatory though they are above us on account of their impeccability, yet they are below us as to the pains that they suffer: and in this respect they are not in a condition to pray, but rather in a condition that requires us to pray for them. (*ST,* II-II, q. 83, art. 11, ad 3)

The real problem presented by St. Thomas Aquinas is that the poor souls in purgatory have no way of knowing of our prayers, that they might be able to answer them. They cannot know them as the blessed in heaven, who see all our needs and prayers in the vision of God, nor can we personally ask for their prayers, as we can of the living on earth:

> Those who are in this world or in purgatory do not yet enjoy the vision of the Word, so as to be able to know what we think or say. Wherefore we do not seek their assistance by praying to them, but ask it of the living by speaking to them. (*ST,* II-II, q. 83, art. 4, ad 3)

This being said, there is no doubt that the poor souls in purgatory are a part of the Communion of the Saints, given that they are members of the Church, united to Christ, the Head, by supernatural charity.

Consequently, there is no reason to affirm that they cannot pray for us, provided that one understands that they cannot merit either for themselves or for us. It is for this reason that many theologians, such as Suarez and St. Robert Bellarmine, maintain that it is possible and permissible to appeal to the poor souls for their intercession. After all, there is no difficulty about God revealing to them in some way the fact of the prayers that are directed towards them, so that they can pray for people on earth.

It is, then, a pious belief that we can pray to the poor souls in purgatory, so that certain synods in the nineteenth century taught that the poor souls can help us by their intercession:

> Leo XIII, in 1889, ratified an indulgenced prayer in which the poor souls are appealed to in dangers to body and soul. (The prayer is not included in the authentic collections of 1937 and 1950.) (Ludwig Ott, *Fundamentals of Catholic Dogma*, p. 323)

It is only in appearance that this pious belief is in contradiction with the teaching of St. Thomas Aquinas given above, based as it is on the fact that the poor souls cannot merit and cannot hear our prayers in God. Although it is not a dogma, Catholics are consequently free to believe that they can pray to poor souls, nor is this belief in any way reprobated by the Church, but, to the contrary, recommended by some theologians.

—*Fr. Scott,* June 2004

Where will unbaptized children and aborted babies go on the day of the Last Judgment?

It is not a doctrine of faith that children dying with original sin only on their soul go to a special place or state called the children's limbo. However, it is the common opinion of the theologians. This is based upon the teaching of Pope Innocent III (and the Fathers of the Church) on the effects of baptism, in which he has this to say: "The punishment of original sin is deprivation of the vision of God, but the punishment of actual sin is the torments of everlasting hell" (*Maiores Ecclesiae Causas*, DS 780).

The state of limbo is consequently a suffering from the pain of loss, or separation from God, but not of the pain of the senses. As St. Thomas Aquinas teaches (*De Malo*, 5, 3), such a pain of loss is compatible with a certain natural happiness. At the Last Judgment, when the bodies will rise to share in the punishment or reward of heaven or hell, the bodies of those who are in limbo will also rise. Although separated from God, in which way they share the punishment of the damned in hell, they will not be tormented by remorse nor will they suffer the pain of the sense which the damned suffer forever in hell.

The denial of this common teaching by the heretical council of Pistoia was condemned by Pope Pius VI as "false, rash, injurious to Catholic schools." Here is his description of the erroneous doctrine:

> The doctrine which rejects as a Pelagian fable that place of the lower regions (which the faithful generally designate by the name of the limbo of children) in which the souls of those departing with the sole guilt of original sin, are punished with the punishment of the condemned, exclusive of the punishment of fire.... (*Auctorem Fidei*, Dz. 1526)

—*Fr. Scott,* March 1998

 ## Does hell exist? What does it seem to mean for some theologians and teachers in the Church today?

Up until recent times no Catholic, however ill-informed or poorly instructed, was ever left in doubt or bewilderment concerning the reality of hell and everlasting punishment should he have the misfortune to die in a state of unrepentant mortal sin. Hell existed. It was a place or state of eternal punishment inhabited by those rejected by God. It is a *de fide* teaching that hell is a reality, that the punishment of hell lasts for all eternity. That the punishment of the damned, however, is proportioned to each one's guilt is the common view of the Church's theologians; it is not *de fide*.

St. Augustine teaches that "in their wretchedness the lot of some of the damned will be more tolerable than that of others" (*Enchiridion* III), a viewpoint illustrated poetically in the *Inferno* of Dante, where he places not only Alexander the Great and Attila the Hun but also Pope Celestine V and Pope Anastasius—the latter mistakenly, for in all probability he refers to the emperor of the same name.

Hell is peopled with damned souls—damned by their own sins and in accordance with the absolute justice and mercy of God. Yes, even hell, with all its torments, is an act of mercy.

Those who teach or give expression to a hell that exists but is surprisingly and comfortingly empty, fly in the face of the entire Tradition of the Church.

These ideas first appeared in the works of Origen and were condemned. In our time they are to be found under the pen of Hans Urs von Balthasar and the convert theologian Sergei Bulgakov, whom the pope confuses, it seems, with the novelist Mikhail Bulgakov in his *Crossing the Threshold of Hope;* similar views, it would appear, are to be found in the writings of the pope himself, as if he doubted or had the greatest reservations concerning the consequences of the doctrine of hell which he upholds elsewhere. (*Catechism of the Catholic Church*, 1033, where, unfortunately, hell is put in quotation marks). Faced with the defined doctrine of the Church in this matter, he says in his new book, faced with the mystery of the damned in hell, "the silence of the Church is therefore the only appropriate position for Christian faith." The Church was never silent, her doctrine is clear as is that of Christ Himself. Hell is for all eternity. Wretched and miserable souls go there to experience the terror of those terrible words of Christ, "Depart from me, you cursed, into everlasting fire" (Mt. 25:41), to experience the horror of Dante's verse: "Abandon hope all you who enter here" (Canto III, 9).

—Father Boyle, January 1995

 ### Can an apostate from the Catholic Church save his soul if he dies in the state of unrepented apostasy?

An apostate is a person who once was a Catholic, and who has now abandoned all practice of religion. Having received and believed the Catholic Faith, and known at least something of the supernatural order of grace, it is not possible for such a person to be in good faith, as it might conceivably be for a Protestant who stopped the practice of his false religion. The reason for this is that good faith presupposes invincible ignorance. Invincible ignorance is only possible for those who have no possibility of knowing the truth concerning divine revelation, and whose ignorance is consequently not culpable. One who has had the theological virtue of faith infused at baptism, and has had at least some instruction in the Catholic Faith, cannot possibly be in invincible ignorance. He may, certainly, be in ignorance as to the true Church and her teachings, but if he is, it is his own fault, and his ignorance is vincible. It seems that the only exceptions to this would be baptized Catholics who had never been taught anything of the Faith, nor had any Catholic examples as role models.

The Catholic Church refuses Christian burial to all public sinners, including public apostates who are unrepentant. If they give some sign of repentance before death, even if it is only a probable sign, such as the expression of sorrow for their stubbornness or the desire to see a priest, the Church can have some hope for their eternal salvation and consequently authorizes Christian burial. Needless to say, however, only God can judge the soul, so that it is still permissible to pray privately and offer Masses privately for such apostates who have given no sign of repentance.

—Fr. Scott, August 2005

ABOUT SCIENCE, MEDICINE, AND MEDICAL MATTERS

 **A friend claims that test-tube babies, which are made by men, have no souls, as God did not create them and breathe life into them. If this is so, then how can they live if they have no soul?**

Your common-sense answer is the best. It is incorrect to say that babies conceived through these means have no souls. To the best of my knowledge, this is another "truth" fostered by the likes of the Bayside "apparitions."

Any child conceived of human seed is human and as such has a human soul. This is not to say that artificial insemination, "test-tube" babies, *etc.*, are legitimate. They are grave offences against nature and the law of God. Though the means may be evil, the child resulting is still human, possessing body and soul, affected by original sin, and capable of redemption.

It is only partially true to say that they are "made by men." It would be better to say that they are the result of men making an attempt to "play God."

—*Fr. Doran,* November 1991

 **Can cloned human babies be used for experiments and for growing spare parts, to help others?**

This is what is called therapeutic cloning, as distinct from reproductive cloning. The clones are to be destroyed, and the living cells recuperated, within a certain number of days, usually fifteen.

The principle here is very simple. The end does not justify the means. It is never permitted to do something evil that good might come from it, for the goodness or evil of a human act is defined by its end more than by anything else.

Clones are true human beings, for they have an immortal soul, just as does a test-tube baby. The human soul is inseparable from the life of a human being, so that whenever the body is organized in such a way as to have human life, the soul is present as the principle of this life. Despite the immorality of the way in which test-tube babies are conceived, and the way in which genetic material of a clone is introduced into the nucleus of the ovum, once this has been done and there is human life, there is a human soul. If the cloned embryo is then frozen, the soul is not frozen. It is just that the processes of life are temporarily interrupted, ready to start again when the temperature environment becomes suitable. A frozen embryo, cloned or otherwise, must consequently be considered alive.

The therapeutic use of human clones for stem cell research or to provide a source of stem cells to regenerate organs in other people requires that the cloned embryo be killed. It is consequently manifestly immoral, and opposed to the natural law and to the fifth commandment. It consequently behooves all Catholics to stand up against this grave insult to Almighty God, and to do all in our power to prevent this great evil of man attempting to raise himself to take God's place.

In principle, a person who actively participates in such cloning procedures incurs the same penalty as one who participates in the procuring of an abortion, namely, an excommunication (Can. 2350, §1 in the 1917 Code of Canon Law and Can. 1398 in the 1983 Code of Canon Law). It is, however, true that a person could maintain that there is a difference between an abortion and the killing of a cloned baby, inasmuch as the clone is in a laboratory, not an infant developing in his mother's womb. In such cases, the Church provides for the interpretation of her penal laws in the most favorable manner (Can. 19 in the 1917 Code and Can. 18 in the 1983 Code), so that in case of doubt the excommunication would not be incurred.

—*Fr. Scott,* September 2004

 **What measures must be taken to preserve one's life, in the case of terminally ill patients or perpetually comatose patients? Who is morally obliged to have health insurance? Who is morally excused from having it?**

It goes without saying that the direct killing of oneself is a grievous sin against the divine and ecclesiastical law. We do not have complete ownership of our bodies, but only the use from God. We are stewards of this life given by the Almighty. For this reason one must take all the ordinary means necessary to preserve health.

Death may never be directly intended as a means to an end—to escape from pain, for example. The patient, therefore, is obliged to use all ordinary means at his disposal to preserve his life. The attending physician must use all the means at his disposal (of probable use) to preserve his patient's life. *Extraordinary* means may be any which entail excessive physical, psychological, or financial burden. These must be judged for each case.

For those patients who are terminally ill, or comatose, it still remains to administer all care necessary to alleviate pain and discomfort.

Under today's circumstances it would seem that if a man could provide for his family's health coverage he should. I say "today's circumstances" because of the astronomical costs involved in health care. One episode of hospitalization could result in the financial ruin of the entire family. A family should at least be covered against catastrophic costs. A single individual would not be under the same obligation to be covered, as his lot does not involve the welfare of others over which he has responsibility.

—*Fr. Doran,* June 1993

 **Is it not excessive to maintain that the providing of fluids and nourishment is always obligatory, regardless of the state of a sick person?**

On the surface of it, it may appear that it would be going to extraordinary lengths, unduly continuing a person's agony, to insist on the duty of providing him with fluids and nourishment, even when he is known to be suffering from a terminal disease or is in an irreversible coma. However, such an opinion fails to consider the wonderful gift of life, of which Almighty God, the Creator, is alone the source. It replaces the God-centered view of human life as a manifestation of God's goodness with a man-centered conception that focuses on the value of life rather than life itself.

The whole question of the distinction between ordinary and extraordinary means in the maintaining of life was treated very thoroughly by Fr. Iscara in the July 1997 issue of *The Angelus,* in which he establishes that feeding and hydration are always ordinary means and consequently obligatory in conscience, regardless of the condition of the person. He there describes the liberal evolution of these concepts. It is certainly true that there is no absolute distinction between ordinary and extraordinary means, and that a means might be extraordinary for some people but ordinary for others as a result of subjective considerations such as excessive cost, pain and discomfort, location and difficulty in using the means, danger of complications, high chance of failure. However, traditionally, and rightly so, the essential consideration is an objective one. An ordinary means is one that can be procured by ordinary effort and diligence, whereas an extraordinary means requires that effort which is out of the common. The distinction is often clear, as is the case with artificial respirators, which are manifestly extraordinary means.

Confusion concerning this distinction has arisen on account of a new emphasis, namely, on the quality of life, which gives undue emphasis to the subjective elements, and which is ultimately a form of humanism. It is considered that if a person is healthy enough to walk around, or has the use of his mind, or has the motive to live, that his life is somehow of more value than that of the person who is in a permanent vegetative state, or afflicted by senility, or suffering pain from terminal cancer, and that consequently the most basic elements of care are no longer ordinary means, since life is just not worth living. This might seem somewhat of a caricature, but it does correspond to the carelessness with which such persons' lives are treated in many nursing facilities.

A balanced response will not consider the subjective condition of the person as irrelevant to the decision as to what is extraordinary means and what is consequently not obligatory in conscience. It will not, however, allow this to be the major determining factor. There are certain basic needs that are not really even medical treatment, properly speaking, but corporal acts of mercy inseparable from the love of our neighbor. They include nursing care and the providing of nourishment and fluids. It was of those who refuse such necessities to their neighbor that our Lord had this to say:

> Lord, when did we see thee hungry, or thirsty, or a stranger, or naked, or sick, or in prison, and did not minister to thee? Then he shall answer them, saying: Amen I say to you, as long as you did it not to one of these least, neither did you do it to me. (Mt. 25:44-45)

Did our Lord place any conditions on the providing of these necessities of life? Did He say that it was not necessary for the insane, the senile, the comatose, or the dying? Far from it. These are precisely those that He instructs us to practice charity towards, for they are the least among us.

One might well object that sometimes the provision for these physical needs is expensive and difficult. It can sometimes be very difficult and time-consuming to feed very sick persons. There is certainly some expense involved in alimentation *via* a naso-gastric tube or a gastrostomy tube directly into the stomach. But what is that compared to a human life that God has created? In fact, by far the most difficult and expensive aspect of caring for the dying, the senile, and the comatose is good nursing care. Yet who would maintain that this is an optional extra that can be withdrawn? Food and fluids fall into exactly the same category. To withdraw such means on account of expense, or inconvenience, or pain, or because a person is dying, is to be indirectly responsible for the death of a person, but in a very real and entirely predictable manner. It is euthanasia. It is immoral, except in the very rare cases that it is impossible to provide food and fluids by such means. The fact that sometimes people died in the past of dehydration or starvation, when these means did not exist, is no excuse at all for refusing to use them when they are possible and available.

Let us put aside, then, all considerations of quality of life when it comes to the consideration of those necessities of human life that common effort and diligence will provide for the sick and dying. Let us fight for the right, in the natural law, of all human persons to the Creator's gift of life, until such time as He calls them, and of our corresponding duty to protect, defend, and nourish that life.

—*Fr. Scott*, November 2004

 **Could you explain the Church's teaching concerning medical treatments given to those who suffer from fatal illnesses? Whilst I am against euthanasia and suicide, I am confused as to what treatments I would be obliged to accept.**

It is not that the moral principles involved in the delicate issue of the terminally ill are in any way unclear. It is that their application has become confusing by the progress of medical technology.

Clearly, we have the obligation to sustain human life, for this life is given by God. Consequently, we can never do anything positive to terminate an innocent human life. The question of "quality of life" as brought up by the liberals is clearly a red herring. It is not because we don't have any "quality time" left that we can treat our life as valueless. The modern secular mentality despises the supernatural value of this "time," which can be used to build up a great measure of merits and glory as well as to do our purgatory here on earth.

Nevertheless, it does not follow from this that we always have the obligation to use all the means at our disposal to maintain life. The other excess of the modern world is the attempt to escape death by the frantic use of modern techniques to prolong life. The essential distinction here is between ordinary means and extraordinary means.

Extraordinary means are those which involve complicated technology, high expenses, many side effects, and much physical and psychological suffering. They include such major procedures as kidney transplants or coronary bypass grafts and such aids as heart-lung machines or dialysis. Ordinary means are those which are commonly used, not complicated or expensive, and which do not produce excessive suffering or side effects. They include such things as hydration and nutrition, simple procedures such as appendectomies and commonly used and effective drugs such as insulin and antibiotics. Ordinary means are always morally obligatory and must always be employed, under pain of sin, for they are simply the sustaining of human life.

The importance of this distinction lies in the principle of double effect for the terminally ill. The prolongation of life is not the only consideration. It is legitimate to desire to reduce the suffering, side effects, discomfort, and high expenses of high tech interventions. That which is desired (less suffering) is good. The negative effect which may sometimes come from this is a slightly shortened life. But since it is not desired in itself, and provided that the good obtained (*i.e.*, less suffering) is not a direct consequence of the bad effect (the possible shortening of life), then this is permissible.

Note that two further conditions are required. The immediate effect must be good. Thus it is never permitted to use a drug to directly suppress respiration, for the immediate effect, death, would be bad. But it is permitted in a case of terminal illness to use morphine derivatives for pain relief, even though they suppress respiration and may ultimately hasten death. Thus the decision not to use life support systems in the terminally ill is permissible, for the immediate effect is not death, but freeing the patient from additional purposeless discomfort and suffering.

The second condition is that a proportionately grave cause must exist for a treatment to be withheld. This would be the suffering, discomfort, and cost along with little or no chance of lasting cure. Thus it would be permissible to withhold strong chemotherapeutic treatment for a terminal cancer patient with little chance of cure.

Note that these considerations have nothing to do with the "quality of life" or "dying with dignity." It is a question of weighing up the good and bad effects of treatments which are not ordinary, easy, and obligatory. A life offered up to God is always quality, regardless of the suffering. But this agony does not always have to be added to by extraordinary means. Dying with dignity in the Catholic sense does not mean taking some action to bring on death without suffering, but willingly accepting suffering as the punishment we have merited for our sins, and thus dying in the state of grace. As much as possible, Catholics will desire to be conscious at the moment of their last agony, so as to receive the sacraments and prayers of the Church with great profit.

A problem does, however, sometimes arise. Sometimes it is not clear whether a treatment is an ordinary or an extraordinary means. Renal dialysis, for example, is an ordinary means for a person who has it regularly, but it would be an extraordinary means for a terminally ill person. In such cases, it is important to consider the proportion which exists between the difficulty and hardship of the treatment and the potential gain. This can help solve some difficult situations, such as the use of blood transfusions or IV treatments in the terminally ill. There may be cases when, in the last days of a terminal illness, for example, a person might be unable to take in sufficient quantities of water and nutrition. It would be quite unreasonable to hospitalize such a dying person so as to give IV nutrition or blood transfusion. The potential gain is practically nonexistent, but more importantly the undue concentration on disproportionate medical means would turn the dying person away from preparing for a holy and edifying death surrounded by his or her family.

After having considered these principles, we can now consider the most acute problem, that of the maintenance of "vegetative functions" in the state of "brain death." The principle is that it is not the quality of life which is important, but the life itself, which is given by God. Consequently, just as it is never permitted to directly cause death, so also is it never permitted to indirectly cause death by stopping such ordinary means as hydration and nutrition. It is not because of brain death that there is no human soul and life. The difficulty in such circumstances is whether or not the turning off of life support systems is a direct cause of death. It is true that medical diagnosis of brain death can be accurate, as also the prognosis that there will be no recovery. Nevertheless, medicine never has the absolute certitude that a person will not continue breathing once the life support is turned off. Consequently, the turning off of such systems can be considered as an indirect cause of death—providing the medical personnel are not "playing God" and there is the proportionate cause of unbelievable expense and effort without any real hope of a cure.

It must be observed that the majority of "living wills" circulating today do not observe these Catholic principles. They permit the person or the relative to judge as to the maintaining of life based on the quality of life of the person. In this way, the question is radically falsified. If it is not always obligatory to use all available means to extend life, it is obligatory to use all reasonable means to maintain life as God's gift, regardless of its so-called quality.

—Fr. Scott, August 1992

 ### Why is sterilization immoral, and is a reversal procedure ever necessary?

Sterilization is a particular form of artificial birth control, characterized by the additional evil intent that the frustration of the marriage act is meant to be permanent. It is surgically accomplished in a man by a double vasectomy, preventing the sperm from having access to the prostate and the seminal fluids. It is done in a woman by tubal ligation, preventing the fertilization of the ovum by the sperm from taking place.

It is a mortal sin and is forbidden by the Church's law precisely because it is against the natural law. The natural law is man's participation in the eternal law of God, and through it every rational creature recognizes in his conscience his own goal and the right means to attain it. It is a secondary but clear precept of the natural law that "the primary end of matrimony is the procreation and the education of children," as is defined by Canon 1013, §1 of the 1917 Code of Canon Law. Sins that frustrate this end, inscribed by the natural law in every man's conscience, are called sins against nature because they are a willful perversion of the order of nature.

Pope Pius XI has this to say about all such forms of artificial birth control:

> No reason, however grave, may be put forward by which anything intrinsically against nature may become conformable to nature and morally good. Since, therefore, the conjugal act is destined primarily by nature for the begetting of children, those who in exercising it deliberately frustrate its natural power and purpose sin against nature and commit a deed which is shameful and intrinsically vicious. Small wonder, therefore, if Holy Writ bears witness that the Divine Majesty regards with greatest detestation this horrible crime and at times has punished it with death....the Catholic Church...through Our mouth proclaims anew: any use whatsoever of matrimony exercised in such a way that the act is deliberately frustrated in its natural power to generate life is an offense against the law of God and of nature, and those who indulge in such are branded with the guilt of a grave sin. (*Casti Connubii*, Pauline Books, pp. 28-29)

All artificial birth control is consequently against the Church's positive law, as well as against the natural law.

Pope Pius XI has this to say in particular about sterilization:

> Furthermore Christian doctrine establishes, and the light of human reason makes it most clear, that private individuals have no power over the members of their bodies than that which pertains to their natural ends; and they are not free to destroy or mutilate their members, or in any other way render themselves unfit for their natural functions, except when no other provision can be made for the good of the whole body. (*Ibid.*, pp. 35-36)

The theologians (*e.g.*, Prummer, II, §6) further explain that a person does not have an absolute dominion or right over his body. He simply has control over its use, as a steward over his master's property. He must consequently always use it according to the will and law of God. Sterilization is a form of self-mutilation, like the cutting off of a hand, and is a grave insult to God who gave the faculty to engender children.

The perversion involved in sterilization is that it is a procedure which is never done for the health of the whole body, but only and simply to frustrate procreation. Even in the case of a mother who already has many children and who is too sick to bear any further children, sterilization (*i.e.*, tubal ligation) is immoral and a mortal sin, for it is only through the frustration of the natural end of the marriage act that her health is helped, that is, only through a perversion of nature. The end does not justify the means. One cannot do evil that good may come of it. In such an instance, a couple must practice abstinence.

It may be objected that sterilization is not such a grave sin as it once was, since this aspect of the natural law has been obscured. It cannot be denied that the modern personalist vision of marriage, namely, that it is primarily "ordered towards the good of the spouses" (Can. 1055, §1 of the 1983 Code of Canon Law; *Catechism of the Catholic Church*, §1601) and only thereafter towards the procreation and education of children, has caused a radical and unnatural change in the manner of thinking. According to this new conception, artificial birth control, in particular sterilization, is seen to be a right instead of a radical perversion of God's plan, and the method of periodic continence is even praised. Although it is true that sterilization is still technically condemned by the post-conciliar church (*CCC*, §2297), it is only in passing, and in an ineffective and watered- down manner. The consequence is obvious. Catholics everywhere have lost the sense of the moral law and feel that they have a "right" to sterilization if they judge that they have had enough children, and it is for their personal good to stop now. Although this may diminish somewhat the subjective culpability of the couples involved, it does not change the fact that these procedures are an objective mortal sin and a perversion.

The question of reversal frequently arises, especially in the cases of couples who have become traditional after having had such a sterilization procedure performed. Fortunately, it is frequently possible to reverse such sterilization procedures. The success of such procedures will depend upon the methods originally used and upon the time that has passed since the original operation. A simple ligation (*e.g.,* of the fallopian tube or of the *vas deferens*) can be repaired. However, the tubes can be destroyed in the procedure, so that reversal is much more difficult. The passage of ten or more years makes the success rate markedly lower, particularly with vasectomy reversal, on account of the slowdown in sperm production which is the consequence of the vasectomy and of the build up of antibodies against the sperm as a result of blowout of the epididymis.

Clearly, however, there is only one way to remedy the defect caused by sterilization, only one means to make restitution for the offense caused to Almighty God; it is the reversal of the procedure. Any Catholic couple that is still of child-bearing age who would maintain that they are sorry for having the procedure done, but would refuse to have it reversed, would be manifestly guilty of hypocrisy and would have no firm purpose of amendment. This is why the confessor will necessarily impose as a condition to the granting of absolution that the penitent accept to have the reversal of the sterilization performed if it is at all possible. If the urologist or the gynecologist insists that it is not possible to reverse the sterilization, or if he maintains that the chances of success in this particular case are extremely low, then the couple is no longer bound in conscience to have the reversal done. Since reversal procedures are expensive and generally not covered by health insurance, it often happens that a couple does not have the funds for a reversal procedure. They should do all in their power to borrow or save up the funds to have the reversal done, but if this truly is not possible and for as long as it is not possible, then they are not bound to do what they cannot do.

Can a couple, of whom one is sterilized, request and render the marriage debt? If it is through no fault of their own that the reversal cannot be done, or if they have the intention to have the reversal performed as soon as it is possible, then it is permissible for both parties to request and render the marriage debt, after having accomplished a suitable penance and made reparation for any scandal that they have caused. A guilty party who would refuse to have the reversal procedure performed (presuming that it is possible) would lose his right to request the marriage debt and would have to be refused absolution if he did.

However, it often happens that an innocent party never consented to his or her spouse's sterilization procedure. Again Pope Pius XI gives us the principle to know what to do:

> Holy Church knows well that not infrequently one of the parties is sinned against rather than sinning, when for a grave cause he or she reluctantly allows the perversion of the right order. In such a case, there is no sin, provided that, mindful of the law of charity, he or she does not neglect to seek to dissuade and to deter the partner from sin. (*Ibid.*, p. 30)

Consequently, it is permissible for the innocent party to request or render the marriage debt to his or her sterilized spouse, in order that the secondary purposes of marriage be fulfilled, namely, mutual help and affection and the calming of the concupiscence.

A further objection is made that the vasectomized man is technically permanently impotent, being unable to provide sperm, and that consequently he cannot enter marriage and has no right to the marriage act if he is married since he will never be able to fully accomplish it. This was the opinion of the older moral theologians, but theologians from the first half of the twentieth century taught that the marriage act is substantially complete even without true sperm since the other seminal fluids are present and suffice for the accomplishment of the secondary end of marriage (Bouscaren and Ellis, *Canon Law: A Text and Commentary* [1946], p. 470). This opinion was confirmed by decree of the Sacred Congregation for the Faith dated May 13, 1977. Consequently, if a reversal procedure should prove impossible, the vasectomized man does not lose the right to the marriage debt.

—*Fr. Scott,* November 2001

Is a vasectomy an immoral operation? When, if ever, is the reversal of this obligatory?

A vasectomy is a form of self-mutilation. Now, self-mutilation is only allowed to save one's life. If it involves a part of the body with little importance, or no vital function, it is a venial sin if done without a sufficient reason. Since a vasectomy is the direct sterilization of the male, it is grave, and as such is a mortal sin.

There is a further complication to this question. Antecedent and perpetual impotency renders a marriage invalid by virtue of the natural law. The Roman Rota declared on October 25, 1945, that a marriage of one who had a double vasectomy, if irreparable by surgery which is not dangerous to life or seriously injurious to health, would be invalid. If the state was remediable, at least at the time of marriage, the marriage would be valid. The whole controversy is over the question of the possibility of the man to generate a child, not just simply the possibility to render the marital debt. Until recently the decisions taken on such a state were negative, but on May 13, 1977, the Sacred Congregation for the Doctrine of the Faith ruled that male seed incapable of begetting children was not an impediment to marriage. If, however, this condition was fraudulently concealed, it could, under certain circumstances, be grounds for challenging the validity of the marriage.

Although a previous double vasectomy directly procured for the purpose of sterilization would not in itself invalidate a marriage, it still remains self-mutilation and a mortal sin. The possibility of reversal of the operation depends on the type of operation which has been performed. When there is a reasonable probability of reversal the man has a grave obligation to do so, remembering his obligations to his family.

—*Fr. Doran,* November 1993

As a Catholic nurse, do I have the right to administer birth control (Depo-Provera) injections?

Clearly, a Catholic does not have the right to help out in the administration of any birth control methods at all, such as Depo-Provera injections. Just as it is wrong for a physician to prescribe such "treatments," when used for birth control, so also is it wrong for a nurse to administer them to patients. You are obliged to make an objection, in conscience, to performing such actions, and see if your employer accepts that you have the right to refuse to do this.

If your hospital or employer refuses to grant this, you would be able to administer such injections, under duress, if it were the only way to keep your job. It would be what is called a material co-operation, which is to help in another's action, not inasmuch as it is a sin, but simply as a physical action, which is not in itself evil, but good or indifferent. The actual act of giving an injection or a medication is not in itself evil, even though the intention of the person and of the physician is immoral. This is permitted for a sufficiently grave reason, such as keeping your employment, and provided that you have an upright intention, namely, to provide for yourself and your family and to help out the sick by the practice of the nursing profession. However, you are obliged to try to find another nursing position, one in which you would not be asked to act against the moral law.

The great tragedy is that nursing is an eminently Christian profession, one which has grown out of the Catholic Church, and the living of the Faith, and the practice of the corporal works of mercy. Traditional Catholics should do all that they can to stay in this field.

—Fr. Scott, September 1999

 ### Can the pill be taken for medical reasons?

Yes, the taking of a hormonal treatment such as the pill is neither moral nor immoral in itself. Clearly it is permissible for an unmarried woman or for a married woman who is not using her marriage right to take such a treatment for the good of her health.

—Fr. Scott, May 1992

 ### Why also could not a married woman using her marriage rights do likewise? Does not the Council of Trent teach that this is permissible, provided that the bad effect (i.e., contraception) is not willed and there is no intention to frustrate life?

It is true that sometimes it is permissible to do things which have bad effects that we do not want in themselves (<i>i.e.,</i> directly), such as to kill an enemy so as to save one's country. However, for such an action to be permissible four conditions must be fulfilled: (1) the action (<i>i.e.,</i> the taking of medication) must not be wrong in itself; (2) the good effect (<i>i.e.,</i> health) must not come from the bad (<i>i.e.,</i> contraceptive or abortifacient) effect; (3) the intention must be upright (<i>i.e.,</i> good health, and not contraception); and (4) there must be a proportionally grave cause (<i>i.e.,</i> in proportion to the possible evil which will happen, even involuntarily).

It is this last question which is the most difficult to judge. There is no doubt that the pill taken by a woman using her marriage right will have a contraceptive effect, <i>i.e.,</i> will prevent ovulation from taking place, thus preventing the principal end of marriage from being attained.

Nevertheless, if there is a very serious health problem (*e.g.*, dysmenorrhea) and this is the only way of treating it, then it could be justified.

There is, however, a further complication. Recent studies have shown that contraceptives do not only suppress ovulation. Moreover, modern contraceptives have greatly reduced the dose of estrogen. But the lower the estrogen dose the higher the rate of breakthrough ovulation. This does not mean that the contraceptive effect fails; for all contraceptives also prevent the ovum, if fertilized, from implanting in the uterine wall—that is they produce *abortions*. If the older high-estrogen dose contraceptives had a 2-10% of breakthrough ovulation rate—and consequently of abortions—the modern lower estrogen dose contraceptives certainly have a much higher rate, although it is not known exactly how high.

CONCLUSION: If you are using your marriage rights and taking oral contraceptives for other medical reasons, there is a good chance that you, like anyone else taking the pill, will have an abortion from time to time without even knowing about it. It doesn't matter if the baby is only six to nine days old. It is still an abortion.

—Fr. Scott, May 1992

 **I have a good Catholic doctor, and he did not tell me I had to abstain.**

You do not have the right to risk an abortion. It is much too serious a thing, even if it is not directly intended and you are not aware of it. Medical practitioners generally do not distinguish the abortifacient effect, which could not be justified for health reasons, from the simple suppression of ovulation, which could.

If, therefore, you are married and you have to take some form of contraceptive for medical reasons, you must abstain for the whole time you are taking it. You must also abstain for a sufficiently long period before beginning it to be sure that you have not conceived.

— *Fr.* Scott, May 1992

 **I know a Catholic woman who took the pill for years. She said that she was advised not to have children during the change of life.**

Another error spread by the medical profession! Women in their forties are perfectly capable of having children. If the risks of complications are slightly higher, they have simply to be more carefully followed by their physician. Of course, they are free to abstain. But the widespread mentality that they have done their duty because they have had several children and that they are consequently justified in using a contraceptive medication for a "woman's problem" or in permanently using NFP is profoundly anti-Catholic.

It is not because they already have children, difficulties, and hardships that they can turn away from the sacred responsibility of using their marriage for the purpose for which Our Lord elevated it to the dignity of a sacrament. As was explained in the March [1992] *Angelus*, only serious reasons of a medical, social, or eugenic nature can justify the use of NFP.

The Couple to Couple League and other organizations are doing untold damage to Catholic families by promoting the indiscriminate use of NFP, condemned by Popes Pius XI and XII. Such couples are no longer at the service of God for the generation of souls, but it is rather they who choose for themselves according to their own desires Where is the Catholic ideal? In fact, and experience clearly proves it, this contraceptive mentality is the open door to liberalism in the home.

—*Fr. Scott,* May 1992

Does the Church approve of surgery for an ectopic pregnancy?

It is never permitted to directly kill an infant (or any other person, for that matter, with the exception of self-defense, just war, and capital punishment), and so consequently, it is immoral to perform an abortion in the case of an ectopic pregnancy, even to save the life of the mother. This is immoral, whether it is done surgically or chemically. There are now available medications (such as methotrexate, or just recently RU-486) that are commonly used for tubular pregnancies and that directly cause the living fetus to be aborted. This is always immoral.

However, if it can be established that the fetus is already dead (by ultrasound examination, for example), then clearly the surgical removal of the already dead fetus for the health of the mother is entirely permissible.

The difficulty arises when the fetus is still alive. The mother's life is endangered through internal hemorrhage at that time. The moral theologians hold different opinions as to whether it is permissible to intervene surgically to remove the ectopic pregnancy before the death of the fetus. Some say that surgical intervention directly kills the fetus, which is immoral. Others say that it is not direct killing at all, but it is the removing of a mass of tissue (including the placenta) which has fixed itself in the wrong place (the fallopian tube instead of the uterus) in such a way as to cause a tumor invading the mother's fallopian tube, rather like a malignant tumor. Just as it is possible to operate on a tumor of the mother, (*e.g.,* in treatment of uterine cancer) even if as a consequence and indirectly the child will die, so also it is moral, they say, to surgically remove this abnormal mass of tissue, which contains the fetus. It is an indirect and unfortunate, though necessary, consequence that the fetus will die, but this is not willed in itself.

The principle used in this second opinion is the application of the principle of double effect, or the indirect voluntary. This is moral, provided that the bad effect, in this case the death of the unborn child, is not directly willed in itself and that there is a proportionate reason (such as saving the life of the mother), and that the good effect, namely, saving the mother's life, does not directly come from the bad effect, the death of the child. The understanding of this solution depends upon the grasping of the gravity of the proportionate reason. The fetus that lodges in the fallopian tube cannot survive in any case, and if the mother is not treated she may very well hemorrhage to death, or she will have to be observed in hospital for several weeks, and her fallopian tubes can be so damaged by the ectopic pregnancy left untreated that she might never be able to conceive again.

Since there are opinions on both sides of this question, both can be safely followed in conscience. Consequently, it is permissible to have surgery, provided that it is not a direct abortion but the removal of invasive tissue; but it is never permissible to take medications to kill the live fetus.

—*Fr. Scott,* February 2001

 ## Is it permissible to induce early delivery in cases of fetal anencephaly?

Anencephaly is a congenital deformity of an unborn fetus in which large parts of the brain and skull are missing. It is always fatal for obvious reasons. The birth can be emotionally upsetting, since the birth defect is quite ugly and obvious. The baby may be stillborn or may survive for a very short period of time before dying. The condition is usually now diagnosed during the second trimester by means of ultrasound. The most frequently advised medical treatment is abortion, the justification being that the baby will not survive and this will diminish the emotional suffering of the wait and the trauma of seeing a deformed baby. However, the fact that the child will die is irrelevant. It is clearly evident that such direct killing of the unborn is not only a mortal sin but also merits for every Catholic the canonical censure of excommunication.

As a consequence, some Catholics devised the plan of early delivery, stating that the principle of double effect applied, and that it was not an abortion, for the death of the baby is not directly willed but rather the relief of the mother's anguish. This is not true, for the early delivery before viability is a direct killing of the infant. Then others came up with the opinion that premature induction could be done for as long as the fetus was viable, namely, at thirty-three weeks. The problem with such a position is that the fetus is likely to die not just of anencephaly but also of the consequences of prematurity, unless extraordinary means are used, which would not normally be the case when there is such a severe defect.

Clearly, then, this is not permissible. At any rate, it is of no advantage to the baby, and there is no real evidence to suggest that there is any relief of parents' emotional distress as a result of such early induction. Consequently, even in such cases in which the infant is viable, there is no proportionate cause, and the principle of double effect cannot be applied to place the baby at such great risk.

Consequently, in 1996 the US Bishops issued a statement that treats of this question quite well, entitled "Moral Principles Concerning Infants with Anencephaly." It declared:

> It is clear that before "viability" it is never permitted to terminate the gestation of an anencephalic child as the means of avoiding psychological or physical risks to the mother. Nor is such termination permitted after "viability" if early delivery endangers the child's life due to complications of prematurity....Only if the complications of the pregnancy result in a life-threatening pathology of the mother may the treatment of this pathology be permitted even at a risk to the child, and then only if the child's death is not a means to treating the mother.

The emotional distress referred to in this whole discussion is none other than the refusal of the mystery of the cross. It is a consequence of original sin that sickness entered into the world, and the particularly distressing sickness of congenital deformities. If the innocence of the baby, who has not personally merited such afflictions, distresses us, yet the existence of such deformities is a necessary reminder of the universality of our inheritance of original sin and of how much we are all in need of the Redemption and of the mystery of the cross. The thought of trying to escape this distress by any other way is nothing less than the running away from the cross that is inseparable from human life in this vale of tears.

Others, however, have proposed early induction not for the comfort of the mother but to assure the birth of a live infant and hence a certainly valid baptism. This is a grave reason but still could not justify doing anything morally wrong, such as delivering a baby before viability, or delivering a baby after viability but not supplying the means necessary to survive. It would seem, at any rate, a false presupposition to think that the baby would be more likely to be born alive with premature induction than with normal birth or Caesarean section at term, and so the Catholic attitude in such a case would be to pray, place all things in divine Providence, and be ready for an emergency baptism as soon as the child is born.

—*Fr. Scott,* July 2007

Is there any moral objection for a Catholic mother to submit to the practice of amniocentesis?

The Catholic Church has no objection in principle to this medical practice provided the intention of doctor and patient is honorable and morally upright. This technique employed in prenatal screening involves using a needle and syringe to remove some of the amniotic fluid from the amniotic sack in which the unborn child is held suspended. The fluid obtained may be analyzed with a view to correcting genetic disorders or maternal fetal blood incompatibility before the birth of the child. Many disorders can be corrected by injecting the unborn child with the appropriate medicine—or by giving the medication to the mother or by performing micro fetal surgery. It is clearly to be seen in this case that the fetus is considered as a patient, *i.e.*, as a person.

However, amniocentesis is also subject to a grave abuse, an immoral usage that every Catholic must deplore. The results obtained frequently permit the doctor to counsel an abortion, a crime against the unborn and crying out to heaven for vengeance.

On the other hand, parents who learn that they may have a potentially deformed child will, of course, be naturally disappointed. At the same time, they should realize in the light and comfort of the Faith, that Almighty God is offering them a very special child and the grace to accept and welcome the infant into their family. How often in a loving Christian home an abnormal child brings out and develops in parents and the other children the finest qualities of love, sacrifice, understanding, and selfless generosity.

In summary, the technique is not opposed to Catholic teaching despite abuses. It is so promising and rich in its possibilities that it truly heralds a breakthrough in medical science and fetal surgery, and Catholics can legitimately profit by it.

—Fr. Boyle, January 1994

Is it licit to allow one's children to be vaccinated for rubella with vaccine manufactured with the help of fetal cells from aborted babies?

There is no doubt that it is illicit to prepare vaccinations by the use of cell cultures from aborted babies. It certainly is a very troublesome situation if the only way of obtaining such necessary vaccines is from cultures prepared from the by-products of abortions.

The question here is whether or not it is permissible to use such vaccines if they are the only ones that are readily available. Can the principles of double effect be applied?—that is, when only a good effect is directly willed and a bad effect is simply permitted but not directly willed in itself? The good effect in this case is the immunization against the infectious disease. The bad effect is the abortion, the killing of the innocent. It is never permitted to do something evil in order that a good can come of it; that is, it is never permitted for the good effect to come from the bad effect. However, it is possible to permit an evil that is not directly willed in itself, and this is called the indirect voluntary.

Here one could argue that the person who seeks the vaccination does not will the abortion but simply uses the cells that are obtained as a consequence. However, the vaccine is not just an indirect effect of the abortion. There is, in fact, a direct line of causality from the abortion to the available fetal cells, to the development of the vaccine, to the immunization. Therefore, the immunization is a direct consequence of the abortion and not just an indirect effect. Consequently, it would be immoral to use a vaccine that one knew was developed in fetal cells no matter how great the advantage to be procured.

Moreover, even if it were to be admitted that the vaccination is not a direct consequence of the abortion, for the abortion is not performed directly in order to obtain fetal cells, and those who use them might claim, as for themselves, that they do not directly will the abortion in itself, the Catholic sense tells the faithful that they can never use the by-products of abortions for any reason at all, for by so doing they promote the mass murder of the innocent which is destroying modern society and all sense of morality. There must always be a proportionate reason to use the indirect voluntary, that is, to permit something evil which is not directly willed. Here the reasonable gain obtained by the use of the double effect (if it truly were indirectly willed only, which it is not) would not in any way be proportionate to the horrible evil of abortion, and the scandal would be immense.

If parents are not aware of the fact that fetal cells are being used in the culture of the vaccines that they are giving to their children, then clearly there is no moral fault involved. However, if they are aware of this, then they are morally obliged to refuse such vaccinations on principle, until such time as they can be obtained from cultures which are morally licit. Furthermore, if civil law should make such vaccinations obligatory (*e.g.*, for attendance at school), then the parents would be obliged to object in conscience to such immoral means of vaccinating their children.

Moreover, it is not permissible to remain in willful ignorance on such a question. If there is a positive reason to suspect that fetal cells are indeed involved in the production of the vaccine, then parents are morally obliged to clarify the matter, and find out if this is indeed true or not.

—*Fr. Scott,* June 2000

Is it wrong to be an organ donor?

There are some occasions in which it is clearly permissible, for example, when a person has a pair of organs, only one of which is really necessary. One can be removed to transplant to another person, such as a kidney transplant. There are other cases in which it is permissible, for example, when the organ can be taken when the person is clearly already deceased, such as eye corneal transplants.

However, it is manifestly immoral to kill a person to take one of his organs, although that person would have died on his own within a short period of time. It is never permissible to kill one person just to help another. Only God has power over life and death.

The problem arises because once a person has really died and his cardiac and respiratory functions have ceased for several minutes, then his organs will be damaged in such a way that they cannot be used for organ transplants. Hence the organs must be removed first.

The big dispute presently concerns when a person is alive or dead. This involves the concept of brain death. The medical profession generally considers that when a person has been proven to be brain dead, for example, by a flat EEG or by the absence of respiration when the respirator has been turned off, then he must be considered to be dead despite the fact that his cardiac and respiratory functions are being artificially maintained. Consequently, it is permitted, so they say, to remove any or all organs from a person who is still breathing and whose heart is still beating, so long as he is proven to be brain dead. This has actually become big business, and a "living corpse" like this is worth probably more than eighty thousand dollars for its internal organs.

This practice is not only disgustingly inhuman. It is manifestly anti-God and immoral. Death is the moment at which the soul leaves the body. This is known only to God, the creator of life. While a person is still breathing, even artificially, and while his heart is still beating, he has many signs of life. His body is being maintained in life by the circulation of blood. He is still a human being. It is true that if his brain is dead he will never think again, and he will not have the reflexes and reactions that depend upon brain function. However, this does not mean that he is not alive. It just means that there is a permanent, irreparable impairment to his human activities. It is not for man to decide that he is not a man and that he is not alive. Consequently, he must be treated as a living person. Hence no essential organs can be removed until well after all respiration and cardiac action have ceased.

—*Fr. Scott,* June 2000

Some physicians use the text of Pope John Paul II's address to the International Congress on Transplants, dated August 29, 2000, to justify "cadaveric" organ transplantation. Can we accept this?

"Cadaveric" transplantation is a misnomer, and is used to describe the removal of organs from a person who has been declared brain dead but who is being kept alive by artificial means.

Note that the pope's address is not a statement of the Church's magisterium, and that it makes no definitions or clear statements on faith or morality. I will pass over the humanistic and naturalistic tone of this discourse, which speaks of the dignity of the human person but not of the salvation of souls. I would, however, like to bring up the crucial statement in this document, which the pope uses to justify his personal opinion that it is licit to harvest organs from brain-dead people, who are being kept alive by artificial means, in order to treat medical conditions by transplantation. The crucial statement is this: "The criterion adopted in more recent times for ascertaining the fact of death, namely, the complete and irreversible cessation of all brain activity, if rigorously applied, does not seem to conflict with the essential elements of a sounds anthropology" (§5).

The pope's very hesitant statement is quite simply wrong. The Church teaches that reason can prove with certitude the spirituality and the immortality of the human soul (DS 2766 and 2812). This means that the soul is not bound to any organ of the body, including the brain. The soul is not dead or absent just because the brain is incapable of functioning, short of a miracle. Death is in fact the separation of the soul from the body. As the pope himself correctly points out, the precise moment of death "is an event which no scientific technique or empirical method can identify directly" (§4). It is for this reason that a priest can conditionally administer the sacrament of extreme unction for up to an hour after a person has been medically declared dead.

The pope's argument is that we can accept that the neurological criteria of death have replaced the cardio-respiratory criteria, namely, the cessation of heart and lung activity for a period of time beyond which it is no longer possible to revive them. It is true that the neurological criteria give the moral certitude that the person will die when the cardio-respiratory life support systems are removed. However, they give absolutely no certitude that the person is already dead in the true sense of separation of soul and body. Moral certitude of this is only possible when corruption takes place, as sure proof that human life is no longer present in the corpse. However, as long as respiration and cardiac function are maintained, albeit artificially, the tissues and cells of the body will certainly stay alive and nourished, and the body remains one organism, with one being—that is to say, one soul. Corruption is the only sure sign that the unity of the being is lost, and that consequently the immortal soul is separated from the body. Once corruption sets in and death is certain, it is certainly permissible to use organs for experimental and other uses, provided that there is a proportionally grave reason. However, since corruption involves some disintegration of the tissues and organs, they cannot normally be used for transplantation purposes.

How can it be said with certitude that the human soul is no longer present in an apparently live body whose brain is dead? And if the human soul is in all probability present, how can the removal of organs necessary for life be justified? The moral certitude that the brain-dead person will die in any case is irrelevant. He is presently, to all appearances and in all likelihood, still alive, and the removal of organs necessary for life could be the direct cause of his death. Surely to be responsible for this is a sin against the fifth commandment. Surely man cannot claim this right to kill another person simply because of the benefit that could accrue to a third person. This is utilitarianism, considering man as a means to an end.

Consequently, the medical diagnosis of brain death cannot be considered as giving the medical profession the right to declare a person as dead, quite simply. Furthermore, it is not permissible to accept organs necessary for life, such as the heart, lung, or liver, removed from a person in such a state. It is consequently my opinion that the present-day practice of "cadaveric" transplantation is immoral and illicit, and it is not permitted for a Catholic to authorize his or another's donation or even to accept organs harvested in this way.

—*Fr. Scott,* August 2001

 ## Is hypnosis permissible as a medical therapy?

Hypnosis is a deliberately induced state of reduced consciousness. It is widely recognized as a means of therapy for a variety of conditions of a psychological nature, including drug and alcohol addiction, insomnia, anxiety, depression, and obsessive-compulsive disorder. However, its most frequent and most successful use is to enable persons to give up smoking who are otherwise unable to do so. The effectiveness of the treatment depends upon the responsiveness of the subject to the therapist's power of suggestion, which is highly variable, depending upon the depth of the hypnosis, the individual character of the subject, and the authority of the therapist. Suggestions not opposed to the will of the individual subject are imprinted deeply into his subconscious, thus strengthening his weak affectivity so that he can think, act, and feel as he desires.

The morality of this method of treatment is dependent upon the modification of the voluntariness of the subject. The loss of voluntariness depicted in the Hollywood representations of hypnosis rarely if ever happens. Experienced hypnotists know full well that nobody can be hypnotized if he does not want to be, and that if the hypnotherapist makes a suggestion opposed to the will of the subject, then the person immediately leaves the state of hypnosis. However, if it were possible through hypnosis, it clearly would be immoral for a person to deliberately allow the voluntariness of his acts to be destroyed, so that he would then act in a programmed way, without responsibility or morality in his acts. This is not the case.

In fact, the modification of voluntariness that hypnosis gives is an increase of voluntariness. It is the willing choice of a method that will increase the effectiveness of the will over the emotional faculties, and the feelings in particular. The therapist repeatedly inculcates the desired feelings, such as the hatred of drugs or alcohol, detestation of smoking, the feeling of happiness, and the like. He is thus an extension of the person's will, indirectly enabling him to have a greater power over the lower faculties that he cannot directly control. Thus a person's feelings come more in line with what he wills, and his actions that follow as a consequence are more deliberate, more willful, and more positively moral than they would have otherwise been.

It is certainly true that like any other therapy, there can be a danger with hypnotherapy. However, this will only take place in the case of particularly immature individuals who do not know what they want, have very little direction, and who are highly suggestible. Consequently, young persons who could fall into this category ought to be accompanied by a parent for hypnotherapy sessions. It is certainly also possible that a therapist could follow a New Age philosophy, but it is neither necessary nor common.

The ideal, of course, would be to find a hypnotherapist who shares the Catholic Faith, for the effectiveness of this treatment is based largely upon trust and confidence, and it is difficult to show such trust and confidence towards those who do not share our religious convictions. This being said, there is no reason why a mature person ought to be afraid of going to a non-Catholic hypnotherapist for the treatment of a particular psychological condition, such as drug addiction, since he knows ahead of time that the suggestions will be limited to that domain, and he will exit the hypnosis if the therapist goes beyond his limits.

—*Fr. Scott,* August 2006

Can a Catholic use acupuncture?

There is obviously an interrelation in the nervous system. The nerves clearly form a network. The main question is whether or not acupuncture solves a problem or merely deadens a nerve. Acupuncture seems to remove pain without necessarily solving the ailment. In itself its practice is indifferent. The only prohibition that would come in would be any association with New Age thinking or practices which very often is the case these days

—*Fr. Doran,* April 1992

Would a person with celiac disease be protected by transubstantiation from being harmed by gluten in the host?

The argument that the accidental qualities of bread cannot harm the intestine of one who suffers from celiac disease (as a result of non-tolerance of gluten in wheat bread) is false. It is, of course, true that the substance of the bread does not remain after the consecration of the sacred species. However, all the accidents remain, which include not just the exterior appearance but everything that is subject to the senses and that science can investigate, including the chemical composition. The chemical effects of the gluten on the intestinal wall will consequently still remain, just as much as will the appearance and texture of bread; for they are just as accidental to the real nature of what is there as the appearance and texture. Here lies the miracle and the mystery of the Blessed Eucharist. It would be a miracle if the accidental qualities of gluten were not to harm the intestine. Although such miracles can happen, we cannot depend upon such an extraordinary intervention of Almighty God. Consequently, a person who suffers from celiac disease needs to ask the priest to give him or her a very small portion of the host. It is never allowed to manufacture the host out of rice or a non-wheaten material that does not contain gluten. Such hosts are not valid matter for the Holy Eucharist.

—*Fr. Scott,* May 2001

Is Alcoholics Anonymous penetrated by the principles of naturalism, and if so, how can it be justifiable for a traditional Catholic to belong to it?

There can be no doubt about the essential accusation of naturalism, nor that it is penetrated by the principles of syncretism, that theory that regards all religions as different aspects of one world religion. It is certainly true that AA has never pretended to be anything else but this. It openly encourages all to believe in their god or power, as they understand it. As such it is a danger to the faith of the weak. In this way it is penetrated with the ideas of Freemasonry. However, it cannot be equated with this condemned organization, which truly is a secret society and has a hidden purpose. AA's purpose is not to promote anti-Catholic philosophies but to help alcoholics, albeit by purely naturalistic means.

I always feel uncomfortable recommending our faithful to attend AA. However, sometimes there is simply no choice. A purely spiritual solution does not work, for these people have a severe personality disorder that requires a natural and psychological help. Anybody who maintains that confession and the spirit of penance suffice to cure alcoholism has absolutely no medical understanding of the condition at all. They are necessary, but not sufficient. The weak character, filled with self-doubt, lack of self-confidence, and poor self-esteem, also needs help. There can be no denying the fact that AA is particularly effective in providing this psychological help. Innumerable are the traditional Catholics who owe their sanity and their ability to live in the state of grace to the psychological support that this organization has given. In actual fact, we have no serious alternative to AA, with the sole exception of regular weekly professional counseling, which can be prohibitively expensive and oftentimes not nearly as effective.

Consequently, I maintain that it is permissible to use AA in cases where the alcoholic has a strong faith, and provided that the danger to the faith be avoided by regular reception of the sacraments and spiritual direction.

—*Fr. Scott,* June 2003

ABOUT THE
STATE AND CIVIC DUTIES

Is there such a thing as the Rights of Man?

Our civilization, the one we used to call Christian but is now thoroughly pagan and Western, has placed a tremendous and unrelenting emphasis on the rights of man to the exclusion of the rights of God. Even the present-day churchmen seem to have ignored, or feign ignorance of, God's rights, yet these two, rights of man and rights of God, can never be in opposition to or deny each other. The rights of man are rooted in the nature God gave him, and that nature must respect the natural law, which is simply a participation in the eternal law.

Since man is a union of body and soul, he has a right to his bodily integrity and the normal development of his physical powers; to food, clothing, shelter, medicine, *etc.* His spiritual integrity in the development of his powers of soul must also be respected. He has a right to life because his life on earth will determine what his eternal destiny will be. He has a right to be treated in accordance with the moral laws, and he has a right to enter into relations with God, the true God, and embrace His truth.

This teaching is clearly set out in the encyclical letter of Pope Pius XI, *Divini Redemptoris*, where the pope speaks of the right to life, the right to bodily integrity, the right to obtain the necessary means of existence, the right of man to tend towards his ultimate goal in the pale marked out for him by God, the right of association, and the right to use property and possess it. Just as matrimony and the right to its natural use are of divine origin, so likewise are the constitution and the fundamental prerogatives of the family fixed and determined by the Creator.

It must be emphasized that rights are not independent of duties, and one cannot really speak of the one without reference to the other, nor can both be treated in disregard of the source of all rights, God Himself.

—*Fr. Boyle,* May 1994

How binding is the "just war" principle on Catholics? Can a Catholic, in good faith, be an absolute pacifist?

A war is an armed conflict between sovereign states, undertaken by public sanction. Every just war is defensive. It must be waged for the defense of some injured rights. War is permissible, just as self-defense is permissible, as war may be the only means of maintaining or defending an independent society's rights, though we must recall that Our Lady of Fatima stated that war is ultimately an effect of sin.

The following conditions must be fulfilled that a war be just:

1) It must be declared by the State itself.

2) It is a last resort after diplomacy has failed.

3) There must be a grave and just reason for it.

4) Its method must be just and according to international law.

5) An upright purpose must be intended.

6) It may not be continued after due satisfaction has been given or offered.

7) Conditions for peace must be just and may not be crushing unless severity is truly necessary to maintain present self-defense.

The reasons for war must be certainly just to be undertaken. Soldiers are usually to presume that their country is in the right, and when in doubt are bound to obey. If a war is obviously unjust, a soldier may not inflict damage to the enemy except for the sake of self-defense. Therefore, a war must be manifestly unjust—not fulfilling the above conditions—before a Catholic can refuse any involvement.

Now, the citizen is both an individual and a person. These two aspects must always be kept in mind to understand basic Catholic social doctrine. The citizen as a rational person is superior to the State. The State thus has the obligation to foster the personal development of the citizen and, indirectly, his spiritual well being. On the other hand, the citizen as an individual is a member of the State and thus at its service. Therefore, the citizen must, if called to duty in a just war, render service. There may be, in some cases, reasons for a non-combatant position, but outright refusal to serve, as an absolute pacifist, would be morally reprehensible.

—*Fr. Doran,* February 1992

Could a US attack on Iraq be considered a just war?

This question is sometimes simplified to the question of whether we condone or condemn the actions of Saddam Hussein. However, this is not the essential question here, even if the legitimacy of his authority were to be questioned.

The morality and conditions for a just war were very well explained by Fr. Iscara in his erudite article in the July 2002 issue of *The Angelus* (pp. 2-16), an article inspired by St. Thomas Aquinas (*ST,* II-II, q. 40, art. 1). In this article, Fr. Iscara points out that the application of these principles to determine the morality of a particular conflict can be very difficult, given the complexity of actual situations.

The *first* condition for a war to be just is that it is declared by a lawful or legitimate authority. It is certainly true that the US Congress has the authority to declare a war for the self-defense of US territory or citizens. It is also certain that its concern for the common good of the US also means that it must have some concern for the common good of the globe as a whole, given the mutual interdependence of nations. However, it does not at all have the authority to act as an international policeman, for the international common good is not its responsibility. For it to do so would be to attack the sovereignty of other nations. No nation has the right to declare war on another nation that is not a threat to it. Furthermore, a body of nations cannot have the authority to make such a declaration of war, since it has no sovereignty. It is true, however, that the people can rebel against an unjust ruler who has lost his right to rule and appeal for foreign aid. This does not appear to be the case in Iraq, with the exception of exiled liberal dissidents. The US would have the moral right to declare war on Iraq only if Iraq posed a real threat to US security (or to that of US allies). This has not at all been demonstrated. The existence of weapons of mass destruction or Iraq's ability to use them has not been demonstrated, nor has the use of Iraq as a base for terrorism.

The *second* condition for a just war is that there must be a just cause, such as defense against an unjust attack or recuperation of what has been unjustly taken. A presumed, imaginary, or even possible problem of terrorist bases or the existence of weapons of mass destruction could not constitute a just cause. Another aspect of the just cause is that it must be proportionate to the evil, death, destruction, and human suffering that could be caused by the war. Since modern wars are indiscriminate and attack civilians just as much as military personnel, it cannot be conceived that a war of this kind could be successful without a great deal of suffering for the citizens of Iraq. There is a manifest lack of proportionality here that makes any reasonable person wonder what the real, underlying reason for such a proposed war or invasion could be. If it were, for example, US self-interest by guaranteeing the supply of oil, then it would be manifestly unjust. Here it is also to be mentioned that a war is only just if there is a good chance of a rapid, successful victory with a minimum of casualties. The specter of Vietnam makes one wonder if this really is the case.

The *third* condition described by St. Thomas for a just war is a right intention, and this in the objective domain, namely, that it be truly the re-establishment of justice which is aimed at. However, this is not at all the case. Iraq has done no injustice to the US. The absence of a right intention is also manifest by the fact the US is not insisting that Israel live up to UN demands as it is with Iraq. To the contrary, the embargo against Iraq has caused the death of many children—as estimated by some, as many as one million. In this regard, a war can only be just if all other avenues of resolution have been exhausted. This does not at all appear to be the case, which is why other nations, that do not stand to gain as much, are not interested in participating.

Consequently, the proposed war on Iraq is not morally licit. This does not mean, however, that American servicemen could not fight in such a conflict, even if they were aware that it is not based on moral principles. It is their duty to defend their country, and once a war were declared it would be necessary for them to do so. It is rather strange that it is the Arab country that has been most tolerant towards its relatively large Chaldean Christian minority which is being threatened in this way. One hopes that it will not be a repeat of Kosovo, in which the NATO invasion brought, as a consequence, the destruction of over a hundred monasteries and churches, most of which had survived five hundred years of Moslem rule.

—*Fr. Scott,* December 2002

Can the use of nuclear weapons in time of war ever be justified?

The traditional principles of Catholic morality manifestly forbid all use of nuclear weapons in time of war. The reason for this is that, as all the authors say, the slaying of the innocent is an illicit and immoral act that cannot be justified for the winning of a war. Noncombatants, who do not contribute either directly or indirectly to the success of the enemy's war effort, must be considered as innocent. To directly attack them for any reason at all, such as to destroy a nation's morale, is an immoral act. It is understood that the killing of the innocent can often happen as a by-product of war, not directly willed in itself. This is not immoral, as long as it is not desired but simply an unavoidable side-effect of an aggressive offensive or of a bombing of military targets.

However, nuclear weapons cause mass destruction of entire civilian populations, nor can they be used to attack localized military targets. Hence, the killing of innocent civilians and non-combatants is not just an unavoidable side-effect. It is what is directly willed. This is manifestly immoral, no matter how just the war might be.

This response must, nevertheless, be modified by the changing nature of war in the modern world. A new barbarism has emerged which goes by the name of total war. Starting with the American War Between the States, and becoming increasingly intense ever since, modern wars are not a conflict simply between the combatants of both sides. The whole resources of a people are now committed to the war effort and to the total destruction of the enemy, including industry, education, and all the infrastructure of a society. This is manifestly an immoral concept of war and cannot possibly be used to justify the killing of the innocent, of noncombatants.

The difficulty arises when an enemy nation employs the techniques of total war. It might happen that the only way to defend oneself against an unjust aggressor in such an immoral war would be to oppose like force to like force, mobilizing all of a country's resources and attacking the enemy's civil targets. (*Cf.* Fagothey, *Right and Reason*, p. 572). The justification for such a response would be that there are no such things as non-combatants, and that since the entire population is involved in the enemy's war effort, all can be the target of aggressive defense. Although this might be admitted as a theoretical possibility, it would certainly be an absolutely frightening decision to have to take.

Hence, the situation could be imagined in which the death of a large number of civilians through the use of nuclear weapons could be justified through the principle of double effect, as a necessary means to win a just war. However, even in such circumstances there would have to be a proportionate reason for the evil of the death of the innocent, namely, the good intended. It is my contention that, in the modern world, such a proportionate reason could never be imagined. The use of one nuclear weapon would bring about the release of other nuclear weapons by the enemy or their allies, and a cycle of unbelievable destruction would be created, which would be a much greater evil than even losing a just war.

Consequently, it seems to me that even allowing the possibility of the theory of total war having to be replied to with total war, in practice the use of nuclear weapons is never permissible.

It is manifestly obvious that the 1945 use of atomic weapons against Hiroshima and Nagasaki was immoral. At that time there was no threat to civilian populations in the allied countries, nor could there truly have been said to be total war. There certainly was no proportionate reason for the civilian suffering, destruction, and misery that resulted, not to mention the public scandal and horror that a "civilized" nation would perpetrate such a barbaric act against the innocent.

—*Fr. Scott,* May 2003

What is the Church's stand on capital punishment?

It is permitted where it is in proportion to the crime committed, such as murder, treason, rape. The Church has always held that a man or woman has the right of self-preservation. If necessary, a person may kill if it is the only way to repulse the unjust attacker. The State, likewise, has a right to protect itself and its people even by the use of reasonable capital punishment.

—*Fr. Carl,* November 1979

Is it morally obligatory to vote?

It is certainly true that the modernists consider democracy and the right to vote as sacrosanct, an immediate consequence of human dignity, directly connected with their humanistic religion.

Reacting against this, knowing as we do how much the electoral system is unjust, realizing how much modern democracy is based upon the false liberal principle of human freedom, escaping from all objective divine and moral law as it does, being aware of how little real choice there is between the candidates and also of how false is the impression that one man's vote is really going to make a difference to such a secular, ungodly system—we might easily conclude that there is no obligation to vote at all.

Yet, the Church's teaching on the subject is not anything new. Without approving the modern system of democracy and its false principle of the sovereignty of the people, the Church nevertheless binds us to contribute towards the common good of society by an obligation of legal justice. This principle is expressed well by Pope Pius XII in his April 20, 1946, discourse to Italian Catholic Action:

> The people is called on to take an always larger part in the public life of the nation. This participation brings with it grave responsibilities. Hence the necessity for the faithful to have clear, solid, precise knowledge of their duties in the moral and religious domain with respect to their exercise of their civil rights, and in particular of the right to vote.

In fact, the pope had clearly explained that it is precisely on account of the anti-Catholic and secular spirit that surrounds Catholics that they have the duty to defend the Church by the correct exercise of their right to vote. It is to prevent a greater evil. He had stated on March 16, 1946, to the parish priests of Rome:

> The exercise of the right to vote is an act of grave moral responsibility, at least with respect to the electing of those who are called to give to a country its constitution and its laws, and in particular those that affect the sanctification of holy days of obligation, marriage, the family, schools, and the just and equitable regulation of many social questions. It is the Church's duty to explain to the faithful the moral duties that flow from this electoral right.

Pope Pius XII was even more explicit two years later, again when speaking to the parish priests of Rome. He explained that in the precise circumstances of the time it was an obligation under pain of mortal sin for all the faithful to use their vote, and this even for women. Although it is certainly true that in the traditional conception of democracy it is only the heads of families who vote, it is perfectly permissible for women to use the right of vote when it is granted, and in fact it becomes an obligation to do so when the common good depends upon all Catholics using their vote correctly.

Here is the text of March 10, 1948:

> In the present circumstances, it is a strict obligation for all those who have the right to vote, men and women, to take part in the elections. Whoever abstains from doing so, in particular by indolence or weakness, commits a sin grave in itself, a mortal fault. Each one must follow the dictate of his own conscience. However, it is obvious that the voice of conscience imposes on every Catholic to give his vote to the candidates who offer truly sufficient guarantees for the protection of the rights of God and of souls, for the true good of individuals, families, and of society, according to the love of God and Catholic moral teaching.

This application of the Church's social teaching to the particular situation of the time is in accord with the teaching of the moral theologians, who speak of the grave sin of omission for those who simply neglect to elect good, Catholic representatives, and of the duty of doing all in our power to encourage suitable laymen to work towards using the electoral system to obtain worthy lawmakers.

However, how far removed we are from this situation! Clearly, we are no longer in the circumstance of having to choose between Catholic and non-Catholic, morally upright and liberal representatives. All the alternatives are liberal, and the deception and the manipulation of the public by the media is rampant. In practice, it generally comes down to the question of whether or not it is permissible to vote for an unworthy candidate (*e.g.*, a candidate who only approves abortion in cases of rape or incest), for he would at least (we suppose) be the lesser evil. In such a case, there can be no obligation to vote, for all the reasons that could oblige, mentioned by Pope Pius XII, no longer apply. Nevertheless, it is still permissible to vote in such a case, provided that one can be sure that there truly is a lesser evil, and that there is a grave reason to do so (*e.g.*, to avoid abortion on demand or promotion of unnatural methods of birth control), and one has the good intention of providing for the good of society as best one can. This is called material cooperation. However, it can never be obligatory.

Consequently, in the rare case that there is a clearly, publicly Catholic candidate who supports the teaching of the Church, there is a strict moral obligation to vote, under pain of mortal sin. Where there is a clear gain possible from the correct use of a vote for some other candidate, it can be recommended or counseled. However, when there is no clear advantage, it would be better to abstain so as not to contribute even to a material participation.

—*Fr. Scott,* February 2007

Is it a mortal sin to vote for a pro-abortion candidate?

The casting of a vote can be a virtuous act, even in our modern liberal democracies, in which so much of the system is not only opposed to our holy religion but even to the natural law itself. However, for a vote to be a virtuous act, it must be directed towards its end, namely, the common good. Consequently, it is in itself a grave sin to vote for an unworthy candidate, for the choice of a candidate whose life or policies are immoral is an illicit cooperation in bringing about a grave evil to society. There can be no doubt that abortion, the murder of the innocent, is one of the greatest evils afflicting modern society, and that it is crying out to heaven for vengeance. Consequently, there cannot in itself be any justification for voting for any candidate who is pro-abortion or in any way tolerant of abortion.

The question arises, however, as to whether there could be sufficient reason to vote for a candidate who might consent to some abortions, for example, to avoid a more serious evil, such as to defeat a candidate who might be in favor of homosexual marriages or who might actively promote abortions or some other great evil, such as unjust wars.

The theologians answer that the act of casting a vote is a material cooperation in the evil that that candidate might cause, and not necessarily a formal cooperation (*cf.* Prummer, III, §604). This means that the person who casts the vote is not necessarily directly responsible for what a bad candidate might do once elected, even if he foresaw that he would perform some evil deeds. In such cases of material cooperation, the Church allows the application of the principles of the indirect voluntary. It is permissible, since the act of casting a vote is not in itself bad, and the end is good, namely, to avoid a greater evil. However, there must be a very grave reason to justify such material cooperation, and all scandal would have to be avoided. This could be the case, for example, if a person were to vote for a Protestant whose platform was in general in accordance with the natural law, but who might have some false principles concerning divorce or the funding of Catholic schools, or on some environmental issue. In such a case, it would be permissible to choose the lesser evil and to vote for a candidate who is not entirely good, on the condition that there is a very grave reason, namely, to avoid a much greater evil.

The question here is whether there could ever possibly be such a grave reason that could justify a person's voting for a pro-abortion candidate. Is it possible for there to be a greater evil that could justify such a participation in this evil of abortion, even only a material participation? I cannot conceive that this could be possible, for abortion is such a perverse and horrible crime.

It is possible to conceive of a greater evil that would allow one to vote for a candidate who would accept (unwillingly) abortions under certain exceptional circumstances such as rape, for this is frequently done in order to prevent the election of a candidate who is positively pro-abortion. This is a frequent occurrence and is certainly permissible. However, it is inconceivable that a Catholic would vote for a politician who is positively pro-abortion simply because he likes his tax scheme or his social policies. In such an instance there would be no proportion at all, and it would certainly be a grave sin, even if the intention were only for a material cooperation.

If in general it is narrow-minded to be a single-issue voter, this certainly does not apply to the abortion question. The common good absolutely and necessarily requires the abolition of abortions from public life, and it is of such overwhelming importance for the good of society that no person could be considered imprudent for voting on the basis of this question alone.

—*Fr. Scott,* February/March 2004

 **Is it permitted for representatives to vote in favor of a law banning partial-birth abortion but permitting some exceptions, such as the protection of the life of the mother?**

The moral dilemma about voting for such a law is that by so doing one actually gives the impression of approving the consequence of the law, namely, that there could be some partial-birth abortions, even if greatly reduced in number. Is it not a cause of scandal to vote for such a law? How can one give one's approval to a law that permits evil? It is certainly understandable that some pro-lifers would refuse to support a local bishop who encourages his faithful to support the law, as does Archbishop Sheehan of Santa Fe for the proposed New Mexico ban on partial abortions.

It is certainly true that "co-operation in evil legislation is sinful" (Jone, *Moral Theology,* p. 140), and that a law that permits any abortions is evil. However, there can be some exceptions to this rule. This can happen when the co-operation is only material, that is, when we do not accept the evil will of the principal agent (here the legislature as a whole) and consequently do not share in the evil. We do not have any intention to make some abortions possible, but our intention is to do all that we can to stop as many abortions, as much evil, as we can.

It is similar to the case in which it is permissible to advise a lesser sin if the sinner cannot otherwise be deterred from committing the greater sin (*i.e.*, all abortions are permitted, *cf.* Jone, p. 90; Slater, *Moral Theology,* p. 131). "To lessen sin is surely to do good. This is the more probable opinion, according to St. Alphonsus."

Here the voting for a law that would occasionally permit abortions (instead of regularly) is not an immediate co-operation, even material. It is only very remotely that our vote would permit the sinful action of some abortions.

> As a rule, this [kind] of co-operation is also wrong. It may be permitted, however, if the rules of the double effect may be applied—if the act performed is not intrinsically evil, for example, and if a correspondingly good reason is present. (Cunningham, *The Christian Life,* p.183)

To participate in a legislative act to stop partial-birth abortions, as much as possible, is not intrinsically evil, and there is a proportionate reason for the unavoidable evil consequence (the occasional abortions on the grounds of the mother's health), namely, that many abortions will be prevented from happening.

Jone admits that this applies to the case of co-operation in evil legislation: "The only exception admitted is the case in which such representatives might avoid a greater evil by their co-operation; in such cases, however, they must make clear their position" (*ibid.*, p. 140). A Catholic representative or voter must make it perfectly clear that he does not support the exceptions involved in the bill to ban partial-birth abortions, so as to avoid giving scandal. However, having done so he is free to vote for it, in order to avoid a greater evil. It is for similar reasons that it is permitted for Catholic representatives to give their approval to laws promoting freedom of religion if they do this in order to avoid a greater evil (*cf.* Prummer, I, 29).

—*Fr. Scott,* July 2000

 ### Can a US citizen swear an oath of loyalty to a foreign Christian prince?

The answer to this question depends upon the question of the submission of subjects to legitimate rulers. This is a duty of justice that derives from the principle contained in sacred Scripture and constantly taught by the Church that the civil power of government comes from God and not from the people:

> Let every soul be subject to higher powers: for there is no power but from God: and those that are, are ordained of God. Therefore he that resisteth the power, resisteth the ordinance of God. And they that resist, purchase to themselves damnation. (Rom. 13:1-2)

This reverence to civil authority requires that no oath be pronounced that be opposed to that authority within the territory of its jurisdiction, or that undermines it. The swearing of an oath of fealty or submission to a foreign power or prince would regularly be considered by all parties to be an infringement of the rights of the civil authority, for no man can serve two masters. The citizen's duty in justice is to defend his own country, its laws, and its civil authority, by the virtue of observance, and not that of another. In general, the swearing of allegiance to a foreign rule means the compromising in some way of one's obligation towards one's own country, or at least the possibility thereof. This very possibility would make the swearing of such an oath immoral, since it would mean an attempt to bind oneself to an obligation that could be in contradiction with a prior obligation in justice.

However, there could be exceptions to this principle. One such exception could take place if a person could establish that the established authority in his country is illegitimate, either because it is opposed to the natural and divine law or because power was seized in an unjust manner. In such a case, one would theoretically not be bound in conscience to obedience to such an authority.

However, this does not seem to me to be the situation with our modern Freemasonic governments. Many of their laws are unjust, immoral, and iniquitous, and no one is bound in conscience to obey them. However, God has given them the authority to rule, and we should respect their authority for as long as they do not request us to do anything against faith and morals. Civil governments would rightly refuse to acknowledge an oath of fealty to a foreign power and would rightly punish a man who would deny his duty in justice to his own country in order to live up to such an oath. Consequently, a US citizen's oath of allegiance to a foreign king ought to be considered unjust, illegal, and null and void, as being opposed to his allegiance to his own country.

A second exception that could exist is the modern situation of dual nationality, which has now become a common occurrence. When a person takes up a second nationality, he must make an oath recognizing submission to the civil authority of the country in which he takes up a second citizenship. This is understood, however, to mean that each government is sovereign in its own domain, that is, in its own country, and that the person with dual citizenship will fulfill his duties in justice towards the governments of both countries without denying either one its rights, and that in case of conflict he will observe the laws and authority of the land in which he is living.

—*Fr. Scott,* August 2007

Am I obliged in conscience to pay my taxes?

This particular issue concerns first and foremost a civil law. It is clear in Catholic theology that those who hold the supreme authority in civil government can for the common good make laws which are binding in conscience upon their subjects. Those laws are not to be in opposition to the demands of the Catholic religion nor the moral teaching of the Gospel. The fact that they are made by pagans or modern liberals does not bring the general principle into doubt, for all authority comes from God. All modern civil laws cannot justly be considered as purely "penal" (*i.e.,* not binding in conscience so that you only pay a penalty if caught infringing them). Tax is any sum of money exacted from the citizens by civil law so as to sustain the public good to meet the public expenses of the State. Today there is almost an unlimited number of taxes, and human invention appears inexhaustible in devising new means to further the burden of taxation whether direct or indirect. Direct taxes are those which an individual must pay, usually deducted at source. They are imposed immediately on a person because of his particular job, profession, or business. Indirect taxes are levied directly upon things, *i.e.*, tobacco, alcohol, *etc.* The payment of such taxes is binding in conscience. The answer made by Christ Himself to the question in the Gospel "Is it lawful to give tribute to Caesar or not?" leaves us in no doubt. "Give to Caesar the things that are Caesar's and to God the things that are God's." Pay every man, then, his dues: taxes, if it be taxes, customs if it be customs. However, if the taxes are manifestly unjust, the obligation in conscience ceases. The justice of taxation is established if the taxes are introduced by the lawful authority, *i.e.*, those who are charged with the welfare of the State; if there is a just reason for the imposition, that is, the common good; and, lastly, if a due proportion in the required payments is observed so that no unjust hardship is inflicted on the individual citizens. In other words, the burden must be justly distributed. To be forgetful on a small scale of manifestly unjust taxes (*e.g.*, where considerable sums are used for immoral purposes), though legally established, should not give rise to any great anxiety in conscience, as many laws relating to indirect taxes are merely penal. There is disagreement over the matter. However, all are urged to pay just taxes. Honesty in filling out tax returns according to their commonly understood interpretation ought to result in our paying our fair average share of the collective burden.

—Fr. Boyle, April 1994

Is slavery evil, and if so, surely the North was right in the American Civil War?

Slavery as an institution can be understood in two ways. The ancient pagans understood it as the right of ownership of one person over another as over a thing or an animal, the slave entirely belonging in every aspect to his master without any recognition of his free will. This is illicit and immoral, for one person can never have the right of control over another's intellect and will, according to which he is made in the image and likeness of God. Such a pagan concept of slavery is manifestly opposed to the natural law and a violation of every man's duty to use his own intellect and will to freely serve God.

However, slavery need not be understood in this sense. It can be simply the ownership of a man's ability to work, his abilities, his productivity. Understood in this sense, it does not violate a man's free will nor his duty to love and serve God, and is consequently not opposed to the natural law.

Furthermore, slavery is not opposed to the divine positive law, *i.e.*, to the law promulgated by God Himself. We consequently find it in this sense allowed in the old law for the Jews. Slavery is also mentioned several times in the New Testament as something licit, slaves not being encouraged to revolt but to maintain their faithful service—for example, by St. Peter: "Servants, be subject to your masters with all fear, not only to the good and gentle, but also to the froward" (I Pet. 2:18). St. Paul says the same: "Servants, be obedient to them that are your lords according to the flesh, with fear and trembling, in the simplicity of your heart, as to Christ" (Eph. 6:5); also, Colossians 3:22. Likewise, masters are not told to free their slaves, but to treat them well: "Masters, do to your servants that which is just and equal: knowing that you also have a master in heaven" (Col. 4:1); also, Ephesians 6:9. Consequently, it cannot be said that God forbids slavery in itself.

The fact that slavery is not in itself intrinsically wrong can also be established from the fact that it is licit for one man or for society to have power over a man's services or his acts. If a man can hire his labor out for a time, he can hire it out for life, as was the case of the serfs in Christendom. Likewise, if society has authority over a man to impose imprisonment or capital punishment for crimes, then it has the authority to impose a lesser sentence, such as the ownership of a man's services.

This being said, it is manifestly obvious that the rise of the Catholic Church little by little put an end to this institution, which it has many times condemned. The problem with slavery is that it is so open to abuse, the slaves having no protection against the infringing of their interior, personal freedom, nor having any guarantee of being treated with kindness, of being supplied with all the necessities of life, of not being overworked, and of respect for their person.

These abuses became horrifically apparent in the slave trade for the New World. Slave-hunting, selling of children into slavery, inhumane treatment in the transports and by slave traders and some slave owners are but some of these immoral conditions. It is for this reason that the popes again and again condemned this slave trade, starting with Pius II in 1462, continuing with Paul III in 1537, Urban VIII in 1639, Benedict XIV in 1741, Gregory XVI in 1839, and Leo XIII in 1888. Gregory XVI had this to say:

> The Roman Pontiffs our predecessors of glorious memory have not at all failed to many times seriously reprehend slavery, as is their duty, as being harmful to their [the black peoples'] spiritual salvation and bringing opprobrium to the Christian name … whence we admonish and order by our Apostolic authority all the faithful of every condition … not to reduce into slavery … or exercise this inhuman trade. (Dec. 3, 1839)

Leo XIII was even more explicit in his letter *In Plurimis* on May 5, 1888, to congratulate the bishops of Brazil on the emancipation of slaves in Brazil on the occasion of the fiftieth anniversary of his priestly ordination:

> This decision was particularly consoling and agreeable to us because we received the confirmation of this news, so dear to us, that the Brazilians desire henceforth to abolish and completely extirpate the barbaric practice of slavery .... For in the midst of so much misery, we must particularly deplore that misery of slavery, to which a considerable part of the human family has been subject for many centuries, thus groaning under the sorrow of abjection, contrary to what God and nature first established.... This inhuman and iniquitous doctrine that slaves must, as instruments lacking reason and understanding, serve the will of their masters in all things, is supremely detestable—so much, indeed, that once it has been accepted there is no oppression, no matter how disgusting or barbarous, that cannot be maintained uncontested with a certain appearance of legality and law.

Consequently, there can be no doubt that the importing of slaves from Africa to the New World, so frequently condemned by the Church as actually practiced, was evil. This does not, however, mean that the Church condemned every slave owner. There were certainly Catholic slave owners who took real care of their slaves, supported their families, provided for all their needs, gave them every facility to become Catholic and save their souls, and who consequently committed no sin, but rather acts of virtue. In practice, however, the multitude of evils and abuses far outweighed the good.

This being said, Catholic historians who have studied the Civil War point out that the real question was not one of slavery at all, but one of economic control. It was the capitalists of the North, with their factories, mines, means of production, forcing an industrial and economic revolution on the agrarian South. The Northerners had long had slaves of their own. However, the Industrial Revolution produced a new kind of slavery, that of the factory workers, who would sweat very long hours for little income, for the profit of their capitalist masters.

The struggles for the rights of workers demonstrate that despite their technical freedom, they were just as oppressed as the slaves of old, and very often more so, for the slaves at least were provided with all the necessities of life. The question of slavery is, consequently, of little importance in the discussion of right and wrong in the Civil War. It really is a question of economic revolution.

—*Fr. Scott,* February 2005

ABOUT SOCIAL JUSTICE, BUSINESS, AND WORK

 **What are the foundations of social justice?**

Pope Pius XI in his encyclical *Divini Redemptoris* states that "the means of saving the world of today from the lamentable ruin into which a moral liberalism has plunged us are neither the class struggle (Karl Marx) nor terror nor yet the autocratic abuse of State power (totalitarianism) but rather the infusion of Social Justice and the sentiment of Christian love into the social economic order." The pope reiterates the necessity of a just wage to support a working man's family; the provision of the opportunity to acquire a modest fortune and the prevention of universal pauperism; and the possibility of making provision for old age, illness, and unemployment. If these needs cannot be met, then social justice has not been fully met. Each man must direct his energies and his actions to the common good.

By his nature man reaches out to others to cooperate in a friendly manner with his neighbor for the good of all. Society is the natural environment in which man develops the gifts bestowed on him by nature. The State, the employer, and the laborer must cooperate in such a way that each individual may enjoy the social goods essential to his development and for the achieving of his end. The State has the serious obligation to supply what the individual or family cannot procure effectively for themselves because the State exists for the good and welfare of the citizens. It must supervise, regulate, and protect so that each one has a due share in the common good. An employer must not exploit the laborer by failing to give him a decent wage, thereby depriving him access to the goods of the earth. In his turn, the worker has obligations towards his employer: "a fair day's work for a just wage."

In these matters it is opportune to remind ourselves that we are also members of the same mystical body of Christ. In this mystical body we are most closely united. "We being many are one body in Christ and everyone members of one another" (Rom. 12:5).

In the mystical body then, all, irrespective of function or trade, are one in Christ. Just as Christ cannot be taken apart by internal schism, so there is no room for mutual hatred and animosity and injustices among those who are united in Him. This is the supernatural aspect and foundation of the common good of social justice, and this also is the source and means of truly uniting man in a harmonious striving for the common good. The promotion of justice alone will not suffice.

—Fr. Boyle, June 1994

 ## What is the Church's understanding of social justice?

This expression is found in an encyclical of Pope St. Pius X, *Jucunda Sane* on St. Gregory the Great, in which he refers to the saint as the public defender of social justice. The phrase cannot be found in *Rerum Novarum* of Leo XIII though the idea is present, but it occurs eight times in *Quadragesimo Anno* of Pope Pius XI, in connection with eight different problems, chief of which are the principle of just distribution of wealth, the question of an adequate and just family wage, the scale of wages in the light of private profit, the true principles that ought to guide and determine economics and economic structures, and, lastly, the violation of the social order.

The theologian distinguishes among commutative justice, which governs the relations between private individuals; social justice, which deals with the relations of citizens to society and of society to its citizens; and international justice, which concerns the relations of one nation to another. The object of social justice is the common good of men.

Pope Pius XI gives the following definition in *Divini Redemptoris*, his encyclical on atheistic communism: "Now it is of the very essence of social justice to demand from each individual all that is necessary for the common good." The common good is the sum total of advantages which all procure for themselves in a well-organized society which enables them to develop their powers to the utmost and to attain their last end. These advantages are of a spiritual, moral, and intellectual nature. They include also material benefits placed at the service of the first and higher category of benefits. These material advantages are proper work and living conditions, opportunities for self-development, *etc.*

Lastly, the State must ensure the promulgation of just laws and maintain peace and order with a view for the common good—which is not the same thing as the public order of Vatican II's *Dignitatis Humanae*, the declaration on religious liberty.

The State must also promote the necessary protection of its citizens against enemies within and without, and finally enable its citizens to enjoy a tranquil and full possession of the spiritual and material blessings to which they have a right. The object of social justice then is clear: it is the general well-being of men as distinct from the particular good and interest of individuals; and concerning this, the Church has a clearly defined doctrine based on the primacy of the common good.

—Fr. Boyle, June 1994

Is usury a sin?

Usury is the charging of interest for the use of money, as if it had some productive power of its own. St. Thomas Aquinas asks himself this question—*i.e.*, is usury a sin?—in the *Summa Theologica* (II-II, q. 78, art. 1) and answers categorically in the affirmative. His reason is that money is not something which remains after it is used (*e.g.*, a house, the use of which is charged for when it is rented out) but which is consumed as it is used (*e.g.*, food, the use of which is not charged for, but just its sale value). These are his exact words:

> He commits an injustice who sells wine or wheat and who asks for double payment, *i.e.*, one, the return of the thing in equal measure, the other the price of the use, which is called usury....Now money, according to the Philosopher, was invented chiefly for the purpose of exchange; and consequently the chief and principal purpose of money is its consumption or alienation whereby it is sunk in exchange. Hence it is by its very nature unlawful to take payment for the use of money lent, which payment is known as usury: and just as a man is bound to restore other ill-gotten goods, so is he obliged to restore the money which he has taken in usury.

There can be no doubt that usury is what is driving modern capitalistic society along its destructive path of materialism, and that it is responsible for world-wide depressions and wars. If, however, usury is always a grave sin, this does not mean that there cannot be legitimate interest, provided that it is not charged for the value of the money itself, for it is a pure means of exchange and has no producing power on its own, as does man's labor or real property. Fr. Walter Farrell, O.P., sums this up quite well in *A Companion to the Summa* (III, 239):

> Wherever usury is found it is wrong; and its evil is manifest. It is absurdly simple to understand that to charge a man twice for the same thing is always unjust; yet that is precisely what usury does, it sells the same thing twice. The trick is possible only when the thing sold or loaned is consumed in its very first use, things like wine or sandwiches, or money. When we demand, over and above the return of the original sum of money loaned, an added amount for the use of the money, our act is the same as selling a man a glass of wine and then charging him for the privilege of drinking it. If we keep this simple statement of usury in mind, it will not be difficult to understand the absolutely necessary distinction between usury and legitimate interest. The latter is charged not for the mere use of the money as in usury, but on some extrinsic title.

Extrinsic titles for legitimate interest could include such things as the risk of losing one's money altogether, the positive damage caused to the creditor by such outside factors as inflation, or the human productivity which becomes possible if money is invested to purchase stock in a business enterprise, thus producing dividends.

The early Fathers of the Church protested against usury in the strongest terms, and numerous ecclesiastical decrees in the twelfth and thirteenth centuries enforced its prohibition under pain of excommunication and denial of Catholic burial. There has been, however, a relaxation of the Church's law on the subject, since the development of Protestantism made it socially acceptable, and *laissez-faire* capitalism in the nineteenth century made it an inescapable reality of daily life. This relaxation of Church law is expressed in the 1917 Code of Canon Law, Canon 1543:

> If a commodity which is consumed by its first use be lent on the stipulation that it becomes the property of the borrower, who is bound to return to the lender not the thing itself, but its equivalent only, the lender may not receive any payment by reason of the loan itself. In the giving or lending of such a commodity, however, it is not in itself unlawful to make an arrangement for the recovery of interest at the rate allowed by the civil law, unless that rate is clearly excessive....

Fr. E. Cahill, S.J., in *The Framework of a Christian State*, comments on and explains this change in the Church's law:

> One may without enquiry or solicitude as to the existence or not of extrinsic titles (such as accidental loss caused by the loan, the risk of not being repaid, *etc.*) receive interest at the rate laid down by the civil law, provided that rate be not clearly excessive. The reason for this change or apparent change in the Church's attitude towards usury is that in modern times, owing to the capitalistic organization of economic life, money has practically become a form of capital, and the Church follows her traditional policy in regulating her attitude towards it. As usual she temporarily adjusts her discipline as far as possible to the needs of the age, even when these needs are the result of a state of things of which she does not approve, and allows the faithful to act in accordance with social customs sanctioned by existing civil law, provided these customs are not manifestly immoral or unjust. (P. 49)

Such would not be the case, however, in a society which recognized and embraced the Social Kingship of Christ.

—*Fr. Scott,* July 1998

Can a Catholic in conscience declare bankruptcy, and if so can he consider his debts as forgiven?

Civil laws allowing the declaration of bankruptcy are just laws, enacted for the common good, for they enable a debtor's creditors to be satisfied in as just a manner as possible and prevent his remaining assets from being squandered or wasted. They consequently oblige in conscience, insofar as they do not conflict with the natural law. Fr. Jone in his *Moral Theology* describes what is allowed by natural law:

> The natural law allows an insolvent person to retain what is required to mod-
> estly support himself and his family according to their social status and to establish
> a small business....To retain more than this is an injustice and makes one subject
> to restitution.... (P. 259)

Consequently, it is morally licit to declare bankruptcy, provided that it is truly impossible to pay one's creditors, and provided that one honestly declares all of one's assets. However, it does not necessarily follow from this that the debtor is freed from all obligation in conscience to make restitution to his creditors.

In fact, ordinarily and of itself, the obligation of restitution is not abolished but only temporarily suspended until such time as it becomes possible. The reason why this is ordinarily the case is that the creditors only very reluctantly accept a partial reimbursement of the debt and can-not be considered as voluntarily condoning it if the former debtor enters into sufficient wealth to pay it off.

However, exceptions to this ordinary rule of justice take place when civil laws explicitly and entirely abolish every obligation of paying a debt after a true legal bankruptcy declaration. This is an accepted exception, for such laws are just laws, very useful for commerce and for the common good. Such persons, having honestly and without any fault of their own fallen into bankruptcy, are then free to begin again their family and busi-ness activities. Fr. Jone has this to say about the United States,

> where the juridical opinion favors complete freedom in case of a *bona fide* bank-
> rupt. According to this more lenient viewpoint, debts are contracted under the
> implied condition that they will cease in case of *bona fide* bankruptcy. Although
> the legal immunity guaranteed in phrases as "forever discharged from all debts and
> claims" does not apply to the internal forum, nonetheless the law for all our States
> and territories "a discharge in bankruptcy shall release a bankrupt from all his prov-
> able debts..." is adduced as proof of the solidly probable opinion that a declaration
> of bankruptcy liquidates a *bona fide* bankrupt's debts also in conscience. (*Ibid.*, pp.
> 259-260)

It seems to me that this opinion can certainly be followed with respect to debts to mortgage companies, credit card companies, and the like, for they calculate on a certain proportion of bad debts. However, it would seem that in the case of a personal loan from a friend, acquaintance, or relative, the implied condition of the cessation of the debt in case of bankruptcy would not exist and that such debts call for restitution in conscience, even if they do not according to civil law.

Furthermore, any person who deliberately brings on a bankruptcy by negligence in administering his finances, or by failure to regularly pay his bills, or by living beyond his means, or by racking up high credit card debts, certainly has the duty in conscience of restitution even after bankruptcy has been declared. For it is taught by all the theologians that when the bankruptcy is brought on by grave fault or fraud on the part of the bankrupt, then the duty of restitution always remains, as soon as it becomes possible to do so (Prummer, II, 210).

It is certain that in our materialistic world this whole question of justice and honor in paying one's debts is taken very lightly, and that many people feel that they are in no way culpable or at fault in bringing about their bankruptcy, or living in such a way as to gravely risk bankruptcy, under the excuse that they can always declare bankruptcy. This is a sin against justice as well as an abuse of the bankruptcy laws. This cardinal virtue of justice is crucial to any upright Catholic life. Grounds of charity cannot be used to excuse from it. Traditional Catholics must make an effort to escape from the slavery of materialism that will lead them to sins against justice by fighting against the mentality of spending all the time and of abusing the facility of credit cards.

—*Fr. Scott,* January 2001

 **Do you accept Belloc's distinction between "productive" and "non-productive" loans?**

I have read and am aware of Belloc's theory that it is licit to charge interest on a loan provided that it is productive, and that in this case it is not truly usurious.

In my opinion, a productive loan is effectively the same thing as what is more traditionally called "extrinsic title for legitimate interest." One of the extrinsic titles that I cited ("Q&A," *The Angelus,* July 1998) was human productivity. Clearly, if the money is used to help man to produce something by his work, the person who provides the funds can share (to a moderate extent) in the productivity of the work. However, it is not the money itself which is productive. That is why the payment of dividends is perfectly moral, but the question of interest is much more delicate. I must confess that I prefer not to give a blanket approval to all "productive loans," as does Hilaire Belloc. I believe that it is very easy to go from that concept to that of modern-day investment, and consequently just to consider as usurious that which is speculative investment. This is not the position of St. Thomas Aquinas and of Catholic Tradition.

—*Fr. Scott,* December 1998

 **Is it permissible for a Catholic to speculate on the stock market or on the international currency exchange market?**

The natural law right to private property brings with it the right to buy and sell, to own, and consequently to trade in property such as shares in public or private companies. Such private investment is, indeed, absolutely essential to the common good, for without capital there can be no production. The fact that the outcome of such investments is highly chancy does not change the morality, provided that a man does not thereby invest the funds necessary for the support of his family. Nor does the fact that one man's gain is another man's loss, provided that there is no deception, fraud, or taking advantage of another's ignorance.

Speculation, though, is not the same thing as investment, but is rather a short term placing of money in stocks or currency to make a quick profit by a rapid sale at a time when the market is strong. Such speculation is not against justice since the terms of the contract are kept, nor can it be considered in itself a sin, given that all the terms of the various contracts of buying and selling and the requirements of civil law are observed. Nevertheless, "they are not morally commendable unless they are required by some commercial necessity" (Merkelbach, *Summa Theologiae Moralis*, II, §604).

The principle is given by Pope Pius XII in a radio message to the entire world on September 1, 1944, in which he condemns not only communism, for its denial of the right to private property, but also "the Capitalism...founded on an erroneous conception that arrogates to itself an unlimited right over property outside of all subordination to the common good" as always having been condemned by the Church "as contrary to the natural law" (PIN [*La paix intérieure des nations*], §831).

The Catholic with an upright conscience ought to make his capital and his investments not only for his own profit but also for the common good of society. It is to be highly doubted whether transient speculations on stock and money markets make any real contribution to the common good, but rather to be wondered that they are selfish and harmful to the common good.

Fr. Merkelbach explains why he does not find such speculation morally commendable, for such speculators

> immoderately retain their capital in intermediary operations that have no real utility; and strive to obtain riches without proportionate labor and *without subordination to the common good*, indeed with loss for others who do not freely expose themselves to chance, but are bound to do so for business reasons. Moreover, the custom of becoming preoccupied with monetary speculations encourages an overwhelming desire for gain, to which they subordinate all things, and every activity. It entrains constant anxiety, and exposes to a great danger of wastefulness, idleness, and the financial ruin of businesses and families. (*Ibid.*)

It is unfortunate that some traditional Catholics consider that such a way of life is compatible with the Social Reign of Jesus Christ, indulging as they do in such trading on the Internet, without consideration of how such speculative trading could serve Christ the King, or possibly following the false principle that the ends justify the means. The mind of the Church is contained in the traditional (1917) Code of Canon Law's interdiction of all such speculation for all clerics and religious, even for the benefit of the Church or other persons (Can. 142).

—*Fr. Scott,* May 2007

 **I have read that the Church has at all times forbidden speculation. I intended to make a career out of commodities trading and am concerned this activity is contrary to Church teaching. Can you respond to my doubts?**

The kind of "speculation" involved in the commodities trade is not necessarily immoral. However, when referring to the usurious practice of using money to make money, which is destroying modern economies, it is indeed morally wrong. In fact, money has of itself no earning or productive power at all but is simply a means of exchange.

"Speculation" in commercial commodities is not in itself morally wrong. It is simply to take advantage of the normal rises and lulls in the prices of various commodities so as to prudently administer one's goods. However, it involves many dangers against the virtues of charity and justice. To falsely bolster and manipulate prices so as to make an undue profit over and above one's investment of time and money is against both justice and charity (*e.g.*, some kinds of land speculation). Honesty in dealing with people is very important for anybody involved in such trade of items. Provided, however, that one has this honesty, it becomes a very honest profession which a Catholic can practice in good conscience.

This is explained in the following brief excerpt from Jone's *Moral Theology* (1956), pp. 207-208:

> 310. —XV. Speculation, as distinguished from regular trade, is the act or practice of buying lands, goods, etc., in the expectation of a rise in price and of selling them at an advantage.
>
> Speculation, in itself, as any other contract, is lawful, but fraught with many dangers of sinning against charity or justice. For these reasons it may often be sinful in practice.
>
> He sins against charity who corners such vast quantities of goods that others thereby suffer need. They sin against justice who raise the price of commodities by means of fraud, e.g., by spreading false reports. Others, however, even those who sell at the increased price, do not seem to sin against justice, since speculation has much in common with games of chance.
>
> Stock and produce exchanges have been used for gambling purposes. However, contracts for the buying and selling of "futures" and of stock "on margin" are, in all but a few of our States, considered as legitimate transac-

tions on the theory that actual future delivery of the property is intended, but, in the case of the "bucket shop," where no delivery is ever intended, the transactions are unenforceable. Not only the fictitious nature of the dealings, but the duress which brokers employ against the producers, condemn gambling in "futures" as morally wrong.

—*Unknown,* February 1994

 **Can a Catholic invest in a company that makes profit from immoral products or activities, such as a drug company?**

Such an investment is generally to be considered a formal cooperation, and not just a material cooperation, since it is deliberately chosen. It is consequently not permissible, provided that the immoral activities are known to the investor.

However, the case could arrive when a person's investment portfolio includes a variety of different companies chosen by his investment or superannuation plan and over which he has no direct control. In such a case it would only be a material cooperation and could be tolerated if there were no choice. Another case of material cooperation would occur if the immoral activity were a very small part of a company's activities and the investment were made rather for the other honest activities. However, this is a more direct material cooperation, especially if the person concerned is aware of the immoral activities, and could only be permissible for a proportionately grave reason.

This being said, Catholics should not be troubled in conscience if they invest in the usual banking institutions, of whose particular investments and activities they are unaware. In modern society, it is impossible to avoid all material cooperation, for it is sometimes very remote and unknown. Nevertheless, how much better it would be to invest one's savings and efforts in Catholic endeavors and businesses, penetrated by the Church's social principles, according to justice and charity.

—*Fr. Scott,* September 2007

 **Is it permissible for a traditional Catholic to teach in a public school?**

It is permissible for a traditional Catholic teacher to teach in a public school, but only provided that he (or she) does not compromise his Catholic principles.

Nevertheless, a Catholic who really loves his Faith would want to teach in a traditional Catholic environment, where the knowledge that he imparts can be integrated into the knowledge of God, religion, and the faith, and can be subordinated to the divine wisdom that we learn from our Catholic Faith. He will also appreciate the moral and disciplinary support that he finds in a Catholic school, and the harmony that exists within the faculty and between the direction and the students of the school.

He will consequently not be deceived by the apparently greater good of being a "lighthouse of truth in the stormy sea of indifferentism." A good Catholic teacher, determined to live a serious and profound spiritual life, will do much more good in a traditional Catholic school, in which he is backed up by his principal and fellow teachers, than in the secular environment of a public school. For in the Catholic school, he can work to form an elite, which elite once formed will continue his own work for souls. However, in a secular environment he is limited to simply touching souls and is unlikely to bring about a profound change in such souls unless he can convince them to enter into a traditional Catholic school.

This having been said, it is certainly true that some teachers do not have the possibility of teaching in a traditional Catholic school or cannot live without the income and benefits that the public school system provides. In such a case, it is permissible provided that there is no danger to their own faith and provided that they stand up publicly for Catholic principles of faith and morality. In this way, they would not be seen to cooperate in any way with the evil and falsehood that are propagated in public schools, nor to support the system without God that is destroying our youth, and could certainly be a blessing to the isolated souls that are seeking the truth.

—Fr. Scott, April 2001

Could you indicate whether I can perform classic country acoustic guitar folk music for income?

1) It is perfectly permissible to perform old-time country folk music for income. It is to be understood, however, that there can be no sensual or immoral themes behind the lyrics used in the songs, and that the style remains that of folk music, refusing the deformations of jazz and rock.

2) It is perfectly permissible to perform old-time country folk music on TV, even on TV run by a heretical organization.

3) It is not permissible to perform Gospel music, either on TV or in public. For this kind of music is an expression of the false Protestant religion and is consequently an active participation in the propagation of a false religion. It is therefore not permissible to perform Gospel music in a nursing home.

4) It is perfectly permissible to adapt the medium of "Gospel" music, that is the style, to Catholic use, and to write Catholic lyrics yourself, to go with commonly known "Gospel"-style tunes. The popular medium could then be used to popularize and propagate the Catholic Faith. Under these conditions you could sing publicly in a nursing home, or on Christian TV, even if the producers or organizers were not aware of the fact that the music that you are singing actually expresses Catholicism and not Protestantism. To do so would be to perform a good deed for the salvation of souls.

5) It is perfectly licit, as a professional performer, to perform at secular ceremonies, including secular marriage ceremonies, that is, when there is really no religious service, even if a minister of religion is present. It is certainly permissible to perform at wedding receptions. It is not permissible to actively participate in a Protestant religious ceremony by which a person would marry. This distinction may sometimes be a little difficult to make.

I do hope that these few remarks help you to decide what to do, and I pray that God will bless you and enable you and your guitar to edify as well as to please.

—*Fr. Scott,* October 1999

 ## What is the purpose of manual labor?

In sacred Scripture we read that "man is born to labor as the bird to fly." Man primarily by his nature rather than by his sin—"in the sweat of thy brow thou shalt earn thy bread"—is ordained to work. Labor is a particularly human activity, and St. Thomas Aquinas enlightens us upon man's natural inclination to manual labor. For St. Thomas, all corporal work was included in the term "manual," and he gives us four reasons for work. First and principally, work is required to obtain food; secondly, work is directed to the removal of idleness, from which many evils come; thirdly, labor is directed to the curbing of concupiscence in so far as it is a means of afflicting the body; and, lastly, it is directed to almsgiving.

God gave man reason and hands by means of which he could ensure for himself the necessities of life. Labor is made possible by this combination of reason and hands. Purpose is recognized in reason, and hands are necessary to bring about the purpose. Before original sin, man obviously had reason and hands. From the very beginning he was naturally ordained to work. After the Fall man did not lose his inclination to work, but it became painful. Work was no longer enjoyable, especially if you also have to pay taxes. However, it is also a means of atonement for sin. Pope Leo XIII in his encyclical *Rerum Novarum* makes the point rather well: "As regards bodily labor, even had man never fallen from the state of innocence, he would not have been wholly unoccupied; but that which would have been his free choice, his delight, became afterwards compulsory and the painful expiation of his sin."

—*Fr. Boyle,* July 1994

 ## Does the Church permit workers to go on strike?

The history of strikes is bound up with that of labor unions. Up until the middle of the nineteenth century, strikes were generally forbidden. Towards the end of the same century, they were legalized in France in 1864, Belgium in 1866, and Germany in 1889. They were given legal recognition in England as early as 1824. Prior to the beginning of the twentieth century, strikes ceased to be illegal throughout Europe except in Russia. By 1940, in the United States there were an average ten strikes a day. The fact that workers make use of an organization to obtain their ends does not make the strike immoral, for the right of association, as Pope Leo XIII points out, is a natural prerogative and is a means of procuring happiness and safeguarding human nature. There are, in fact, several important conditions laid down by the Church for a lawful strike.

The strike must be undertaken for a just cause; the laborers must have a genuine claim in justice. A just cause would include the following: protection of life, health, morals; unsanitary conditions, disease, *etc.*; the recognition of labor unions, reasonable hours of labor, and a minimum living wage.

The advantages anticipated must outweigh the evil effects which are the inevitable consequence of a strike. The evils envisaged must be compensated by the greater good to be obtained. Such evils are loss of trade, damage done to general interests of the public, disorder, and even violence. Recourse to strike action is permitted only after all peaceful solutions have been attempted and have clearly failed to resolve grievances in justice. There must also be a reasonable hope that the strike will succeed. Lastly, only lawful means may be used in the conduct of the strike. The workers must use persuasion, not intimidation; for moral persuasion is an attempt to direct and influence the thinking of another, not a violation of human liberty. Once these conditions are met, it is permissible to strike.

—*Fr. Boyle,* May 1994

 ## Should a Catholic plan his or her retirement?

The only true retirement is that of the eternal happiness of heaven, where the soul has the leisure to enjoy the goodness and holiness of the Most Holy Trinity without any distraction or interruption at all. This is the retirement that a Catholic has to plan for by his faithful accomplishment of the commandments of God, the precepts of the Church, and the duties of his state, especially towards his family; by his fidelity to the true Mass, by the frequent reception of the sacraments, and by his daily prayers, meditations, spiritual reading, and rosaries.

However, retirement from the active workforce is also something that has to be planned. If not all of us will experience this privileged time, and many of us will be taken beforehand, it nevertheless has the potential of being the most serious, most profound, most contemplative, most God-centered period of one's life, as well as the most helpful for others. It is that period of life that most directly prepares for eternity. And yet, for so many of the elderly, it is the emptiest and most aimless and meaningless time, without any other goal than the temporary joy of the rapidly passing moments.

Plan, then, for a retirement not to be spent in continual vacation but in doing all those things that the necessities of work and family life previously made impossible. Try to live close to a traditional priest so that you can attend daily Mass and devotions. Donate your time to charity, to teaching and helping out in schools, to work around the church, or to being of assistance to poor families or widows. Stay close to your children, so that you can be of assistance in their own difficulties in raising their own children. Be the extended family that they need. Be the stabilizing influence and the valuable asset that senior members of the community ought to be. Live in the present, and your experience from the past will be of value to the whole community. Use your leisure to teach true moral values and detachment, and you will fight against the feverish hyperactivity of our materialistic world. Use prudence in planning for the retirement years, that you might have the means to support yourself so that you might not be a burden on others. Yet, at the same time remember that there is no purpose in heaping up huge mounds of savings for some far off time that might never come, for "Lay not up to yourselves treasures on earth: where the rust and moth consume, and where thieves break through and steal. But lay up to yourselves treasures in heaven" (Mt. 6:19-20).

—*Fr. Scott,* September 2000

 ## How should a traditional Catholic plan for retirement?

Two excesses are to be avoided on this question. There are those who cannot bring themselves to retire. They live to work, have become attached to their own endeavors, and do not appreciate the value of well-earned leisure in old age. More frequent is the attitude that equates retirement with sloth, as if retired persons no longer have any duties or responsibilities.

The truth is that retirement is a special time of life, when a person can escape some from the incessant demands of the rat race and concentrate on higher goals that would be impossible without the extra leisure of retirement. It gives a person the opportunity to think of his soul, to pray and meditate more regularly, to attend extra Masses and devotions, and to prepare his soul for its last end. However, it is also a time when a person can devote more time and energy to the practice of the spiritual and corporal works of mercy, whether they be directed towards one's family members (children or grandchildren) or whether they be directed towards others. Thus retirement has a real purpose, in total opposition to the modern concept of retirement as a well-earned right to unlimited sloth, pleasure, and self-indulgence for as long as one's health holds out, as practiced by snowbirds—winter Floridians and winter Texans.

Decisions concerning planning for retirement will depend upon the understanding of this purpose. It is certainly true that it is prudent to provide a nest egg for medical and other expenses, and to arrange a good pension fund. It would be imprudent not to provide for old age in such a way. However, it would be just as wrong for this to become a fetish, a preoccupation.

On the one hand, retired persons should desire to locate themselves close to a traditional chapel so that they can have ready access to the Mass and sacraments, even during the week, and so that the priest can easily get to them if they are sick. On the other hand, they need to play an essential role in society by the help that they give to their children and grandchildren, to the community at large, and to other traditional Catholics in particular. In the present crisis, these two aspects of retirement can sometimes be in conflict, and it can be difficult to resolve this conflict and to decide whether to relocate or not. In such cases no general rule can be given since the decision of prudence will differ in each particular case, according to the circumstances. However, if a retired couple does intend to relocate, they should have a plan as to how they will help those in need, whether family, parishioners, or others. To opt out of such duties of charity would be to opt out of the responsibility and care for the common good that ought to be particularly developed in older, retired persons.

—*Fr. Scott,* March 2003

 ### Is it permissible for a landlord to rent an apartment or house to an unmarried couple living in sin?

This is a case of material cooperation in somebody else's sin. This is not normally permissible, for obvious reasons, and a Catholic ought to refuse to rent an apartment if he knows that a couple is not married and is going to live in sin in that apartment.

However, material cooperation is not the same as formal cooperation. The difference is that in material cooperation the Catholic (in this case, the landlord) does not want the sin to happen, whereas in formal cooperation he does. This is why it is permissible to rent to such persons for a proportionately serious reason, for example, if the civil law made it an offense to "discriminate," and one did not have any other "legal" reason to refuse, so that the refusal to rent would mean a real possibility of civil or criminal action being initiated against the landlord.

This being said, a Catholic should do everything in his power, including accepting a lower rent from good tenants, or using other legally approved reasons to exclude such tenants, in order to avoid even material cooperation in such a sin. However, if a Catholic were trying to do this, but got caught and was afraid of being sued, then he could rent it to such a couple, as effectively having no choice. Here the principles of the indirect voluntary apply. What is directly willed is not the cooperation in another's sin but the gaining of a just return for his investment.

This very real possibility ought not to dissuade Catholics from owning rental properties. For to do so is to provide a service for the poor, underprivileged members of society, less able to take care of themselves. Understood in this sense, it is an act of charity, especially when the landlord is willing to give the needy a break on their monthly rent.

—*Fr. Scott,* May 2006

 **Is it licit to sell on the Internet auction site eBay relics (first, second, and third class), blessed articles, statues and sacred vessels, and items of intrinsic value secondarily containing a blessed item or a relic?**

The principle to always keep in mind is that once they have been blessed or consecrated, holy pictures and sacred vessels are of their nature set aside for the worship of God and for the honor of the saints, as also are relics of the Passion of Our Lord and of the saints. They must consequently "not be used for profane purposes" (Can. 1296 of the 1917 Code of Canon Law) and must be kept in a sacristy or other decent and safe place.

Blessed or consecrated objects can be owned by private persons, but they may not be used for profane or non-religious purposes. However, if they lose their blessing or consecration they may be, provided that these are not sordid uses (Can. 1510 of the 1917 Code of Canon Law). This law still exists in the 1983 Code of Canon Law, eliminating, however, the precision that even when they lose their blessing they still must not be used for improper or anti-Catholic purposes.

The 1917 Code of Canon Law is very explicit about the fact that exposing blessed or consecrated items to public sale or auction does cause them to lose their blessing (Can. 1305). There is no equivalent in the 1983 Code of Canon Law. Clearly, the advertising for sale on eBay constitutes a public auction, so that objects that are sold in this way do need to be re-blessed.

The 1917 Code of Canon Law (only) is very explicit about the vice of simony, the will and intention to buy or sell spiritual things for a temporal price (Can. 727, §1). It describes two types: simony of divine law and of ecclesiastical law. Simony of divine law exists when intrinsically spiritual things (*e.g.*, sacraments, indulgences) are sold for a price, or when a spiritual thing is made the partial object of a contract, such as when a chalice is sold for more money because it is consecrated (Can. 727, §1). Simony of ecclesiastical law does not concern us here, for it consists in requiring some kind of exchange for a spiritual benefice or favor, such as letters of recommendation or Christian burial.

The 1917 Code of Canon Law (Can. 730) is also very specific in excluding from simony the giving of payment for a temporal object which has something spiritual joined to it. Thus it is that it is not simony, and consequently perfectly moral, to sell a chalice for the value of the metal, provided that there is no increase in price because it is consecrated (*e.g.*, for a private sale, where the consecration is not lost), or the sale of the reliquary in which relics are contained. However, this would not be licit unless it could be foreseen that all profane uses were to be excluded (in the case of blessed items or relics) and unless all anti-Catholic uses could be excluded for those formerly blessed or consecrated items which are solid publicly, as on eBay.

From this it follows that it would be moral to sell historic or antique religious items for their real value on the market, provided that no additional price was requested because of their former blessing or use, or the relic that might be attached or included within the item.

It is never permitted to sell relics, as relics, for their spiritual value as a relic, whether they be first, second, or third class. This is clear from Canon 1289 of the 1917 Code of Canon Law, which states that "it is a horrible thing to sell sacred relics," which prescription is renewed in the 1983 Code of Canon Law, Canon 1190, §1. However, it is permissible to sell the reliquary in which the relic is contained for its artistic or historical value. It would, though, be entirely against the spirit of the Church to make this a legal fiction by calling it a price for the reliquary and simply taking advantage of the demand for a particular relic and charging for it, calling it a price for the reliquary. This is simony.

A further distinction is made in the Church's Code of Canon Law, and that is of important relics, which are held in great veneration by the people, such as an entire body, head, forearm, heart, *etc.* from other relics. Important relics such as these cannot be moved into private houses or oratories without the authorization of the Holy See (Can. 1282 of the 1917 Code of Canon Law and 1190, §2 of the 1983 Code of Canon Law). Other relics can be kept, but *with due honor*, in private homes, and even carried piously on their persons by the faithful.

The wisdom of all these prescriptions of the Church, to protect the honor and reverence due to holy things, is a part of the sacredness of the Church's life that we all must do our utmost to preserve in this time of secularism, in which the sacred has become so defiled.

—*Fr. Scott,* August 2000

 ## Can a Catholic telephone operator give out telephone numbers to Planned Parenthood and immoral movie theaters?

This is a question of material cooperation. A person who would willingly and knowingly give out such numbers would be guilty of formal cooperation, and would consequently have the guilt of the sin, and if it concerned a woman seeking an abortion, the guilt and the excommunication of the subsequent abortion, if it took place. However, the moral dilemma arises when the Catholic telephone operator abhors such crimes and would do anything to avoid them.

Clearly, such a person ought to do his utmost to avoid even material cooperation and should, if possible, refuse or side-step giving out such numbers. However, this is not always possible, for he could easily lose his job by such a refusal. In such a case, the principles of the indirect voluntary apply. It is permissible to perform an act in itself good or indifferent (giving out a telephone number), provided that the evil is not willed and comes from the good (doing one's job), and provided that there is a proportionately grave reason, depending upon the gravity of the sin and the proximity of the material cooperation. Such a grave reason could be the necessity to do this to keep one's job and to support one's family. It would much more easily apply to the giving out of a number for an immoral movie theater, since the evil is not so great nor the cooperation so immediate as giving out the number of Planned Parenthood, effectively an abortion mill.

It would consequently seem possible, in order to keep one's job, to give out numbers to places where sins are frequently but not necessarily committed, such as movie theaters. It would also be possible to give out numbers to a person making a general request, for example, for advertising purposes, even to Planned Parenthood. However, it would be illicit to use the principle of material cooperation to give out the number of Planned Parenthood to a woman suspected of wanting to have an abortion performed. In such case, one would have to risk losing one's job rather than perform this action.

It goes without saying that a person who is regularly placed in such qualms of conscience through known material cooperation in evil actions ought to seek a different employment.

—Fr. Scott, September 2007

ABOUT NAMES AND MEANINGS OF WORDS AND PHRASES

Is it correct to speak of our "Judeo-Christian" heritage?

The term "Judeo-Christian" is not a recent invention of the ecumenical age, as it would first seem. It is a very ancient term, dating from the beginning of Christianity. The Judeo-Christians were originally converts to the Faith from Judaism, but who still practiced circumcision and observed the Mosaic law and attempted to impose this upon the converts from amongst the Gentiles. They were first condemned by the Council of Jerusalem in the year 49, as told in Chapter 15 of the Acts of the Apostles.

Thereafter, two groups of Judeo-Christians emerged. There were those who simply kept the Mosaic law themselves, but who did not attempt to impose it upon other Christians and who were not heretical. They were called Nazarenes, and rapidly disappeared after the destruction of Jerusalem in the year 70. The other group of Judeo-Christians were also called Ebionites. They were truly heretical, considered the Mosaic law obligatory, and denied the divinity of Christ, the virgin birth, and the work and writings of St. Paul. They also gave rise to various Gnostic sects. It is for this reason that the title "Judeo-Christian" is a pejorative one, opposed to doctrinal orthodoxy.

The attempt to describe one's morality or principles as "Judeo-Christian" is consequently not at all traditional. It could theoretically be used to describe one's attachment to the moral principles of the Bible, including the Ten Commandments, as being the principles of all moral life and which the Church received from the Israelites. However, there are a couple of problems. The first one is that the Jews themselves in the time of Our Lord did not keep the moral principles of the Old Law, as Our Lord did not cease reiterating. How could one possibly use the title of "Judeo-Christian heritage" to express one's attachment to these principles when the Jews themselves practiced polygamy and divorce; when the Jews did not hesitate to undermine the first and great commandment of the love of God and neighbor by teaching the exact opposite, "love your neighbor and hate your enemy" (Mt. 5:43) or "an eye for an eye and a tooth for a tooth" (Mt. 5:38)? How could we possibly use this title when the vast majority of Jews have no problem with euthanasia, abortion, birth control, divorce, homosexuality, and even the elimination of God and love towards our neighbor from public life, politics, education, and the courts? What could this title "Judeo-Christian heritage" consequently really mean?

If it is used to indicate those who observe the Ten Commandments and keep them as the foundation of all morality, then let that be said explicitly: our heritage is the Ten Commandments. Let there be no ambiguity. However, it is not Jewish. It is our Catholic heritage. The Catholic Church has in fact succeeded the Israel of the Old Testament, as being the true people of God. Present-day Jews are not a part of this heritage, nor are they our older brothers in the faith, as the pope has, alas, stated. They do not have the true faith, the faith of the Catholic Church, for they explicitly reject and refuse to believe in Christ, the Son of God made man, despite the fact that He fulfilled all the prophecies of the Old Testament. By refusing to believe in the Holy Trinity, they refuse to believe in God as He has revealed Himself. They consequently have not had the faith of Abraham, who believed everything that God revealed to him, since Christ revealed this mystery of the Trinity.

The existence in the Church of a modern, liberal, ecumenical concept of a Judeo-Christian heritage dates back to the Vatican II document on the relation of the Church to non-Christian religions, *Nostra Aetate*. This declaration mentions twice that *"Christians and Jews have a common spiritual heritage"* (§4), without explaining what that is. If by this is meant that we share that part of sacred Scripture that we call the Old Testament, it is partly right (the Jews reject seven inspired books of the Old Testament). If, however, by this is meant that there is something common with respect to our spiritual life, faith, and moral principles, then it is entirely wrong, for present-day Judaism is based upon the denial of the most basic truths of the Catholic Faith.

Consequently, this politically correct term "Judeo-Christian heritage" must be regarded as vague, deliberately ambiguous, liberal, favoring indifferentism and ecumenism, and not at all orthodox.

—*Fr. Scott,* April 2005

What is the origin of the word "Lent"?

We get the word "Lent" from the old Anglo-Saxon language: Lententide meant springtime, and "Lent" is the spring fast.

In Latin this season is called Quadragesima, which means "fortieth" and comprises the number of the days of the fast. It recalls the forty days and nights of Our Lord's fasting when he was led by the Spirit into the desert.

—*Fr. Boyle*, April 1994

What is meant by the expression *"sensus fidei"*?

This expression is not properly speaking theological, nor is it consequently precisely defined. However, it is used to mean a "way of thinking that is governed by the truths of the faith." It is in this sense that it is used, for example, by Archbishop Lefebvre when speaking of the *Novus Ordo Missae* and how it is rejected as by a kind of supernatural instinct by those who still think as the Church has always thought, governed by the principles of the Faith. Allow me to quote the following text, written by Archbishop Lefebvre for the *Cor Unum* newsletter on February 16, 1980 (§269):

> We had always said that we consider the *Novus Ordo Missae* to be dangerous for the faith of both priests and faithful, and that, consequently, it was inconceivable to group and form young aspirants to the priesthood around this new altar. The facts prove us to be right. The *sensus fidei* of the faithful, there where it is not yet corrupt, gives us total approval....

Understood in this sense, the "spirit of the faith" is directly analogous to St. Ignatius's "Rules for Thinking with the Church." These eighteen rules contained in the book of the exercises of St. Ignatius of Loyola are a treasure, a summary of the attitudes, convictions, way of thinking that characterize the profoundly supernatural man who is penetrated by the principles of the Faith. They describe perfectly well the sense of the Faith as being a spirit of submission to the Church's judgment and way of thinking, and include such things as the praising of frequent sacramental confession and Holy Communion, the frequent assistance at Mass, the recitation of long prayers and the Divine Office, the religious life and its three vows, the relics of the saints and their veneration, the precepts of the Church and acts of exterior and interior penance, the veneration of sacred images, and so on.

It follows from this that a person can have the faith without the "spirit of the faith." For the Catholic Faith itself is destroyed only by formal heresy, the pertinacious denial of a revealed dogma. However, the spirit of the faith is lost by any way of thinking that is contrary to the Church's way of thinking, that does not take into account divine revelation and supernatural truth. This is particularly the case of the modernists and those who promote the New Mass. They are not, in general, heretics, and are careful not to deny a defined dogma of faith. However, little by little the assistance at the New Mass undermines the convictions of faith that ought to govern the lives and, in particular, the prayers of Catholics. They become humanistic, man-centered, directed towards personal experience rather than towards the salvation of the soul and the greater honor and glory of God. It was for this reason that St. Pius X condemned the Sillon movement in 1910. He did not say that it was heretical, but rather that "judging the words and deeds, we feel compelled to say that in this action as well as in its doctrine, the Sillon does not give satisfaction to the Church" (§30). Archbishop Lefebvre comments on this observation that the spirit of the Sillon was not the spirit of the Church:

> In the same way, when he [St. Pius X] says that Modernism is the synthesis of all the heresies, he does not add that all those favorable to Modernism are heretics. He only says that it is the synthesis of all the heresies in its doctrine. (*Against the Heresies*, p. 281)

However, that the various manifestations of modernism, whether it be the New Mass; whether it be ecumenism; whether it be secularism, indifferentism, or religious liberty, demonstrate clearly the loss of the spirit of the faith. This is well described by Romano Amerio:

> For the new theology, it is not stability that characterizes real faith, but rather the mobility of an endless searching. People even go so far as to say that an authentic faith must go into crisis.…This dynamic view of faith is immediately derived from modernism, which holds that faith is procured by a feeling for the divine, and that conceptual truths that the intellect produces are merely changeable expressions of that feeling.…The mistake in this position lies in regarding as humble an attitude that is really an intense form of pride.…In short, the Object is being valued less than the subject and an anthropocentric view is being adopted that is irreconcilable with religion.… (*Iota Unum*, p. 375)

In this way the spirit of the faith, the objective submission of the intellect to divinely revealed truth, is destroyed.

The importance of this spirit of the faith in present day Catholics can, consequently, escape no one. Without it, we will fall to the novelties of the post-conciliar church. In another of his newsletters (June 26, 1982), Archbishop Lefebvre pointed out that the spirit of faith is identical with the spirit of the Church: "The spirit of the Society is the spirit of the Church, the spirit of faith in Our Lord Jesus Christ and His redemptive work." He goes on to explain that this spirit of faith is the fruit of prayer, by which the faith penetrates into our souls:

This spirit of faith is essentially a spirit contemplating the crucified and glorified Jesus. The faith is the seed of the beatific vision, which is an eternally blessed contemplation.

He further points out that the spirit of faith is to be found where the life of the Church is to be found:

If the teaching that is contained in the liturgical life is so admirable and draws us towards an ever greater sanctification of soul, then the practical directives of the Church throughout its history, as well as its approval of the many foundations destined to sanctify souls, not to mention the examples of the saints, are all equally precious guidelines for our souls. In following them, according to the grace God grants us, we can be sure of not deceiving ourselves. Contemplation, obedience, and humility are all the elements of one sole reality: the imitation of Jesus Christ and participation in His infinite love.

This passage holds the key to understanding whether or not we have the spirit of faith. The love of the Church's traditional spiritual teachings, and saints, and the longing for contemplation, obedience, and humility are the sign that we are truly seeking the spirit of faith. For it really is the fruit of the gift of the Holy Ghost that we call the gift of understanding, through which we penetrate into the depth of supernatural truths and unveil their secrets. This is well explained by Archbishop Martinez:

It is the gift of understanding given to every Christian which makes him apprehend supernatural truths when this is necessary for the attainment of his salvation. And as it increases, this gift produces things even more wonderful in our souls; it makes us penetrate into the very mysteries of religion; by it we understand the beautiful harmonies in spiritual things. (*The Sanctifier*, p. 183)

—*Fr. Scott,* March 2008

Where do we get the word "collation" from?

The universal fast preceding the great solemnity of Easter was not in the beginning observed everywhere in a uniform way. Over the centuries, relaxation in the discipline was allowed. The one meal during the Lenten fast began to be taken at 3:00 p.m. in the afternoon, that is, the hour of None instead of after Vespers. In the tenth century, this was the universal practice, but Vespers were earlier and still before the meal. At the end of the thirteenth century, Vespers and the fasting meal were at midday. As a result of the meal's being earlier, it is not surprising to learn that a "collation" was deemed necessary in the evening. The use of the word comes from the rule of St. Benedict.

There a distinction is made between the fast of the Church and that of the Benedictine rule. On days of monastic fast, the dinner was at 3:00

p.m. In the summer and autumn months when work in the fields was heavy and the heat induced much fatigue, the abbot permitted the monks a small measure of wine before Compline during the reading of the "Conferences of Cassian." Now, the Latin word for conference is *collatio*, and from this name the evening refreshment on fasting days came to be called "collation."

We are permitted two such collations in the present discipline and, if I may say so, what a joy it is to presume the abbatical permission of the traditional Benedictine "collation"!

—*Fr. Boyle*, April 1994

 **Please explain what "slain in the Spirit" is, and how far back does this date in the history of the Catholic Church?**

"Slain in the Spirit" is a term taken from Pentecostalism. It refers to the phenomenon when the person, supposedly under the influence of the Holy Ghost, collapses at a prayer meeting. This Pentecostalism was borrowed by Catholics in the so-called Charismatic Movement, dating only from the early 1960's. It is therefore not a Catholic term, nor is it very old in the Church, as it is foreign to Catholicism. Most of this movement is based on emotionalism. And even if it were truly from the Holy Ghost, the gifts are subordinate to the theological virtue of charity and for the benefit usually of those outside the Church—not for a spiritual "high" at a Wednesday prayer meeting.

—*Fr. Doran*, February 1992

ABOUT OTHER CONCERNS

 **What do you think of *The Poem of the Man God* by Maria Valtorta?**

These books have never received an imprimatur. I have in my possession a statement of Archbishop Lefebvre advising against their reading. These books appeal too much to the sensitivity. But worse, they contain several passages impossible to be from God—passages which are tantamount to blasphemy. For instance, Maria Valtorta presents Mary as asking her mother Anne: "Tell me, mummy, can one be a sinner out of love of God?...I mean to commit a sin in order to be loved by God, Who becomes Savior." How could the Immaculate Virgin even think such a thing, since she was full of that charity which "dealeth not perversely, ...thinketh no evil" (I Cor. 13:4-5)? She knew too well that "the damnation of those who say, 'let us do evil, that there may come good, is just'!" (Rom. 3:8).

In another place, Valtorta presents Mary as being ignorant of the gifts she had received from God: "I did not know I was without stain!" How could this be in her who had received to the fullness the Spirit of God, "that we may know the things that are given us from God" (I Cor. 2:12). In her *Magnificat*, Our Lady manifests that she knew "the great things" which the Lord had done in her.

Other statements are even worse, which reverence for God and even mere decency prevent us printing here. Conclusion: these books must not be read!

—*Fr. Laisney,* January 1991

CONTRIBUTORS

FR. LEO BOYLE

Fr. Leo Boyle was ordained at Ecône in 1991. After several posts in the United States, he returned to England at the turn of the century, where he is now a retreat master at St. Saviour's House, Bristol.

FR. JAMES DORAN

Fr. James Doran was ordained in 1988 at Ecône, Switzerland. From 1988-1990, he was assistant headmaster in St. Marys, Kansas. From 1990-1991 he was prior in St. Louis, Missouri. In 1991 he became editor of Angelus Press and moved its office to Kansas City, where he also became the founding prior of Kansas City. In 1992 he was named prior of Post Falls, where he laid the cornerstone of St. Dominic's School. In 1996, he was appointed professor at St. Thomas Aquinas Seminary in Winona, Minnesota, where he became vice-rector in 1998. In 2005 he was appointed prior of Geneva, Switzerland, where he is working on his graduate degree.

FR. FRANÇOIS LAISNEY

Father François Laisney was born on December 5, 1957. He entered Ecône in October 1976, and was ordained on June 29, 1982. He was first assigned as an assistant priest in Australia; then on May 13, 1984, he was appointed district superior of the United States for six years. He later became bursar in Australia for one year, then district superior in Australia for three years, until the General Chapter of 1994. He was then bursar general for eight years, prior of Hampton (Australia) for two years, and now prior of Wanganui, New Zealand, for four years.

He is the author of the book *Is Feeneyism Catholic?* and compiled another book, *Archbishop Lefebvre and the Vatican,* which gives (almost) all documents relevant to the episcopal consecrations by Archbishop Lefebvre in 1988. Both are available through Angelus Press.

FR. CARL PULVERMACHER

Father Carl Pulvermacher, R.I.P. 2006, was the founder of Angelus Press and *The Angelus*. It was during the first years of *The Angelus* that he began "Ask Me," which would later become the "Questions and Answers" column that inspired this book. A Capuchin for fifty-six years, he spent the last thirty-one years of his life working with the Society of Saint Pius X.

FR. PETER SCOTT

Born in Sale, Victoria, Australia, in 1957, and raised outside the Catholic Church, Father Scott converted to the Catholic Faith whilst in medical school in 1979, being received into the Church by Reverend Father Augustine Cummins, C. Ss. R., the traditional Catholic priest who founded many of the traditional chapels in Australia and New Zealand. Having completed his degree in 1980, it was in 1982 that he was accepted into the Saint Pius X Seminary in Ecône, Switzerland. He there completed the six years of priestly formation, being ordained to the priesthood on June 29, 1988. His first assignment was as a professor at St. Thomas Aquinas Seminary in Winona, Minnesota, where he taught a variety of subjects, including Philosophy, Dogmatic Theology, History and Latin. In June 1990, he was named district superior of the United States District of the Society of Saint Pius X, whose headquarters was at that time at Queen of the Holy Rosary in Webster Groves, a suburb of St. Louis. It was in December 1991 that he moved the District Headquarters to Kansas City. After having completed two terms as district superior, he was assigned as rector of Holy Cross Seminary in August 2002. He spent six years at that post, during which time he extended the major seminary to include the full six year program, Theology as well as Philosophy, and founded a minor seminary. He is presently assigned as principal of Our Lady of Mount Carmel Academy, New Hamburg, Ontario, Canada.